Harvey Washington Wiley

**Sugar**

molasses and sirup, confections, honey and beeswax

Harvey Washington Wiley

**Sugar**
*molasses and sirup, confections, honey and beeswax*

ISBN/EAN: 9783337130039

Printed in Europe, USA, Canada, Australia, Japan

Cover: Foto ©Andreas Hilbeck / pixelio.de

More available books at **www.hansebooks.com**

U. S. DEPARTMENT OF AGRICULTURE.

DIVISION OF CHEMISTRY.

BULLETIN                                          No. 13.

# FOODS

AND

# FOOD ADULTERANTS.

INVESTIGATIONS MADE UNDER DIRECTION OF

## H. W. WILEY,

CHIEF CHEMIST,

WITH THE COLLABORATION OF H. A. HUSTON, H. H. NICHOLSON,
W. B. RISING, M. A. SCOVELL, S. P. SHARPLES, W. C. STUBBS
SHIPPEN WALLACE, F. G. WIECHMANN, H. A. WEBER,
AND K. P. McELROY.

### PART SIXTH.

SUGAR, MOLASSES AND SIRUP, CONFECTIONS,
HONEY AND BEESWAX.

PUBLISHED BY AUTHORITY OF THE SECRETARY OF AGRICULTURE.

WASHINGTON:
GOVERNMENT PRINTING OFFICE.
1892.

# LETTER OF TRANSMITTAL.

U. S. DEPARTMENT OF AGRICULTURE,
DIVISION OF CHEMISTRY,
*Washington, D. C., February* 23, 1892.

SIR: I have the honor to submit, for your inspection and approval the manuscript of Part 6 of Bulletin No. 13, embracing the subjects of sugars, molasses and sirups, confections, and honeys and beeswax, and their adulterations.

Respectfully,

H. W. WILEY,
*Chemist.*

Hon. J. M. RUSK,
*Secretary of Agriculture*

# FOODS AND FOOD ADULTERANTS.

## PART VI.—SUGAR, MOLASSES, CONFECTIONS, AND HONEY, AND THEIR ADULTERATIONS.

### SCOPE AND CHARACTER OF THE WORK.

In the study of the adulteration of these common articles of table use an attempt has been made to determine not only the character of the adulterant used, but to a certain extent the scope and extent of the adulteration. In this respect a slight departure has been made from the rule adopted at the beginning of this work, viz, to restrict the investigations chiefly to the study of the character of the adulterants and the methods of detecting them. In the cases under consideration it has been thought wiser to devote less time to the methods of detecting adulteration, which for the most part are simple operations and well understood, and to give greater attention to the extent of the practice of the adulteration. This idea has been followed out except in the case of beeswax, with which a complete study has been given of the methods proposed for analysis and the detection of adulterations. To this end the coöperation of chemists in different parts of the country was secured and a general scheme of investigation adopted, which it was proposed to carry into effect simultaneously in different parts of the country. As collaborators in the work there were secured the following-named gentlemen: In Boston, Dr. Stephen P. Sharples; in New York, Dr. F. G. Wiechmann; in Philadelphia, Dr. Shippen Wallace; in New Orleans, Dr. W. C. Stubbs; in San Francisco, Prof. W. B. Rising; in Lincoln, Nebr., Prof. H. H. Nicholson; in Lexington, Ky., Prof. M. A. Scovell; in Columbus, Ohio, Prof. H. A. Weber; in La Fayette, Ind., Prof. H. A. Huston. After securing the coöperation of these gentlemen the following instructions were sent them, under date of December 9, 1890:

U. S. DEPARTMENT OF AGRICULTURE,
DIVISION OF CHEMISTRY,
*Washington, D. C., December* 9, 1890.

DEAR SIR: In continuation of the work of the chemical division relating to the adulteration of foods, I am authorized by the Secretary to secure the aid of analysts interested in such work in different parts of the country.

I therefore ask your coöperation in this work in the examination of one hundred and seventy-five samples of saccharine products, as follows:

*Fifty samples of molasses:* Polarization before and after inversion; sucrose; reducing sugar before inversion; qualitative test for tin; water; ash.

*Fifty samples of liquid honey:* Polarization before and after inversion; sucrose; reducing sugar before inversion; water; ash; fermentation; polarization of residue after fermentation.

*Fifty samples low-grade sugars:* Polarization; water; ash.

*Twenty-five samples of cheap confections (candies, etc.)* : Sucrose before and after inversion; reducing sugars; matters insoluble in water; water, ash, and coloring matters (mineral or non-mineral). Get a few highly colored samples.

You will be authorized to purchase the samples in open market and without indicating the purpose for which they are to be used.

The molasses should be purchased in packages of about 1 quart, the honey and sugar in about 1 pound lots.

The sugar when purchased is to be immediately put in air-tight packages, so as to avoid loss of moisture.

In every case the name of the dealer from whom the purchase is made is to be entered, together with the name of the firm manufacturing the product, and labels or descriptions on the package, and such other descriptions as will give any information concerning the sample.

The itemized bill for the samples is to be sent to the Department, and you will be compensated therefor.

It is not required that the whole of the analytical work is to be performed by you personally, but it must be under your personal direction and responsibility. Full directions for conducting the analyses will be sent. The work is to be finished and reported to me by March 1, 1891.

Respectfully,

H. W. WILEY,
*Chemist.*

## DIRECTIONS FOR ANALYSIS OF SUGARS, HONEYS, AND CONFECTIONS.

It was thought proper to leave to each analysist as large a degree of independent action as possible in carrying on the work, and therefore only a general outline of the method of conducting the work was supplied.

The reading of the polariscope employed is to be given for the 200 mm and 100 mm tubes, with the sample of sugar sent, weighing 26.048 g. in the air, and making up to 100 cc in a flask graduated at that mark to hold 100 g distilled water at 17.5° for instruments with a Ventzke scale, or 16.19 g sugar weighed in air in flask graduated at 100 cc, with 100 g water at 4° for Laurent scale. These readings of the instrument are to accompany the analytical data.

The direct polarizations are to be made in the usual way, using lead subacetate for clarifying the solutions, neutralizing with acetic acid, and rejecting first part of the filtrate. Bone black is only to be used in extreme cases. If dried at 100° to 105° it can be added directly to the solution after the volume is completed. If moist, it must be placed on the filter paper and the first half of the filtrate rejected.

For inversion 50 cc of the normal solution are to be heated for ten minutes to 68° with 5 cc strong hydrochloric acid, cooled quickly to constant temperature, and polarized. The percentage of sucrose is calculated from Clerget's formula. The polarization should be made at the same temperature as the direct polarization of the same sample.

*Reducing sugars.*—The alkaline copper solution should be set by the sample of (practically) pure sugar sent. The operations should be conducted on solutions containing about 1 per cent of reducing sugar, and under precisely similar conditions as those used in setting the copper solution.

*Water.*—The substance is to be dried in quantities of about 1 gram for each 5 square centimeters of bottom, in flat dishes, first at lower temperature, and, when nearly dry, for one hour at 102° to 103°.

*Ash.*—By incineration of residue from above at *low* redness until all carbon is consumed.

*Tin.*—Incinerate 25 to 50 g of the molasses in a porcelain dish, and extract ash with hot HCl. Filter and test for tin in filtrate with H₂S.

*Coloring matters.*—Incinerate and examine ash for Cu, Pb, etc. If arsenic is suspected, test with Marsh apparatus in original sample, after treatment with HCl and KClO₃.

Coloring matters destroyed by incineration are of vegetable or animal origin or coaltar colors. It will be sufficient to discriminate between the two great classes of colors as indicated above.

*Fermentation.*—Make a 10 per cent solution of the honey (25 to 50 g) and treat with yeast; keep at temperature of about 30° until evolution of CO₂ ceases.

*Treatment of fermentation residue.**—Filter the residue after fermentation, evaporate to a thin sirup, measure volume, filter through bone black if necessary, take half of the total volume, and, polarize. Give polarization in degrees, sugar scale, and calculate to a basis of 26.048 (16.19) g of the original honey to 100 cc.

*Matter insoluble in cold water.*—Dry at 100° to 103°, weigh and examine for starch, terra alba, etc.

At the same time a similar examination was undertaken in the chemical laboratory of the Department of Agriculture and the work of carrying on these investigations was chiefly done by Mr. K. P. McElroy and Mr. E. G. Runyan. Thus in all, ten sets of samples were secured at practically the same time in ten localities representing pretty well the general distribution of these articles of diet over the United States.

In regard to the examination of honey, in addition to the work of a routine character mentioned before, extensive researches were undertaken in the laboratory of the Department in regard to additional methods of detecting honey adulterants, and also of the methods of examination of the wax, both natural and commercial. It was thought that it would be of great interest to consumers of honey in general to have a careful study made of the wax as well as of the honey contained therein. The detailed results of this examination will be found in the following pages.

The chief points to be considered in respect of molasses were the use of glucose as an adulterant in so-called cane molasses and the occurrence of tin. This latter substance is introduced into the molasses in brightening sugar crystals in the centrifugals and in making yellow (Demerara) crystals. Stannous chloride in some form is the salt of tin generally employed for this purpose, and this is sold in the trade under various misleading names.

In confections the chief points to be considered were the presence of adulterating agents such as chalk, terra alba, glucose, etc., and especially the character of the pigments used in coloring candies.

Many confections are quite as highly regarded for their delicate and

---

* The examination by the method of fermentation was subsequently omitted.

pleasing tints as for the taste of the sweets which they contain, and therefore it becomes a matter of sanitary importance to determine the character of the coloring matters used.

It is a matter of regret that other and more insistent duties have prevented an earlier arrangement and study of the results, but their value depends rather in the patient and painstaking labors of those engaged in the investigations than on their chronological appearance. This part of Bulletin No. 13 is preëminently one of data rather than of deductions.

### LETTERS OF TRANSMITTAL FROM THE ANALYSTS ENGAGED IN THE WORK.

A general idea of the character of the examinations made and the methods employed therein can be had from a perusal of the letters from the several analysts transmitting the results of the analyses.

PURDUE UNIVERSITY,
*La Fayette, Ind., March* 19, 1891.

DEAR SIR: I have to-day forwarded to you report on honey, sirup, sugar, and candies. I have made out the report as I understood from directions furnished. Should any changes be required of course I shall take pleasure in making the same.

The information regarding the origin of the samples was very difficult to obtain. This is particularly true of the sugars which are usually removed from the packages and sold from bins in the stores.

In addition to the work reported I have tested fifteen samples of the honey, and find that nine out of fifteen contain tin or some metal precipitated by $H_2S$ and having the same general appearance as the tin precipitate found in the molasses.

I have also examined the soda test for molasses, but find that a mixture of molasses and glucose will also give tests.

The best informed honey man that I met stated that every genuine strained honey would granulate if left open and exposed to the air for eight days. I have not yet had an opportunity to test this matter.

In regard to candies I am informed by manufacturers that there are now very few boilers of candy who can make candy without the addition of a small amount of glucose; about 10 per cent is the amount mentioned. I understand this to mean a minimum amount.

The itemized bill for samples will follow.

Very truly yours.

H. A. HUSTON.
Dr. H. W. WILEY,
*Chief Chemist U. S. Department of Agriculture, Washington, D. C.*

UNIVERSITY OF NEBRASKA, DEPARTMENT OF CHEMISTRY,
*Lincoln. Nebr., March* 7, 1891.

MY DEAR DOCTOR: I inclose to you to-day reports of analyses of sugars, sirups, honeys, and candies, together with vouchers for purchase money. I inclose also bills for expenses incurred in making purchases outside of this city. If these last can not be allowed I will be out just that amount. I am very sorry for the delay, but it has been absolutely unavoidable.

Since January 1 we have been in the midst of a legislative session, and the outside drafts on my time have been considerable. This, with the hundred and one things that have the faculty of precipitating themselves on one when he is in a pinch, is the reason for not being more prompt.

Mr. Horton, who has made all of the polarizations and the reducing sugar determinations, has had considerable difficulty in bringing some of these substances into a proper condition for examination. This, as you well know, brings vexatious delays. Should you wish any of these determinations repeated we will gladly do it for you at any time.

The methods of analyses employed follow.

Hoping that our delay has not seriously incommoded you, I am, yours, very truly,

H. H. NICHOLSON.

H. W. WILEY,
 *Chief Chemist, Department of Agriculture, Washington, D. C.*

METHODS OF ANALYSIS EMPLOYED.

*Clarification.*—Very light products use $Al_2 (OH)_6$. Dark products tannic acid in excess and exact precipitation with a solution of normal lead acetate as in the method proposed by Scheibler.

*Readings.*—With one or two exceptions all readings made in 2 dem tube.

*Inversion.*—50 cc of solution used for direct polarization, 5 cc HCl (sp. g. 1. 18). Heated slowly to 70°, and kept at this point for ten to twelve minutes, when cooled in stream of water to 17½° and filled to mark. Polarized in 22 dem jacketed tube to control temperature.

*Reducing sugar.*—5 g in 100 cc, thereby giving burette reading of over 13 cc.

The inversion work was carefully conducted but the results are not satisfactory. Formerly I heated for fifteen minutes and allowed solution to cool slowly to near the proper temperature, but ten minutes or twelve have been recommended and so I adopted this time limit. You will notice that Dr. Spencer has given this time as ten minutes.

I have made the following experiments to determine the effect of time:

 I. 50 cc of Sol.
  5 cc HCl (1. 18).

  10 min. at 70°.  Reading $\dfrac{\alpha \text{ Series.}}{12.10}$  $\dfrac{\beta \text{ Series.}}{12.10}$

 II. 50 cc of Sol.
  5 cc HCl (1. 18).

  15 min. at 70°.  Reading $\dfrac{\alpha \text{ Series.}}{11.52}$  $\dfrac{\beta \text{ Series.}}{11.48}$

  Difference...... 0.58  0.62

I am at present carrying through samples giving fifteen minutes as recommended and hope to find some interesting results.

*Sirups, molasses.*—Clarification, inversion, readings, reducing sugars as with sugars.

I have been amazed at the high right-hand p̣ ., ɪization of these sirups. The number obtained are to a certain extent inaccurate, as we had the Schmidt & Haensch instrument to work with. In every case where the high polarization was found the two halves of field of vision in instrument were tinted and not light and shadow, pointing conclusively to presence of substances having different power of refrangibility from quartz or sugar. In inversion these solutions did not color as did solution having approximately + 50° polarization, but could be read without any preparation.

The color and viscosity of these ultra right-hand sirups are characteristic.

From a few observations I think that dextrin in the sirups is the cause of the high numbers.

*Honeys.*—In examining the honeys I have used 26,048 g to 100 cc, and have obtained perfect clarification with $Al_2 (OH)_6$.

I was greatly surprised at the high right-hand polarization of the honeys. The percentage of reducing sugars from these samples looks interesting, there being a marked difference between (+) honeys and (−) honeys.

I have become interested in the honey question and I have arranged for several "swarms" of Italians, and you may expect to hear of my discomfort before many weeks. I have collected a number of samples of "straight" honey, some from my own place in Massachusetts and some from this State, and when at leisure shall work out something. Will you make some suggestions for me to look up in connection with honeys?

*Candies.*—I never saw more fluorescent solutions than some of the candies gave, one in particular I should think was colored with fluorescein. Several samples nothing could be done with—they were gums coated with sugar.

The names given to the molasses and sirups are misleading, *e. g.*, a very dark "black strap" is labeled "N. O. molasses." The maple sirups are a surprise to me and will doubtless be to you.

OFFICE OF STATE ANALYST,
*Berkeley, Cal., April* 17, 1891.

DEAR SIR: Accompanying this note please find report of examination of sugar, molasses, sirup, honeys, and candies.

A supplement containing the examination for tin, etc., will follow soon.

Very truly yours,

W. B. RISING.

Prof. H. W. WILEY.

KENTUCKY AGRICULTURAL EXPERIMENT STATION,
*Lexington, Ky., April* 18, 1891.

MY DEAR SIR : I send you herewith my report containing the results of the analysis of 50 samples of sirups, 50 samples of sugars, 50 samples of honeys, and 25 samples of candies.

The samples were collected from retail houses in Lexington and Louisville, Ky., and Cincinnati, Ohio. A few samples of honeys were obtained in Bowling Green, and one in Franklin, Ky.

It was difficult to get low-grade sugars at the time I was collecting them, in the first part of March, as buyers were holding off until April on account of the tariff reduction.

Strained honey seemed to be obtained as readily in March as it was in December, when I made the first collection. In collecting the samples of sirups I endeavored to get a fair average of the different brands sold in the three markets named above. I append a statement on test of apparatus and chemicals.

Yours very truly,

M. A. SCOVELL, *Director.*

Dr. H. W. WILEY,
*Department of Agriculture, Washington, D. C*

TEST OF APPARATUS AND CHEMICALS.

*First.* 100 *cc flask.*—The 100 cc flask was graduated in the usual manner with 100 grams distilled water at 17.5° C.

*Second.* Polariscope tubes used were tested by a normal solution of the test sugar sent for the purpose. Temperature of the solution at the time of testing being 24.8°. The readings were as follows :

First, 200 mm metal tube, 99.8.

Second, 100 mm glass tube, 49.9.

Third, 220 mm glass tube, 110.

Tests in each case were made in triplicate. From the above results it will be seen that the 220 mm tube is a trifle long. No correction was made for this, however, in the readings of the inverts. Most of invert readings were made in the 220 mm tube.

*Third. The Fehling Solution.*—Violette's formula was used. To test it, 0.95 grams of the test sugar was dissolved in 50 cc of water and inverted with 5 cc of hydrochloric acid at 68° C. This solution was diluted to 100 cc. After neutralizing, 10 cc of Fehling's solution was put in a small Erlenmeyer flask, and to this 30 cc of water was added and the solution boiled. The diluted sugar solution was gradually added to the copper solution until the copper was entirely reduced as indicated by ferrocyanide of potash in the acetic acid solution. The following are the results obtained:

4.9 cc sugar solution added to copper solution ; copper not all reduced.

5 cc sugar solution added ; copper all reduced.

4.9 cc sugar solution added ; reaction for copper.

50 cc sugar solution added ; no copper in solution.

## METHODS.

The instructions sent out by you were strictly followed.

The detailed method for detection of tin was sent in a former letter.

The sucrose was calculated by the following formula :

$$\text{Per cent sucrose} = \left\{ \frac{\text{Direct reading} - \text{indirect reading}}{142.4 - \dfrac{\text{T}}{2}} \right\} 100.$$

The direct readings were all made approximately at 25° C.

---

BOSTON, *March* 5, 1891.

DEAR SIR : I herewith transmit the report on the sugars, sirups, honeys, and candies examined at your request.

I have endeavored, in making my selections, to get as fair a representation of the market as possible, except in the case of the candies. In these the articles most likely to be adulterated were examined. As a result of the investigation, with the exception of tin in some of the samples of molasses, I have failed to find any injurious adulteration.

My thanks are due to my assistant, F. W. Bennet, for the able manner in which he has assisted me during this investigation.

Respectfully,

S. P. SHARPLES.

Dr. H. W. WILEY,
*Washington, D. C.*

---

NEW ORLEANS, LA., *March* 22, 1891.

DEAR SIR : I send you herewith analyses of 50 molasses, 50 low-grade and white pulverized sugars, 50 honeys, and 25 low-grade candies. These samples were purchased in this city according to your instructions. Great difficulty was encountered in the collection of these samples, and, in many instances, either from ignorance or from an indisposition to accommodate, the wholesale or manufacturers' names could not be obtained. Seven days were spent in trying to obtain samples with a known history, but at last many had to be taken with only the name of the dealer.

In the analyses performed your instructions have been followed, with two slight modifications :

First, as to clarification for polariscopic readings ; and second, in giving a greater superficial area to the amount required for determination of moisture in the dishes used.

It was found difficult to prepare some samples of honeys, candies, etc., for the polariscopic readings by the method prescribed. Resort was had to a 10 per cent sodic sulphate solution and basic acetate lead and acetic acid. Sometimes a drop or two of aluminic hydrate cream was used. No bone black was used. Whenever possible, basic acetate of lead, neutralized with acetic acid, was used.

Great difficulty was experienced in properly determining the moisture, especially with molasses and honeys. This was enhanced by the weather, as it has rained here almost continuously since January 1, and the hygroscopic tendencies of our samples have not been completely prevented even though every sample has been kept in stoppered bottles. In fact, the determination of moisture has required more time and labor than all of the other constituents. As many as five or six determinations in some instances had to be made before we could feel sure of their correctness. I now have every reason to believe that they are correct.

The sugar sent us by you read in 200 mm tube exactly 100°, and in 100 mm tube exactly 50°. We have two excellent Schmidt & Haensch polariscopes, and upon these all the readings were made.

The molasses analyzed represented every form sold in this city; syrop de batterie, open kettle molasses, centrifugal molasses from small three-roller mills, from large five roller mills, from diffusion houses; mixed goods, i. e., when Louisiana molasses has been mixed with corn glucose sirup; and doctored goods, i. e., when very dark centrifugal molasses have been brightened by artificial processes. I learn that there are many houses in this city where the mixing of Louisiana molasses and corn glucose sirup is made. I also learn that there are several houses where dark centrifugal molasses is brightened. Each house claims to have a special method (of course secret) by which this brightening is performed. In conversation with a gentleman engaged in this business, a few days since, he said that he was contracting to brighten 20,000 barrels of centrifugal molasses next year. These practices are generally known and no attempt is made to cover them with secrecy, save the process peculiar to each house performing the bleaching.

The sugars examined are all pure goods. Several samples of white pulverized sugar were examined to determine whether they contained any appreciable amount of starch sugar, but in every instance with negative results.

Not so with the candies and honeys. The latter, as you will see, were, as a rule, very impure. The people of this city must eat very little honey, judging from the absence of this article from nearly every grocery. They had to be procured from the drug stores and, in some instances, were believed to have been compounded after being called for. Some of these honeys are, however, pure goods.

Only low-grade candies were purchased. Since nearly every manufacturer of candies in this city has a retail department attached to the works, it was deemed best to go there and buy largely of the samples used. It is found that starch sugar enters largely into the composition of low-grade candies, and I am told that by the use of a vacuum pan, as high as 60 per cent of dextrose or starch sugar may be advantageously mixed in the candies. Of coloring matter copper and ultramarine were found. Other coloring matter found was organic.

This work has been performed with great care, assisted by two chemists, Mr. W. Wipprecht and Mr. T. P. Hutchinson, both of whom have had considerable experience in sugar work.

I trust it may be acceptable to you.

Yours truly,

WM. C. STUBBS.

Dr. H. W. WILEY,
    *Washington, D. C.*

PHILADELPHIA, PA., *February* 25, 1891.

MY DEAR SIR: I hereby submit my report on the analyses of molasses, honey, low-grade sugars and cheap confections, agreeable to your request of December 9, 1890. Of the 50 samples of low-grade sugars which I have analyzed no adulteration was detected. By reference to the tables, it will be found that the polarization is quite uniform, varying not more than 4 per cent. The greatest difference is in the amount of ash. This is caused undoubtedly by the sugars being in a number of instances made from raw beet as it is well known that the ash of raw beet sugars is greater than that from raw sugars from cane. In some instances there can be but little doubt that the sugars are made from raw cane alone. There is one refinery in this city which claims not to use any raw beet in the making of its product, while other refineries use both raw beet and cane. The soft sugars are made from the sirup resulting from the making of the centrifugal or granulated sugars, as they are commercially known. Consequently, there is more or less invert sugar present, and for all practical purposes I think the amount can be asserted to be the difference between the sum of cane sugar, water, and ash, and 100. A few years since an attempt was made to adulterate soft sugars with glucose sugar. This, however, did not prove to be a commercial success. When the glucose sugar was mixed with the soft, the product absorbed moisture and in only a short time after the barrel was opened it was more or less in a "mushy" condition and could not be sold. It was impossible, as a rule, to obtain the name of the makers of the sugars, since wholesale dealers, when they purchase from refineries, have their names stenciled on the head of the barrel as being sugar refiners, which they are not. I have consequently only noted the names of the persons from whom the sugar was purchased, together with, in some instances, the name of a sugar, such as "Keystone," "Continental," etc. These names, however, will indicate more or less the refinery, since the different refineries have their own names for the different grades of soft sugar.

The table will also show the price per pound.

## MOLASSES.

Of the 50 samples of molasses analyzed there were only 19 pure; all the others were adulterated with more or less glucose sirup. There was no tin detected in any of the samples; the only adulteration besides glucose sirup being the fact that they had been bleached by means of sulphurous acid or a sulphite, some of the samples smelling very strongly of sulphurous acid, and a sediment in the bottle on examination being shown to be a sulphite. At the same time the molasses had an acid reaction, indicating that in all probability this resulted from an acid being made use of to liberate the sulphurous acid from the sulphite, there being in the market a preparation which is sold with directions how to use it, with the object of bleaching dark-colored sirups.

All of these samples when bought were sold under the name of "New Orleans" or, "sirup" or "mixed goods," but in only a few instances did the seller sell them for "mixed" goods. By reference, however, to the table it will be noticed that a large number of those which were sold for New Orleans molasses were really glucose sirup. One reason, I think, for the few samples of pure molasses which I obtained was owing to the fact that a firm in this city makes a business of manufacturing mixed goods, and they naturally sell the greatest bulk of their product in this city and vicinity. There is no trouble in detecting the addition of glucose sirup to molasses. The polarization will indicate this, if it exceeds 56, without the necessity of inversion, and while I have met with molasses, polarizing about 50, which contained glucose sirup, it is a very rare case, the polarization being, when glucose sirup is added, from 75 up.

In case of molasses it was not possible to obtain the name of the maker, and only the name of the seller is given. The table will show polarization before and after inversion, reducing sugar before inversion, sucrose calculated by means of Clerget's formulas and the amount of ash.

As the result of the investigation as well as the experience we have met with in New Jersey, I consider that it is difficult to find in the market a sample of pure molasses such as could have been obtained some years since. If it is not adulterated with glucose sirup, it has been treated with chemicals in order to lighten its color. This latter method is quite as much an adulteration as the former, and is, in my opinion, to be protested against much more than the use of glucose sirup. There is nothing deleterious in glucose and its object is simply to make a sirup not only pleasing to the eye but more pleasant, in the opinion of many, to the taste.

### CHEAP CONFECTIONS.

Of the 25 samples of candies bought they were all purchased from stands on the street or from small stores, the object being to obtain candies which would be more likely to be adulterated than if purchased from larger stores. All the samples were more or less colored, some very highly, but in no instance was any mineral coloring matter detected, the coloring agent in all cases being an aniline color. This was determined by dissolving some of the candy in water and noting the absorption bands as shown by a small pocket spectroscope. There was no terra alba detected, the candies being composed of cane sugar, glucose, starch, or flour.

The candies purchased consisted of sticks, broken candy, caramels, and such as are usually seen on stands or in small stores. It will be seen on reference to the table that there was a very small amount of " matters insoluble in water," this fact showing that they were much purer than one would anticipate from the various statements which have been published. Where the matters insoluble in water have been large, it has been in cases where the candies have been composed of an admixture of starch or flour or cocoanut, or some similar material, but not from the addition of any mineral substances. From the fact that the coloring agent used was aniline, I examined very carefully for the presence of arsenic, but failed to obtain any reaction. While a few years since aniline colors contained arsenic, at the present time there is no difficulty in obtaining them perfectly free; in fact they are sold with the guarantee to this effect.

It will be noticed from the price which was paid for these candies that they must have been, as they were, of a low grade. They were all more or less flavored, the flavoring agent being artificial and not natural and consisting of the higher ethers.

### LIQUID HONEY.

This substance can be classed with molasses in the difficulty of obtaining the pure article. The effort was made to obtain as many different brands as possible, and I succeeded in obtaining 31 samples from as many different makers and 19 unknown makers. In doing this there were 132 stores visited, of which 103 sold a brand which was shown to be adulterated. The adulterant used is cane sugar or glucose, or both, while in some instances it appears as if a solution of invert sugar had been used. I have not been able to learn whether such an article is manufactured, although it would be a simple matter for a maker to produce it. Judging from the labels on the various bottles, one is struck with the fact that those samples which claim to be of the greatest purity are as a rule adulterated, and a sample which lays no claim to purity, but is simply marked "honey," is as often pure. All the samples obtained were liquid honey, although there are to be found in the market jars containing portions of comb. These, however, as is well known, are adulterated, the only honey being the small piece of comb. The makers of the adulterated honey do not always use the same formula. This fact is shown from the analysis of different samples bearing the same brand. Makers also have different brands for different grades of their honey, all being adulterated, one manufacturer in this city producing four and perhaps more different brands, they varying from pure glucose sirup, with a flavor, to a mixture of glucose and cane sugar in varying proportions—none of them containing a particle of honey.

The result of this examination has been to show that there is quite as much adulterated honey in the market as there was in 1886, when I made a very extensive investigation for the New Jersey dairy commissioner, and that the adulteration is now the same as it was then. The manufacturer in this city of mixed sirups also makes a honey. The flavor and taste are very similar to the pure article, and a number can not detect the difference. How he makes it, or how the flavoring is obtained, is of course known only to him. The substance consists of a mixture of cane sugar, sirup, and glucose sirup, and he has quite an extensive sale for it.

The method of analyses for determining whether the sample is pure or not is the same as that for molasses. Pure honey will seldom on a direct polarization indicate more than + 3 in my experience, although it has been stated that there are honeys which have indicated as much as + 7. All the adulterated honeys on the direct polarization indicate from + 25 to over 100, according to the amount of cane sugar or glucose which has been used. On inversion if only cane sugar has been used the polarization will be to the left, whereas if glucose is used it will be to the right.

The following are the names and the marks on the bottle:

Pure California White Clover Honey, P. J. Ritter Company, Philadelphia.

XX White Clover Honey, no maker.

White Clover Honey, Sleeper, Wells & Aldrich.

Honey, Arthur Todd, Philadelphia.

Virgin Honey, Philadelphia Pickling Company.

Pure Extracted Honey, T. S. Borden, Burlington.

Honey, Phildelphia Pickling Company.

Pure Honey, Philadelphia Pickling Company.

Pure Honey, W. G. Griffiths.

Pure Honey, Anderson & Co.

Pure Honey, Henry Bassett, Salem, N. J.

California Honey, no maker.

White Rose Honey, New Jersey Preserving Company.

Choice Extracted Northern Honey, Geo. D. Powell.

Superior Extracted Honey, Walker, McCord & Co.

XXX White Clover California, J. O'Schimmel Company.

Pure Honey, Stevenson Bros.

Strictly Pure Extracted, Austin Nichols & Co.

California Honey, E. T. Coudoncy Company.

Choice Honey, Wm. Collins, New York.

Los Angeles California Honey, John Long, New York.

Ritter's Pure California Honey, Ritter & Co., Philadelphia.

Old Virginia Pure Honey, Geo. K. McMechen.

Pure Clover Honey, no maker.

XX White Clover Honey, G. & R.

Honey, Chas. G. F. Denk.

Golden Rod Honey, Wm. Thompson, New York.

Superior Honey, Witimans Bros., Philadelphia.

Pure California Honey, Thos. Martindale & Co., Philadelphia.

Extracted Honey, C. H. Luttgens, Hammonton, N. J.

Pure Honey, P. A. Garretson, Hillsboro, N. J.

Old Virginia Honey, Geo. K. McMechen & Son.

Strained Honey, Francis H. Leggett & Co.

Pure Honey, Max Ams, New York.

The method of analysis has been as directed in your letter of instructions. The polariscope made use of is a Soleil-Ventzke, made by Dr. C. Scheibler, of Berlin. The sample of sugar received from you polarized 99.8 in a 200mm tube. The half tube polarized 49.9. I have a quartz plate indicating 99 with which it is my custom to test the instrument. All readings which I have given have been based on the basis of 100 and not 99.8. The determinations of the amount of reducing sugar were made with a Fehling's solution, 10 cc equaling 0.05 dextrose. The amount of sucrose was calculated by Clerget's formula, the temperature being 20° C.

By an examination of the amount of reducing sugar in the molasses, some curious results are shown, which can only be accounted for by the fact that the glucose which has been made use of as an adulterant contained varying amount of dextrin. This fact is well known to me, as I have been called on to examine the commercial glucose and have found that frequently there is a quantity of dextrin present. The same specific gravity of two glucoses will frequently show as much as 40 points difference on the polariscope. The numbers given on the table of the various samples will show by reference to the numbers on the tables of soft sugars from whom they were obtained, since in the purchase of the samples the effort was made to obtain from the same person a sample of sugar, molasses, and honey. Consequently, I have not repeated the name of the seller on the tables giving the result of the molasses and honey analyses. The determination of the amount of ash was, as a rule, made by taking three grammes of substance in a platinum dish of about 2.5 inches in diameter. The reducing sugar has in all cases been calculated as dextrose. In giving the results of the honey analyses I have given one table containing them all, and a subsequent one where I have separated and classified the honeys as to their purity and the adulterant made use of.

List of those from whom purchased:

C. H. Rambo, Gloucester, N. J.
L. Fowler, Gloucester, N. J.
James McLaughlin, Gloucester, N. J.
R. K. Jester, Burlington, N. J.
Samuel Burr, Burlington, N. J.
George F. Worth, Burlington, N. J.
Sherman Bros., Burlington, N. J.
G. F. Fort, Burlington, N. J.
William Sherwood, Burlington, N. J.
George W. Kimball, Burlington, N. J.
Samuel Emmons, Burlington, N. J.
Shinn & Son, Burlington, N. J.
Ivins, Pettit, Burlington, N. J.
G. W. Swaney, Camden, N. J.
Charles Warner, Camden, N. J.
Horner & Son, Camden, N. J.
C. K. Morris, Camden, N. J.
A. McAllister, Ninth and Dickinson, Philadelphia.

J. Murriel, 1345 South Eighth street, Philadelphia.
Samuel P. Hehner, 723 Dickinson street, Philadelphia.
C. J. Rollins, 716 Tasker street, Philadelphia.
John McDonnell, Eighth and Wharton, Philadelphia.
Purdy Bros., Fifth and Dickinson, Philadelphia.
C. H. Wescott, Philadelphia.
John Wilson, Philadelphia.
County East End Grocery, Philadelphia.
Deacon & Frey, Philadelphia.
Callowhill Street Market.
G. W. Jenkins.
A. Honget.
L. Blacss.
Shengle & Smull.

From some of the above there were two samples obtained, and samples of sirup obtained from all.

The accompanying tables give the result of the analyses, and in the case of honeys I have separated those which appear to be pure from those which are adulterated. The numbers of the different samples indicate by reference to the list of samples what the brand or mark was, as well as from whom purchased.

All of which is respectfully submitted.

SHIPPEN WALLACE, *Chemist.*

Dr. H. W. WILEY,
  *Chemist, U. S. Department of Agriculture, Washington, D. C.*

————

COLUMBUS, OHIO, *March* 1, 1891.

SIR: The undersigned has the honor to submit the following report of the investigation of saccharine products, made under your direction for the U. S. Department of Agriculture.

Very respectfully,

H. A. WEBER.

Dr. H. W. WILEY,
  *U. S. Department of Agriculture, Washington, D. C.*

26.048 grams of the sugar were dissolved in a flask holding 100 grams of water at 17.5° C. when filled to the mark :

Polarization of 200 mm tube......................................... 99. 4
Polarization of 100 mm tube......................................... 49. 7

### TEST FOR COMMERCIAL GLUCOSE.

It is convenient in the examination of sirups, honeys, etc., to have an easy preliminary test for the presence of commercial glucose. As commercial glucose always contains about 50 per cent of dextrin, the writer has employed the dextrin reaction with iodine for this purpose. The test is applied in the following manner : A watch glass, placed upon white paper, is half filled with sirup, etc., to be tested. Eight or ten drops of a saturated solution of iodine in 50 per cent alcohol are allowed to fall upon the surface. If no glucose is present the iodine will dissipate in a short time and the original color of the sirup will be restored. If glucose is present a permanent brown color or precipitate will remain. In the case of thick honeys it is best to add a few drops of water and mix before the tincture of iodine is applied. Candies and sugars may be tested in the same way after dissolving a portion to the consistency of sirup.

### SUGARS.

The 50 samples of low-grade sugars were collected in the city of Columbus, and fairly represent the quality of sugars as sold on this market. As the analyses show, none of these sugars was adulterated.

### SIRUPS.

The 50 samples of sirups collected in the city of Columbus, Ohio, embrace New Orleans molasses, maple molasses, and table sirups. Of the 17 samples of New Orleans molasses examined, 3 were found to be adulterated with commercial glucose.

Among the 17 samples of maple molasses 6 were found to be adulterated with commercial glucose. This fact was a surprise to the writer, since two years ago the dairy and food commission of Ohio had succeeded in driving all of these spurious brands of maple sirup from the State. By referring to the analyses of the remaining 11 samples of maple sirup it will be seen that some of the samples have a considerable proportion of reducing sugars, and at the same time a low content of ash. In the manufacture of maple sirup and sugar, the salts contained in the sap are not separated from the finished product. The writer has never found the ash of genuine maple sirups to fall below 0.5 per cent. It would seem, therefore, that some of the samples not adulterated with glucose were contaminated with cane sugar or sirup having a low content of ash.

### HONEYS.

As the itemized bill sent with this report will show, the price paid for the 50 samples of honey purchased in various parts of the State was uniformly that of pure honey, or 20 cents per pound. The immense fraud perpetrated upon the consumer in the sale of this one article is evident from the fact, as shown by the analyses, that of the 50 samples examined 20 were found to be adulterated with commercial glucose costing about 3 cents per pound. Only two of the samples, Nos. 14 and 48, contained an exceptional amount of cane sugar. This would suggest a contamination with cane sugar or sirup.

### CANDIES.

Not a single sample of the 25 candies examined consisted of pure cane sugar. They were all mixtures of cane sugar with commercial glucose or starch, or both. No mineral contamination, either for bulk or color, was present. All of the colors, with the exception of cochineal, turmeric, and lampblack, were aniline dyes.

METHOD FOR DETERMINATION OF SUCROSE IN PRESENCE OF GRAPE SUGAR, AND DEXTRIN OR SOLUBLE STARCH.

(1) *For sirups and honeys.*—Five grams are weighed and diluted to 500 cc, grape or reducing sugar, determined by Fehling's solution; 250 cc of the solution are boiled in sand bath for one hour with 5 cc commercial acetic acid, allowed to cool neutralized with sodium carbonate, and again diluted to 250 cc. The total reducing sugar is now determined and the sucrose calculated in the usual manner.

(2) *For candies.*—Five grams are weighed, dissolved in water and diluted to 200 cc ; 100 cc of this solution are diluted to 250 cc and boiled on sand bath for one hour with 5 cc commercial acetic acid. Total reducing sugar determined by Fehling's method. In the other portion the reducing sugar is determined if the solution is of the proper strength ; if not, 5 to 20 grams, as may be necessary, are weighed and diluted to 100 cc for this purpose. From the data obtained the percentage of sucrose is calculated. That the dextrin is not converted into reducing sugar by this process may be seen from the analyses of honey, No. 17, 19, etc. That the cane sugar is inverted will be seen by the examination of the analyses of candy, all of which were made by this method.

———

NEW YORK, *March* 1, 1891.

SIR : Herewith please find my report on 175 samples of sugars, confections, honeys, sirups, and molasses, purchased in New York City and its immediate vicinity, and examined at your request and by authority of the Secretary of Agriculture.

Allow me to take this opportunity of acknowledging my obligations to Mr. Theodore A. Havemeyer, New York, for his kindness and courtesy in granting the facilities of one of the laboratories of the American Sugar Refining Company for the prosecution of this work. I append a statement on collection of samples, etc.

Respectfully,

FERDINAND G. WIECHMANN.

Prof. H. W. WILEY,
   *Washington, D. C.*

### COLLECTION OF SAMPLES.

All samples were purchased by myself. My efforts were directed to procuring them from the different districts of New York City in order to make the collection a fairly representative one. Some samples were obtained in Brooklyn, eastern division.

*Sugars.*—In buying these I generally asked for "brown" sugar in order to secure the lowest grade in the market. In only one or two instances, however, was I successful in obtaining the article desired, as there is apparently no longer a demand for this quality. A few samples of powdered sugar were selected, in some of the poorer quarters of New York, as popular belief holds this grade especially liable to adulteration.

*Confections.*—With few exceptions these were bought directly from the manufacturers. Brightly colored samples were preferred ; specimens, red, blue, green, and yellow in color, are represented in the series analyzed.

*Honeys.*—In selecting these I aimed to secure as many different brands as possible. The 50 samples secured represent 17 different manufacturers.

*Molasses and sirups.*—New Orleans and Porto Rico molasses, and sirups, varying from a dark brown to a bright yellow, constitute the series.

### METHODS OF ANALYSIS.

*Treatment of samples.*—The sugars and confections were thoroughly crushed and mixed and preserved in air-tight jars ; the honeys, molasses, and sirups were kept in the bottles in which they were purchased, and thoroughly mixed before analysis.

*Examination of polariscope.*—The polariscope used, a half-shade instrument made by Schmidt & Haensch, was examined with the test sugar furnished by the Department. The weighing of the sugar, 26.048 grams, was made on a balance indicating tenths of a milligram. The sample was dissolved in distilled water at 17.5° C. and made up to 100 cc in a flask graduated to contain 100 05 grams of pure water at 17.5° C. The polariscope having been correctly set at zero, the above sugar solution polarized in—

The 100 mm tube ......................................... 49.9
The 200 mm tube ......................................... 99.9

*Composition and standardizing of Fehling's solution.*—The Fehling's solution used was prepared according to the following formula:

Sulphate of copper, cryst...........34.639 g in 500 cc of water.
Rochelle salts ...................173.000 g in 400 cc of water.
. Sodium hydrate ................: 50.000 g in 100 cc of water.

To standardize this solution the test sugar sent by the Department was used.

Of this there was weighed out 0.9500 gram. This was dissolved in about 75 cc of distilled water, 2.5 cc. concentrated C. P. hydrochloric acid were added, the mixture warmed up to 68° C. and kept for five minutes at between 68° and 70° C.

The flask with its contents was then quickly cooled, the solution was neutralized with sodium carbonate, and then made up to 100 cc. Of this solution exactly 5.0 cc were required to precipitate all of the copper in 10 cc of the above Fehling solution.

10 cc Fehling solution contain 0.0877 copper.

5 cc of the above invert sugar solution contain 0.050 grams invert sugar.[*]

As 0.0877 copper were precipitated by 0.050 invert sugar,

$$0.0877 \div 0.05 = 1.754$$

that is, the ratio of invert sugar to copper is as 1: 1.754 with a 1 per cent solution of invert sugar.

PREPARATION OF SOLUTIONS FOR POLARIZATION.

*Polarizations.*—Whenever possible the solutions were prepared for polarization solely by addition of basic acetate of lead, together with a few drops of acetic acid. In numerous instances, however, in the analysis of confections—honeys and molasses—the addition of two to three cubic centimeters of alumina cream was found to be indispensable.

With many of the confections, sirup, and molasses samples, dry blood carbon had also to be used in order to effect decolorization. This carbon was perfectly dry and always added after making the solution up to 100 cc. All readings in the polariscope were made at 20° C., and the observations were in most instances made by two observers.

*Polarization after inversion.*—The inversion was made on 50 cc of the solution used for the direct polarization. The inversion was effected by the addition of 5 cc of concentrated hydrochloric acid; the solution, about 75 cc in volume, was heated to between 67° and 68° and kept at that temperature for five minutes. It was then quickly cooled, made up to 100 cc, and some of this solution was placed in an observation tube provided with a thermometer and the reading taken at 20° C.

*Sucrose.*—The following is the calculation by which the sucrose was found wherever recorded.

$$\text{Sucrose} = \frac{100\ S}{142.66 - \frac{1}{2}\ t}.$$

S = sum of the two polarizations of the normal weight solution, before and after inversion, the minus sign being neglected.

t = temperature in degrees C. at which the polarization of the inverted solution was observed. In all of the analyses here reported, $t = 20°$ C.

[*] 95 sucrose correspond to 100 invert sugar. (U. S. Department of Agriculture, Division of Chemistry, Bulletin No. 24, p. 199.) If 0.9500 grams sucrose are dissolved up to 100 cc, 1 cubic centimeter = 0.01 grams invert-sugar, and 5 cubic centimeters = 0.05 grams invert sugar.

*Reducing sugar.*—This was determined by dissolving 1 gram of the sample in 100 cc of water. Each cc of the solution contains therefore 0.01 gram of substance. This test was carried out in the usual manner by allowing so much of this solution to flow into 10 cc of the Fehling solution, kept at the boiling-point, until all of the copper had been precipitated as cuprous oxide.

The end of the test was determined by aid of a ferrocyanide of potassium and acetic acid solution ; the amount of invert sugar present is found by dividing 500 by the number of cubic centimeters of saccharine solution used to precipitate all of the copper. This value obtained records the amount of reducing sugar in percentage.

*Water.*—On the sugar and confection samples the water determinations were made on 5 grams ; in the honey, the sirup, and molasses samples 2 grams were used.

With all of the confection, honey, sirup, and molasses samples sand had to be mixed, in order to insure a perfect desiccation. The drying was accomplished in a water-jacketed air bath, the water in which was cold at the start, and which was gradually raised to the boiling point.

The sugars and confections were dried from three and a half to four hours ; the honey, sirup, and molasses samples received ninety-one consecutive hours' drying in a fresh-water bath, and were then placed for two to four hours more in a salt-water bath, there being maintained at a constant temperature of between 102° and 103° C.

*Ash.*—For the determination of the ash there were used of all samples 2.5 grams. These were burned off with ether and sulphuric acid, and from the weight found one-tenth was deducted. The incineration was in every instance made at dull-red heat in platinum dishes placed within a platinum muffle.

*Coloring matters.*—The test for coloring matters was applied to the confections. Five grams were dissolved in distilled water, made up to 100 cc, and filtered through paper or through asbestos.

In nearly all of the samples the coloring matter was completely soluble in water. A portion of the filtrate was evaporated, the residue incinerated, and the ash taken up with distilled water.

In the very few instances where the coloring matter was not completely soluble in water it was removed from the filter and examined. In some cases copper, lead, and iron were looked for.

*Matter insoluble in cold water.*—Five grams of the confection samples were dissolved in cold distilled water, and the solution made up to 100 cc. The samples were left in the water for two and a quarter hours, being frequently stirred. The insoluble matter was then removed by filtration through weighed filters of paper or asbestos. These, with their contents, were then thoroughly dried at the temperature of boiling water, reweighed, and the amount of insoluble matter calculated and recorded in percentage.

*Tin.*—This metal was tested for in all of the sirup and molasses samples. About 50 grams of the sample were incinerated, the ash was boiled with hydrochloric acid, and sulphuretted hydrogen was passed into the solution. When a precipitate was formed this was separated by filtration and further examined for tin by attempted reduction to the metallic state.

RECORD OF ANALYSES.

The total number of samples analyzed was 178.

There were required :

Samples.

Group   I. Sugars ........................................ 50

        II. Sirups and molasses ........................... 50

      III. Honeys ..................................... 50

      IV. Confections ................................. 25

In addition to these, two samples of undoubtedly genuine honey and one sample of "commercial dextrin" were examined for comparison with the samples purchased.

Special tests, whenever made, and such comments as seemed called for, will be found appended to the full record of analysis of each group.

## EXAMINATION OF SUGARS.

A sample of pure granulated sugar, of a polarimetric value of ap·proximately 99.7, was sent to the analysts, in order that they might use it in testing their polariscopes and setting their solutions of copper. Thus the same sample was used by all the analysts, and a comparison of the polariscopes used can be easily made.

The polarizations obtained by the several analysts were as follows :

|  | In 200 mm tube. | In 100 mm tube. | In 220 mm tube. |
|---|---|---|---|
| H. A. Huston | 99. 7 | 49. 9 | |
| H. H. Nicholson | 100. 0 | 50. 0 | |
| W. B. Rising | 100. 0 | | |
| M. A. Scovell | 99. 8 | 49. 9 | 110.0 |
| S. P. Sharples | 90. 9 | 50. 0 | |
| W. C. Stubbs | 100. 0 | 50. 0 | |
| Shippen Wallace | 99. 8 | 40. 9 | |
| H. A. Weber | 99. 4 | 49. 7 | |
| F. G. Wiechmann | 99. 9 | 49. 9 | |
| Chemical division, Department of Agriculture | 99. 73 | | |

The reading, 99.73, was obtained by the examination of two solutions of sugar, weighed separately. These solutions were read independently by three skilled observers, and thirty-six readings were made. The mean of these closely agreeing readings was 99.93.

Checked with a standard quartz plate it was found that the instrument read 0.2° too high. The true polarization of the sample sugar was therefore 99.73 for the 200 mm tube.

Comparing this number with the results obtained, the following observations may be made :

  Mr. Huston—instrument .......................... 0.03 too low.
  Mr. Nicholson—instrument........................ 0.27 too high.
  Mr. Rising—instrument........................... 0.27 too high.
  Mr. Scovell—instrument .......................... 0.07 too high.
  Mr. Sharples—instrument ......................... 0.17 too high.
  Mr. Stubbs—instrument........................... 0.37 too high.
  Mr. Wallace—instrument.......................... 0.07 too high.
  Mr. Weber—instrument............................ 0.33 too low.
  Mr. Wiechmann—instrument...................... 0.17 too high.

The data of all the analyses following have been carefully examined and in some instances appear to be anomalous. An attempt has been made to have these anomalous results corrected by the several analysts, but not always with success. For those that are still uncorrected the editor disclaims responsibility

# ANALYSIS OF SUGARS

## ANALYSES BY H. A. HUSTON.

### Description of samples.

| No. | Bought of. | Manufacturer or brand. | Description. | Price per pound. |
|---|---|---|---|---|
| 101 | Chas. H. Slack, Chicago ........... | Armelise X D C...... | New Orleans sugar, open kettle. | $0.0600 |
| 102 | ......do............................ | Standard Sugar Refinery, Boston. | Extra Yellow C; Dakota C . | .0600 |
| 103 | W. G. Brown, La Fayette........... | ........................ | Yellow C .................... | .0500 |
| 104 | .....do............................ | ........................ | A sugar ..................... | .0050 |
| 105 | ......do............................ | ........................ | New Orleans sugar........ | .0600 |
| 106 | .....do............................ | ........................ | Pressed Loaf sugar ........ | .0300 |
| 107 | ...:..do............................ | ........................ | Powdered sugar.... ....... | .0800 |
| 108 | A. B. Braden, La Fayette........... | Mallor, Serrick & Co., New York. | Confectioners' sugar........ | .1250 |
| 109 | ......do............................ | Sugar Trust .......... | Yellow C .................... | .0600 |
| 110 | Schwarm & Heinmiller........... | ........................ | Powdered sugar ............ | .1000 |
| 111 | Beck & Frasch, La Fayette ...... | ........................ | .....do ..................... | .1000 |
| 112 | ......do............................ | ........................ | A sugar ..................... | .0700 |
| 113 | ......do............................ | ........................ | Yellow C .................... | .0600 |
| 114 | P. Feeley, LaFayette....... ...... | Havemeyer & Elder .. | ....do .:.................... | .0600 |
| 115 | ......do............................ | ....do ............... | Ideal C .................... | .0700 |
| 116 | .....do............................ | ........................ | Powdered sugar ............ | .0850 |
| 117 | Emsing Brothers .................. | ........................ | Extra C..................... | .0625 |
| 118 | .....do............................ | ........................ | Ridgewood A............... | .0700 |
| 119 | .....do............................ | ........................ | Powdered sugar ........:... | .1000 |
| 120 | .....do............................ | ........................ | Dark C ..................... | .0500 |
| 121 | C. Jevne & Co., Chicago .......... | ........................ | New Orleans sugar ......... | .0600 |
| 122 | .....do............................ | ........................ | Powdered sugar........... | .0750 |
| 123 | .....do............................ | ........................ | C sugar..................... | .0600 |
| 124 | .....do............................ | ........................ | Demerara sugar ............ | .0600 |
| 125 | Rockwood Brothers, Chicago .... | .................-........ | Maple sugar................ | .2200 |
| 126 | ......do............................ | ........................ | Powdered sugar ............ | .0750 |
| 127 | Joyce & Co., Chicago............. | ........................ | ......do .................... | .0800 |
| 128 | .....do ............................ | ........................ | A sugar ..................... | .0700 |
| 129 | ......do ........................... | ........................ | Yellow C.................... | .0600 |
| 130 | .....do ............................ | ........................ | Maple sugar................ | .1300 |
| 131 | Hassett's, Chicago ............... | ........................ | Powdered sugar ............ | .0800 |
| 132 | .....do............................ | ........................ | Light C sugar .............. | .0600 |
| 133 | .....do ............................ | ........................ | Dark C sugar ... .......... | .0600 |
| 134 | .... do ............................ | ........................ | A sugar..................... | .0600 |
| 135 | H. H. Lee & Co., Indianapolis..... | ........................ | Windsor C sugar .......... | .0600 |
| 136 | ......do............................ | ........................ | Confectioners' sugar........ | .0800 |
| 137 | .....do............................ | ........................ | New Orleans sugar ........ | .0600 |
| 138 | .....do............................ | ........................ | Ridgewood A sugar ........ | .0700 |
| 139 | .....do............................ | ........................ | Empire A sugar ............ | .0700 |
| 140 | .....do............................ | ........................ | 4 X powdered sugar ........ | .1000 |
| 141 | ......do ........................... | ........................ | Powdered sugar ... ........ | .1000 |
| 142 | J. W. Power, Indianapolis ........ | ........................ | A sugar..................... | .0800 |
| 143 | .....do............................ | ........................ | Extra C sugar............... | .0800 |
| 144 | .....do ............................ | ........................ | Powdered sugar............ | .1000 |
| 145 | Henry Swain, Indianapolis ....... | J. H. Barker & Co., Rutland. | Maple sugar................ | .2600 |
| 146 | L. Kimmel, Indianapolis ......... | ........................ | Powdered sugar ............ | .1000 |
| 147 | .....do ............................ | ........................ | A sugar ..................... | .0700 |
| 148 | Joseph Bock, La Fayette........... | ........................ | C sugar..................... | .0700 |
| 149 | ......do ........................... | ........................ | A sugar ..................... | .0600 |
| 150 | ......do ........................... | ........................ | Powdered sugar .:.......... | .1000 |

*Analytical data.*

| No. | Direct polarization. | Indirect polarization. | Temperature ° C. | Sucrose by factor 144. | Water. | Ash. |
|---|---|---|---|---|---|---|
| 101 | 89.90 | | | | 4.420 | 0.440 |
| 102 | 88.40 | | | | 3.980 | 0.890 |
| 103 | 90.80 | | | | 3.820 | 0.700 |
| 104 | 94.11 | | | | 4.630 | 0.220 |
| 105 | 93.54 | | | | 1.230 | 0.740 |
| 106 | 99.90 | | | | 0.004 | 0.004 |
| 107 | 100.00 | | | | 0.004 | 0.004 |
| 108 | 99.10 | | | | 0.108 | 0.024 |
| 109 | 88.60 | | | | 2.130 | 1.028 |
| 110 | 99.90 | | | | 0.012 | 0.001 |
| 111 | 99.00 | | | | 0.036 | 0.004 |
| 112 | 93.10 | | | | 5.436 | 0.140 |
| 113 | 86.97 | | | | 3.160 | 4.280 |
| 114 | 81.45 | | | | 5.568 | 0.566 |
| 115 | 93.11 | | | | 4.440 | 0.380 |
| 116 | 99.00 | | | | 0.260 | 0.134 |
| 117 | 74.56 | | | | 4.400 | 2.076 |
| 118 | 89.94 | | | | 4.328 | 0.424 |
| 119 | 99.00 | | | | 0.024 | 0.002 |
| 120 | 78.44 | | | | 3.316 | 2.048 |
| 121 | 79.44 | | | | 3.304 | 0.123 |
| 122 | 99.90 | | | | 0.003 | 0.002 |
| 123 | 90.10 | | | | 8.150 | 0.936 |
| 124 | 93.40 | | | | 1.506 | 0.764 |
| 125 | 84.11 | | | | 4.344 | 3.876 |
| 126 | 99.80 | | | | 0.092 | 0.092 |
| 127 | 99.00 | | | | 0.300 | 0.008 |
| 128 | 90.59 | | | | 0.005 | 0.306 |
| 129 | 88.41 | | | | 0.664 | 0.101 |
| 130 | 84.21 | | | | 0.080 | 0.612 |
| 131 | 99.20 | | | | 0.120 | 0.044 |
| 132 | 88.30 | | | | 0.060 | 1.260 |
| 133 | 86.44 | | | | 4.370 | 3.552 |
| 134 | 96.10 | | | | 3.144 | 0.028 |
| 135 | 87.40 | | | | 4.286 | 0.840 |
| 136 | 96.70 | | | | 2.564 | 0.064 |
| 137 | 90.40 | | | | 1.400 | 0.864 |
| 138 | 84.11 | | | | 4.966 | 1.404 |
| 139 | 87.50 | | | | 4.964 | 0.312 |
| 140 | 100.00 | | | | 0.001 | 0.006 |
| 141 | 99.80 | | | | 0.001 | 0.003 |
| 142 | 97.10 | | | | 1.040 | 0.060 |
| 143 | 89.90 | | | | 2.668 | 0.001 |
| 144 | 99.20 | | | | 0.090 | 0.040 |
| 145 | 81.40 | | | | 6.688 | 0.120 |
| 146 | 99.10 | | | | 0.008 | 0.004 |
| 147 | 90.40 | | | | 6.396 | 0.304 |
| 148 | 90.10 | | | | 5.272 | 1.580 |
| 149 | 90.50 | | | | 5.868 | 0.008 |
| 150 | 99.60 | | | | 0.004 | 0.005 |

## ANALYSES BY H. H. NICHOLSON.

### Description of samples.

| No. | Name of dealer. | Manufacturer. | Label. |
|---|---|---|---|
| 1 | Wm. Fleming, Omaha, Nebr | Havemeyer | Extra C. |
| 2 | .....do .. | ......do | Brown C. |
| 3 | Miner Bros , Red Cloud, Nebr | | Do. |
| 4 | Gladstone Bros., Omaha, Nebr | Havemeyer | Light brown. |
| 5 | Little & Williams, Omaha, Nebr | | Brown C. |
| 6 | B. F. Mizner, Red Cloud, Nebr | New Orleans | N. O. |
| 7 | Jones & Evans, Red Cloud, Nebr | | Light brown C. |
| 8 | Thompson & Pettinger, Beatrice, Nebr | New Orleans | N. O. |
| 9 | .....do | | C. |
| 10 | Long & Moschel, Beatrice, Nebr | New Orleans | N. O. |
| 11 | Anderson & Co., Beatrice, Nebr | | Extra C. |
| 12 | Geo. Bosselmann, Lincoln, Nebr | New Orleans | N. O. |
| 13 | S. P. Stevens & Co., Lincoln, Nebr | ......do | N. O. |
| 14 | Sparrett Bros., Lincoln, Nebr | | Pure cane. |
| 15 | H. R. Nissley & Co., Lincoln, Nebr | New Orleans | N. O. |
| 16 | Jas. Miller, Lincoln, Nebr | ......do | N. O. |
| 17 | Geo. Bosselmann, Lincoln, Nebr | | Extra C. |
| 18 | McShane & Benner, Lincoln, Nebr | New Orleans | N. O. |
| 19 | Cook & Johnson, Lincoln, Nebr | Spreckels | Extra C. |
| 20 | Scott, Ashland, Nebr | | Brown C. |
| 21 | Wm. Hotaling, Lincoln, Nebr | | Extra C. |
| 22 | .....do | New Orleans | N. O. |
| 23 | James Britton, Lincoln, Nebr | | C. |
| 24 | .....do | New Orleans | N. O. |
| 25 | G. W. Closson, Lincoln, Nebr | Spreckels | C. |
| 26 | Maxwell & Co., Lincoln, Nebr | ......do | Extra C. |
| 27 | J. Monroe, Omaha, Nebr | Havemeyer | C. |
| 28 | Henry Billin & Co., Omaha, Nebr | ......do | C. |
| 29 | D. L. Carpenter, Omaha, Nebr | | C. |
| 30 | Henry Billin & Co., Omaha, Nebr | New Orleans | N. O. |
| 31 | A. L. Root, Omaha, Nebr | Havemeyer & Elder | N. O. |
| 32 | J. Monroe, Omaha, Nebr | Havemeyer | Extra C. |
| 33 | William Gentleman, Omaha, Nebr | Havemeyer & Elder | P o. |
| 34 | .....do | ......do | Light Brown C. |
| 35 | John Swoboda, Omaha, Nebr | Havemeyer | C. |
| 36 | H. Blumstan, Omaha, Nebr | Spreckles | C. |
| 37 | .....do | ......do | Light Brown C. |
| 38 | H. Moeller, Omaha, Nebr | ......do | Extra C. |
| 39 | Henry Billin & Co., Omaha, Nebr | Havemeyer | C. |
| 40 | Heimrod & Co., Omaha, Nebr | ......do | Extra C. |
| 41 | J. Slatter, Omaha, Nebr | D. M. Steele & Co. | Do. |
| 42 | Spot Cash Grocery, Omaha, Nebr | New Orleans | N. O. |
| 43 | J. Slatter, Omaha, Nebr | ......do | Brown C. |
| 44 | Heimrod & Co., Omaha, Nebr | Havemeyer | N. O. |
| 45 | J. Neuman, Omaha, Nebr | ......do | Extra C. |
| 46 | Viers Bros., Omaha, Nebr | Spreckles | C. |
| 47 | L. N. Brown, Omaha, Nebr | ......do | C. |
| 48 | J. W. Pennell, Omaha, Nebr | ......do | C. |
| 49 | Heimrod & Henson, Omaha, Nebr | Havemeyer | Light Brown C. |
| 50 | .....do | ......do | C. |

*Analytical data.*

| No. | Direct polarization. | Indirect polarization. | Temperature, °C. | Sucrose by factor 144. | Water. | Ash. |
|-----|------|------|------|------|------|------|
| 1 | 90.1 | | | | 2.06 | 0.54 |
| 2 | 85.6 | | | | 2.20 | 1.27 |
| 3 | 85.3 | | | | 2.95 | 1.46 |
| 4 | 89.9 | | | | 1.08 | 0.73 |
| 5 | 82.8 | | | | 3.16 | 3.63 |
| 6 | 87.7 | | | | 3.03 | 2.47 |
| 7 | 89.1 | | | | 2.58 | 2.33 |
| 8 | 89.1 | | | | 4.44 | 0.97 |
| 9 | 87.8 | | | | 2.96 | 1.98 |
| 10 | 77.3 | | | | 3.73 | 1.95 |
| 11 | 89.8 | | | | 3.21 | 1.14 |
| 12 | 88.6 | | | | 1.55 | 0.63 |
| 13 | 83.9 | | | | 4.23 | 1.43 |
| 14 | 88.6 | | | | 3.16 | 0.99 |
| 15 | 84.4 | | | | 4.33 | 1.59 |
| 16 | 88.2 | | | | 3.49 | 0.89 |
| 17 | 91.2 | | | | 2.50 | 0.79 |
| 18 | 88.6 | | | | 3.43 | 1.33 |
| 19 | 89.6 | | | | 4.40 | 0.84 |
| 20 | 93.4 | | | | 1.77 | 0.72 |
| 21 | 88.8 | | | | 4.68 | 0.74 |
| 22 | 88.1 | | | | 4.24 | 1.38 |
| 23 | 88.2 | | | | 3.83 | 1.43 |
| 24 | 89.2 | | | | 4.28 | 0.91 |
| 25 | 100.0 | | | | 0.13 | 0.06 |
| 26 | 90.7 | | | | 2.05 | 1.06 |
| 27 | 86.3 | | | | 3.68 | 0.66 |
| 28 | 93.2 | | | | 3.71 | 0.57 |
| 29 | 93.5 | | | | 2.21 | 0.68 |
| 30 | 95.3 | | | | 0.76 | 0.84 |
| 31 | 86.7 | | | | 1.63 | 1.09 |
| 32 | 84.1 | | | | 4.17 | 1.05 |
| 33 | 89.6 | | | | 3.58 | 0.56 |
| 34 | 80.8 | | | | 3.22 | 1.52 |
| 35 | 90.8 | | | | 3.59 | 1.02 |
| 36 | 84.4 | | | | 2.72 | 2.03 |
| 37 | 91.1 | | | | 3.20 | 0.87 |
| 38 | 88.3 | | | | 3.85 | 0.65 |
| 39 | 86.7 | | | | 3.01 | 1.53 |
| 40 | 90.1 | | | | 3.59 | 0.65 |
| 41 | 92.3 | | | | 1.05 | 0.57 |
| 42 | 100.2 | | | | 1.07 | 1.88 |
| 43 | 89.8 | | | | 1.93 | 2.30 |
| 44 | 92.9 | | | | 1.31 | 0.93 |
| 45 | 88.1 | | | | 3.43 | 1.98 |
| 46 | 93.3 | | | | 1.95 | 0.89 |
| 47 | 94.6 | | | | 1.58 | 0.46 |
| 48 | 90.4 | | | | 3.38 | 1.02 |
| 49 | 87.6 | | | | 3.90 | 0.99 |
| 50 | 87.6 | | | | 2.07 | 1.10 |

ANALYSES BY W. B. RISING

*Description of samples.*

| No. | Label. | Where bought. | Color. |
|---|---|---|---|
| 4 | Extra C, California Refinery ...... | McLain & Co., Berkeley................ | White. |
| 5 | Granulated, California Refinery .. | ......do................................ | Do. |
| 47 | Extra C, American Refinery ...... | P. Banne, 15th and Mission, San Francisco. | Light. |
| 48 | Extra C............................ | P. A. Holst, 17th and Howard, San Francisco. | Do. |
| 49 | Golden C.......................... | Shotwell and 16th, San Francisco....... | Yellow. |
| 50 | ................................ | ................................ | Dark brown. |
| 51 | Louisiana ........................ | 17th and Howard, San Francisco ....... | Do. |
| 52 | Golden C.......................... | W. Ahren, Folsom and 16th, San Francisco. | Yellow. |
| 53 | Extra .:....,.................... | Kattleman & Rippe, Howard and 16th, San Francisco. | Light. |
| 54 | Extra C.......................... | W. W. Buckmann, Mission and 15th, San Francisco. | Do. |
| 90 | ................................ | J.O.Holst, Minna and 1st, San Francisco. | Light yellow. |
| 91 | ................................ | Clementina and Mission, San Francisco. | Yellow brown. |
| 92 | ................................ | Natoma and 1st, San Francisco........ | Light. |
| 93 | ................................ | D. Tietjen, San Francisco ...... ...... | Dark yellow. |
| 94 | ................................ | Mission and 2d, San Francisco .......... | Light yellow. |
| 95 | ................................ | C. Giese, San Francisco, Pacific and Battery. | Yellow. |
| 96 | American Refinery .............. | 217 2d............................ | Brown. |
| 97 | Extra C.......................... | Pacific and Front, San Francisco........ | Light. |
| 98 | Golden C ........................ | Davis and Pacific, San Francisco....... | Yellow. |
| 99 | ................................ | Cohn Bros., Clementina and 1st ......... | Brown. |
| 100 | American Refinery.............. | Hayes and Dwyer, Mission and 2d ...... | Very light. |
| 101 | American Refinery .............. | Mission and 1st...................... | Do. |
| 102 | ................................ | Mission and 3d...................... | Light. |
| 103 | American........................ | Folsom and 1st .................... | Yellow. |
| 104 | ................................ | Mission and 2d...................... | Do. |
| 105 | American Refinery .............. | Kunder & Westphal, corner Jackson and Drumm, San Francisco. | Light. |
| 106 | American........................ | Derrie and Ecker .................... | Do. |
| 107 | ................................ | Natoma and 2d street, San Francisco ... | Do. |
| 144 | American Refinery .............. | Geary and Larkin streets, San Francisco | Do. |
| 145 | ......do ...................... | A. Buttelman, Howard and 11th streets, | Do. |
| 146 | ......do ...................... | 709 Larkin, San Francisco.............. | Do. |
| 147 | ......do ...................... | Ellis and Larkin streets, San Francisco | Do. |
| 148 | California Refinery .............. | 117 9th street, San Francisco........... | Brown yellow. |
| 149 | American Refinery .............. | Mission and 9th, San Francisco......... | Light yellow. |
| 150 | ......do ...................... | M. Offert, Howard and Folsom streets.. | Light. |
| 151 | ......do ...................... | H. Kayser, 9th and Folsom streets...... | Light yellow. |
| 152 | ................................ | McVicker & Co., 27 9th, San Francisco.. | Yellow. |
| 153 | American Refinery .............. | A. Nachman, Geary and Larkin streets | Do. |
| 154 | ................................ | F. Riecke, Eddy and Larkin streets, San Francisco. | Gray crystalline. |
| 155 | ................................ | Folsom and 11th, San Francisco........ | Light. |
| 156 | ................................ | 1319 Folsom, San Francisco ............ | Do. |
| 157 | American Refinery .............. | Golden Gate Avenue and Larkin, San Francisco. | Yellow. |
| 158 | .... do ...................... | Folsom and 9th, San Francisco.......... | Very white. |
| 159 | ......do ...................... | M. Shea, 1405 Folsom, San Francisco.... | Do. |

*Description of samples*—Continued.

| No. | Label. | Where bought. | Color. |
|---|---|---|---|
| 160 | California Refinery | J. S. Phillips, Folsom and 10th, | Yellow |
| 161 | | 9th and Mission, San Francisco | Do. |
| 162 | American Refinery | Natoma and 9th, San Francisco | Very light. |
| 163 | | O. J. Shehan, 9th and Clementina | Brown. |
| 164 | | La Frenze and Wrage, San Francisco | Very light. |
| 165 | American Refinery | 68 9th, San Francisco | Yellow. |
| 166 | ......do | H. Holting, Port and Larkin, San Francisco. | Very light. |
| 167 | ......do | J. Lane, 9th and Mission, San Francisco | Light. |
| 168 | Golden C | H. Rothschild, 9th and Howard, San Francisco. | Yellow. |
| 169 | ......do | Stevenson and 9th | Do. |
| 170 | | Heller Bros., Natoma and 5th | Light yellow. |
| 171 | | | |
| 172 | | Bœckelman & Co., Mission and 5th | Dark brown. |
| 173 | | Kaufman & Feldman | |
| 174 | | Natoma and 5th | Light brown. |
| 175 | Golden C | J. W. Ryan, Minna and 5th | Light yellow. |

*Analytical data.*

| No. | Direct polariza- tion. | Indirect polariza- tion. | Temper- ature, °C. | Sucrose by Factor 144. | Water. | Ash. |
|---|---|---|---|---|---|---|
| 4 | 85.70 | | | | 4.07 | 5.03 |
| 5 | 98.10 | | | | 0.15 | 0.02 |
| 47 | 91.40 | | | | 3.52 | 0.96 |
| 48 | 89.00 | | | | 3.88 | 1.68 |
| 49 | 82.60 | | | | 5.33 | 2.70 |
| 50 | 86.24 | | | | 4.34 | 0.98 |
| 51 | 87.10 | | | | 4.13 | 1.82 |
| 52 | 82.90 | | | | 4.03 | 1.81 |
| 53 | 86.80 | | | | 4.28 | 1.30 |
| 54 | 82.70 | | | | 4.98 | 1.78 |
| 90 | 86.30 | | | | 4.41 | 1.16 |
| 91 | 85.80 | | | | 3.63 | 1.30 |
| 92 | 90.20 | | | | 4.40 | 0.78 |
| 93 | 84.64 | • | | | 4.24 | 1.54 |
| 94 | 84.60 | | | | 3.60 | 1.26 |
| 95 | 84.70 | | | | 5.31 | 1.83 |
| 96 | 85.20 | | | | 3.61 | 2.42 |
| 97 | 87.90 | | | | 3.10 | 1.36 |
| 98 | 84.15 | | | | 4.20 | 1.41 |
| 99 | 82.50 | | | | 6.66 | 1.63 |
| 100 | 87.70 | | | | 3.85 | 0.63 |
| 101 | 87.20 | | | | 3.75 | 0 68 |
| 102 | 88.50 | | | | 4.08 | 0.77 |
| 103 | 82.30 | | | | 4.88 | 2.93 |
| 104 | 85.70 | | | | 4.64 | 1.21 |
| 105 | 90.20 | | | | 3.68 | 0.76 |
| 106 | 89.70 | | | | 3.29 | 2.13 |
| 107 | 83.27 | | | | 5.23 | 1.23 |

*Analytical data*—Continued.

| No. | Direct polarization. | Indirect polarization. | Temperature, °C. | Sucrose by Factor 144. | Water. | Ash. |
|---|---|---|---|---|---|---|
| 144 | 82.72 | | | | 4.62 | 3.93 |
| 145 | 81.50 | | | | 4.61 | 1.15 |
| 146 | 83.60 | | | | 4.78 | 2.79 |
| 147 | 85.80 | | | | 5.11 | 1.91 |
| 148 | 82.50 | | | | 6.51 | 1.29 |
| 149 | 86.10 | | | | 5.25 | 1.30 |
| 150 | 85.00 | | | | 4.89 | 0.97 |
| 151 | 86.00 | | | | 4.34 | 1.31 |
| 152 | 86.00 | | | | 4.42 | 1.31 |
| 153 | 82.90 | | | | 5.66 | 1.56 |
| 154 | 98.50 | | | | 0.39 | 0.15 |
| 155 | 86.80 | | | | 4.12 | 1.04 |
| 156 | 86.20 | | | | 4.57 | 1.15 |
| 157 | 82.40 | | | | 5.32 | 1.76 |
| 158 | 87.80 | | | | 3.82 | 0.88 |
| 159 | 90.60 | | | | 3.25 | 0.82 |
| 160 | 84.20 | | | | 5.53 | 1.08 |
| 161 | 80.50 | | | | 5.82 | 1.97 |
| 162 | 85.50 | | | | 4.53 | 2.10 |
| 163 | 81.50 | | | | 6.57 | 2.10 |
| 164 | 90.00 | | | | 3.94 | 1.03 |
| 165 | 84.00 | | | | 5.07 | 1.48 |
| 166 | 88.60 | | | | 3.82 | 1.10 |
| 167 | 88.60 | | | | 3.68 | 1.00 |
| 168 | 84.60 | | | | 4.46 | 1.59 |
| 169 | 83.90 | | | | 4.18 | 0.85 |
| 170 | 84.30 | | | | 5.76 | 1.73 |
| 171 | 79.60 | | | | 6.32 | 2.65 |
| 172 | 86.80 | | | | 3.95 | 1.32 |
| 173 | 87.60 | | | | 4.86 | 1.11 |
| 174 | 82.60 | | | | 2.16 | 3.47 |
| 175 | 93.20 | | | | 5.01 | 1.76 |

## ANALYSES BY M. A. SCOVELL

*Description of samples.*

Sample 51. Powdered sugar. Sold by "Griffith," Cincinnati. Made by the Franklin Sugar Refinery, Philadelphia, Pa.

Sample 52. Coffee Crushed. A light C sugar, soft grained. Made by F. O. Matthiessen & Weichers. Sold by Hamilton Grocery Company, Cincinnati, Ohio.

Sample 53. Havemeyer & Elder's Y. C., a straw-colored soft sugar. Sold by R. J. McCombs, Cincinnati, Ohio.

Sample 54. Havemeyer & Elder's Y. C., a soft-grained yellow sugar, brighter colored than 53. Sold by the Hamilton Grocery Company, Cincinnati, Ohio.

Sample 55. Prairie C. Made by F. O. Matthiessen & Weichers. Sold by Henry Vogt, Lexington. A light soft-grained sugar.

Sample 56. Powdered XXX. Havemeyer & Elder. Sold by Joseph R. Peeble's Son's Co., Cincinnati, Ohio.

Sample 57. Dark C. Havemeyer & Elder. Sold by R. J. McCombs, Cincinnati, Ohio. A dark soft-grained sugar. The sample taken from a sugar bin and brand given by the seller.

Sample 58. Y. C. Red Star Brand sugar. Spreckel's Sugar Refinery, Philadelphia, Pa. Sold by Joseph R. Peeble's Son's Co., Cincinnati, Ohio. Taken from bin; brand given by seller.

Sample 59. New Orleans. Open kettle. Sold by Hamilton Grocery Company, Cincinnati, Ohio. A dark, fairly well-grained sugar having a greenish tint.

Sample 60. Y. C. Havemeyer & Elder. Sold by the Great Atlantic and Pacific Tea Company, 663 Pearl street, Cincinnati, Ohio. Sample taken from bin.

Sample 61. Crescent C. F. O. Matthiessen & Weichers. Sold by D. H. B. Coffin, Cincinnati, Ohio. A soft-grained, light straw-colored sugar. From barrel.

Sample 62. Y. C. New Orleans Sugar Refinery Company, New Orleans. A dark-yellow soft-grained sugar. Sold by Thomas Foster, Cincinnati, Ohio. From bin. Description given by seller.

Sample 63. Green Star Brand C. Spreckel's Sugar Refinery, Philadelphia, Pa. Sold by D. H. B. Coffin, Cincinnati, Ohio. From bin. A dark, wet sugar.

Sample 64. Extra C. Havemeyer & Elder. Sold by the Joseph Peeble's Son's Company, Cincinnati, Ohio. From the bin.

Sample 65. Y. C. Havemeyer & Elder. Sold by A. "Barnes," Cincinnati, Ohio. Soft grained, straw colored. From the bin.

Sample 66. New Orleans. Open kettle sugar. Sold by Henry Hineke Company, Cincinnati, Ohio, through Heitmeyer & Company, Cincinnati, Ohio. In barrel.

Sample 67. Orange Yellow. Louisiana Refinery, American Sugar Refining Company, New Orleans. Sold by John Hutchinson, Lexington, Ky. In sacks.

Sample 68. Ridgewood B. Havemeyer & Elder. Sold by C. W. Jefferson, Louisville, Ky. A very light, soft sugar. In barrel.

Sample 69. New Orleans. Open kettle. Sold by Sterritt, Cincinnati, Ohio. In barrel. A fine-grained greenish straw color.

Sample 70. Dark C. From Thurber, Whyland & Co., New York. Sold by C. Sack, Cincinnati, Ohio. A hard, lumpy, dark sugar.

Sample 71. Traders' Brand. F. O. Matthiessen & Weichers. Sold as "Blackberry" sugar, by G. H. Kinnear, Lexington, Ky. A very dark, soft sugar. In barrel.

Sample 72. Extra C. Franklin Sugar Refinery Company, Philadelphia, Pa. Sold by Colter & Co., Cincinnati, Ohio. A light, straw colored, soft sugar.

Sample 73. New Orleans. Open kettle. Saidia Plantation. Sold by John Hutchinson, Lexington, Ky.

Sample 74. Prairie C. F. O. Matthiessen & Weichers. Sold by G. H. Kinnear, Lexington, Ky. In barrel.

Sample 75. Crescent C. F. O. Matthiessen & Weichers. Sold by Scully & Yates, Lexington, Ky. In barrel. Light and soft.

Sample 76. Crescent C. F. O. Matthiessen & Weichers. Sold by John Hutchinson, Lexington, Ky. In bin. Light, soft.

Sample 77. Extra C. Havemeyer & Elder. Sold by Colter & Co., Cincinnati, Ohio. Light and soft. In barrel.

Sample 78. Extra C. Havemeyer & Elder. Sold by W. H. May, Lexington, Ky. In barrel.

Sample 79. New Orleans. Open kettle. A wet dark brown crystallized sugar. Sold by C. W. Jefferson, Louisville, Ky. Wholesaler, Torbitt & Castleman, Louisville, Ky.

Sample 80. Off A. Havemeyer & Elder. Sold by G. T. Sterritt, Cincinnati, Ohio. A white soft sugar.

Sample 81. New Orleans. Open kettle. A light straw-colored crystallized sugar, wet. Sold by M. J. Doyle, Louisville, Ky.

Sample 82. Metropolitan Extra C. F. O. Matthiessen & Weichers. Sold by Eiseman & Co., Cincinnati, Ohio. A soft light sugar, in barrel.

Sample 83. Extra C Coffee sugar. Havemeyer & Elder. Sold by T. J. Cassell, Lexington, Ky. A light soft sugar, in barrel.

Sample 84. Maple sugar. Manufactured for Joseph R. Peebles' Sons' Co., Cincinnati, and sold by Joseph R. Peebles' Sons' Co., Cincinnati, Ohio. A light-colored cake.

Sample 85. Maple sugar. Made by G. G. Ehrmann & Son, Louisville, Ky. Sold by T. N. McClelland, Lexington, Ky. A dark-colored cake.

Sample 86. Caramel sugar. From Thurber, Whyland & Co., New York. Sold by T. N. McClelland, Lexington, Ky. A very dark lumpy sugar, in barrel.

Sample 87. New Orleans. Open kettle. Through Torbitt & Castleman, Louisville, Ky. Sold by Lindsay & Nugent, Lexington, Ky. In barrel.

Sample 88. New Orleans. Open kettle. Sold by Isaac Hutchinson, Lexington, Ky. A well-grained open-kettle sugar, in barrel.

Sample 89. Green Star C. Spreckels. Sold by C. W. Jefferson, Louisville, Ky. From bin.

Sample 90. Extra C. Knight Sugar Refinery. Sold by M. J. Doyle, Louisville, Ky.

Sample 91. Y. C. New Orleans Sugar Refinery Co. Sold by T. Menamara, Cincinnati, Ohio. In bin.

Sample 92. Red Star A. Spreckels. Sold by Montgomery & Bailey, Louisville, Ky. In barrel.

Sample 93. Demerara sugar. Sold by T. H. Watkins, Louisville, Ky. Wholesaler, Creole & Co., Louisville, Ky. A very large-grained yellow sugar. Looks like first centrifugal Louisiana sugars. In bin.

Sample 94. Y. C. New Orleans "Homestead Plantation, J. N. Hill." Sold by C. W. Jefferson, Louisville, Ky. In barrel.

Sample 95. New Orleans sugar. "Glencoe Plantation W. R. K." First centrifugal. Sold by Montgomery & Bailey, Louisville, Ky.

Sample 96. Extra C. Havemeyer & Elder. Sold by "Frank," Cincinnati, Ohio. In bin.

Sample 97. New Orleans. Open kettle. Sold by "Barnes," Cincinnati, Ohio. In barrel.

Sample 98. Y. C. Spreckles. Sold by Berry & Shelby, Lexington, Ky. In barrel. No head. Brand given by sellers.

Sample 99. New Orleans. Open kettle. Sold by J. P. Baunhan, Lexington, Ky., through Torbitt & Castleman, Louisville, Ky. In barrel.

Sample 100. Traders' Brand. F. O. Matthiessen & Weichers. Sold by J. C. Berryman, Lexington, Ky. A very dark sugar. In barrel.

*Analytical data.*

| No. | Direct polariza- tion. | Indirect polariza- tion. | Tempera- ture, °C. | Sucrose by Factor 144. | Water. | Ash. |
|---|---|---|---|---|---|---|
| 51 | 09.75 | .............. | .............. | .............. | 0.02 | 0.02 |
| 52 | 89.5 | .............. | .............. | .............. | 4.87 | 0.64 |
| 53 | 89.2 | .............. | .............. | .............. | 3.42 | 0.88 |
| 54 | 86.7 | .............. | .............. | .............. | 4.72 | 1.87 |
| 55 | 87.3 | .............. | .............. | .............. | 5.04 | 1.11 |
| 56 | 90.7 | .............. | .............. | .............. | 0.03 | Trace. |
| 57 | 88.1 | .............. | .............. | .............. | 2.01 | 1.21 |
| 58 | 88.3 | .............. | .............. | .............. | 3.24 | 0.75 |
| 59 | 92.6 | .............. | .............. | .............. | 4.18 | 1.10 |
| 60 | 88.5 | .............. | .............. | .............. | 2.96 | 0.61 |
| 61 | 89.6 | .............. | .............. | .............. | 3.38 | 0.96 |
| 62 | 88.7 | .............. | .............. | .............. | 2.73 | 0.86 |
| 63 | 88.4 | .............. | .............. | .............. | 3.77 | 3.32 |
| 64 | 85.9 | .............. | .............. | .............. | 4.95 | 0.64 |
| 65 | 91.2 | .............. | .............. | .............. | 3.03 | 1.85 |
| 66 | 93.0 | .............. | .............. | .............. | 1.89 | 0.53 |
| 67 | 86.4 | .............. | .............. | .............. | 3.47 | 1.00 |
| 68 | 84.8 | .............. | .............. | .............. | 6.00 | 0.66 |
| 69 | 92.9 | .............. | .............. | .............. | 1.73 | 0.65 |
| 70 | 88.0 | .............. | .............. | .............. | 3.81 | 1.11 |
| 71 | 85.5 | .............. | .............. | .............. | 4.61 | 1.84 |
| 72 | 85.6 | .............. | .............. | .............. | 5.25 | 0.66 |
| 73 | 90.0 | .............. | .............. | .............. | 5.01 | 0.65 |
| 74 | 85.8 | .............. | .............. | .............. | 4.64 | 0.50 |
| 75 | 86.3 | .............. | .............. | .............. | 5.54 | 0.98 |
| 76 | 85.7 | .............. | .............. | .............. | 4.64 | 0.58 |
| 77 | 84.8 | .............. | .............. | .............. | 4.45 | 0.70 |
| 78 | 87.0 | .............. | .............. | .............. | 5.14 | 0.93 |
| 79 | 86.4 | .............. | .............. | .............. | 5.85 | 0.96 |
| 80 | 87.7 | .............. | .............. | .............. | 5.70 | 0.44 |
| 81 | 93.1 | .............. | .............. | .............. | 4.26 | 0.61 |
| 82 | 90.7 | .............. | .............. | .............. | 4.59 | 0.79 |
| 83 | 85.8 | .............. | .............. | .............. | 3.83 | 0.63 |
| 84 | 74.4 | .............. | .............. | .............. | 4.88 | 0.67 |
| 85 | 79.0 | .............. | .............. | .............. | 4.46 | 1.03 |
| 86 | 85.2 | .............. | .............. | .............. | 4.98 | 1.58 |
| 87 | 92.1 | .............. | .............. | .............. | 4.58 | 0.97 |
| 88 | 92.3 | .............. | .............. | .............. | 3.99 | 0.70 |
| 89 | 84.1 | .............. | .............. | .............. | 6.10 | 1.34 |
| 90 | 88.2 | .............. | .............. | .............. | 3.88 | 0.75 |
| 91 | 88.7 | .............. | .............. | .............. | 2.58 | 0.62 |
| 92 | 98.0 | .............. | .............. | .............. | 0.91 | 0.24 |
| 93 | 99.2 | .............. | .............. | .............. | 0.20 | 0.11 |
| 94 | 98.9 | .............. | .............. | .............. | 0.15 | 0.09 |
| 95 | 99.6 | .............. | .............. | .............. | 0.05 | 0.04 |
| 96 | 90.1 | .............. | .............. | .............. | 3.36 | 0.93 |
| 97 | 91.9 | .............. | .............. | .............. | 1.90 | 0.89 |
| 98 | 85.5 | .............. | .............. | .............. | 4.86 | 0.64 |
| 99 | 92.0 | .............. | .............. | .............. | 4.69 | 0.63 |
| 100 | 90.2 | .............. | .............. | .............. | 2.27 | 2.50 |

## ANALYSES BY S. P. SHARPLES.

### Description of samples.

| No. | Color. | Price per pound. | Bonght from— |
|---|---|---|---|
| 9302 | Light brown............... | $0.060 | Robert McCullagh, Boston Highlands. |
| 9303 | Medium brown............. | 0.060 | Do. |
| 9304 | .....do .................... | 0.055 | E. W. Favor, Cambridge street, Boston, Mass. |
| 9305 | .....do .................... | 0.055 | Charles Smith, Cambridge street, Boston, Mass. |
| 9306 | Dark brown ............... | 0.060 | Cobb, Bates & Yerxa, Dock square, Boston, Mass. |
| 9307 | Medinm brown ............ | 0.060 | Bullard, South Boston. |
| 9308 | Light brown............... | 0.070 | Bullard, Broadway, South Boston. |
| 9309 | Powdered white ........... | 0.060 | Bullard, South Boston. |
| 9310 | Dark brown ............... | 0.100 | Broadway Market, South Bosto... |
| 9311 | White .................... | 0.075 | W. S. Melcher, 65 Warren street, Boston, Mass. |
| 9312 | .....do ................... | 0.060 | Cobb, Aldrich & Co., Roxbury, Mass. |
| 9313 | Very light brown.......... | 0.065 | C. D. Swain, Roxbury, Mass. |
| 9314 | Dark brown ............. .. | 0.070 | Cobb, Aldrich & Co., 2233 Washington street, Roxbury, Mass. |
| 9315 | Medium brown ............ | 0.070 | Harlow & Gledden, Cambridgeport, Mass. |
| 9316 | Very light brown.......... | 0.065 | John Gilbert, Court street, Tremont Row, Boston, Mass. |
| 9317 | .....do ................... | ....... | Cobb, Aldrich & Co., 2233 Washington street, Roxbury, Mass. |
| 9318 | Dark brown ............... | 0.065 | J. R. Bampton, Roxbury, Mass. |
| 9319 | .....do ................... | 0.060 | W. S. Melcher, 65 Warren street, Roxbury, Mass. |
| 9320 | Medium brown ............ | 0.060 | S. F. Rand, 208 Washington street, Roxbury, Mass. |
| 9321 | Dark brown ............... | 0.060 | C. F. Swain, 2364 Washington street, Boston, Mass. |
| 9322 | Light brown............... | 0.065 | F. O. White, 135 Dudley street, Roxbury, Mass. |
| 9323 | Dark brown ............... | 0.070 | S. D. Ware, Eliot square, Roxbury, Mass. |
| 9324 | Very light brown.... ...... | 0.070 | E. F. Sibley, 1339 Tremont street, Boston, Mass. |
| 9325 | Medium brown ............ | 0.065 | B. F. Ansart, 1408 Tremont street, Roxbury, Mass. |
| 9326 | Light brown............... | 0.065 | Cobb's, 1249 Tremont street, Boston, Mass. |
| 9327 | Dark brown ............... | 0.065 | B. F. Ansart, 1408 Tremont street, Roxbury, Mass. |
| 9328 | .....do ................... | ....... | B. F. Jerome & Co., 1447 Tremont street, Roxbury, Mass. |
| 9329 | ... .do ................... | 0.060 | E. D. Wood, 1265 Tremont street, Roxbury, Mass. |
| 9330 | .....do ................... | 0.060 | Cobb's, 1249 Tremont street, Boston, Mass. |
| 9331 | .... do ................... | 0.065 | J. B. Lyons, 1414 Tremont street, Boston, Mass. |
| 9332 | Medium brown ............ | 0.060 | Cobb's, 1249 Tremont street, Boston, Mass. |
| 9333 | Dark brown ............ .. | 0.055 | Do. |
| 9334 | Medium brown ............ | 0.060 | Highland Flour Store, 1257 Tremont street, Boston, Mass. |
| 9335 | Dark brown ............... | 0.065 | E. F. Sibley, 1339 Tremont street, Boston, Mass. |
| 9336 | .....do ................... | 0.060 | Wm. Hoghes, 211 Main street, Charlestown, Mass. |
| 9337 | White (damp sugar)........ | 0.065 | E. S. Gilmore, 29 Main street, Charlestown, Mass. |
| 9338 | Medinm brown ............ | 0.065 | Do. |
| 9339 | Dark brown ............... | 0.060 | Do. |
| 9340 | .......do ................. | 0.060 | A. N. Swallow, 12 City Square, Charlestown, Mass. |
| 9341 | Medium brown ............ | 0.060 | C. D. Cobb & Co., 1 Thompson Square, Charlestown, Mass. |
| 9342 | Very light brown .......... | 0.065 | Do. |
| 9343 | White a..................... | 0.068 | Mr. Porter, Spreckles' granulated, made in Philadelphia. |
| 9344 | Gray b .................... | 0.300 | Shu Ying Tank & Co., 18 Harrison avenue, Boston, Mass. |
| 9345 | White c .................... | 0.068 | Revere Sugar Refinery, Boston, Mass. |
| 9346 | White d ................... | ....... | Do. |
| 9347 | Yellow e ................... | ....... | Do. |
| 9348 | White f.................... | ....... | American Sugar Refining Company, Boston, Mass. |
| 9349 | White g.................... | ....... | Do. |
| 9350 | White h ................... | ....... | Do. |
| 9351 | Dark yellow i............... | ....... | Do. |

a A very handsome sugar, but very irregular grains.
b Chinese sugar: Very sour odor and unlike any other raw sugar on the market.
c Druggists' granulated: This sugar is made expressly for making sirups for druggists, and is entirely free from coloring.
d Belmont A: A soft white sugar used to some extent by confectioners.
e Revere yellow: Only a small amount of this sugar is made.
f Granulated: This is the principal sugar used in this market.
g Diamond A: Pure white sugar made expressly for confectioners' use.
h Standard A: Made in New York.
i Made in New York.

*Analytical data.*

| No. | Direct polarization. | Indirect polarization. | Tempera- ture °C. | Sucrose by factor, 144. | Water. | Ash. |
|---|---|---|---|---|---|---|
| 9302 | 87.2 | | | | 4.50 | 0.47 |
| 9303 | 89.3 | | | | 2.74 | 1.84 |
| 9304 | 91.1 | | | | 2.18 | 0.60 |
| 9305 | 89.1 | | | | 3.24 | 2.55 |
| 9306 | 87.2 | | | | 3.44 | 2.65 |
| 9307 | 94.6 | | | | 1.52 | 0.94 |
| 9308 | 86.0 | | | | 4.60 | 1.24 |
| 9309 | 90.7 | | | | none. | none |
| 9310 | 83.5 | | | | 4.25 | 1.67 |
| 9311 | 99.9 | | | | none. | none. |
| 9312 | 90.7 | | | | none. | none. |
| 9313 | 87.4 | | | | 4.67 | 0.96 |
| 9314 | 83.9 | | | | 3.34 | 1.88 |
| 9315 | 88.4 | | | | 3.14 | 2.38 |
| 9316 | 87.1 | | | | 5.02 | 1.08 |
| 9317 | 87.0 | | | | 5.50 | 1.10 |
| 9318 | 86.6 | | | | 3.68 | 2.60 |
| 9319 | 87.2 | | | | 3.38 | 2.68 |
| 9320 | 85.4 | | | | 4.64 | 1.20 |
| 9321 | 86.9 | | | | 3.25 | 0.81 |
| 9322 | 83.4 | | | | 3.58 | 1.16 |
| 9323 | 82.7 | | | | 4.04 | 1.60 |
| 9324 | 89.3 | | | | 4.05 | 0.66 |
| 9325 | 82.2 | | | | 4.96 | 1.06 |
| 9326 | 86.4 | | | | 4.63 | 0.32 |
| 9327 | 83.3 | | | | 5.18 | 2.16 |
| 9328 | 85.0 | | | | 3.68 | 2.13 |
| 9329 | 87.0 | | | | 3.76 | 1.74 |
| 9330 | 81.5 | | | | 4.10 | 1.44 |
| 9331 | 88.0 | | | | 3.44 | 2.22 |
| 9332 | 85.5 | | | | 4.78 | 2.30 |
| 9333 | 86.0 | | | | 3.86 | 2.76 |
| 9334 | 85.0 | | | | 4.42 | 1.78 |
| 9335 | 86.0 | | | | 3.92 | 2.89 |
| 9336 | 87.8 | | | | 3.32 | 2.36 |
| 9337 | 82.2 | | | | 4.50 | 0.18 |
| 9338 | 83.6 | | | | 4.32 | 1.62 |
| 9339 | 87.0 | | | | 3.83 | 2.28 |
| 9340 | 86.1 | | | | 3.52 | 2.02 |
| 9341 | 88.7 | | | | 2.80 | 1.02 |
| 9342 | 87.7 | | | | 3.02 | 1.28 |
| 9343 | 99.0 | | | | none. | none. |
| 9344 | 80.8 | | | | 3.12 | 0.44 |
| 9345 | 99.0 | | | | none. | none. |
| 9346 | 95.6 | | | | 3.46 | 0.02 |
| 9347 | 89.9 | | | | 1.93 | 1.23 |
| 9348 | 96.6 | | | | 0.22 | none. |
| 9349 | 99.8 | | | | 0.15 | none. |
| 9350 | 92.3 | | | | 5.41 | 0.20 |
| 9351 | 84.3 | | | | 6.22 | 1.82 |

# FOODS AND FOOD ADULTERANTS.

## ANALYSES BY W. C. STUBBS.

### *Description of samples.*

| No. | Bought at— | Description. |
|---|---|---|
| 1 | Mrs. Rapp, Magazine street, New Orleans, La ..................... | Centrifugal seconds. |
| 2 | Christ Hoppe, Magazine street, New Orleans, La................... | Open kettle. |
| 3 | M. Smith, 1360 Magazine street, New Orleans, La................ | Centrifugal seconds. |
| 4 | J. J. Hecker, 1352 Magazine street, New Orleans, La............. | Open kettle. |
| 5 | Mrs. Murphy, Dufossat street, New Orleans, La ................... | Centrifugal seconds. |
| 6 | Du Mont's grocery, Magazine street, New Orleans, La ............ | Do. |
| 7 | Frank J. Marone, 441 Dryades street, New Orleans, La............ | Open kettle. |
| 8 | Patrick Egan, Villere street, New Orleans, La..................... | Centrifugal seconds. |
| 9 | F. Martin, Conti street, New Orleans, La ........................ | Do. |
| 10 | Jules O. Lalarain, Perdido street, New Orleans, La ................ | Do. |
| 11 | ......do....................................................... | Do. |
| 12 | George Klimert, Rampart street, New Orleans, La................. | Do. |
| 13 | C. Redersheimer, 141 South Rampart street, New Orleans, La...... | Open kettle. |
| 14 | C. Feahnay, Poydras street, New Orleans, La..................... | Do. |
| 15 | John J. Driscoll, 227 South Rampart street, New Orleans, La...... | Do. |
| 16 | William Cunningham, 271 South Rampart street, New Orleans, La.. | Centrifugal seconds. |
| 17 | M. H. Riddlo, South Rampart street, New Orleans, La............. | Open kettle. |
| 18 | ......do....................................................... | Do. |
| 19 | Neel Pannental, Jackson street, New Orleans, La................. | Centrifugal seconds. |
| 20 | ——, Erato street, New Orleans, La ............................ | Do. |
| 21 | F. W. Theisman, 361 Magazine street, New Orleans, La .......... | Do. |
| 22 | H. Hammet, 552 Magazine street, New Orleans, La ............... | Do. |
| 23 | A. J. Kernan, 578 Magazine street, New Orleans La .............. | Open kettle. |
| 24 | G. F. Stanfield, St. Andrew street, New Orleans, La .............. | Do. |
| 25 | Henry Butner, Arabella street, New Orleans, La .................. | Do. |
| 26 | ......do ....................................................... | White powdered. |
| 27 | John D. King, Laurel street, New Orleans, La.................... | Centrifugal seconds. |
| 28 | John W. Frank, Soniab street, New Orleans, La . ............... | Do. |
| 29 | ......do....................................................... | White powdered. |
| 30 | H. B. Gilson, Valence street, New Orleans, La ................... | Centrifugal seconds. |
| 31 | J. P. Schmidt, 1091 Magazine street, New Orleans, La ........... | Do. |
| 32 | Fred. Denny, 1093 Magazine street, New Orleans, La ............. | White powdered. |
| 33 | ......do ....................................................... | Yellow clarified. |
| 34 | ......do ....................................................... | White powdered. |
| 35 | E. A. Žataim, 1071 Magazine street, New Orleans, La ........... | Do. |
| 36 | Charles Worth, 894 Magazine street, New Orleans, La .......... | Do. |
| 37 | ......do ....................................................... | Open kettle. |
| 38 | Jaeckel & Magnetzky, Third street, New Orleans, La ........... | White powdered. |
| 39 | Joseph Vigo, Laurel street, New Orleans, La..................... | Centrifugal seconds. |
| 40 | ......do ....................................................... | White powdered. |
| 41 | Philip Mcnendez, Jackson street, New Orleans, La............... | Do. |
| 42 | T. J. & Wm. Byrnes, 395 Dryades street, New Orleans, La........ | Do. |
| 43 | ......do....................................................... | Open kettle. |
| 44 | Pitcheloup's grocery, Washington street, New Orleans, La ...... | White powdered. |
| 45 | F. A. Volkmann, Washington street, New Orleans, La............ | Do. |
| 46 | J. Pentat, Dauphine street, New Orleans, La..................... | Do. |
| 47 | A. Marechal, St. Anne street, New Orleans, La .................. | Do. |
| 48 | James Dwyer, St. Charles street, New Orleans, La ............... | Do. |
| 49 | James Wilson & Co., Prytania street, New Orleans, La .......... | Do. |
| 50 | L. Sillers, Laurel and Calhoun streets, New Orleans, La ......... | Off white. |

*Analytical data.*

| No. | Direct polarization. | Indirect polarization. | Temperature °C. | Sucrose by Factor 144. | Water. | Ash. |
|---|---|---|---|---|---|---|
| 1 | 85.60 | | | | 6.07 | 0.54 |
| 2 | 83.60 | | | | 6.96 | 0.58 |
| 3 | 90.80 | | | | 4.27 | 0.35 |
| 4 | 88.85 | | | | 6.23 | 0.37 |
| 5 | 86.10 | | | | 6.21 | 0.37 |
| 6 | 91.05 | | | | 2.89 | 0.48 |
| 7 | 80.20 | | | | 10.04 | 0.86 |
| 8 | 91.60 | | | | 4.42 | 0.32 |
| 9 | 86.40 | | | | 6.57 | 0.74 |
| 10 | 96.10 | | | | 2.17 | 0.48 |
| 11 | 90.50 | | | | 6.01 | 0.46 |
| 12 | 87.90 | | | | 5.46 | 0.28 |
| 13 | 83.80 | | | | 7.71 | 0.70 |
| 14 | 90.30 | | | | 5.80 | 0.43 |
| 15 | 80.20 | | | | 8.05 | 1.14 |
| 16 | 87.40 | | | | 6.81 | 0.76 |
| 17 | 86.60 | | | | 7.52 | 0.76 |
| 18 | 86.60 | | | | 5.35 | 0.52 |
| 19 | 88.50 | | | | 6.48 | 0.53 |
| 20 | 89.50 | | | | 5.57 | 0.73 |
| 21 | 88.20 | | | | 6.11 | 0.68 |
| 22 | 93.50 | | | | 2.60 | 0.37 |
| 23 | 79.40 | | | | 10.05 | 1.05 |
| 24 | 80.30 | | | | 6.04 | 0.58 |
| 25 | 90.50 | | | | 4.57 | 0.56 |
| 26 | 99.90 | | | | 0.16 | 0.02 |
| 27 | 90.50 | | | | 6.89 | 0.57 |
| 28 | 87.30 | | | | 7.40 | 0.66 |
| 29 | 99.80 | | | | 0.08 | ......... |
| 30 | 89.70 | | | | 7.18 | 0.54 |
| 31 | 90.80 | | | | 6.64 | 0.52 |
| 32 | 99.10 | | | | 0.16 | 0.27 |
| 33 | 97.30 | | | | 1.26 | 0.21 |
| 34 | 99.00 | | | | 0.07 | 0.00 |
| 35 | 99.40 | | | | 0.16 | 0.06 |
| 36 | 99.50 | | | | 0.12 | 0.05 |
| 37 | 89.00 | | | | 7.25 | 0.71 |
| 38 | 99.40 | | | | 0.13 | 0.04 |
| 39 | 89.30 | | | | 6.04 | 0.58 |
| 40 | 99.80 | | | | 0.08 | 0.01 |
| 41 | 90.80 | | | | 0.18 | 0.01 |
| 42 | 100.00 | | | | 0.11 | 0.00 |
| 43 | 88.90 | | | | 8.50 | 0.70 |
| 44 | 99.90 | | | | 0.10 | 0.02 |
| 45 | 99.80 | | | | 0.24 | 0.03 |
| 46 | 100.00 | | | | 0.14 | 0.01 |
| 47 | 99.70 | | | | 0.05 | 0.01 |
| 48 | 99.70 | | | | 0.05 | 0.01 |
| 49 | 99.50 | | | | 0.13 | 0.01 |
| 50 | 98.70 | | | | 0.53 | 0.01 |

## ANALYSES BY SHIPPEN WALLACE.

*Description of samples.*

| No. | Seller. | No. | Seller. |
|---|---|---|---|
| 1 | C. H. Rambo, Gloucester, N. J. | 26 | C. K. Morris, Camden, N. J. |
| 2 | Do. | 27 | Gifford & Co., Camden, N. J. |
| 3 | L. Fowler, Gloucester, N. J. | 28 | Thomas Malone, Camden, N. J. |
| 4 | James McLaughlin, Gloucester, N. J. | 29 | Thomas Westacott, Philadelphia, Pa. |
| 5 | Do. | 30 | Cousty's Grocery, Philadelphia, Pa. |
| 6 | R. K. Jester, Burlington, N. J. | 31 | Do. |
| 7 | Samuel Burr, Burlington, N. J. | 32 | Do. |
| 8 | George F. Worth, Burlington, N. J. | 33 | Do. |
| 9 | Sherman Brothers, Burlington, N. J. | 34 | L. Blaess, Philadelphia, Pa. |
| 10 | Do. | 35 | Deacon & Fry, Philadelphia, Pa. |
| 11 | George F. Fort, Burlington, N. J. | 36 | Callowhill Street Market, Philadelphia, Pa. |
| 12 | Do. | 37 | A. McCallister, Philadelphia, Pa. |
| 13 | William Sherwood, Burlington, N. J. | 38 | S. Merriel, Philadelphia, Pa. |
| 14 | George W. Kimball, Burlington, N. J. | 39 | Wm. Cunningham & Co., Philadelphia, Pa. |
| 15 | Do. | 40 | Samuel P. Helmer, Philadelphia, Pa. |
| 16 | Samuel Emmons, Burlington, N. J. | 41 | C. S. Rollins, Philadelphia, Pa. |
| 17 | Do. | 42 | John McDonald & Son, Philadelphia, Pa. |
| 18 | Shinn & Son, Burlington, N. J. | 43 | Purdy Brothers, Philadelphia, Pa. |
| 19 | Ivins Pettit, Burlington, N. J. | 44 | Do. |
| 20 | Charles-Ettenger, Burlington, N. J. | 45 | Crippen & Son, Philadelphia, Pa. |
| 21 | George A. Anthony, Burlington, N. J. | 46 | John Willson & Co., Philadelphia, Pa. |
| 22 | R. S. Dutton, Burlington, N. J. | 47 | South Second Street Market, Philadelphia, Pa. |
| 23 | G. W. Swaney, Camden, N. J. | 48 | Do. |
| 24 | Charles Warner, Camden, N. J. | 49 | Do. |
| 25 | Horner & Son, Camden, N. J. | 50 | Do. |

Price paid, 5½ cents per pound.

*Analytical data.*

| No. | Direct polarization. | Indirect polarization. | Tempera- ture, °C. | Sucrose by factor 144. | Water. | Ash. |
|---|---|---|---|---|---|---|
| 1 | 86.7 | | | | 3.200 | 1.500 |
| 2 | 91.3 | | | | 4.117 | 0.216 |
| 3 | 86.0 | | | | 3.200 | 1.500 |
| 4 | 87.0 | | | | 3.717 | 0.830 |
| 5 | 88.3 | | | | 3.834 | 1.260 |
| 6 | 88.0 | | | | 3.870 | 1.200 |
| 7 | 91.0 | | | | 3.500 | 0.150 |
| 8 | 87.0 | | | | 3.884 | 0.830 |
| 9 | 87.0 | | | | 3.875 | 0.820 |
| 10 | 88.5 | | | | 4.100 | 0.725 |
| 11 | 89.0 | | | | 3.915 | 0.530 |
| 12 | 87.0 | | | | 3.900 | 0.845 |
| 13 | 88.0 | | | | 4.000 | 0.153 |
| 14 | 88.2 | | | | 4.000 | 1.522 |
| 15 | 86.8 | | | | 3.915 | 1.572 |
| 16 | 88.5 | | | | 4.100 | 1.520 |
| 17 | 85.0 | | | | 3.280 | 1.600 |
| 18 | 86.5 | | | | 3.200 | 0.890 |
| 19 | 86.2 | | | | 3.200 | 0.890 |
| 20 | 89.7 | | | | 6.100 | 0.333 |
| 21 | 90.3 | | | | 3.920 | 0.290 |
| 22 | 91.3 | | | | 3.750 | 0.210 |
| 23 | 92.0 | | | | 3.000 | 0.115 |
| 24 | 92.7 | | | | 2.850 | 1.500 |
| 25 | 91.5 | | | | 3.100 | 0.200 |
| 26 | 93.3 | | | | 3.700 | 0.110 |
| 27 | 87.2 | | | | 3.884 | 1.100 |
| 28 | 93.0 | | | | 3.700 | 0.233 |
| 29 | 92.5 | | | | 4.112 | 1.500 |
| 30 | 89.0 | | | | 6.167 | 0.333 |
| 31 | 94.0 | | | | 3.975 | 0.100 |
| 32 | 93.7 | | | | 4.235 | 1.222 |
| 33 | 86.3 | | | | 4.115 | 0.785 |
| 34 | 86.5 | | | | 4.120 | 0.785 |
| 35 | 85.8 | | | | 5.110 | 0.822 |
| 36 | 86.0 | | | | 5.225 | 0.820 |
| 37 | 86.7 | | | | 5.200 | 0.775 |
| 38 | 86.5 | | | | 5.200 | 0.775 |
| 39 | 87.5 | | | | 5.000 | 0.580 |
| 40 | 88.2 | | | | 4.100 | 0.725 |
| 41 | 88.0 | | | | 4.115 | 0.725 |
| 42 | 88.5 | | | | 4.115 | 1.520 |
| 43 | 88.3 | | | | 4.200 | 1.225 |
| 44 | 88.7 | | | | 4.000 | 0.725 |
| 45 | 88.8 | | | | 3.900 | 1.120 |
| 46 | 88.0 | | | | 4.110 | 0.740 |
| 47 | 87.5 | | | | 4.225 | 0.560 |
| 48 | 87.7 | | | | 4.350 | 0.570 |
| 49 | 88.0 | | | | 4.350 | 0.720 |
| 50 | 86.5 | | | | 5.200 | 1.520 |

FOODS AND FOOD ADULTERANTS.

ANALYSES BY II. A. WEBER.

*Description of samples.*

| No. | Bought from— | Labels. |
|---|---|---|
| 1 | J. G. & S. Brown, Hunter street and 5th avenue, Columbus. | Off A, Havemeyer & Elder. |
| 2 | ......do........................................... | C, Havemeyer & Elder. |
| 3 | ......do........................................... | Brown sugar, Spreckels' raw sugar. |
| 4 | Henry Thropp, 345 South High street, Columbus. | Off A, Franklin Sugar Refinery Company, Philadelphia. |
| 5 | ......do........................................... | C, Franklin Sugar Refinery Company, Philadelphia. |
| 6 | ......do........................................... | Brown sugar, Spreckels' raw, Franklin Sugar Refinery Company, Philadelphia. |
| 7 | Esper & Sons, 403 South High street, Columbus. | Off A, Franklin Sugar Refinery Company, Philadelphia. |
| 8 | ......do........................................... | C sugar, Franklin Sugar Refinery Company, Philadelphia. |
| 9 | ......do........................................... | Brown sugar, Franklin Sugar Refinery Company, Philadelphia. |
| 10 | William Schaw, South High street, Columbus... | Brown sugar. |
| 11 | Preinkens Bros., 391 South High street, Columbus. | Light C. |
| 12 | ......do........................................... | Yellow C. |
| 13 | R. M. Babb, 297 South High street, Columbus.. | C sugar, Franklin Sugar Refinery Company, Philadelphia. |
| 14 | R. M. Babb, 297 South High street, Columbus.. | Yellow C, Franklin Sugar Refinery Company, Philadelphia. |
| 15 | R. M. Babb, 297 South High street, Columbus.. | Franklin Sugar Refinery Company, Philadelphia. |
| 16 | ......do........................................... | Coffee C, Franklin Sugar Refinery Company, Philadelphia. |
| 17 | Wheeler's, 15 North High street, Columbus .... | C, Franklin Sugar Refinery Company, Philadelphia. |
| 18 | ......do........................................... | Yellow C, Franklin Sugar Refinery Company, Philadelphia. |
| 19 | ......do........................................... | Brown sugar, Havemeyer & Elder. |
| 20 | F. E. Hayden, 16 North High street, Columbus | Yellow C, Franklin Sugar Refinery Company, Philadelphia. |
| 21 | ......do........................................... | Brown sugar, Franklin Sugar Refinery Company, Philadelphia. |
| 22 | J. II. Bachus, 205 South High street, Columbus. | Yellow C, Franklin Sugar Refinery Company, Philadelphia. |
| 23 | A. J. Evans, 236 East Long street, Columbus... | Off A, Franklin Sugar Refinery Company, Philadelphia. |
| 24 | ......do ........................................... | C sugar, Franklin Sugar Refinery Company, Philadelphia. |
| 25 | ......do........................................... | Brown sugar, Franklin Sugar Refinery Company, Philadelphia. |
| 26 | ......do........................................... | New Orleans, Franklin Sugar Refinery Company, Philadelphia. |
| 27 | Bowman Bros., corner Long and Grant avenues, Columbus. | Off A. |
| 28 | ......do........................................... | Brown sugar. |
| 29 | M. A. Montgomery, 618 East Long street, Columbus. | Yellow C, standard. |
| 30 | ......do........................................... | Brown sugar, standard. |

*Description of samples*--Continued.

| No. | Bought from— | Labels. |
|---|---|---|
| 31 | M. Theado & Co., 234 and 236 South 4th street, Columbus. | Off A. |
| 32 | ......do...... | C. |
| 33 | ......do...... | Brown sugar. |
| 34 | Fraas & Fooks, 174 and 176 South 4th street, Columbus. | Off A, Havemeyer & Elder. |
| 35 | ......do...... | C, Havemeyer & Elder. |
| 36 | ......do...... | N. O. sugar. |
| 37 | Chris. Have, Main street, Columbus............ | C. |
| 38 | ......do...... | N. O. sugar. |
| 39 | ......do...... | C sugar. |
| 40 | Saul & Eberly, 74, 76, and 78 Main st., Columbus. | C, Spreckels. |
| 41 | ......do...... | Brown sugar, Spreckels' very dark. |
| 42 | ......do...... | N. O. sugar. |
| 43 | J. B. & L. Zettler, South 4th street, Columbus.. | Light C. |
| 44 | ......do...... | Brown. |
| 45 | George Babb, 32 East Main street, Columbus... | Off A. |
| 46 | ......do...... | Yellow C. |
| 47 | ......do...... | Brown. |
| 48 | Holden Bros., North High street, Columbus.... | Brown sugar. |
| 49 | Aug. Boesel, 1352 North High street, Columbus. | Do. |
| 50 | J. L. Guthridge, 1444 N. High street, Columbus. | Do. |

*Analytical data.*

| No. | Direct polarization. | Indirect polarization. | Temperature, °C. | Sucrose by factor 144. | Water. | Ash. |
|---|---|---|---|---|---|---|
| 1 | 89.7 | —27.0 | 16.5 | 86.99 | 5.42 | 0.41 |
| 2 | 82.9 | —26.5 | 19.0 | 82.32 | 5.29 | 0.03 |
| 3 | 86.8 | —26.7 | 19.0 | 85.70 | 3.48 | 3.25 |
| 4 | 92.0 | —28.7 | 19.0 | 90.99 | 6.53 | 0.19 |
| 5 | 85.5 | —28.0 | 19.0 | 85.32 | 5.71 | 0.88 |
| 6 | 88.1 | —28.0 | 19.0 | 87.37 | 3.04 | 3.17 |
| 7 | 92.0 | —29.0 | 19.0 | 91.00 | 6.08 | 0.22 |
| 8 | 85.8 | —28.1 | 19.0 | 85.70 | 5.49 | 0.85 |
| 9 | 86.7 | —27.8 | 19.0 | 86.15 | 4.06 | 0.31 |
| 10 | 85.7 | —28.7 | 19.0 | 86.08 | 5.50 | 1.07 |
| 11 | 90.3 | —28.3 | 19.0 | 89.24 | 6.51 | 0.27 |
| 12 | 81.8 | —28.5 | 22.0 | 86.22 | 5.37 | 0.74 |
| 13 | 85.0 | —28.0 | 22.0 | 85.99 | 5.14 | 0.76 |
| 14 | 84.6 | —27.5 | 22.0 | 85.31 | 5.73 | 1.02 |
| 15 | 85.4 | —27.8 | 22.0 | 86.14 | 4.06 | 3.56 |
| 16 | 90.0 | —30.0 | 22.0 | 91.32 | 6.08 | 0.30 |
| 17 | 87.3 | —29.5 | 17.0 | 86.48 | 5.95 | 0.34 |
| 18 | 83.4 | —28.0 | 17.0 | 83.19 | 4.70 | 1.08 |
| 19 | 81.3 | —28.0 | 17.0 | 81.55 | 5.14 | 2.17 |
| 20 | 83.0 | —28.0 | 17.0 | 82.82 | 3.80 | 0.68 |
| 21 | 85.7 | —28.0 | 17.0 | 84.01 | 5.20 | 3.68 |
| 22 | 87.8 | —27.0 | 21.0 | 87.11 | 5.22 | 0.48 |
| 23 | 92.6 | —29.0 | 21.0 | 92.19 | 6.12 | 0.33 |
| 24 | 92.0 | —28.2 | 21.0 | 91.12 | 3.52 | 0.67 |
| 25 | 89.0 | —26.4 | 21.0 | 87.40 | 3.20 | 1.71 |
| 26 | 92.5 | —28.8 | 21.0 | 91.96 | 1.89 | 0.27 |
| 27 | 91.9 | —28.1 | 19.0 | 90.20 | 6.78 | 0.28 |
| 28 | 86.3 | —27.1 | 19.0 | 85.32 | 4.46 | 3.60 |
| 29 | 86.8 | —28.8 | 19.0 | 86.98 | 5.61 | 0.76 |
| 30 | 85.3 | —27.5 | 19.0 | 84.87 | 7.67 | 2.46 |
| 31 | 95.1 | —30.0 | 20.0 | 95.56 | 4.21 | 0.09 |
| 32 | 87.3 | —27.2 | 23.0 | 87.70 | 6.44 | 1.10 |
| 33 | 92.5 | —29.0 | 23.0 | 87.01 | 3.72 | 3.50 |
| 34 | 86.9 | —28.0 | 23.0 | 87.77 | 5.55 | 0.11 |
| 35 | 86.9 | —28.0 | 23.0 | 87.77 | 6.84 | 1.30 |
| 36 | 91.6 | —29.7 | 19.0 | 91.19 | 2.55 | 0.91 |
| 37 | 86.6 | —28.5 | 19.0 | 86.60 | 6.50 | 1.45 |
| 38 | 94.5 | —20.5 | 19.0 | 93.80 | 3.05 | 0.42 |
| 39 | 95.7 | —29.5 | 19.0 | 94.20 | 4.09 | 0.52 |
| 40 | 88.2 | —28.3 | 19.0 | 88.48 | 4.00 | 0.97 |
| 41 | 86.1 | —27.1 | 19.0 | 85.17 | 4.08 | 3.50 |
| 42 | 93.4 | —29.7 | 19.0 | 92.62 | 1.18 | 0.59 |
| 43 | 87.5 | —27.5 | 19.0 | 86.53 | 6.48 | 1.00 |
| 44 | 87.8 | —27.9 | 19.0 | 87.05 | 4.06 | 3.18 |
| 45 | 90.1 | —29.2 | 19.0 | 89.76 | 4.01 | 0.38 |
| 46 | 88.0 | —28.4 | 19.0 | 88.03 | 4.03 | 1.01 |
| 47 | 82.1 | —27.2 | 19.0 | 80.75 | 5.38 | 1.79 |
| 48 | 86.8 | —27.8 | 19.0 | 86.23 | 4.14 | 4.17 |
| 49 | 90.7 | —29.0 | 19.0 | 90.06 | 3.14 | 1.18 |
| 50 | 88.5 | —28.2 | 19.0 | 87.81 | 4.45 | 2.10 |

## ANALYSES BY F. G. WIECHMANN.

### *Description of samples.*

| No. | Character. | Price per pound. | Bought at— |
|---|---|---|---|
| 1.... | Soft ............... | $0.07 | H. Boeslager, 794 3d avenue, New York. |
| 2.... | ...do .............. | .07 | L. Eicke, 4th avenue and 11th street, New York. |
| 3.... | ...do .............. | .07 | F. C. Rahe, Broome and Forsyth streets, New York. |
| 4.... | ....do .............. | .07 | Steinberg, Wythe avenue and South 2d street, Brooklyn, E. D. |
| 5.... | ....do .............. | .07 | 38 Grand street, Brooklyn, E. D. |
| 6.... | Powder ........... | .10 | A. Balfauz, 54 Grand street, Brooklyn, E. D. |
| 7.... | Soft............... | .07 | L. Gieseler, Wythe avenue and South 1st street, Brooklyn, E D. |
| 8.... | ....do .............. | .06 | P. U. Montorsi, 60 South 5th avenue, New York. |
| 9.... | ... do . ............ | .06 | Tompkins, 70 South 5th avenue, New York. |
| 10.... | ....do ............. | .06 | Schaefer & Son, 95 West Houston street, New York. |
| 11.... | Powder ........... | .09 | Malatesta, 133 South 5th avenue, New York. |
| 12.... | ...do .............. | .10 | Piatt, 160 Spring street, New York. |
| 13.... | Soft............... | .07 | Bergonzi Bros., 58 Grand street, New York. |
| 14.... | ....do ............. | .07 | Hanley & Glynn, 59 Whitehall street, New York. |
| 15.... | ...do .............. | .07 | Fajen & Co., 17 South street, New York. |
| 16.... | ....do .............. | .07 | C. Meyer, 29 Coenties slip, New York. |
| 17.... | ....do .............. | .07 | R. C. Hewitt, 201 3d avenue, New York. |
| 18.... | ....do .............. | .07 | Koch & Semke, 185 3d avenue, New York. |
| 19.... | Powder........... | .09 | Behrens, 273 avenue A, New York. |
| 20.... | Soft ............... | .07 | A. Becker, 283 avenue A, New York. |
| 21.... | ....do .............. | .08 | D. Müller, 307 avenue A, New York. |
| 22.... | ....do .............. | .07 | Junghertchon, 310 avenue A, New York. |
| 23.... | ...do .............. | .07 | L. Dwingelo, 778 2d avenue, New York. |
| 24.... | ....do .............. | .06 | The Great Overland Tea Company, 748 2d avenue, New York. |
| 25.... | ....do .............. | .07 | W. F. Vogel, 739 2d avenue, New York. |
| 26.... | ....do .............. | .06 | Kerr Brothers, 738 2d avenue, New York. |
| 27.... | ....do .............. | .06 | People's Tea Company, 722 2d avenue, New York. |
| 28.... | ....do .............. | .07 | F. Hardy, 718 2d avenue, New York. |
| 29.... | ...do .............. | .07 | G. A. Wuerfel, 690 2d avenue, New York. |
| 30.... | ....do .............. | .07 | 659 2d avenue, New York. |
| 31.... | ....do .............. | .06 | J. Butler, 643 2d avenue, New York. |
| 32.... | ....do .............. | .07 | C. C. Sievers, 641 2d avenue, New York. |
| 33.... | ....do ............. | .06 | New York and China Tea and Coffee Company, 604 2d avenue, New York. |
| 34.... | ....do ............. | .08 | Fresher & Donolley, 337 East 33d street, New York. |
| 35.... | ....do ........... . | .07 | Charles & Co., 50 East 43d street, New York. |
| 36.... | ....do ............. | .08 | J. N. Galway, 42d street and Vanderbilt avenue, New York. |
| 37.... | ....do ............. | .06 | H. Middendorf, 415 3d avenue, New York. |
| 38.... | ....do ............. | .06 | The Great Atlantic and Pacific Tea Company, 8th avenue and 53d street, New York. |
| 39.... | ....do ............. | .07 | Wright & Ryer, 891 8th avenue, New York. |
| 40.... | ....do . ........... | .07 | E. and P. Gerety, 880 8th avenue, New York. |
| 41.... | ....do . .......... | .07 | H. W. Krumwiede, 870 8th avenue, New York. |
| 42.... | ...do ............. | .07 | A. S. Bedell, 847 8th avenue, New York. |
| 43.... | ....do ............. | .07 | G. L. Schroeder, 836 8th avenue, New York. |
| 44.... | ....do ............. | .07 | H. Bremer & Son, 790 8th avenue, New York. |
| 45.... | ....do ............. | .08 | A. Birnbaum, 780 8th avenue, New York. |
| 46.... | ....do ............. | .07 | D. H. Tonjes, 740 8th avenue, New York. |
| 47.... | ....do ............. | .08 | W. De Mott, 732 8th avenue, New York. |
| 48.... | ....do ............. | .07 | W. H. Maxwell, 706 8th avenue, New York. |
| 49.... | ....do ............. | .07 | H. Rixmann, 684 8th avenue, New York. |
| 50.... | ....do ............. | .07 | J. Kelleher, 681 8th avenue, New York. |

*Analytical data.*

| No. | Direct polarization. | Indirect polarization. | Temperature, ° C. | Sucrose by factor 144. | Water. | Ash. |
|---|---|---|---|---|---|---|
| 1 | 88.3 | | | | 5.95 | 1.213 |
| 2 | 87.9 | | | | 4.99 | 0.997 |
| 3 | 91.3 | | | | 5.49 | 0.511 |
| 4 | 84.7 | | | | 5.01 | 2.365 |
| 5 | 90.7 | | | | 5.04 | 0.511 |
| 6 | 99.7 | | | | 0.03 | 0.003 |
| 7 | 86.8 | | | | 2.59 | 0.979 |
| 8 | 93.2 | | | | 2.69 | 1.350 |
| 9 | 87.2 | | | | 5.69 | 1.609 |
| 10 | 86.6 | | | | 5.04 | 1.699 |
| 11 | 99.7 | | | | 0.07 | 0.007 |
| 12 | 99.9 | | | | 0.02 | 0.003 |
| 13 | 85.3 | | | | 5.45 | 1.440 |
| 14 | 87.6 | | | | 4.79 | 1.134 |
| 15 | 87.4 | | | | 3.01 | 1.440 |
| 16 | 87.0 | | | | 5.44 | 1.278 |
| 17 | 87.3 | | | | 3.45 | 1.227 |
| 18 | 90.9 | | | | 5.47 | 0.659 |
| 19 | 99.9 | | | | 0.03 | 0.007 |
| 20 | 85.3 | | | | 4.15 | 0.745 |
| 21 | 86.7 | | | | 4.86 | 0.497 |
| 22 | 91.0 | | | | 4.72 | 1.699 |
| 23 | 86.4 | | | | 4.08 | 1.310 |
| 24 | 88.6 | | | | 4.72 | 1.414 |
| 25 | 89.0 | | | | 4.85 | 0.903 |
| 26 | 89.5 | | | | 2.27 | 1.685 |
| 27 | 86.3 | | | | 4.53 | 2.304 |
| 28 | 84.7 | | | | 3.80 | 1.080 |
| 29 | 86.5 | | | | 4.79 | 1.998 |
| 30 | 88.3 | | | | 5.72 | 1.170 |
| 31 | 92.1 | | | | 4.80 | 0.684 |
| 32 | 86.4 | | | | 4.68 | 1.058 |
| 33 | 88.4 | | | | 5.16 | 1.375 |
| 34 | 87.0 | | | | 4.04 | 1.422 |
| 35 | 83.3 | | | | 4.70 | 2.160 |
| 36 | 89.9 | | | | 4.80 | 0.601 |
| 37 | 85.8 | | | | 4.14 | 1.144 |
| 38 | 89.2 | | | | 4.81 | 0.604 |
| 39 | 86.3 | | | | 3.99 | 2.142 |
| 40 | 90.0 | | | | 5.54 | 0.864 |
| 41 | 89.3 | | | | 4.01 | 0.544 |
| 42 | 89.7 | | | | 6.39 | 0.817 |
| 43 | 89.7 | | | | 3.82 | 0.504 |
| 44 | 86.9 | | | | 3.85 | 2.203 |
| 45 | 86.1 | | | | 4.34 | 1.735 |
| 46 | 91.6 | | | | 4.26 | 1.162 |
| 47 | 91.6 | | | | 5.69 | 0.540 |
| 48 | 90.0 | | | | 4.68 | 0.648 |
| 49 | 86.9 | | | | 4.00 | 2.077 |
| 50 | 87.7 | | | | 4.70 | 0.648 |

## SUGAR ANALYZED IN CHEMICAL DIVISION.

### Description of samples.

| No. | Where bought. | Character. | Price per pound. |
|---|---|---|---|
| 8559 | A. A. Winfield, 215 13½ street SW | Brown sugar | $0.06 |
| 8533 | 327 13th street NW | Cut sugar | .10 |
| 8564 | 324 13th street NW | White sugar | .08 |
| 8565 | ......do | Brown sugar | .07 |
| 8567 | 1219 E street | ......do | .07 |
| 8570 | W. E. Abbott, corner 11th and H streets | ......do | .06 |
| 8571 | ......do | Powdered sugar | .08 |
| 8574 | J. H. Semmes, 740 12th street | Brown sugar | .06 |
| 8577 | Franklin Barrett, New York avenue and 12th street | ......do | .06 |
| 8581 | Hart & Higgins | ......do | .06 |
| 8583 | Russell & Co., 9th and I streets | ......do | .06 |
| 8586 | W. H. Combs, 934 9th street | ......do | .06 |
| 8587 | Wilson & Schultz, corner I and 7th streets | White sugar (granulated) | .07 |
| 8589 | C. D. Kenny, corner 7th and I streets | Granulated sugar | .07 |
| 8590 | ......do | Powdered sugar | .08 |
| 8591 | ......do | Off A sugar | .06 |
| 8593 | China and Japan Tea Store, 731 7th street | Granulated white sugar | .06 |
| 8594 | ......do | Black sugar | .05 |
| 8595 | ......do | Brown | .06 |
| 8596 | H. L. Keyworth, 531 7th street | Cut | .10 |
| 8568 | 1367 C street SW | Brown sugar | .06 |
| 8590 | ......do | Black sugar | .06 |
| 8600 | J. W. Brewer, corner C and 13½ streets SW | Granulated sugar | .07 |
| 8601 | Estler & Co., corner C and 13½ streets SW | Brown sugar | .06 |
| 8602 | ......do | Powdered sugar | .08 |
| 8620 | F. Lawrence, 523 Lexington avenue, Baltimore, Md | Brown sugar | .06 |
| 8621 | Corner Linden avenue and Rose street, Baltimore, Md | A sugar | .06 |
| 8622 | Geo. E. French, corner North Paca and Lexington, Baltimore, Md. | Brown sugar | .05 |
| 8623 | Bryant & Clarvoe, Baltimore, Md | ......do | .06 |
| 8624 | Rider & Co., 739 Baltimore street, Baltimore, Md | ......do | .06 |
| 8625 | Ed. Reese & Son, 412 Baltimore street, Baltimore, Md | ......do | .06 |
| 8626 | L. H. Reitz, 237 Hanover street, Baltimore, Md | ......do | .06 |
| 8627 | 720 North Eutaw street, Baltimore, Md | ......do | .06 |
| 8628 | E. T. Carter, 180 Camden street, Baltimore, Md | ......do | .05 |
| 8629 | United States Tea Company, corner Lexington and Pearl, Baltimore, Md. | ......do | .06 |
| 8630 | L. Strauss, 226 North Eutaw street, Baltimore, Md | ......do | .06 |
| 8631 | Randall, 410 Baltimore street, Baltimore, Md | ......do | .06 |
| 8632 | 611 Lexington street, Baltimore, Md | ......do | .06 |
| 8633 | Hopper, McGaw & Co., 222 Charles street, Baltimore, Md. | B sugar | .06 |
| 8634 | Atlantic and Pacific Tea Company, 615 West Lexington street, Baltimore, Md. | Pulverized sugar | .08 |
| 8635 | Simms & Co., 116 Eutaw street, Baltimore, Md | Brown sugar | .06 |
| 8636 | Atlantic and Pacific Tea Company, 615 West Lexington street, Baltimore, Md. | Columbia A sugar | .06 |
| 8637 | Greene, 412 Baltimore street, Baltimore, Md | Soft white sugar | .06 |
| 8638 | Rider & Co., 709 Baltimore street, Baltimore, Md | A sugar | .06 |
| 8639 | R. R. Howard, Camden and Howard streets, Baltimore, Md. | Cut sugar | .08 |
| 8640 | T. M. Reese & Sons, corner North Charles and Mulberry streets, Baltimore, Md. | Louisiana sugar | .07 |
| 8641 | L. Strauss, 226 North Eutaw street, Baltimore, Md | A sugar | .06 |
| 8642 | S. Edmonds & Sons, corner Lexington and Pearl streets, Baltimore, Md. | Confectioners' sugar | .10 |
| 8643 | C. L. Gabeler, 524 Lexington street, Baltimore, Md | Pulverized sugar | .08 |
| 8644 | L. H. Reitz, 227 Hanover street, Baltimore, Md | ......do | .08 |

*Analytical data.*

| No. | Direct polariza- tion. | Indirect polariza- tion. | Temper- ature ° C. | Sucro-e by factor 14i. | Water. | Ash. |
|---|---|---|---|---|---|---|
| 8559 | 87.1 | —29.6 | 18.5 | 87.6 | 6.45 | .09 |
| 8563 | 99.9 | —34.6 | 17.6 | 99.5 | .04 | .03 |
| 8564 | 98.2˙ | —33.2 | 17.4 | 97.1 | 1.44 | .23 |
| 8565 | 84.1 | —28.0 | 19.8 | 83.5 | 4.23 | 2.02 |
| 8567 | 85.0 | —27.7 | 20.6 | 84.3 | 5.52 | 1.02 |
| 8570 | 83.7 | —29.7 | {17.4 | 83.8 | 5.12 | 1.21 |
| 8571 | 99.5 | —32.3 | 20.0 | 98.3 | .05 | .05 |
| 8574 | 88.4 | —30.1 | 15.8 | 87.1 | 5.08 | 1.27 |
| 8577 | 85.0 | —29.0 | {19.8 | 85.0 | 4.89 | 1.80 |
| 8581 | 87.0 | —28.6 | 20.6 | 85.8 | 4.64 | .67 |
| 8583 | 85.1 | —28.9 | 19.0 | 84.8 | 4.87 | 1.18 |
| 8586 | 87.0 | —28.3 | 21.0 | 86.3 | 3.78 | 1.07 |
| 8587 | 99.0 | —33.0 | 20.0 | 98.5 | .03 | .05 |
| 8589 | 100.0 | —34.2 | 17.6 | 98.9 | .00 | .05 |
| 8590 | 100.1 | —32.9 | 20.6 | 99.5 | .00 | .04 |
| 8591 | 93.0 | —30.3 | 20.6 | 92.2 | 5.93 | .18 |
| 8593 | 90.2 | —31.4 | 17.8 | 90.0 | 5.85 | .36 |
| 8594 | 80.6 | —29.3 | 20.2 | 82.1 | 7.98 | .11 |
| 8595 | 85.7 | —27.6 | 18.6 | 84.1 | 5.92 | .19 |
| 8596 | 100.1 | —33.4 | 18.8 | 99.2 | .11 | .03 |
| 8598 | 86.0 | —29.0 | 20.5 | 86.0 | 6.20 | .80 |
| 8599 | 81.1 | —27.6 | 20.0 | 81.1 | 7.97 | .14 |
| 8600 | 100.0 | —33.1 | 20.8 | 99.8 | .06 | .01 |
| 8601 | 87.5 | —27.7 | 20.6 | 86.2 | 5.00 | 1.57 |
| 8602 | 100.1 | —32.8 | 19.8 | 99.9 | .06 | .02 |
| 8620 | 85.0 | —29.6 | 19.4 | 85.3 | 5.60 | 1.46 |
| 8621 | 93.9 | —31.2 | 19.6 | 93.2 | 4.83 | .26 |
| 8622 | 86.8 | —29.2 | 19.8 | 86.5 | 6.22 | .58 |
| 8623 | 84.6 | —29.0 | 20.0 | 84.7 | 4.87 | 2.30 |
| 8624 | 83.4 | —29.3 | 20.0 | 84.1 | 5.27 | 1.66 |
| 8625 | 84.0 | —28.9 | 20.0 | 84.3 | 4.73 | .89 |
| 8626 | 85.3 | —28.6 | 20.4 | 84.4 | 6.71 | .93 |
| 8627 | 85.8 | —29.3 | 20.4 | 86.0 | 5.65 | .82 |
| 8628 | 87.0 | —29.1 | 20.4 | 86.8 | 4.04 | 3.33 |
| 8629 | 88.0 | —29.5 | 20.4 | 87.8 | 3.52 | 2.94 |
| 8630 | 85.8 | —29.1 | 20.8 | 86.0 | 6.63 | 1.34 |
| 8631 | 84.0 | —29.1 | 22.0 | 85.0 | 7.17 | .89 |
| 8632 | 83.5 | —28.2 | 22.0 | 84.0 | 3.96 | 2.11 |
| 8633 | 88.6 | —30.8 | 22.0 | 89.8 | 4.40 | .88 |
| 8634 | 100.0 | -32.6 | 22.0 | 99.7 | .01 | .02 |
| 8635 | 85.2 | —29.2 | 22.0 | 86.0 | 6.11 | 1.51 |
| 8636 | 93.3 | —31.5 | 22.0 | 93.6 | 3.63 | .47 |
| 8637 | 86.7 | —29.0 | 22.0 | 87.0 | 6.64 | .80 |
| 8638 | 92.2 | —30.7 | 22.0 | 92.4 | 5.52 | .22 |
| 8639 | 99.4 | —32.7 | 22.2 | 99.3 | .17 | .01 |
| 8640 | 98.3 | —33.0 | 22.2 | 98.8 | .33 | .40 |
| 8641 | 92.2 | —30.0 | 22.4 | 92.0 | 5.81 | .38 |
| 8642 | 100.0 | -83.0 | 22.4 | 99.6 | .30 | .03 |
| 8643 | 100.0 | —33.0 | 22.4 | 99.7 | .29 | .05 |
| 8644 | 99.6 | —32.4 | 22.8 | 99.5 | .01 | .02 |

## NOTES ON ANALYSES.

### GENERAL.

The total absence of any added matters to the sugars of commerce is plainly shown by the five hundred analyses of samples purchased in open market in different parts of the country.

A few years ago an attempt was made to adulterate cane sugar, then worth nearly 10 cents a pound, with sugar made from cornstarch, worth from 3 to 5 cents a pound. This sugar was sold in considerable quantities under the name of new-process sugar. It is needless to say that it passed into consumption under the impression that it was genuine cane sugar. The cornstarch sugar, on account of the difficulty of drying it, made the whole mass sticky and difficult to handle. This variety of sugar, therefore, did not find a ready sale, and its manufacture never assumed very large proportions.

Attempts were then made to manufacture pure anhydrous cornstarch sugar, and these attempts were successful from a chemical, but not from a commercial, point of view. In point of fact, however, considerable quantities of this dry dextrose were put on the market, and I believe it is still made under the patents of Dr. Arno Behr.

The low price of cane sugar, however, has heretofore prevented the profitable adulteration of cane sugar with any article made from starch. It is also gratifying to know that the powdered sugars of commerce were not found adulterated with starch or terra alba; at least, in so far as the limited examination of them extended.

The chief adulterant of low-grade sugars, if it can properly be so called, is water. By modern methods of sugar-boiling a great deal of low-grade sugar and water can be incorporated in low-priced sugars, which still show an almost white color. This is due to the combined influence of bone black, and low temperature in the vacuum pan. By means of bone black the sirups are nearly or quite decolorized; and by boiling at a low temperature (115° to 120° F.) a soft crystal of sugar is formed which is capable of holding a large percentage of water and reducing sugar. The resulting sugar is, nevertheless, almost white, and finds a ready sale for many culinary operations. These sugars are easily detected by noticing the polarizations below 90° in the tables of analyses.

The question of the use of these sugars is one of economy only, for they are certainly not injurious to health. In general it may be said that for a given sum a greater quantity of saccharine matter can be purchased by taking the high-grade sugars. In respect of maple sugar there is a general impression that it is largely adulterated with cheaper varieties. At the present time the resources of chemistry are powerless to detect such an adulteration. The sugar of the maple sap is identical in composition with that of the sugar cane, sorghum, and sugar beet. No discrimination in such cases can be made by analysis. If the ethereal substance which gives to maple sugar its peculiar flavor could be detected and quantitatively determined, then adulteration with a sugar containing none of this substance might be detected. Extract of hickory bark is said to contain the same flavor as maple sap, and, therefore, even in case of being able to measure the quantity of this substance, it might be added as an adulterant.

In regard to the price of the sugars, molasses, etc., it should be remembered that they were purchased early in the year 1891, before sugar was admitted to our ports free of duty.

### THE COLORING OF SUGARS.

White and yellow sugars usually receive a special treatment, either in the vacuum pan or the centrifugal, in order to prevent a gray or "dead" appearance. In the case of white sugars blue ultramarine is the substance usually employed for this purpose. The coloring matter is suspended in water and is applied as final wash in the centrifugal immediately before stopping the machine. This process is termed "bluing." A very small amount of the color adheres to the crystals, giving the sugar a whiter and brighter appearance. Some sugar makers suspend a small amount of ultramarine in water and draw it into the vacuum pan a few minutes before the strike is finished. In addition to this treatment in the pan the sugar is also blued in the centrifugal. It is not unusual to find sugars which have been excessively blued, and which, on solution, yield a blue sirup. Fortunately ultramarine is not poisonous and no injury to health can result from its use.

The yellow clarified sugars of the plantations are always treated with a wash containing chloride of tin, commercially known as tin crystal. The yellow sugars not treated with tin, soon after leaving the centrifugal, lose their bright color and become a dead or grayish yellow. Such sugars are only manufactured for the refiner, and do not enter directly into the consumption. The tin crystal is dissolved in water and, as in the case of ultramarine, is employed as a final wash shortly before stopping the centrifugal. The depth of the yellow color of the sugar depends largely upon the strength of the tin solution and is modified by the manufacturers to suit the demands of the market.

The principal constituent of the various sugar colors known as "rock compound," "Smith's sugar color," etc., is chloride of tin. The tin chloride is not in itself a coloring matter. Tin can rarely be detected in sugars known to have been colored by means of tin chloride. The yellow color produced by this substance is probably a result of its action on the sugar itself.

Tin crystal is also employed in the vacuum pan, but not generally in this country. In the manufacture of the beautiful sugar known as "Demerara crystals," chloride of tin is employed in the vacuum pan. Sulphuric acid was formerly used for this purpose, but it has been superseded by the tin compound.

The chloride of tin passes into the molasses and becomes an objectionable constituent of this product. Messrs. Lock & Newlands Brothers* mention a harmless yellow color of organic origin, which is used in the manufacture of imitation Demerara crystals. So far as the writer is aware this color is not used on the sugar plantations of this country.

## SPECIAL NOTES.

### ANALYSES BY H. A. HUSTON.

The samples of sugar were purchased in La Fayette, Ind., Indianapolis, and Chicago. A glance at the descriptions of the samples will show that all the common commercial sugars are represented in the samples.

*Open-kettle sugar.*—One sample of marked open-kettle sugar is found in the list. Open-kettle sugar is made largely in Louisiana by planters, having only a small area in cultivation and inexpensive factory facilities. The boiling is accomplished without the aid of vacuum apparatus and in open kettles. The molasses is separated without the use of centrifugals and by simple drainage from the hogsheads, into which the mush sugar is placed after granulation. Open-kettle molasses is the best and highest priced molasses in the New Orleans market. Very little open-kettle sugar is found in commerce outside of the region of its production. There is some demand for it, especially among bakers, and many like its aromatic flavor and taste. For this reason there might be some inducement to brand with that name the low-grade yellow cane sugars of a refinery.

*Maple sugar.*—Three samples of maple sugar are included in the list, viz, 125, polarizing 84.11 and costing 22 cents a pound; 130, polarizing 84.21 and costing 13 cents a pound; and 145, polarizing 81.40 and costing 20 cents a pound.

The price of maple sugar, as is well known, is out of all proportion to the saccharine matter which it contains, and is due to its peculiar and pleasant taste, derived presumably from some ethereal matter exuded with the sap. The nature of this substance has not, to my knowledge, been definitely determined. It is not wholly volatile, since it remains in the sugar and molasses after they have been kept for a long time at a high temperature during the process of concentration. Nevertheless, a distinctly agreeable odor marks the process of maple sap evaporation, as every one can attest who has visited the primitive sugar factories which are operated in the maple-sugar industry.

As has before been intimated, there is a popular belief that maple sugar is largely adulterated with cane sugar derived from other sources. The chemical identity of these sugars, however, prevents any chemical detection of such alleged adulteration. The great stores of maple sugar and sirup offered for sale in comparison with the very limited supply is the chief basis for the popular suspicion. It must be remem-

---

* Sugar: Lock & Newlands Brothers, p. 291.

bered, however, that the annual output of maple sugar in this country approximates 20,000 tons, and this would be sufficient to supply a great demand. Maple sugar is chiefly used, outside of the area of its manu- facture, as a delicacy and not in general consumption.

No. 117—*Extra C.*—This sample is distinguished by having the lowest polarization of any in the list, viz, 74.56°. It shows in a marked way how much water and molasses can be incorporated in a sugar with fair color and merchantable conditions. This sugar was selling for 6¼ cents a pound when sugar of 99.5° purity was bringing only 8 cents. The relative value of the sugar in the two samples at 9 cents a pound for pure sugar is as follows;

Value of 99.5° sugar at 9 cents for pure 100° sugar, 8.96 cents.

Value of 74.56° sugar at 9 cents for pure 100° sugar, 6.71 cents.

At the rate of 6¼ cents per pound for 74.56° sugar, 100° sugar would cost 8.38 cents a pound. At the rate of 8 cents for 99.5° sugar, 100° sugar would cost 8.04 cents a pound. It is seen at once, therefore, that in respect of the quantity of pure sugar obtained the purchaser of the low-grade sugar is at a disadvantage. This, however, is an extreme case. In most cases prices and purity are so adjusted as to give approximately the same quantity of pure sugar for the same price.

*High polarizing sugars.*—A pure sugar under certain definite condi- tions corresponds with the 100° mark on the polariscopic scale. This scale is fixed arbitrarily, and the quantity of pure sugar required to read 100° in a given volume of solution varies with different instru- ments. When, however, in a given accurate instrument, a reading of more than 100° is obtained for a sample of sugar, it shows either some analytical error or else the presence in the sugar of some body having a higher specific rotatory power than sucrose. It was noticed that sev- eral samples of granulated sugar examined in the laboratory of the Department of Agriculture showed a rotation slightly greater than 100°. These values will be discussed below. In the case of No. 139 of the samples now under discussion, a polarization of 100° is noticed with a trace of moisture and ash. This may have been due to a slight error in reading, which may sometimes amount to as much as 0.2°, or to some high rotating material in the sugar under examination. Mr. Hus- ton's polariscope was almost exactly correct, giving a reading of 99.7° with the sugar sent, against 99.73°, the mean of numerous readings in the Department laboratory, checked by a quartz plate, standardized by the office of weights and measures, U. S. Coast and Geodetic Survey.

### ANALYSES OF H. H. NICHOLSON.

*Samples.*—The samples examined by Prof. Nicholson were purchased at Red Cloud, Beatrice, Lincoln, and Omaha, Nebr. They consist chiefly of low-grade sugars, only two, Nos. 25 and 40, reaching the grade of pure granulated sugars.

*Lowest polarization.*—No. 10, marked New Orleans sugar, shows the lowest polarization of any of the samples, viz, 77.3°. It is low even for an open-kettle sugar. It is more likely to be a very low grade of refinery product.

*Highest polarization.*—The highest polarization shown by any of the samples is 100.2° by No. 42, also marked New Orleans. This sample is shown to have also 1.07 per cent water and 1.88 per cent ash. The number, 100.2°, representing the polarization is necessarily erroneous. All plus polarizing sugars are of a high grade of purity and have but little ash. The only possible explanation of this high number is that the sample is beet sugar made from material rich in raffinose and not well purified. This might account for the excess of polarization and also for the presence of so large a quantity of ash. A sugar polarizing 99° and over should have only a trace of ash.

This polarization should also be diminished 0.3, on account of error in the instrument. But even 99.9 polarization is entirely too high for a sugar containing nearly 3 per cent of foreign matter, unless, as above intimated, it may also contain raffinose.

## ANALYSES BY W. B. RISING.

*Samples.*—The samples were purchased in Berkeley and San Francisco, Cal. They were mostly low-grade refinery samples, and one, of which there was some doubt, was said to be New Orleans sugar.

*Lowest polarization.*—Sample No. 171 showed the lowest polarization, viz, 79.6°. It was a yellow sugar with 6.32 per cent water and 2.65 per cent ash. The place of its manufacture and the name under which it was sold are not given.

*Highest polarization.*—The purest sugar of this lot is No. 5, a granulated sugar purchased in Berkeley. It shows a polarization of 98.10°, with only .15 per cent water and .02 per cent ash.

*Highest ash.*—Sample No. 4 is remarkable in having so high a content of ash. Scarcely more than this would be expected in molasses. The color of this sugar, however, was white and its polarization only 85.7°. From the large quantity of ash contained in it there is reason to suspect that it was made from beets. The small quantity of beet sugar used on the Pacific coast, however, would make it difficult to accept such an explanation.

*Accuracy of instrument.*—Mr. Rising has failed to report the reading of the sample sugar sent him; therefore the accuracy of the polariscope used by him is not known.

## ANALYSES BY M. A. SCOVELL.

*Samples.*—The samples were purchased in Lexington and Louisville, Ky., and in Cincinnati, Ohio. After the analytical work had all been finished Prof. Scovell's laboratory was destroyed by fire and his notes and samples destroyed. With great energy and ability he soon reestablished his laboratory, purchased new samples, and repeated the work. The data given are of course from the second set of samples.

*Temperature.*—The solutions were all made up and read at approximately 25°.

*Standard of the instrument.*—The sample of test sugar sent to Mr. Scovell polarized on his instrument 99.8°. By standard quartz plate, 99.73°. Error, .07°. The instrument, therefore, was correctly graduated, reading only a trifle too high.

*Lowest polarization.*—Sample No. 84 showed the lowest polarization, viz., 74.4°. This sample had 4.88 per cent water and .67 per cent ash. It was labeled maple sugar, and was a light-colored cake, similar in form to the most common shape in which maple sugar is sold.

### ANALYSES BY S. P. SHARPLES.

The sugars on this (Boston and suburbs) market, as sold at the retail stores, come from the two refineries which are situated at this place. A small amount is bought from Spreckels' refinery at Philadelphia.

Almost the whole of the sugar used in this part of the State is of the quality known as granulated. I have procured three or four samples of this to show the grade of the sugar.

The only yellow sugar made at present here is that numbered 9437, and known as the Revere yellow. The Revere Sugar Refinery uses only high-grade centrifugal sugars, made from cane. The American Sugar Refining Company uses all grades of sugar that come into the market, including some beet sugars. This winter they have been using some New Orleans sugars and some little sorghum.

The yellow sugars now on the market here are mainly of New York make, and are sold through the American Sugar Refining Company.

I have endeavored to give as fully as possible the exact condition of the market here in selecting these sugars, giving the sugars as found in the retailers' hands and also the sugars as sold by the refiners.

Many of the retail dealers do not keep the yellow sugars, dealing only in the granulated sugars. These are generally of three grades, fine, medium, and coarse.

They are all alike and made at the same time, but the consumers here very generally prefer the fine granulated, and quite frequently it brings a shade more at wholesale. There is generally an insufficient supply of this grade. The three grades are prepared by passing the dried sugar through a sizing machine.

### TEST SUGAR RECEIVED FROM WASHINGTON.

| | |
|---|---|
| Moisture | 0.08 |
| Polarized in 200 mm tube | 99.90 |
| Polarized in 100 mm tube | 50.00 |
| After inversion (read at 21° C.) | −31.80 |

50 cc of Violette solution required 35.5 cc of inverted sugar solution containing 6.847 grams to the litre.

1 cc of Violette solution =0.00486 grams of invert sugar.

The above value has been used throughout this report.

ANALYSES BY W. C. STUBBS.

These analyses are particularly interesting on account of being made on samples which are supposed to represent very accurately the raw sugars produced in Louisiana.

In the description of the samples we find the terms which are used in that State in describing raw sugars. Some of these, perhaps, merit a more extended definition.

The term "open-kettle sugar" is applied to raw sugars made in the old-fashioned way of boiling the juices in open kettles to proof. The juice is then drawn off in tanks and allowed to crystallize. The mixture of sugar and molasses thus formed is transferred to hogsheads, with perforated bottoms and allowed to stand until the molasses drains off. Open-kettle sugars are highly prized by many on account of their fine odor and taste. They are, however, moist and likely to become hard on drying. In many respects, especially in baking cakes, the sugar is of great value.

The term "centrifugal seconds" is applied to sugar made by the modern process, reboiled from the molasses obtained in the first crystallization. This sugar is sometimes grained in the vacuum pan, but more often is boiled to string proof and allowed to crystallize in wagons in the hot room. In polarization, this sugar is generally higher than open-kettle sugar, but in flavor it is inferior to that sugar. For refining purposes, however, it is probably a little more valuable than ordinary open-kettle sugars.

"Yellow clarified sugar" is a first product of high grade and a delicate yellow color. It was formerly produced very largely on all the plantations in the State where modern processes are employed. It found a ready market without passing through a refinery. The delicate yellow color is imparted by treating the juices with sulphur fumes before the process of clarification is completed. The juices are then boiled in the clarifying pans and swept until very clean. After granulation in the vacuum pans, they are washed in the centrifugal and brightened by being sprayed with a solution of chloride of tin in some form or other. Since the change in the fiscal policy of the Government in regard to sugar duties and the institution of the bounty, yellow clarified sugars are made in much less quantities than before.

The highest polarizing sugar examined by Mr. Stubbs was No. 46, polarizing 100°. When the instrument, however, is corrected to correspond with the proper polarization, it is seen that this number is not too high. becoming, instead of 100, 99.70.

## ANALYSES BY SHIPPEN WALLACE.

The samples examined by Mr. Wallace were of low-grade sugars for which he paid a uniform price of 5½ cents per pound. They were purchased in Philadelphia and vicinity, and represent undoubtedly the low-grade sugars from the refineries of that city. The only clew to the origin of these low-grade sugars will probably be found in the percentage of ash which they contain. Those which contain over 1 per cent of ash are certainly raw sugars derived from the sugar beet. The same is possibly true of those where the ash runs above one-half of 1 per cent, but in these cases it is probable the raw sugar is derived from a mixture of sugars made from cane and beet. I believe it is the custom in some refineries not to attempt to keep the raw beet sugars and cane sugars separate during refining. In this case, both the refined article and low-grade sugars would be mixtures of the two.

## ANALYSES BY II. A. WEBER.

The samples examined by Mr. Weber were all purchased in Columbus in the localities mentioned in the table. These were also uniformly low-grade sugars and presumably low-grade sugars from refiners. Many of them, however, were marked New Orleans sugar, but this label does not always indicate the origin of the sample. In many localities New Orleans sugars are much in demand, and from the quantity of such sugar which is sold, it is to be presumed that much of the low-grade sugar of refineries is sold under the name of New Orleans sugar.

As indicated in the communication of Mr. Weber in transmitting his samples, he determined the sugar by chemical methods as well as by polarization. He seems to rely more upon the chemical method than upon the method by polarization, in which respect his opinion differs from that of most chemists familiar with this class of work. The differences, in many instances in his figures, are quite marked. In sample No. 1 there is a difference of nearly 3 per cent between the result of the polarization and of the sugar determined by chemical means. In most of the other instances the two results are nearly identical.

## ANALYSES BY F. G. WIECHMANN.

In one of the sugars examined, No. 23, there were found grains of rice, whole and broken. The presence of this rice, however, was probably only accidental, due to carelessness, as the market-price of this article is almost the same as that of sugar, thus offering no inducement for its use as an adulterant.

With this exception, all of the samples examined must be pronounced non-adulterated, as polarization, water, and ash are in every case within the test limits of these grades of refined sugars.

Particular attention must be called to the percentages of ash found in the samples examined by Mr. Wiechmann, especially as compared with the content in the samples analyzed by Mr. Stubbs. As before intimated, an excess of ash in raw sugars would point to a beet-sugar origin. The presumption in favor of the New Orleans sugars is that they are all made from cane. On the other hand, it is known that large quantities of raw beet sugar are imported into New York and the greatly increased percentage of ash in the New York samples possibly indicates the use of considerable quantities of raw beet sugar by the refineries supplying the New York and Brooklyn markets.

## THE SAMPLES OF SUGAR EXAMINED AT THE LABORATORY OF THE DEPARTMENT.

These samples were purchased in Washington and Baltimore. Numbers 8559 to 8602, inclusive, were purchased in Washington; numbers 8620 to 8644, inclusive, were purchased in Baltimore.

An attempt was made not only to get fair samples of the low-grade sugars, but also a considerable number of high-grade sugars. It is interesting to note that a number of these sugars polarized 100° or slightly over. In every case, these high polarizing sugars had the peculiar odor characteristic of beet sugar. A possible explanation of this high polarization is found in the supposition that they may have contained traces of raffinose.

The low-grade sugars represented all the various kinds of such sugars which the market would afford. Considerable time and effort were spent in getting absolutely fair market samples both from Washington and Baltimore.

In the table of analyses are given, in addition to the ordinary data, the percentages of sugar contained in each sample when calculated after inversion by the factor 144. Apparently the factor 144 gave more accurate results than the factor 142.6, the results of which tend to be, as would be expected, too high.

From a general review of the analyses of sugar purchased in all parts of the country we may safely assume that the adulteration of sugar with sand or terra alba which is said to exist in other countries is not practiced to any appreciable extent in this. The addition of other sugars than cane sugar to the sugars of commerce is also extremely doubtful. The only things which could be construed as an adulteration is in making sugars almost white but with soft grain capable of absorbing a considerable quantity of molasses and retaining it and the use of excessive quantities of ultramarine. The soft sugars mentioned form a considerable quantity of the low-grade sugars of commerce. From the calculations made, in one or two instances, it is seen that the purchaser scarcely gets as much saccharine matter in buying these low-grade sugars at a low price as he does in buying high-grade sugars at a slightly higher price. The difference, however, is so slight as to be unimportant. The trade in low-grade sugars, therefore, can not be considered fraudulent, as the purchaser is fully aware at the time of buying that he is getting an inferior quality of sugar for which he is paying a lower price. So long as the price of sugar continues at its present low figure, it may be said that the danger of adulteration is extremely small. The very best way of all to prevent the adulteration of an article of food is to have the price of this article so low as to exclude the possibility of any kind of adulteration proving profitable.

Attempts to find the origin of the sugar samples usually proved fruitless, inasmuch as they were, as a rule, bought in small groceries, the proprietors of which knew no more about them than that they came from the wholesale houses. One sample of Louisiana yellow clarified (No. 8640) was found in Baltimore. Many of the granulated white sugars, after standing in corked bottles for some time, developed the foul odor characteristic of beet products. The sugars now called "brown sugar" by the grocers are moist, fine-grained, light-yellow products, while by "black sugar" is understood a yellowish-brown sugar, such as was sold as "brown sugar" five or six years ago. It was attempted to get some very cheap samples, but none were found which varied much from the average price.

For direct polarization duplicate samples of 26.048 grams ($\pm 0.5$ mg) were weighed out in a sugar dish, washed into a 100 cc flask, with water of room temperature, dissolved in about 75 cc. of water by giving the flask a gentle rotary motion, and from 1 drop to 1 cc of concentrated solution of basic acetate of lead added, the smaller quantity being for very high-grade sugars, the greater for correspondingly low; 1 or 2 cc of alumina cream was also always added. High-polarizing sugars seldom give a flocky, readily filtering precipitate with basic acetate as do lower grades, the precipitate formed being as a rule scanty and slimy, passing readily through the filter. Addition of alumina cream flocks this suspended finely-pulverulent precipitate together, much facilitating filtration and insuring clear filtrates. For the sake of uniformity all sugar samples received this addition. After making the solution up to the mark it was filtered through a fluted filter and polarized in a 200 mm tube. The polariscope used was a 600 mm half-shade Schmidt & Haensch. Six readings were made on each solution, the average being recorded. For invert readings a 50 to 55 cc. flask was filled to the 50 cc mark with the solution which had been polarized, room temperature being noted, 5 cc of strong hydrochloric (sp. g. 1.2) added, and the flask, together with another containing water and having a thermometer standing in it, placed in a pan of water kept heated to 68 to 70 by a steam bath. As soon as the thermometer in the flask showed 69, time was noted and that temperature kept up for ten minutes. After this lapse of time the flasks were plunged in another pan of cold water, to be again removed when the thermometer showed room temperature. Polarization was made in a 220 mm tube. The tube was laid in the polariscope over a delicate thermometer. Readings were then made at short intervals until they ceased to vary, the final reading being recorded and, at the same time, the temperature recorded on the thermometer was noted. The old value for Clerget's constant, 144, was used instead of the newer but not yet established values 142.4 and 142.6-7. Bone-black was not used with sugar samples.

# MOLASSES AND SIRUPS.

## ANALYSES BY H. A. HUSTON.

*Description of samples.*

| No. | Bought of— | Price per gallon. | Manufacturer or brand. | Kind. | Remarks. |
|---|---|---|---|---|---|
| 51 | Chas. H. Slack, Chicago. | $0.80 | " Leighton " .......... | New Orleans molasses. | |
| 52 | ....do ............. | .60 | Diamond Gilt Edge... | Sugar sirup.......... | |
| 53 | Whitsel & Co., West La Fayette. | ........ | Harvey's Nursery, Tippecanoe Co., Ind. | Sorghum ............ | |
| 54 | Chas. H. Slack, Chicago. | 2.20 | D. C. Leonard & Son, Wilmington, Vt. | Pure Vermont maple sirup. | Ash light green in color. |
| 55 | ....do ............. | .30 | Bee Hive ............ | Black Strap molasses. | |
| 56 | ....do ............. | .60 | ..................... | Porto Rico molasses.. | |
| 57 | ....do ............. | .60 | Bellview............. | New Orleans molasses | |
| 58 | ....do ............. | .60 | Stanley.............. | ......do ........... | |
| 59 | A. Botsford & Co., Chicago. | ..... | ..................... | Ohio maple sirup ..... | Made up from maple sugar. |
| 60 | ....do ............. | ..... | ..................... | ......do ............ | Made up from maple sugar and glucose. |
| 61 | A. B. Braden, La Fayette. | 1.25 | Sugar-Growers' Association, Chardon, Ohio. | ......do ............ | |
| 62 | ... do ............. | .75 | ..................... | Boston Refinery sugar drips. | |
| 63 | ....do............. | .60 | Open-kettle goods ... | New Orleans molasses. | |
| 64 | ....do ............. | 2.00 | Crown Cordial and Extract Co., New York. | Tu Fru * ............. | In tin can from stock. (See No. 80.) |
| 65 | Schwarm & Heinmiller, Chicago. | 1.20 | Put up for Pottlitzer Bros., Fort Wayne and La Fayette, Ind. | Maple sirup ......... | Pottlitzer Bros. stated 65 was better than 66, and 66 better than 67, but gave no statement that either was genuine maple sirup. |
| 66 | Pottlitzer Bros., La Fayette. | 1.00 | Put up for Baldwin & Co., New Haven. | Orange County, Vt.. homemade maple sirup. | |
| 67 | ....do ............. | 1.00 | Canned by National Sirup Co. | Western New York... | |
| 68 | Beck & Frasch, La Fayette. | .50 | Bradshaw & Wait, Chicago, Ill. | Silver drips........... | |
| 69 | ....do ............. | .75 | ..................... | New Orleans molasses. | |
| 70 | ....do ............. | 1.25 | Bradshaw & Wait, Chicago, Ill. | Maple sirup........... | |
| 71 | P. Feeley, La Fayette. | 1.20 | (No name) Indianapolis, Ind. | Ohio maple sirup ..... | |
| 72 | ....do ............. | .40 | (No name) Chicago, Ill. | Excelsior sirup ....... | |

* Label states: " A pure, delicious, fruity table sirup for griddle and pan cakes, made from fine selected fruit and best grade of sugar."

683

*Description of samples—Continued.*

| No. | Bought of— | Price per gallon. | Manufacturer or brand. | Kind. | Remarks. |
|---|---|---|---|---|---|
| 73 | P. Feeley, La Fayette. | $0.40 | (No name) Chicago, Ill. | Sirup ............... | Said to be "stronger" sirup than No. 72. |
| 74 | ....do ............ | .50 | (No name) Tippecanoe Co., Ind. | Sorghum............. | |
| 75 | ....do ............ | .65 | ................... | New Orleans molasses. | |
| 76 | Ensing Bros., La Fayette. | 1.10 | Reid, Murdock & Co, Chicago, Ill. | Michigan maple sirup. | |
| 77 | ... do ............ | .45 | ................... | Silver drips .......... | |
| 78 | ....do ............ | .70 | ................... | New Orleans molasses. | |
| 79 | ....do ............ | .50 | ................... | Fancy honey sirup ... | |
| 80 | A. B. Braden, La Fayette. | 2.00 | Crown Cordial and Extract Co, Chicago. | Tu Fru ............... | Same as No. 64, but put up in glass and marked "Sample purchased because tin was found in No. 64." |
| 81 | C. Jevne & Co., Chicago. | ........ | ................... | New Orleans molasses. | |
| 82 | .. do ............ | ........ | ................... | Confectioners' sirup .. | |
| 83 | ...do ............ | ........ | ................... | Maple sirup ......... | |
| 84 | ....do ............ | ........ | ................... | Corn sirup ........... | |
| 85 | .. do ............ | ........ | I. Calvin Shafer Co., New York. | Standard strawberry sirup. | |
| 86 | D. B. Scully, Chicago. | .75 | Woodstock .. ....... | New Orleans molasses. | |
| 87 | Sprague, Warner & Co., Chicago. | .90 | ................... | No. 1 maple sirup ..... | |
| 88 | ...do ............ | .60 | White Rose ......... | New Orleans molasses. | |
| 89 | .. do ............ | .80 | Magnolia ........... | ......do ............. | |
| 90 | .. do ............ | .60 | Woodlawn ........... | .... do ............... | |
| 91 | ...do ............ | .50 | ................... | Boston standard sirup. | |
| 92 | ...do ............ | .50 | ................... | Perfection sirup ...... | |
| 93 | Cruckelbans, Indianapolis. | 1.00 | Canned by Bradshaw & Wait, Chicago. | First-run selected maple sirup. | |
| 94 | Louis Schism, La Fayette. | .60 | Sprague, Warner & Co., Chicago. | Honey Drop sirup .... | |
| 95 | Wells & Schilling, La Fayette. | .40 | ................... | Good Luck sirup ..... | |
| 96 | ....do ............ | .70 | ................... | New Orleans molasses. | Sold as being free from tin. |
| 97 | Wm. Beck, La Fayette. | .70 | ................... | ......do ............. | Do |
| 98 | Louis Kemmel, La Fayette. | 1.40 | F. G. Strohmeyer & Co., New York. | Pure maple sirup, "delicious and wholesome." | |
| 99 | Jos. Beck, La Fayette. | 1.40 | ................... | Maple sirup from Vermont. | |
| 100 | Ja. O'Neil & Co., Chicago. | ........ | Delgado & Co., New Orleans, La. | New Orleans molasses. | |

*Analytical data.*

| No. | Polarization. | | Tempera-ture ° C. | Sucrose. | Reducing sugars. | Water. | Ash. | Tin or other metals. |
|---|---|---|---|---|---|---|---|---|
| | Direct. | Indirect. | | | | | | |
| | | | | *Per cent.* | *Per cent.* | *Per cent.* | *Per cent.* | |
| 51 | .......... | .......... | .......... | 41.23 | 26.92 | 20.24 | 2.75 | Absent. |
| 52 | .......... | .......... | .......... | 23.94 | 33.27 | 16.47 | 0.92 | Present. |
| 53 | .......... | .......... | .......... | 39.34 | 36.01 | 20.88 | 1.87 | Absent. |
| 54 | .......... | .......... | .......... | 65.71 | 00.05 | 24.15 | 0.40 | Present. |
| 55 | .......... | .......... | .......... | 26.40 | 17.21 | 22.64 | 0.13 | Do. |
| 56 | .......... | .......... | .......... | 21.73 | 30.00 | 24.18 | 2.75 | Do. |
| 57 | .......... | .......... | .......... | 40.23 | 29.52 | 18.10 | 3.61 | Absent. |
| 58 | .......... | .......... | .......... | 21.89 | 30.00 | 20.27 | 3.61 | Do. |
| 59 | .......... | .......... | .......... | 51.00 | 13.46 | 34.93 | 0.32 | Present. |
| 60 | .......... | .......... | .......... | 40.55 | 27.63 | 38.80 | 0.31 | Do. |
| 61 | .......... | .......... | .......... | 65.23 | 00.29 | 32.37 | 0.27 | Do. |
| 62 | .......... | .......... | .......... | 39.19 | 37.85 | 11.12 | 2.79 | Absent. |
| 63 | .......... | .......... | .......... | 54.28 | 14.58 | 21.90 | 2.18 | Do. |
| 64 | .......... | .......... | .......... | 9.44 | 51.14 | 23.18 | 0.06 | Present. |
| 65 | .......... | .......... | .......... | 27.76 | 36.45 | 20.89 | 0.33 | Do. |
| 66 | .......... | .......... | .......... | 31.01 | 32.81 | 23.49 | 0.43 | Absent. |
| 67 | .......... | .......... | .......... | 26.07 | 39.77 | 21.97 | 0.70 | Present. |
| 68 | .......... | .......... | .......... | 21.83 | 52.50 | 16.24 | 0.99 | Absent. |
| 69 | .......... | .......... | .......... | 17.82 | 41.01 | 20.84 | 1.13 | Do. |
| 70 | .......... | .......... | .......... | 63.26 | 1.98 | 35.82 | 0.55 | Present. |
| 71 | .......... | .......... | .......... | 23.11 | 35.76 | 26.68 | 0.44 | Do. |
| 72 | .......... | .......... | .......... | 31.44 | 41.53 | 21.26 | 0.94 | Do. |
| 73 | .......... | .......... | .......... | 26.47 | 23.75 | 25.29 | 2.95 | Do. |
| 74 | .......... | .......... | .......... | 36.14 | 31.39 | 23.15 | 2.56 | Absent. |
| 75 | .......... | .......... | .......... | 31.44 | 26.34 | 24.22 | 4.25 | Present. |
| 76 | .......... | .......... | .......... | 13.30 | 42.19 | 27.59 | 0.25 | Do. |
| 77 | .......... | .......... | .......... | 18.65 | 41.53 | 23.25 | 0.89 | Absent. |
| 78 | .......... | .......... | .......... | 32.19 | 27.68 | 22.90 | 8.90 | Present. |
| 79 | .......... | .......... | .......... | 16.14 | 47.78 | 16.79 | 0.43 | Do. |
| 80 | .......... | .......... | .......... | 12.66 | 52.93 | 22.01 | 0.08 | Do. |
| 81 | .......... | .......... | .......... | 43.87 | 29.67 | 24.16 | 1.95 | Absent. |
| 82 | .......... | .......... | .......... | 14.38 | 51.42 | 20.03 | 0.85 | Present. |
| 83 | .......... | .......... | .......... | 30.33 | 38.28 | 30.75 | 0.45 | Do. |
| 84 | .......... | .......... | .......... | 14.41 | 42.06 | 19.47 | 0.78 | Do. |
| 85 | .......... | .......... | .......... | 0.00 | 60.78 | 39.10 | 0.02 | Do. |
| 86 | .......... | .......... | .......... | 40.57 | 30.00 | 21.23 | 2.48 | Do. |
| 87 | .......... | .......... | .......... | 32.48 | 28.42 | 29.31 | 0.46 | Do. |
| 88 | .......... | .......... | .......... | 37.34 | 32.53 | 24.81 | 1.69 | Do. |
| 89 | .......... | .......... | .......... | 48.47 | 18.30 | 25.25 | 2.81 | Absent. |
| 90 | .......... | .......... | .......... | 38.12 | 18.00 | 23.73 | 3.72 | Do. |
| 91 | .......... | .......... | .......... | 40.90 | 34.17 | 18.13 | 2.93 | Do. |
| 92 | .......... | .......... | .......... | 28.16 | 44.26 | 21.53 | 0.62 | Do. |
| 93 | .......... | .......... | .......... | 29.57 | 31.19 | 27.19 | 0.61 | Present. |
| 94 | .......... | .......... | .......... | 26.58 | 35.94 | 21.66 | 0.99 | Do. |
| 95 | .......... | .......... | .......... | 15.15 | 40.53 | 23.24 | 0.44 | Absent. |
| 96 | .......... | .......... | .......... | 43.77 | 32.14 | 24.63 | 4.24 | Present. |
| 97 | .......... | .......... | .......... | 11.43 | 39.13 | 27.86 | 1.96 | Do. |
| 98 | .......... | .......... | .......... | 54.72 | 28.48 | 32.64 | 0.60 | Do. |
| 99 | .......... | .......... | .......... | 30.19 | 21.60 | 35.40 | 0.41 | Do. |
| 100 | .......... | .......... | .......... | 51.31 | 18.95 | 25.09 | 4.78 | Absent. |

ANALYSES BY II. II. NICHOLSON.

*Description of samples.*

| No. | Bought of— | Wholesaler or manufacturer. | Label. |
| --- | --- | --- | --- |
| 1706 | Starrett Bros., Lincoln........ | A. B. Smith, Fairfield .......... | Sorghum. |
| 1707 | ......do ........................ | Boston........................... | Crystal drips. |
| 1708 | ......do ........................ | New Orleans .................... | New Orleans molasses. |
| 1709 | ......do .................. ...... | .................................. | Rock candy sirup. |
| 1710 | ......do ........................ | L. G. Yoe & Co., Chicago........ | Maple sirup. |
| 1711 | G. W. Closson, Lincoln........ | New Orleans .................... | New Orleans molasses. |
| 1712 | ..,...do ..........,.... ........ | ......do ........................ | New Orleans molasses, second grade. |
| 1713 | ......do ........................ | Coulten, N. Y .................... | Honey drip sirup. |
| 1714 | ......do ........................ | Fairfield, Nebr.................. | Sorghum. |
| 1715 | Cook & Johnson................ | Farmer ......................... | Do. |
| 1716 | ......do ........................ | .................................. | New Orleans molasses. |
| 1717 | ......do ........................ | Sprague & Co., Chicago......... | Sugar sirup. |
| 1718 | ......do ........................ | ......do ........................ | |
| 1719 | ......do ........................ | Vermont......................... | Vermont maple sirup. |
| 1720 | ......do ........................ | .................................. | New Orleans sirup. |
| 1721 | Jas. Miller, Lincoln ........... | .................................. | Do. |
| 1722 | Britton, Lincoln .............. | .................................. | New Orleans, second best. |
| 1723 | ......do ........................ | .................................. | New Orleans, best. |
| 1724 | ......do .............. ......... | Paxton & Gallagher ........... | Golden drip. |
| 1725 | ......do ........................ | Murdoch & Co., Chicago....... | Maple sirup. |
| 1726 | Maxwell, Sharpe & Ross, Lincoln. | Raymond Bros., Lincoln ........ | Crystal drops. |
| 1727 | ......do ........................ | Plummer & Perry, Lincoln..... | Tip Top sirup. |
| 1728 | ......do ........................ | ......do ........................ | Honey Dew. |
| 1729 | ......do ........................ | .................................. | Sorghum. |
| 1730 | ......do ........................ | New Orleans .................... | New Orleans molasses. |
| 1731 | ......do ........................ | ...do ........................... | New Orleans molasses, second grade. |
| 1732 | Viers Bros., Omaha............ | St. Louis Preserving Company | Golden drip. |
| 1733 | ......do ........................ | .................................. | New Orleans molasses. |
| 1734 | II. Blumstein, Omaha......... | St. Louis Preserving Company.. | Golden sirup. |
| 1735 | D. L. Carpenter, Omaha....... | L. G. Yoe & Co.................. | Honey drips. |
| 1736 | ......do ........................ | New Orleans .................... | New Orleans molasses. |
| 1737 | John Swoboda, Omaha....... | ......do ........................ | Common sirup. |
| 1738 | ......do ........................ | ......do ........................ | New Orleans molasses. |
| 1739 | Heimrod & Co., Omaha ....... | Farrell & Co.................... | Corn sirup, No. 7. |
| 1740 | H. Moeller, Omaha............ | S. B. Bachelder................. | Sorghum. |
| 1741 | ......do ........................ | Farrell & Co.................... | Sirup No. 70. |
| 1742 | Henry Bollin ................. | .................................. | New Orleans molasses. |
| 1743 | Viers Bros., Omaha .......... | Paxton & Gallagher ........... | Ohio maple sirup. |
| 1744 | J. W. Fennell, Omaha......... | New Orleans..................... | Choice New Orleans. |
| 1745* | H. Moeller, Omaha............ | ......do ........................ | New Orleans, first grade. |
| 1746 | ......do ........................ | ......do ........................ | New Orleans, second grade. |
| 1747 | II. Blumstein, Omaha ........ | ......do ........................ | New Orleans sirup. |
| 1748 | Heimrod & Co., Omaha....... | ......do ........................ | Do. |
| 1749 | J. Neumann, Omaha .......... | .................................. | Corn sirup, Climax Drip. |
| 1750 | James Miller, Lincoln ........ | .................................. | Sorghum. |
| 1751 | John Swoboda, Lincoln ....... | Paxton & Gallagher .......... | Ohio maple sirup. |
| 1752 | II. Blumstein, Lincoln ........ | J. H. Feilbach, Omaha .......... | Do. |
| 1753 | J. Neuman, Lincoln........... | Cresson Sugar Refining Co...... | Vermont maple sirup. |
| 1754 | Henry Moeller, Lincoln....... | A. R. Bremer & Co., Chicago... | Do. |
| 1755 | Viers Bros., Lincoln.......... | Paxton & Gallagher ........... | Ohio maple sirup. |

* " Black strap " pure and simple, and next to impossible to decolorize sufficiently to read.

*Analytical data.*

| No. | Polarization. | | Temperature °C. | Sucrose. | Reducing sugars. | Water. | Ash. | Tin, or other metals. |
|---|---|---|---|---|---|---|---|---|
| | Direct. | Indirect. | | | | | | |
| | | | | Per cent. | Per cent. | Per cent. | Per cent. | |
| 1706* | + 46.1 | — 21.0 | 12 | 49.7 | 9.91 | 22.03 | 3.74 | None. |
| 1707 | +140.0 | +133.2 | .......... | .......... | 19.60 | 20.59 | 1.28 | Do. |
| 1708 | + 45.1 | — 25.5 | 11.5 | 51.6 | 9.62 | 25.48 | 2.17 | Do. |
| 1709 | + 58.4 | — 24.4 | 12 | 60.6 | 3.50 | 27.57 | 1.17 | Do. |
| 1710 | + 89.7 | + 72.9 | 11 | .......... | 14.82 | 33.88 | 0.25 | Do. |
| 1711 | +133.5 | +123.9 | 15 | .......... | 17.24 | 25.81 | 1.58 | Do. |
| 1712 | +102.5 | + 86.6 | 10.5 | .......... | 16.94 | 27.00 | 2.52 | Do. |
| 1713 | +124.2 | +118.3 | 12 | .......... | 20.40 | 22.87 | 1.82 | Do. |
| 1714 | + 37.1 | — 19.8 | 10.5 | 41.3 | 13.88 | 21.56 | 2.77 | Do. |
| 1715 | + 99.6 | + 81.2 | 12 | .......... | 16.00 | 27.22 | 1.63 | Do. |
| 1716 | + 43.0 | — 22.8 | 12 | 48.7 | 9.76 | 27.80 | 0.69 | Do. |
| 1717 | +136.5 | +128.3 | 12.5 | .......... | 19.20 | 22.47 | 1.68 | Do. |
| 1718 | +131.8 | +121.1 | 12 | .......... | 12.56 | 27.26 | 4.20 | Trace. |
| 1719 | + 86.5 | + 31.8 | 11.5 | 39.9 | 6.34 | 31.73 | 0.54 | None. |
| 1820 | + 73.7 | + 74.6 | 14.5 | .......... | 27.80 | 18.15 | 0.22 | Do. |
| 1721 | + 33.5 | — 13.8 | 10.5 | 35.1 | 13.88 | 28.91 | 5.58 | Do. |
| 1722 | + 9.8 | — 27.3 | 10.5 | 26.9 | 27.00 | 25.50 | 6.00 | Do. |
| 1723 | + 37.3 | — 26.7 | 12 | 47.1 | 12.50 | 28.28 | 2.81 | Do. |
| 1724 | +147.5 | +123.0 | 12 | .......... | 16.52 | 20.50 | 1.24 | Do. |
| 1725 | +125.5 | +103.9 | 12 | .......... | 14.38 | 30.00 | 0.35 | Do. |
| 1726 | +128.5 | +123.6 | 11.5 | .......... | 20.40 | 22.43 | 1.58 | Do. |
| 1727 | +148.3 | +110.7 | 12 | .......... | 20.20 | 18.20 | 1.60 | Do. |
| 1728 | +148.9 | .......... | .......... | .......... | 16.66 | 21.10 | 1.35 | Do. |
| 1729 | + 19.2 | — 19.1 | 12 | 27.0 | 13.60 | 26.85 | 4.38 | Do. |
| 1730 | + 41.1 | — 27.1 | 11.5 | 49.7 | 11.36 | 35.51 | 3.11 | Do. |
| 1731 | +126.9 | +122.5 | 12 | .......... | 20.40 | 26.36 | 1.54 | Do. |
| 1732 | +134.9 | +120.6 | 12 | .......... | 14.70 | 26.76 | 1.56 | Do. |
| 1733 | +136.1 | +126.0 | 11 | .......... | 17.24 | 27.30 | 1.20 | Do. |
| 1734 | +131.0 | +117.5 | .......... | .......... | 16.66 | 23.71 | 1.54 | Do. |
| 1735 | +134.2 | +119.5 | 11.5 | .......... | 18.00 | 24.49 | 1.90 | Do. |
| 1736 | + 30.9 | — 27.0 | 11 | 42.2 | 12.98 | 29.65 | 4.96 | Do. |
| 1737 | +132.1 | +126.4 | 11 | .......... | 17.10 | 24.83 | 1.44 | Do. |
| 1738 | + 83.5 | + 64.3 | 11 | .......... | 17.54 | 26.78 | 4.15 | Do. |
| 1739 | +148.3 | +127.8 | 12 | .......... | 25.60 | 19.28 | 1.11 | Do. |
| 1740 | + 40.2 | — 21.4 | 12 | 45.0 | 12.04 | 28.41 | 4.10 | Do. |
| 1741 | +122.1 | +115.1 | 12 | .......... | 15.38 | 28.52 | 1.44 | Do. |
| 1742 | +125.5 | +120.0 | 11.5 | — | 15.62 | 30.88 | 1.51 | Do. |
| 1743 | +114.5 | + 99.5 | 12 | .......... | 19.20 | 26.27 | 1.50 | Do. |
| 1744 | + 74.2 | + 68.2 | 11.5 | .......... | 13.08 | 30.56 | 2.30 | Do. |
| 1745* | + 4.0 | — 5.4 | 11 | 6.9 | 23.80 | 29.35 | 6.27 | Do. |
| 1746 | + 67.5 | + 37.8 | 11 | 76.7 | 17.38 | 28.88 | 4.40 | Do. |
| 1747 | + 48.1 | — 16.9 | 11 | 47.7 | 9.62 | 29.81 | 3.60 | Do. |
| 1748 | + 34.9 | — 28.4 | 11.5 | 46.3 | 16.94 | 26.22 | 3.40 | Do. |
| 1749 | +137.6 | +125.3 | 11.5 | .......... | 19.00 | 20.21 | 4.69 | Do. |
| 1750 | +128.5 | +123.8 | 13 | .......... | 14.92 | 27.74 | 2.07 | Do. |
| 1751 | +129.5 | +110.5 | 12 | .......... | 14.50 | 28.69 | 0.33 | Do. |
| 1752 | +134.5 | +120.3 | 14 | .......... | 16.40 | 27.79 | 0.29 | Do. |
| 1753 | +131.5 | +108.3 | 14 | .......... | 14.70 | 28.73 | 0.60 | Do. |
| 1754 | +115.6 | + 87.5 | 13 | .......... | 12.98 | 30.97 | 0.45 | Do. |
| 1755 | +137.6 | +120.0 | 14 | .......... | 15.88 | 26.57 | 0.27 | Do. |

* This sample could not be clarified sufficiently well to get a reliable reading.

FOODS AND FOOD ADULTERANTS.

## ANALYSES BY W. B. RISING.

*Description of samples.*

| No. | Label. | Where bought. | Price per quart. | Color, etc. |
|---|---|---|---|---|
| 3 | Golden Drip, Haas Bros., San Francisco. | Congden & Co., Berkeley ....... | ........ | Light brown. |
| 6 | New Orleans molasses .......... | A. Wallman, 14th and Adeline, Oakland. | ........ | Dark red. |
| 7 | Golden Sirup, Wellman Peck & Co. | Eichwede, Muhr & Co., 7th and Adeline, Oakland. | ........ | Red-brown. |
| 8 | New Orleans molasses, Wellman, Peck & Co., San Francisco. | ......do ...................... | ........ | Dark brown. |
| 9 | Sirup, Tillmann & Bendel, San Francisco. | Hadler Bros., 17th and Mission, San Francisco. | ........ | Yellow-brown. |
| 10 | New Orleans molasses, F. E. T .. | ......do ...................... | ........ | Greenish-brown. |
| 13 | Golden sirup, California Refinery. | Stewart & Trowbridge, Berkeley | ........ | Yellow-brown. |
| 40 | Golden sirup, American Refinery. | Burns Bros., 16th and Mission, San Francisco. | ........ | Do. |
| 41 | New Orleans molasses, Tillman & Bendel, San Francisco. | ......do ...................... | ........ | Dark greenish. |
| 42 | New Orleans molasses .........: | W. P. Wheeler, San Pablo and 14th streets, Oakland. | ........ | Dark reddish-brown. |
| 43 | Golden sirup, California Refinery. | Agard & Co., Broadway and 13th street, Oakland. | ........ | Light yellow. |
| 44 | New Orleans molasses .......... | ......do ...................... | ........ | Light yellow crystallized. |
| 45 | ......do ...................... | Phelan & Fish, 11th and Washington, Oakland. | ........ | Muddy brown. |
| 46 | Golden sirup, California Refinery. | ......do ...................... | ........ | Dark red. |
| 55 | ......do ...................... | D. Brune, 15th and Mission ...... | $0.10 | Light amber. |
| 56 | Extra New Orleans clarified molasses, Tillman & Bendel, San Francisco (in 1-gallon cans). | C. Paulsen, Valencia and 18th streets, San Francisco. | .30 | Dark brown. |
| 57 | New Orleans molasses .......... | 18th and Mission, San Francisco. | .10 | Red-brown. |
| 58 | ......do ...................... | Cluff & Co., 18th and Mission, San Francisco. | .15 | Dark green. |
| 59 | New Orleans molasses, Albert Mau & Co., San Francisco. | Wood & Ferguson, Valencia and 17th, San Francisco. | .25 | Red-brown. |
| 60 | Golden drip, American Refinery | 18th and Mission, San Francisco. | .10 | Light brown. |
| 61 | ......do ...................... | Kattelman & Rippe, northwest corner 16th and Howard, San Francisco. | .15 | Do. |
| 62 | Molasses ...................... | ......do ...................... | .15 | Dark, almost black |
| 63 | Sirup ......................... | W. W. Beckmann .............. | .15 | Light brown. |
| 66 | Golden sirup .................. | Northeast corner Broadway and Kearny, San Francisco. | .20 | |
| 67 | Sirup ......................... | Dupont and Green streets, San Francisco. | .15 | |
| 68 | ......do ...................... | Northeast corner Filbert and Powell, San Francisco. | .15 | |
| 69 | ......do ...................... | J. L. Williams, 533 New Montgomery. | .20 | |
| 70 | Molasses ...................... | .............................. | .15 | Black. |

*Description of samples*—Continued.

| No. | Label. | Where bought. | Price per quart. | Color, etc. |
|---|---|---|---|---|
| 71 | Molasses......................... | New York Tea Company, south-west corner 14th and Mission, San Francisco. | $0.15 | Very dark brown. |
| 72 | Golden sirup .................... | A. S. Barboro, 531 Washington street, San Francisco. | .10 | Light red. |
| 73 | Sirup ..................... ........ | 1st and Mission, San Francisco. | .15 | Do. |
| 74 | R. von d. Mehden ............... | Corner 2d and Mission, San Francisco. | .15 | Do. |
| 75 | New Orleans molasses.......... | New York Tea Company, south-west corner 4th and Mission, San Francisco. | .25 | Reddish yellow. |
| 76 | Sirup .......... ..... ......... | Powell & Greenwich ............ | .10 | Yellow. |
| 77 | ......do ....................... | H. Shattuck, 2d and Minerva, San Francisco. | .15 | Yellow-red. |
| 78 | ......do ......................... | J. H. Gobbenboske, southwest corner 2d and Howard, San Francisco. | .15 | Dark red. |
| 79 | ......do ......................... | Mission and Howard, San Francisco. | .15 | Reddish. |
| 80 | New Orleans molasses.......... | Cluff Bros., 9 New Montgomery, San Francisco. | .30 | Red-brown. |
| 81 | Sirup ..................... ........ | Kunnecke & Co., 539 Howard street, San Francisco. | .15 | Reddish. |
| 82 | ......do ......................... | Northeast corner Everett and 3d streets, San Francisco. | .20 | Light yellow. |
| 84 | ......do ......................... | Everett and 4th.................., | .10 | Red-brown. |
| 85 | New Orleans molasses .......... | Hayes & Dwyer, 50 2d street, San Francisco. | .40 | Black. |
| 86 | Sirup ...... .................. | Natoma and First, San Francisco. | .15 | Almost black. |
| 87 | Sirup said to be from Sandwich Islands. | Irvin Brose, 570 Howard ........ | .20 | Do. |
| 88 | Sirup ...... .................... | B. H. Bore, 137 4th street........ | .15 | Red. |
| 119 | Sirup, American refinery ....... | Robohm & Kinoma, Howard and 8th, San Francisco. | .10 | Greenish. |
| 120 | ......do ......................... | Riecher & Zimmer, 7th and Stevenson, San Francisco. | .15 | Red. |
| 121 | New Orleans molasses.......... | W. B. Cluff & Bro., Stevenson and 6th street, San Francisco. | .40 | Turbid-brown. |
| 122 | Sirup......................... | Northwest corner 6th and Jessie | .15 | Yellow-brown. |
| 123 | ......do ......................... | 8th and Jessie, San Francisco... | .15 | Red-brown. |

*Analytical data.*

| No. | Polarization. | | Temp., ° C. | Sucrose. | Reducing sugars. | Water. | Ash. | Tin or other metals. |
|---|---|---|---|---|---|---|---|---|
| | Direct. | Indirect. | | | | | | |
| | | | | *Per cent.* | *Per cent.* | *Per cent.* | *Per cent.* | |
| 3 | 111.05 | 88.77 | .......... | 16.71 | 29.85 | 17.47 | 1.03 | .......... |
| 6 | 40.15 | —19.25 | .......... | 43.64 | 24.51 | 20.08 | 3.18 | .......... |
| 7 | 91.00 | 63.80 | .......... | 20.00 | 28.57 | 17.00 | 1.51 | .......... |
| 8 | 105.38 | 72.27 | .......... | 24.21 | 30.30 | 20.06 | 1.79 | .......... |
| 9 | 40.92 | —18.81 | .......... | 44.06 | 24.39 | 24.78 | 3.72 | .......... |
| 10 | 45.43 | —19.47 | .......... | 48.00 | 27.17 | 26.12 | 2.94 | .......... |
| 13 | 37.30 | —25.30 | .......... | 46.00 | 72.50 | 16.92 | 2.84 | .......... |
| 40 | 42.24 | —18.04 | .......... | 44.28 | 22.70 | 17.30 | 4.98 | .......... |
| 41 | 67.10 | 28.60 | .......... | 28.20 | 23.40 | 24.32 | 2.10 | .......... |
| 42 | 77.66 | 25.63 | .......... | 38.07 | 24.06 | 26.77 | 1.84 | .......... |
| 43 | 40.70 | —27.83 | .......... | 50.20 | 22.99 | 22.88 | 2.16 | .......... |
| 44 | 39.71 | —23.65 | .......... | 46.28 | 23.25 | 23.71 | 2.58 | .......... |
| 45 | 92.62 | 61.27 | ....... .. | 23.00 | 28.17 | 25.01 | 2.46 | .......... |
| 46 | 38.51 | —14.30 | .......... | 39.10 | 83.01 | 20.87 | 6.72 | .......... |
| 55 | 36.85 | —19.03 | .......... | 41.35 | 24.06 | 19.36 | 4.18 | .......... |
| 56 | 86.90 | 40.17 | .......... | 27.35 | 31.00 | 22.27 | 2.35 | .......... |
| 57 | 47.72 | —18.70 | .......... | 50.00 | 19.90 | 25.02 | 4.29 | .......... |
| 58 | 93.50 | 46.10 | .......... | 34.90 | 35.00 | 22.65 | 2.13 | .......... |
| 59 | 47.96 | —23.54 | .......... | 52.57 | 16.67 | 24.19 | 1.82 | .......... |
| 60 | 38.83 | —19.80 | .......... | 43.00 | 21.55 | 20.19 | 5.13 | .......... |
| 61 | 41.47 | —17.10 | .......... | 43.10 | 17.54 | 18.59 | 8.08 | .......... |
| 62 | 39.93 | —19.58 | .......... | 44.07 | 19.68 | 25.61 | 4.04 | .......... |
| 63 | 40.92 | —17.60 | .......... | 42.35 | 24.75 | 18.54 | 7.25 | .......... |
| 66 | 42.24 | —18.48 | .......... | 44.28 | 24.51 | 19.95 | 4.24 | .......... |
| 67 | 41.25 | —17.60 | .......... | 43.57 | 18.18 | 26.78 | 4.94 | .......... |
| 68 | 36.85 | —16.28 | .......... | 38.80 | 27.78 | 23.85 | 4.26 | .......... |
| 60 | 37.73 | —18.70 | .......... | 41.64 | 19.23 | 27.49 | 3.53 | .......... |
| 70 | 18.15 | —16.30 | .......... | 25.42 | 30.10 | 80.26 | 5.20 | .......... |
| 71 | 33.00 | —18.81 | .......... | 38.21 | 13.50 | 23.26 | 8.99 | .......... |
| 72 | 36.00 | —19.36 | .......... | 40.35 | 19.20 | 21.40 | 4.85 | .......... |
| 73 | 39.93 | —15.73 | .......... | 40.42 | 21.31 | 20.88 | 6.42 | .......... |
| 74 | 36.00 | —18.70 | .......... | 39.92 | 19.45 | 16.35 | 4.23 | .......... |
| 75 | 83.49 | 49.06 | .......... | 25.35 | 32.00 | 20.79 | 2.26 | .......... |
| 76 | 41.86 | —22.33 | .......... | 46.90 | 22.23 | 20.06 | 3.46 | .......... |
| 77 | 27.17 | —17.80 | .......... | 35.21 | 21.22 | 17.86 | 5.72 | .......... |
| 78 | 36.96 | —16.50 | .......... | 39.42 | 26.10 | 21.80 | 7.31 | .......... |
| 79 | 38.77 | —20.68 | .......... | 43.75 | 22.70 | 21.35 | 2.28 | .......... |
| 80 | 39.16 | —22.00 | .......... | 44.71 | 26.20 | 24.90 | 3.99 | ....... ... |
| 81 | 37.84 | —17.82 | .......... | 41.07 | 21.10 | 19.87 | 4.68 | .......... |
| 82 | 37.40 | —18.26 | .......... | 40.14 | 18.94 | 21.12 | 0.14 | .......... |
| 84 | 36.30 | —15.95 | .......... | 38.02 | 25.38 | 20.79 | 4.14 | .......... |
| 85 | 36.00 | —12.10 | .......... | 35.00 | 23.81 | 23.79 | 4.38 | .......... |
| 86 | 41.00 | —17.00 | .......... | 43.07 | 25.64 | 18.76 | 4.15 | .......... |
| 87 | 29.70 | —18.15 | .......... | 35.50 | 19.23 | 26.08 | 5.90 | .......... |
| 88 | 49.70 | —22.88 | .......... | 53.35 | 20.83 | 26.37 | 1.93 | .......... |
| 119 | 42.26 | —15.40 | .......... | 42.21 | 17.50 | 23.11 | 5.50 | .......... |
| 120 | 43.01 | —17.05 | .......... | 44.04 | 27.20 | 24.95 | 3.55 | .......... |
| 121 | 77.00 | 36.08 | .......... | 30.00 | 24.00 | 24.22 | 2.45 | .......... |
| 122 | 41.58 | —14.74 | .......... | 41.21 | 20.41 | 21.18 | 5.04 | .......... |
| 123 | 39.82 | —13.53 | .......... | 39.00 | 24.39 | 23.58 | 4.10 | .......... |

## ANALYSES BY M. A. SCOVELL.

### *Description of samples.*

Sample  1. New Orleans.  Light color, some sugar.  Seller, R. J. McCombs, Cincinnati, Ohio.  Manufacturer, Raceland Plantation, Louisiana.

Sample  2. Sugarhouse Sirup.  Bright, light color, thick, clean.  Seller, Hamilton Grocery Company, Cincinnati, Ohio.  Manufacturer, American Preserve Company, Cincinnati, Ohio.

Sample  3. Rock-candy Drips.  White, thin.  Seller, Joseph R. Peebles' Sons' Company, Cincinnati, Ohio.  Manufacturer, R. A. Hulden, Cincinnati, Ohio.

Sample  4. New Orleans.  Light color, medium consistency.  Seller, Joseph R. Peebles' Sons' Company, Cincinnati, Ohio.  Manufacturer, "S. & A." Plantation, Louisiana.

Sample  5. Golden Sirup.  Very light color, thick.  Seller, Joseph R. Peebles' Sons Company, Cincinnati, Ohio.  Manufactured through "Hogard," New York.

Sample  6. Maple Sirup.  Light color, thin.  Seller, R. J. McCombs, Cincinnati.  Manufacturer, Henry E. Crane, Garrettsville, Ohio.

Sample  7. McMeehen's Old Virginia Tree Maple Sirup.  Dark color, medium thickness.  Seller, Schwabacher, Louisville, Ky.  Made by Geo. R. McMeehen, Wheeling, W. Va.

Sample  8. King Drips.  Light color, thick.  Seller, R. J. McCombs, Cincinnati.  Wholesaler or manufacturer, Thurber, Whyland & Co., New York.

Sample  9. Clymer's Select Maple.  Put up by the Buckeye Sirup Refinery, Cincinnati, Ohio, in quart tin caus.  Seller, Hamilton Grocery Company, Cincinnati, Ohio.  Color light, medium thickness.

Sample 10. Old Time Maple Sirup.  Put up by L. G. Yoe & Co., Chicago, Ill., in quart tin cans.  Sold by P. Tracy, Cincinnati, Ohio.  Light color, medium thickness.

Sample 11. Vermont Maple Sirup.  Put up by the Crescent Sugar Refinery Company.  Sold by H. D. Gosa, Cincinnati, Ohio.  Fair color, medium consistency.

Sample 12. Maple Sirup.  Put up at the camp for Jos. R. Peebles' Sons' Company, Cincinnati, Ohio.  Very light, thin.

Sample 13. New Orleans, Avon Plantation.  By E. W. B.  Sold by Henry Huneke & Co., Cincinnati, Ohio.  Light-colored, some sugar.

Sample 14. Maple Molasses.  Made by Crane Brothers, Garrettsville, Ohio.  The label states: "We guarantee this to be perfectly pure maple molasses, purchased by us of responsible farmers, and hermetically sealed in cans, under our own supervision.  It is justly denominated the best of all and is unequaled by any other brands.  Colter & Co., northwest corner Sixth and Main streets, Cincinnati, Ohio."

Sample 15. Sugarhouse Molasses.  Dark-colored, saltish taste, clear.  Made by Havemeyer & Elder.  Bought of Sterritt, Cincinnati, Ohio.

Sample 16. Sugarhouse Molasses.  Very dark, thick, turbid, greenish; has the smell of New Orleans.  Sold by W. H. May, Lexington, Ky.  Wholesaler, Mosley, Raum & Gogreve, Cincinnati, Ohio.

Sample 17. New Orleans Molasses.  Dark, with much sugar.  Seller, Lindsay & Nugent, Lexington, Ky.  Maker, J. N. R. Plantation, Louisiana.

Sample 18. New Orleans Molasses.  Light colored, some sugar, fine flavor.  Voiron Plantation.  Sold by G. H. Kinnear, Lexington, Ky.

Sample 19. Bartino Sirup.  "Made for winter use."  Smell and flavor of New Orleans.  Made by Hopple, Flasche & Co., Cincinnati, and sold by G. H. Kinnear, Lexington, Ky.

Sample 20. Clover Drips.  "Pure sugar sirup."  Dark, turbid, saltish.  From Hobart, New York City.  Sold by Colter & Co., Cincinnati, Ohio.

Sample 21. Sorghum. Dark colored, very acid taste. Made by Mr. Hurst, Fayette County, Ky. Sold by J. T. Honaker, Lexington, Ky.

Sample 22. Bartino Sirup. Dark colored, New Orleans flavor. Made by Hopple, Flasche & Co., Cincinnati, Ohio, and sold by T. J. Cassell, Lexington, Ky.

Sample 23. Phœnix Drips. A bright, thick, light sirup. Made by Bradshaw & Waite, Chicago, Ill. Sold by Mrs. Clark, Lexington, Ky.

Sample 24. New Orleans Molasses. Open kettle. Sold by Cozine, Lexington, Ky., through Mosley, Raum & Co., Cincinnati, Ohio.

Sample 25. Sorghum. From the Big Sandy River, Kentucky. Fair color, fermenting slightly. Sold by W. H. May, Lexington, Ky.

Sample 26. New Orleans. Fair color, no sugar. In cypress barrels marked "D. A. Brand." Bought through Curry, Howard & Co., Lexington, Ky., by T. J. Cassell, and sample obtained of T. J. Cassell.

Sample 27. New Orleans. Dark-colored, turbid molasses, thick. Seller, McClelland, Lexington, Ky. Made by the Cedar Grove Plantation, Louisiana.

Sample 28. New Orleans. Open kettle. In cypress barrels, marked "Ser. pt." Seller, W. H. May, Lexington, Ky. Wholesaler, Torbitt & Castleman, Louisville, Ky. Very light colored sirup. Very little sugar.

Sample 29. Caramel Drips. A light transparent sirup, made by Bradshaw & Waite. Sold by W. H. May, Lexington, Ky.

Sample 30. Bartino. A very reddish black thick sirup. Made by Hopple, Flasche & Co., Cincinnati. Sold by Vogt, Lexington, Ky.

Sample 31. Sorghum. A fair-colored bright molasses, with sorghum taste. Seller, Henry Vogt, Lexington, Ky. Wholesaler, J. T. Heitmeyer & Son, Cincinnati, Ohio.

Sample 32. Open Kettle. A fair New Orleans molasses, with much sugar. Sold by H. Vogt, Lexington, Ky. Wholesaler, Torbitt & Castleman, Louisville, Ky.

Sample 33. New Orleans. A light-colored molasses, with fine flavor. Sold by McClelland, Lexington, Ky. Wholesaler, Torbitt & Castleman, Louisville, Ky. Said to be branded "Magnolia Plantation."

Sample 34. Maple Sirup. A bright, thin sirup. Put up in quart jugs by Thurber, New York. Sold by John Hutchinson, Lexington, Ky.

Sample 35. Old Time Maple Sirup. Bright, medium thickness. Put up in quart cans by L. G. Yoe & Co. Sold by John Hutchinson, Lexington, Ky.

Sample 36. Milton Maple Sirup. Light colored, thin. Said to be put up by L. G. Yoe & Co., Chicago, Ill., although there is no manufacturer's name on the can. In quart cans. Sold by John Hutchinson, Lexington Ky.

Sample 37. Bartino. A medium-colored thick sirup. New Orleans flavor. Made by Hopple, Flasche & Co., Cincinnati, Ohio. Sold by John Hutchinson, Lexington, Ky.

Sample 38. Sweet Clover Sirup. A very light straw-colored, thick sirup, made by L. G. Yoe & Co., Chicago, Ill. Sold by A. J. Ross, Louisville, Ky.

Sample 39. Sorghum. Horseshoe brand. A fair colored sorghum flavored molasses. Sold by John Hutchinson, Lexington, Ky. Wholesaler, Hopple, Flasche & Co., Cincinnati, Ohio.

Sample 40. Melrose Sirup. A light-colored, clear, thick sirup. Manufacturer, T. Willard & Co., New York City. Sold by J. B. Wnrach, Louisville, Ky.

Sample 41. New Orleans reboiled. Barrel marked "Union." Blackstrap. Sold by John Hutchinson, Lexington, Ky. Wholesaler, Torbitt & Castleman, Louisville Ky.

Sample 42. New Orleans Molasses. Magnolia Plantation. Light colored, some sugar. Sold by John Hutchinson, Lexington, Ky.

Sample 43. New Orleans Sugar-House molasses. Dark colored. In barrels branded "Mrs. A. A. B." Sold by Scully & Yates, Lexington, Ky.

Sample 44. New Orleans Centrifugal. A blackstrap. Alice B. Plantation. Sold by Cozine, Lexington, Ky.

Sample 45. Golden Sirup. A bright, transparent thick syrup made by the Buckeye Sirup Refinery, Cincinnati, Ohio. Sold by Hamilton Grocery Company, Cincinnati, Ohio.

Sample 46. Sorghum. Light-colored, sorghum taste. Sold by McClelland, Lexington, Ky. Wholesaler, Hopple, Flasche & Co., Cincinnati, Ohio.

Sample 47. Maple Sirup. In quart tin cans, thin, bright. Labeled as follows: Guaranteed pure Maple Sirup, canned for C. W. Jefferson, Louisville, Ky. Manufacturer's name not on the can. C. W. Jefferson states that it was made by L. G. Yoe, Chicago, Ill.

Sample 48. Rock Candy Drips. A white sirup of medium consistency, made by L. G. Yoe & Co., Chicago, Ill. Sold by A. J. Ross, Louisville, Ky.

Sample 49. New Orleans. A light-colored sugar sirup, made by Church (A. W. S.) Plantation. Sold by Scully & Yates, Lexington, Ky.

Sample 50. California Golden Sirup. Made from pure cane sugar of Spreckels. Sunset brand. None genuine without the brand. Sold by J. C. Berryman, Lexington, Ky.

*Analytical data.*

| No. | Polarization. | | Temperature, ° C. | Sucrose. | Reducing sugars. | Water. | Ash. | Tin or other metals. |
| --- | --- | --- | --- | --- | --- | --- | --- | --- |
| | Direct. | Indirect. | | | | | | |
| | | | | Per cent. | Per cent. | Per cent. | Per cent. | |
| 1 | 42.4 | -- 20.6 | 24.0 | 48.31 | 18.52 | 25.41 | 2.51 | Tin. |
| 2 | 130.4 | 117.0 | 28.8 | 10.31 | 40.81 | 16.69 | 0.72 | Do. |
| 3 | 46.6 | — 21.0 | 24.0 | 52.53 | 16.13 | 28.82 | 0.03 | |
| 4 | 44.2 | — 18.5 | 24.0 | 48.09 | 18.18 | 26.32 | 2.33 | Tin. |
| 5 | 41.5 | — 5.1 | 24.6 | 35.82 | 30.30 | 18.13 | 2.45 | |
| 6 | 62.8 | — 20.8 | 25.2 | 64.41 | 2.53 | 25.28 | 0.58 | |
| 7 | 83.4 | 16.9 | 24.2 | 51.04 | 12.54 | 23.29 | 0.33 | Trace. |
| 8 | 36.0 | -- 12.3 | 24.8 | 37.15 | 34.48 | 15.05 | 3.25 | |
| 9 | 92.0 | 46.4 | 24.8 | 35.08 | 20.20 | 25.24 | 0.39 | Tin. |
| 10 | 104.8 | 76.1 | 24.6 | 22.06 | 25.15 | 26.70 | 0.29 | Do. |
| 11 | 128.2 | 112.0 | 24.8 | 12.46 | 32.25 | 23.23 | 0.46 | Do. |
| 12 | 61.4 | — 21.4 | 24.8 | 63.70 | 1.56 | 29.72 | 0.63 | |
| 13 | 42.4 | — 20.4 | 24.8 | 48.30 | 18.35 | 25.47 | 2.05 | |
| 14 | 59.8 | — 20.0 | 25.2 | 61.48 | 1.31 | 30.67 | 0.74 | Tin. |
| 15 | 64.2 | 23.3 | 24.0 | 31.36 | 31.25 | 18.70 | 3.14 | |
| 16 | 25.0 | — 20.5 | 24.6 | 34.97 | 32.26 | 20.37 | 4.82 | |
| 17 | 62.4 | — 23.6 | 24.4 | 66.05 | 10.52 | 16.68 | 1.87 | |
| 18 | 38.0 | — 21.2 | 24.8 | 45.54 | 25.00 | 20.28 | 3.68 | |
| 19 | 130.8 | 120.1 | 24.4 | 8.22 | 35.39 | 18.80 | 1.13 | Tin. |
| 20 | 38.0 | — 15.8 | 24.8 | 41.39 | 30.30 | 15.03 | 2.83 | Copper. |
| 21 | 30.4 | — 12.5 | 25.0 | 33.02 | 31.74 | 27.83 | 3.46 | |
| 22 | 123.6 | 116.2 | 24.4 | 5.08 | 37.73 | 21.73 | 1.19 | Tin. |
| 23 | 153.8 | 144.1 | 25.6 | 7.48 | 34.78 | 16.40 | 0.65 | |
| 24 | 47.2 | -- 20.0 | 25.6 | 52.54 | 16.81 | 22.69 | 3.15 | |
| 25 | 42.8 | — 14.2 | 24.6 | 43.81 | 21.05 | 27.50 | 2.58 | |
| 26 | 39.6 | — 20.2 | 24.8 | 46.00 | 20.41 | 25.63 | 2.70 | |
| 27 | 30.6 | — 16.4 | 24.8 | 36.16 | 31.25 | 17.68 | 4.80 | |
| 28 | 35.4 | — 15.6 | 24.8 | 39.32 | 28.98 | 21.84 | 2.63 | |
| 29 | 121.0 | 108.5 | 25.0 | 9.62 | 40.82 | 17.33 | 1.17 | |
| 30 | 125.6 | 116.6 | 24.8 | 6.92 | 41.24 | 13.69 | 1.42 | Tin. |
| 31 | 122.2 | 112.6 | 24.8 | 7.38 | 40.00 | 17.79 | 1.52 | |
| 32 | 52.8 | — 24.0 | 24.8 | 50.07 | 17.86 | 17.17 | 1.86 | |
| 33 | 44.0 | — 18.0 | 26.0 | 48.60 | 20.20 | 24.13 | 2.09 | Do. |
| 34 | 60.4 | — 20.0 | 24.8 | 61.53 | 4.00 | 30.24 | 0.28 | |

*Analytical data—Continued.*

| No. | Polarization. | | Tempera-ture, ° C. | Sucrose. | Reducing sugars. | Water. | Ash. | Tin or other metals. |
|---|---|---|---|---|---|---|---|---|
| | Direct. | Indirect. | | | | | | |
| | | | | *Per cent.* | *Per cent.* | *Per cent.* | *Per cent.* | |
| 35 | 109. 8 | 78. 1 | 24. 8 | 24. 38 | 25. 31 | 26. 05 | 0. 31 | Tin. |
| 36 | 115. 6 | 98. 6 | 24. 6 | 13. 06 | 27. 31 | 31. 53 | 0. 22 | Do. |
| 37 | 125. 2 | 113. 9 | 25. 4 | 8. 82 | 39. 22 | 18. 98 | 1. 02 | Do. |
| 38 | 153. 0 | 145. 6 | 25. 2 | 5. 67 | 40. 81 | 14. 89 | 0. 32 | |
| 39 | 106. 4 | 86. 0 | 24. 8 | 15. 69 | 34. 48 | 21. 84 | 1. 17 | |
| 40 | 39. 2 | — 11. 6 | 24. 8 | 39. 08 | 33. 33 | 13. 78 | 2. 63 | |
| 41 | — 8. 0 | — 18. 3 | 24. 8 | 7. 92 | 54. 05 | 20. 11 | 4. 84 | Trace of tin. |
| 42 | 41. 0 | — 18. 9 | 24. 6 | 46. 04 | 18. 35 | 25. 70 | 3. 05 | |
| 43 | 34. 4 | — 21. 6 | 24. 2 | 42. 97 | 25. 32 | 18. 81 | 2. 50 | Tin. |
| 44 | 28. 2 | — 19. 8 | 25. 2 | 36. 97 | 28. 57 | 19. 30 | 4. 36 | Do. |
| 45 | 142. 2 | 138. 6 | 24. 2 | 2. 76 | 40. 82 | 18. 47 | 0. 64 | |
| 46 | 102. 0 | 76. 1 | 24. 6 | 19. 91 | 29. 70 | 27. 30 | 1. 93 | |
| 47 | 61. 6 | — 20. 0 | 24. 8 | 62. 77 | 5. 81 | 28. 32 | 0. 33 | Do. |
| 48 | 67. 6 | — 21. 1 | 24. 8 | 68. 23 | 0. 53 | 23. 81 | 0. 16 | |
| 49 | 38. 4 | — 20. 7 | 24. 8 | 45. 46 | 23. 25 | 24. 50 | 3. 16 | Trace of tin. |
| 50 | 36. 6 | — 13. 0 | 25. 6 | 38. 27 | 31. 25 | 20. 44 | 2. 20 | |

## ANALYSES BY S. P. SHARPLES.

*Description of samples.*

| No. | Bought of— | Price per quart. | Label. | Remarks. |
|---|---|---|---|---|
| 9352 | Walter Swan & Co., Boston, Mass. | ........ | No. 1, New Orleans, Ange-lina. | Said to be pure open-kettle sirup. |
| 9353 | ......do ..................... | ........ | No. 2, New Orleans, H. A.... | Supposed to be bleached; has a poor flavor and tastes of sulphur. |
| 9354 | ......do . ................... | ........ | No. 3, New Orleans (mark) Home, N. W. F. | Supposed to be bleached. |
| 9355 | ......do ..................... | ........ | No. 4, New Orleans Armelie, B. H. H. & Co. | |
| 9356 | ......do . ................... | ........ | No. 5, New Orleans Armelie, N. B. M. | |
| 9357 | ......do ..................... | $0.07½ | No. 6, New Orleans Magno-lia, N. W. F. | |
| 9358 | Robert McCullagh, Boston Highlands. | . 13 | ..................... | |
| 9359 | ......do ..................... | .35 | Maple Sirup ............... | |
| 9360 | Roxbury market .......... | .15 | New Orleans............... | |
| 9361 | Cobb, Bates & Yerka, Dock Square, Boston, Mass. | . 17 | ......do ................... | |
| 9362 | ......do ..................... | .15 | Porto Rico............... | |
| 9363 | S. D. Ware, Eliot Square, Roxbury, Mass. | .15 | Golden Drips ............. | Probably consists of about 50 per cent sirup and 50 per cent glucose. |
| 9364 | Low Bros., 84 Blue Hill ave-nue, Roxbury, Mass. | .15 | Golden Sirup ............. | Do. |
| 9365 | F. A. McCobb, 45 Rockland street, Roxbury, Mass. | .15 | Porto Rico............... | . |

*Description of samples*—Continued.

| No. | Bought of— | Price per quart. | Label. | Remarks. |
|---|---|---|---|---|
| 9366 | Mendnm, 141 H a m p d e n street, Boston, Mass. | $0.10 | Porto Rico .................. | Low grade. |
| 9367 | ......do ..................... | .15 | New Orleans............... | High grade article, full of sugar. |
| 9368 | F. H. Haynes, Blue Hill avenue, Roxbury, Mass. | .15 | Porto Rico.................. | Probably adulterated with about 10 per cent glucose to improve color and body. |
| 9369 | A. A. Whidden, Central street, Boston, Mass. | .07½ | New Orleans............... | |
| 9370 | M. Casbin, Clark street, Boston, Mass. | .37½ | Porto Rico.................. | About 50 per cent glucose and 50 per cent low grade Porto Rico. |
| 9371 | French Bros., 392 Hanover street, Boston, Mass. | .45 | Ideal Table Sirup........... | Mainly glucose ........... |
| 9372 | ......do ..................... | .45 | New Orleans............... | |
| 9373 | Viveiras & Casta, 27 Prince street, Boston, Mass. | .37½ | Porto Rico................. | |
| 9374 | William J. Shea & Co., 377 Hanover street, Boston, Mass. | .15 | ......do ...................... | Probably about 10 per cent glucose added to improve color and body. |
| 9375 | E. Robinson & Co., 63 Warren street, Roxbury, Mass. | .35 | Warranted Pure Sap Sirup, W. J. Lamb. Medford, Mass. Maple sirup in flask. | Sirup of this brand was found last year to be adulterated with glucose. |
| 9376 | Tisdale, Roxbury, Mass..... | .25 | Maple sirup in fancy pressed glass jug. | |
| 9377 | St. Cloud Market, 561 Tremont street, Boston, Mass. | .35 | Pure Maple Sirup, A. J. Raymond, Everett, Mass. In wine bottle. | |
| 9378 | E. Robinson & Co., 63 Warren street, Roxbury, Mass. | .35 | (On neck) Challenge brand. (On side) Pure Maple Sirup, Orange County, Vt. | Very probably made from granulated or other high-grade cane sugar and flavored with maple sirup. |
| 9379 | S. E. Wilson & Co., corner Worcester and Washington streets, Boston, Mass. | .30 | Pure Maple Sirup, put up by J. G. Turner, Medford, Mass. In wine bottle. | |
| 9380 | C. C. Howland & Co., 652 Shawmut avenue, Boston, Mass. | .35 | Boyd's Green Mountain Maple Sirup, warranted pure sap sirup, bottled expressly for our family trade | In wine bottles. |
| 9381 | James H. Wythe & Co., Brattle street, Cambridge, Mass. | .30 | Maple sirup in wine bottles. | Made near Montpelier, Vt.; guaranteed pure and reliable. |
| 9382 | D. D. Pickard, 566 Shawmut avenue, Boston, Mass. | .35 | Boyd's Green Mountain maple sirup, warranted pure sap sirup, bottled expressly for our family trade, D. D. Pickard. | In wine botttles. |
| 9383 | Benney, Eliot Square, Roxbury, Mass. | .30 | Pure Maple Sirup from Mapleton, Vt., D. H. Geer. | In wine bottles. About one-fifth glucose. |
| 9384 | C. D. Swain & Co., 2364 Washington street, Boston Highlands. | .35 | Superior Maple Sirup. Unequaled for buckwheat, griddle cakes, etc., from C. D. Swain & Co., Boston Highlands. | In wine bottles. |

*Description of samples—Continued.*

| No. | Bought of— | Price per quart. | Label. | Remarks. |
|---|---|---|---|---|
| 9385 | C. C. Howland & Co., 652 Shawmut avenue, Boston, Mass. | $0.35 | Boyd's Green Mountain Maple Sirup, put up by C. C. Howland & Co., 652 Shawmut avenue, Boston, Mass. | In wine bottles. |
| 9386 | A. A. Davenport, Warren street, Roxbury, Mass. | .25 | Mapleine Sirup for table use. Put up by Reid & Co., Boston, Mass. | In wine bottle. Probably a cane-sugar solution flavored with maple sirup. |
| 9387 | Richard Tubman, Washington street, Roxbury, Mass. | .30 | Pure Maple Sirup, Woodstock, Vt., F. P. Adams & Co., Boston, Mass. | In wine bottle. |
| 9388 | W. S. Melcher, 35 Warren street, Roxbury, Mass. | .30 | Warranted Strictly Pure Sap, from Woodstock, Vt. Maple Sirup. F. P. Adams & Co., Boston, Mass. | |
| 9389 | F. S. Pisteen, 529 Tremont street, Boston, Mass. | .35 | On neck : Gilt Edge Brand. On side : Pure Maple Sirup. Put up by J. G. Turner, Medford, Mass. | Do. |
| 9390 | J. F. Johnson, 256 Shawmut avenue, Boston, Mass. | .30 | No label.................... | Maple sirup. This sample was partly crystallized in the bottle. |
| 9391 | Cobb, Aldrich & Co., 2233 Washington street, Roxbury, Mass. | .26 | Improved Maple Sirup, Woodstock, Vt. Compound. | In wine bottle. Adulterated with glucose. |
| 9392 | Revere Sugar Refinery...... | .07½ | Diamond Sirup ............ | Sample of this sirup was said to have been stopped at Canadian customhouse. I analyzed it then, with about same results as at present. |
| 9393 | Thomas Dana & Co., Boston, Mass. | ........ | Texas Clear ............... | |
| 9394 | ......do ...................... | ........ | Fancy Ponce .............. | A very handsome, good flavored Porto Rico. |
| 9395 | ......do ...................... | ........ | Texas A ................... | A heavy dark sirup. |
| 9396 | ......do ...................... | ........ | Texas B ................... | A very dark thick sirup. |
| 9397 | ......do ...................... | ........ | New Orleans Matilda ....... | A low grade New Orleans. |
| 9398 | American Sugar Refinery Company. | ........ | Standard Sirup ............ | |
| 9399 | Butcher & Sons, Philadelphia, Pa. | .05 | Sirup ..................... | Sold for use in curing meat. |
| 9400 | James Bliss & Co., 328 Atlantic avenue, Boston, Mass. | .15 | New Orleans................ | Dark colored. |
| 9401 | C. Foster & Son, 338 Atlantic avenue, Boston, Mass. | .10 | Porto Rico................. | A very low grade black molasses. |
| ...... | S. S. Pierce & Co., Tremont and Court streets, Boston, Mass. | ........ | Pure Maple Sirup, put up hot in Vermont sugar orchards, expressly for S. S. Pierce & Co., Importers and grocers. | This is supposed to be perfectly pure article. |

*Analytical data.*

| No. | Polarization. | | Tempera-ture, °C. | Sucrose. | Reducing sugars. | Water. | Ash. | Tin or other metals. |
|---|---|---|---|---|---|---|---|---|
| | Direct. | Indirect. | | | | | | |
| | | | | *Per cent.* | *Per cent.* | *Per cent.* | *Per cent.* | |
| 9352 | 38.00 | —12.00 | 23 | 38.20 | 24.28 | 23.80 | 2.64 | Absent. |
| 9353 | 41.50 | —21.00 | 20 | 47.21 | 19.36 | 24.12 | 2.56 | Do. |
| 9354 | 46.50 | —21.00 | 20 | 50.90 | 13.68 | 22.53 | 2.88 | Do. |
| 9355 | 39.50 | —20.80 | 20 | 45.54 | 18.68 | 22.14 | 2.61 | Present. |
| 9356 | 42.00 | —18.00 | 20 | 45.33 | 17.67 | 23.14 | 2.28 | Absent. |
| 9357 | 42.40 | —19.50 | 24 | 47.45 | 18.68 | 25.28 | 1.93 | Do. |
| 9358 | 43.00 | —11.00 | 24 | 41.39 | 20.24 | 24.49 | 1.74 | Do. |
| 9359 | 59.00 | —19.70 | 20 | 59.54 | 2.21 | 27.48 | 0.38 | Do. |
| 9360 | 42.60 | —12.50 | 24 | 42.23 | 21.12 | 24.22 | 1.74 | Do. |
| 9361 | 39.70 | —16.60 | 24 | 43.15 | 28.12 | 20.60 | 2.10 | Do. |
| 9362 | 50.30 | —14.00 | 28 | 50.08 | 14.72 | 24.76 | 1.49 | Present. |
| 9363 | 92.80 | 70.00 | 27 | 17.79 | 32.40 | 21.02 | 1.20 | Absent. |
| 9364 | 96.50 | 74.60 | 27 | 16.99 | 36.00 | 25.02 | 0.86 | Do. |
| 9365 | 41.70 | —15.00 | 27 | 43.98 | 23.12 | 21.28 | 1.00 | Present. |
| 9366 | 22.00 | —17.50 | 29 | 30.89 | 28.60 | 23.44 | 4.66 | Do. |
| 9367 | 43.80 | —22.00 | 19 | 49.52 | 22.48 | 18.55 | 1.00 | Absent. |
| 9368 | 56.40 | — 6.50 | 20 | 47.50 | 17.36 | 23.44 | 1.08 | Do. |
| 9369 | 25.00 | —16.70 | 19 | 31.39 | 29.44 | 25.38 | 3.04 | Present. |
| 9370 | 83.90 | 70.20 | 19 | 10.46 | 35.20 | 24.62 | 1.56 | Absent. |
| 9371 | 112.60 | 96.60 | 19 | 19.56 | 31.20 | 24.60 | 0.86 | Do. |
| 9372 | 42.40 | —18.70 | 17 | 45.63 | 19.60 | 23.52 | 1.90 | Do. |
| 9373 | 32.00 | —16.10 | 24 | 36.87 | 29.40 | 23.94 | 2.68 | Present. |
| 9374 | 46.30 | — 6.50 | .......... | 40.18 | 18.00 | 26.22 | 1.99 | Do. |
| 9375 | 59.70 | —21.00 | 16 | 60.04 | 2.34 | 30.04 | 0.18 | Absent. |
| 9376 | 58.80 | —20.00 | 16 | 58.62 | 6.20 | 27.35 | 0.32 | Do. |
| 9377 | 53.00 | —19.40 | .......... | 53.30 | 4.67 | 30.92 | 0.58 | Do. |
| 9378 | 59.40 | —20.20 | 18 | 59.87 | 2.53 | 32.00 | 0.12 | Do. |
| 9379 | 58.00 | —19.80 | 18 | 58.35 | 3.27 | 29.88 | 0.30 | Do. |
| 9380 | 61.50 | —19.40 | 21 | 61.04 | 2.10 | 29.64 | 0.50 | Do. |
| 9381 | 59.90 | —10.20 | 16 | 58.85 | 3.12 | 27.70 | 0.42 | Do. |
| 9382 | 63.00 | —20.60 | 17 | 62.44 | 1.38 | 32.46 | 0.46 | Do. |
| 9383 | 77.00 | 4.60 | 17 | 53.78 | 6.57 | 28.28 | 0.26 | Do. |
| 9384 | 61.00 | —20.20 | 21 | 61.27 | 2.19 | 28.02 | 0.32 | Do. |
| 9385 | 54.10 | —16.90 | 24 | 54.42 | 2.83 | 35.20 | 0.46 | Do. |
| 9386 | 54.80 | —15.90 | 24 | 54.19 | 5.40 | 34.20 | 0.14 | Do. |
| 9387 | 58.00 | —18.70 | 23 | 58.59 | 3.27 | 30.82 | 0.38 | Do. |
| 9388 | 60.00 | —20.90 | 19 | 60.89 | 3.27 | 28.28 | 0.38 | Do. |
| 9389 | 59.00 | —20.30 | 19 | 59.66 | 3.99 | 25.52 | 0.31 | Do. |
| 9390 | 64.90 | —21.70 | 19 | 65.18 | 2.58 | 20.52 | 0.17 | Do. |
| 9391 | 86.50 | 43.50 | 19 | 32.36 | 20.68 | 32.88 | 0.24 | Do. |
| 9392 | 35.90 | —12.70 | 19 | 36.58 | 26.28 | 19.66 | 5.90 | Do. |
| 9393 | 20.80 | —20.00 | 20 | 30.81 | 29.48 | 22.86 | 3.06 | Do. |
| 9394 | 48.00 | —15.50 | 19 | 47.79 | 16.48 | 26.37 | 1.74 | Do. |
| 9395 | 34.00 | —20.00 | 19 | 40.64 | 21.12 | 21.34 | 6.50 | Do. |
| 9396 | 21.50 | —19.00 | 19 | 30.48 | 22.60 | 21.82 | 6.96 | Do. |
| 9397 | 29.10 | —23.50 | 19 | 39.59 | 27.80 | 20.52 | 2.20 | Do. |
| 9398 | 37.20 | —14.50 | 19 | 38.91 | 22.08 | 22.76 | 6.44 | Do. |
| 9399 | 45.40 | —12.80 | .......... | 44.23 | 7.68 | 26.44 | 7.68 | Do. |
| 9400 | 39.90 | —20.20 | 19 | 42.22 | 26.28 | 19.90 | 2.54 | Do. |
| 9401 | 30.20 | —14.20 | 19 | 33.41 | 18.32 | 27.02 | 4.38 | Do. |
| ........ | 62.50 | 22.60 | 19 | 64.05 | 2.58 | 22.34 | 0.51 | Do. |

FOODS AND FOOD ADULTERANTS.

## ANALYSIS BY W. C. STUBBS.

### Description of sample.

| No. | Bought of— | Where wholesaled or manufactured. | Remarks. |
|---|---|---|---|
| 1 | Mrs. N. Smith, 1360 Magazine street, New Orleans, La. | Rodd Bros. & Co., New Orleans. | Mixture of glucose, sirup, and Louisiana molasses. |
| 2 | DaMonte Grocery, Magazine street, New Orleans, La. | Origin unknown ............ | Louisiana centrifugal molasses. |
| 3 | Rose Johnson, Dryades street, New Orleans, La. | Marianna Plantation ....... | Do. |
| 4 | Sugar Levee .................... | Poplar Grove Plantation.... | Do. |
| 5 | ......do ........................... | Marked "H" ................ | Do. |
| 6 | ......do ........................... | Star Plantation ............. | Do. |
| 7 | ......do ........................... | Justinia Plantation......... | Do. |
| 8 | ......do ........................:. | Julia Plantation ............ | Open kettle. |
| 9 | ..:...do ........................... | Horse Shoe Brand .......... | Do. |
| 10 | Louisiana Sugar Refinery No. 38. | Louisiana Sugar Refinery .. | Refinery molasses. |
| 11 | Louisiana Sugar Refinery No. 36. | ......do ..................... | Do. |
| 12 | Louisiana Sugar Refinery No. 37. | ......do ..................... | Do. |
| 13 | Jno. Barclay & Co ............ ..... | Justinia Plantation......... | Louisiana centrifugal molasses. |
| 14 | ......do ........................... | Evan Hall Plantation....... | Do. |
| 15 | ......do ........................... | Des Lignes Plantation...... | Louisiana centrifugal molasses, diffusion process. |
| 16 | ......do ........................... | Enreka Plantation.......... | Louisiana centrifugal molasses. |
| 17 | ......do ........................... | Belle Alliance Plantation... | Do. |
| 18 | ......do ........................... | McManor Plantation ...... | Do. |
| 19 | ......do ........................... | Marianna Plantation . ...... | Do. |
| 20 | ......do ........................... | Cora Plantation............. | Do. |
| 21 | ......do ........................... | L. & M. Central Factory .... | Do. |
| 22 | ......do ........................... | Waveland (Bayou Teche)... | Do. |
| 23 | ......do ........................... | Stella Plantation............. | Do. |
| 24 | Emile E. Hatery, Camp and Julia streets. | Sugar Levee ............... | Mixture glucose sirup and Louisiana molasses. |
| 25 | A. A. McGinnis's Sons.......... | Hermitage Plantation ...... | Louisiana centrifugal molasses. |
| 26 | Wm. Hart, Rampart and Gravier streets. | Unknown.................... | Louisiana centrifugal molasses, perhaps mixed. |
| 27 | Jules O. Zalarain, Rampart and Perdido streets. | ......do ..................... | Open kettle. |
| 28 | C. Redersheimer, 141 S. Rampart street. | ......do ..................... | Mixture of glucose sirup and Louisiana molasses. |
| 29 | C. Foabney, Poydras and Rampart streets. | ......do ..................... | Louisiana open kettle. |
| 30 | ......do ...................... | ......do ..................... | Do. |
| 31 | Jno. J. Driscoll, 227 South Rampart street. | Chinango Plantation........ | Do. |
| 32 | Lollinger & Fnerty, 291 Rampart street. | Unknown.................... | Mixture of glucose sirup and Louisiana molasses. |
| 33 | T. F. McMahon, 483 Dryades street. | ......do ..................... | Louisiana centrifugal molasses (?). |
| 34 | Noel Parmental, Dryades and Jackson streets. | ......do ..................... | Mixture of glucose sirup and Louisiana molasses. |
| 35 | H. Haunmeth, 552 Magazine street. | ......do ..................... | Do. |
| 36 | A. J. Kernan, 580 Magazine street. | ......do ..................... | Louisiana open kettle and (?). |
| 37 | G. L. Stanfield, Magazine and St. Andrew streets. | ......do ..................... | Mixture of glucose sirup and Louisiana molasses. |

## ANALYSIS BY W. C. STUBBS.

*Description of sample—Continued.*

| No. | Bought of— | Where wholesaled or manufactured. | Remarks. |
|---|---|---|---|
| 38 | F. Magintzgy, 133 Magazine street. | Unknown | Mixture of glucose sirup and Louisiana molasses. |
| 39 | A. W. Skarden, Magazine and Jackson streets. | ......do | Louisiana centrifugal molasses and (?). |
| 40 | Harry Butner, Laurel and Arabella streets. | Louisiana Sugar Refinery... | Mixture of glucose sirup and Louisiana molasses. |
| 41 | I. E. King, Valmot and Laurel streets. | Unknown | Louisiana "syrop de batterie." |
| 42 | G. W. Dunbar's Sons | ......do | Do. |
| 43 | Jas. Wilson & Co., Prytania and Felfnty streets. | ......do | Mixture glucose sirup and Louisiana molasses. |
| 44 | H. B. Gilson, 28 Valence street .. | ......do | Louisiana "syrop de batterie." |
| 45 | ......do | ......do | Mixture glucose sirup and Louisiana molasses. |
| 46 | J. P. Schmidt, 1094 Magazine street. | Rodd Bros. & Co | Do. |
| 47 | Fred Denny, 1093 Magazine street. | ......do | Do. |
| 48 | ......do | ......do | Louisiana centrifugal molasses. |
| 49 | Smith Bros. & Co., 106 Poydras street. | Unknown | Mixture glucose sirup and Louisiana molasses. |
| 50 | ......do | ......do | Do. |

*Analytical data.*

| No. | Polarization. Direct. | Polarization. Indirect. | Temperature ° C. | Sucrose. | Reducing sugars. | Water. | Ash. | Tin or other metals. |
|---|---|---|---|---|---|---|---|---|
| | | | | Per cent. | Per cent. | Per cent. | Per cent. | |
| 1..... | 46.00 | 00.88 | 21 | 33.79 | 28.77 | 29.97 | 0.84 | .......... |
| 2....., | 40.40 | — 24.86 | 20 | 48.70 | 23.52 | 23.10 | 1.75 | .......... |
| 3..... | 25.00 | — 17.82 | 20 | 31.95 | 34.48 | 26.75 | 3.53 | .......... |
| 4..... | 30.50 | — 22.C0 | 17 | 38.74 | 27.00 | 25.05 | 4.32 | .......... |
| 5..... | 36.10 | — 23.32 | 18 | 44.01 | 25.64 | 24.74 | 4.01 | .......... |
| 6..... | 30.36 | — 18.36 | 16 | 36.55 | 20.60 | 31.11 | 4.77 | .......... |
| 7..... | 36.20 | — 23.54 | 18 | 44.25 | 21.50 | 26.04 | 3.37 | .......... |
| 8..... | 42.25 | — 22.22 | 15 | 47.23 | 20.00 | 27.58 | 2.56 | .......... |
| 9..... | 38.00 | — 21.78 | 18 | 44.28 | 25.31 | 25.67 | 2.67 | .......... |
| 10..... | 35.50 | — 22.22 | 13 | 42.70 | 28.60 | 22.60 | 3.11 | .......... |
| 11..... | 38.40 | — 14.96 | 18 | 36.70 | 32.30 | 24.04 | 3.74 | .......... |
| 12..... | 36.40 | — 14.74 | 18 | 30.47 | 29.40 | 31.96 | 4.57 | .......... |
| 13..... | 33.20 | — 26.18 | 6 | 42.11 | 25.00 | 25.94 | 3.75 | .......... |
| 14..... | 24.60 | — 23.98 | 8 | 34.70 | 25.97 | 31.17 | 4.83 | .......... |
| 15 .... | 23.00 | .......... | .......... | 31.70 | 35.70 | 26.27 | 3.93 | .......... |
| 16 ... | 23.00 | .......... | .......... | 33.58 | 29.29 | 29.11 | 4.53 | .......... |
| 17..... | 23.80 | ....:...... | .......... | 31.10 | 31.20 | 29.08 | 4.55 | .......... |
| 18..... | 28.60 | .......... | .......... | 35.60 | 29.40 | 23.11 | 3.88 | .......... |
| 19..... | 22.20 | .......... | .......... | 30.50 | 35.70 | 23.43 | 3.96 | .......... |
| 20..... | 27.80 | — 24.43 | 10 | 37.56 | 25.00 | 29.18 | 4.95 | .......... |
| 21.... | 33.00 | — 23.10 | 10 | 40.36 | 26.31 | 26.35 | 3.90 | .......... |
| 22..... | 23.80 | — 21.12 | 20 | 33.52 | 31.25 | 27.34 | 3.34 | .......... |
| 23..... | 27.20 | — 21.56 | 20 | 36.38 | 25.00 | 26.83 | 6.28 | .......... |
| 24..... | 112.00 | 96.14 | 20 | 12.28 | 34.66 | 27.20 | 1.57 | .......... |
| 25..... | 29.20 | — 22.44 | 16 | 37.90 | 23.50 | 24.54 | 6.02 | .......... |
| 26..... | 19.20 | — 20.68 | 12 | 28.80 | 37.81 | 28.09 | 2.58 | .......... |
| 27..... | 40.00 | — 23.98 | 13 | 41.53 | 23.63 | 24.50 | 2.78 | .......... |
| 28..... | 120.40 | 97.90 | 14 | 16.42 | 33.00 | 33.31 | 1.72 | .......... |
| 29..... | 49.20 | — 23.54 | 14 | 53.09 | 17.00 | 28.69 | 0.85 | .......... |
| 30..... | 48.60 | — 22.20 | 14 | 51.89 | 17.55 | 26.55 | 1.52 | .......... |
| 31..... | 55.40 | — 22.44 | 14 | 56.81 | 17.33 | 22.90 | 0.89 | .......... |
| 32..... | 67.50 | 31.24 | 16 | 26.66 | 34.66 | 25.04 | 3.54 | .......... |
| 33..... | 34.00 | — 1.65 | 19 | 26.50 | 33.00 | 22.90 | 2.63 | .......... |
| 34..... | 62.80 | 27.28 | 16 | 26.11 | 32.50 | 28.56 | 2.52 | .......... |
| 35..... | 61.40 | 9.68 | 15 | 37.89 | 25.81 | 26.18 | 2.21 | .......... |
| 36..... | 43.20 | — 10.56 | 19 | 39.97 | 26.00 | 30.19 | 2.41 | .......... |
| 37..... | 115.20 | 95.48 | 16 | 14.50 | 38.51 | 29.17 | 1.51 | .......... |
| 38..... | 122.40 | 98.56 | 14 | 17.40 | 34.66 | 28.14 | 4.61 | .......... |
| 39..... | 30.20 | — 7.70 | 20 | 22.28 | 36.49 | 27.20 | 4.34 | .......... |
| 40..... | 124.20 | 104.50 | 10 | 14.17 | 31.01 | 29.66 | 1.97 | .......... |
| 41.... | 44.00 | — 23.54 | 10 | 48.58 | 16.52 | 27.38 | 2.22 | .......... |
| 42..... | 50.80 | — 20.20 | 25 | 53.85 | 12.44 | 24.89 | 1.45 | .......... |
| 43..... | 98.20 | 79.20 | 10 | 13.66 | 38.32 | 29.93 | 1.12 | .......... |
| 44..... | 52.40 | — 23.89 | 9 | 54.68 | 12.00 | 29.22 | 1.27 | .......... |
| 45 .... | 116.80 | 99.00 | 25 | 13.53 | 35.74 | 30.67 | 0.65 | .......... |
| 46 .... | 120.80 | 99.22 | 20 | 16.41 | 31.11 | 28.81 | 0.59 | .......... |
| 47.... | 123.00 | 105.60 | 25 | 13.23 | 32.51 | 30.00 | 0.72 | .......... |
| 48.... | 27.40 | — 21.56 | 25 | 37.23 | 27.84 | 26.07 | 1.38 | .......... |
| 49 .... | 87.70 | 62.15 | 25 | 19.42 | 33.37 | 31.33 | 2.38 | .......... |
| 50 .... | 86.00 | 62.70 | 25 | 18.17 | 22.60 | 26.38 | 1.41 | .......... |

ANALYSES BY SHIPPEN WALLACE.

*Analytical data.*

| No. | Polarization. | | Temperature, °C. | Sucrose. | Reducing sugars. | Water. | Ash. | Tin or other metals. |
|---|---|---|---|---|---|---|---|---|
| | Direct. | Indirect. | | | | | | |
| | | | | Per cent. | Per cent. | Per cent. | Per cent. | |
| 1..... | 96.8 | 70.0 | .......... | 20.00 | 27.50 | .......... | 1.89 | .......... |
| 2..... | 122.0 | 108.0 | .......... | 10.40 | 33.50 | .......... | 1.53 | .......... |
| 3..... | 115.0 | 99.0 | .......... | 11.90 | 34.00 | .......... | 1.52 | .......... |
| 4..... | 134.0 | 121.4 | .......... | 9.40 | 35.30 | .......... | 1.37 | .......... |
| 5..... | 117.8 | 92.0 | .......... | 19.20 | 32.28 | .......... | 1.50 | .......... |
| 6 .... | 50.2 | — 13.0 | .......... | 47.10 | 12.85 | .......... | 2.75 | .......... |
| 7..... | 67.8 | 26.0 | .......... | 31.10 | 19.50 | .......... | 3.10 | .......... |
| 8..... | 110.5 | 87.0 | .......... | 17.50 | 29.85 | .......... | 1.55 | .......... |
| 9..... | 133.0 | 104.0 | .......... | 31.60 | 35.60 | .......... | 1.92 | .......... |
| 10..... | 51.7 | — 12.0 | .......... | 47.53 | 13.08 | .......... | 4.00 | .......... |
| 11..... | 112.3 | 77.0 | .......... | 26.20 | 30.90 | .......... | 1.33 | .......... |
| 12..... | 40.7 | — 14.0 | .......... | 39.20 | 16.10 | .......... | 4.75 | .......... |
| 13..... | 37.8 | — 11.0 | .......... | 36.41 | 17.20 | .......... | 4.85 | .......... |
| 14..... | 97.3 | 76.0 | .......... | 15.80 | 28.10 | .......... | 1.90 | .......... |
| 15..... | 138.0 | 136.0 | .......... | 1.40 | 35.80 | .......... | 1.45 | .......... |
| 16.... | 44.3 | — 16.0 | .......... | 45.00 | 21.50 | .......... | 4.38 | .......... |
| 17..... | 129.0 | 101.4 | .......... | 20.50 | 32.50 | .......... | 1.48 | .......... |
| 18 .... | 60.0 | 31.4 | .......... | 28.00 | 27.40 | .......... | 2.50 | .......... |
| 19..... | 46.0 | — 18.0 | .......... | 44.70 | 11.85 | .......... | 4.25 | .......... |
| 20..... | 111.2 | 76.0 | .......... | 20.20 | 29.47 | .......... | 1.45 | .......... |
| 21..... | 44.2 | — 16.0 | .......... | 44.90 | 21.50 | .......... | 4.40 | .......... |
| 22..... | 38.5 | — 13.6 | .......... | 38.40 | 22.20 | .......... | 4.95 | .......... |
| 23..... | 45.0 | — 15.0 | .......... | 44.70 | 19.10 | .......... | 4.75 | .......... |
| 24..... | 126.2 | 111.2 | .......... | 11.10 | 33.75 | .......... | 1.50 | .......... |
| 25..... | 38.7 | — 13.0 | .......... | 38.50 | 22.00 | .......... | 4.90 | .......... |
| 26.... | 62.3 | 28.4 | .......... | 25.30 | 28.85 | .......... | 3.75 | .......... |
| 27..... | 105.3 | 86.0 | .......... | 13.90 | 30.35 | .......... | 1.35 | .......... |
| 28.... | 43.5 | — 15.0 | .......... | 43.50 | 18.50 | .......... | 5.50 | .......... |
| 29..... | 107.2 | 86.0 | .......... | 15.80 | 29.75 | .......... | 1.40 | .......... |
| 30.... | 89.3 | 48.0 | .......... | 30.80 | 31.62 | .......... | 3.25 | .......... |
| 31..... | 146.4 | 138.0 | .......... | 6.20 | 36.71 | .......... | 1.25 | .......... |
| 32..... | 55.0 | — 14.0 | .......... | 51.40 | 12.10 | .......... | 4.06 | .......... |
| 33..... | 116.0 | 92.5 | .......... | 17.50 | 32.50 | .......... | 1.60 | .......... |
| 34..... | 32.8 | — 17.0 | .......... | 37.10 | 17.35 | .......... | 5.90 | .......... |
| 35..... | 44.0 | — 16.0 | .......... | 44.70 | 21.41 | .......... | 4.40 | .......... |
| 36..... | 44.3 | — 16.0 | .......... | 45.00 | 21.85 | .......... | 4.40 | .......... |
| 37..... | 120.0 | 113.0 | .......... | 5.20 | 34.80 | .......... | 1.38 | .......... |
| 38..... | 122.0 | 106.0 | .......... | 11.90 | 34.00 | .......... | 1.44 | .......... |
| 39..... | 42.5 | — 12.0 | .......... | 40.60 | 15.32 | .......... | 4.50 | .......... |
| 40..... | 120.0 | 113.0 | .......... | 5.20 | 34.50 | .......... | 1.40 | .......... |
| 41..... | 148.4 | 146.0 | .......... | 1.70 | 37.53 | .......... | 1.25 | .......... |
| 42..... | 40.5 | — 12.0 | .......... | 39.10 | 16.50 | .......... | 4.50 | .......... |
| 43..... | 53.0 | — 14.6 | .......... | 50.50 | 11.92 | .......... | 4.00 | .......... |
| 44 .... | 122.0 | 113.0 | .......... | 6.70 | 33.45 | .......... | 1.50 | .......... |
| 45..... | 42.5 | — 15.0 | .......... | 42.90 | 18.22 | .......... | 4.75 | .......... |
| 46..... | 117.0 | 93.0 | .......... | 17.90 | 30.80 | .......... | 1.90 | .......... |
| 47.... | 93.0 | 29.0 | .......... | 47.70 | 33.33 | .......... | 2.00 | .......... |
| 48..... | 104.5 | 45.5 | .......... | 44.00 | 28.75 | .......... | 3.50 | .......... |
| 49..... | 123.4 | 55.5 | .......... | 50.60 | 32.15 | .......... | 3.10 | .......... |
| 50..... | 82.0 | 25.3 | .......... | 42.30 | 30.22 | .......... | 4.00 | .......... |

FOODS AND FOOD ADULTERANTS.

*Analytical data.*

| No. | Polarization. | | Temperature °C. | Sucrose. | Reducing sugars. | Water. | Ash. | Tin or other metals. |
|---|---|---|---|---|---|---|---|---|
| | Direct. | Indirect. | | | | | | |
| | | | | Per cent. | Per cent. | Per cent. | Per cent. | Per cent. |
| 1 | 29.7 | —10.0 | 16.5 | 29.60 | 28.20 | 28.68 | 5.00 | 0.0074 |
| 2 | ......... | ......... | ......... | ......... | 40.98 | 21.00 | .58 | ......... |
| 3 | 30.4 | —10.0 | 15 | 30.17 | 28.56 | 27.51 | 5.17 | 0.0134 |
| 4 | 34.0 | —6.0 | 15 | 29.87 | 27.80 | 31.15 | 4.54 | 0.0200 |
| 5 | 90.0 | ......... | ......... | 12.14 | 32.68 | 25.52 | 1.93 | 0.0028 |
| 6 | 44.5 | —10.0 | 15 | 40.70 | 21.82 | 23.45 | 5.05 | 0.0100 |
| 7 | 44.3 | —10.0 | 15 | 40.00 | 22.44 | 23.27 | 4.17 | 0.0180 |
| 8 | 56.8 | —21.5 | 18 | 58.60 | 0.24 | 30.25 | 0.24 | ......... |
| 9 | 82.0 | 21.0 | 18 | 40.22 | 14.50 | 29.70 | 0.33 | 0.0020 |
| 10 | ......... | ......... | ......... | 3.32 | 37.60 | 26.25 | 0.41 | ......... |
| 11 | 55.4 | —21.7 | 18 | 57.79 | 5.26 | 31.40 | 0.55 | 0.0080 |
| 12 | 65.5 | —23.0 | 18 | 66.34 | 1.32 | 30.85 | 0.45 | ......... |
| 13 | 62.6 | —21.3 | 20 | 63.43 | 1.43 | 30.87 | 0.53 | Trace. |
| 14 | 63.5 | —21.9 | 20 | 64.50 | 1.26 | 30.12 | 0.50 | ......... |
| 15 | ......... | ......... | ......... | 1.50 | 44.60 | 20.53 | 1.17 | ......... |
| 16 | 64.5 | —22.5 | 18 | 65.22 | 1.26 | 33.13 | ......... | ......... |
| 17 | 58.4 | —20.9 | 20 | 59.99 | 5.88 | 32.17 | 0.28 | 0.0100 |
| 18 | ......... | ......... | ......... | 34.78 | 14.92 | 30.86 | 0.11 | 0.0200 |
| 19 | 57.0 | —20.9 | 20 | 58.83 | 5.70 | 33.12 | 0.32 | 0.0100 |
| 20 | 28.5 | —18.0 | 20 | 35.04 | 26.74 | 23.99 | 4.70 | 0.0260 |
| 21 | ......... | ......... | ......... | 29.79 | 18.64 | 28.20 | 2.54 | 0.0060 |
| 22 | ......... | ......... | ......... | 1.71 | 37.58 | 24.00 | 1.02 | ......... |
| 23 | 130.8 | 110.0 | 20 | 9.37 | 33.32 | 25.85 | 0.35 | ......... |
| 24 | ......... | ......... | ......... | 30.44 | 14.28 | 32.55 | 0.42 | ......... |
| 25 | ......... | ......... | ......... | 7.14 | 38.46 | 28.59 | 2.68 | ......... |
| 26 | 35.0 | —18.9 | 22 | 41.17 | 25.38 | 26.44 | 3.50 | 0.0200 |
| 27 | ......... | ......... | ......... | 5.16 | 33.33 | 28.06 | 1.60 | Trace. |
| 28 | ......... | ......... | ......... | 8.49 | 30.12 | 25.71 | 4.12 | 0.0100 |
| 29 | ......... | ......... | ......... | 2.07 | 40.00 | 20.86 | 0.64 | ......... |
| 30 | 48.2 | —21.9 | 22 | 53.34 | 13.33 | 30.45 | 0.17 | ......... |
| 31 | 49.4 | —19.4 | 22 | 52.35 | 8.19 | 35.64 | 0.74 | ......... |
| 32 | 60.3 | —21.0 | 22 | 61.87 | 1.66 | 31.37 | 0.71 | 0.0060 |
| 33 | ......... | ......... | ......... | 2.42 | 41.66 | 17.90 | 0.76 | ......... |
| 34 | 33.2 | —18.0 | 23 | 39.11 | 26.88 | 25.60 | 2.85 | 0.0140 |
| 35 | 31.4 | —18.6 | 23 | 38.12 | 27.03 | 24.98 | 4.31 | 0.0040 |
| 36 | ......... | ......... | ......... | 1.92 | 40.00 | 22.14 | 1.03 | ......... |
| 37 | ......... | ......... | ......... | 43.76 | 10.75 | 30.48 | 0.30 | ......... |
| 38 | ......... | ......... | ......... | 2.07 | 40.65 | 26.33 | 1.03 | ......... |
| 39 | 43.0 | —18.4 | 23 | 46.90 | 22.22 | 23.35 | 4.31 | 0.0120 |
| 40 | ......... | ......... | ......... | 4.65 | 38.56 | 24.10 | 1.26 | ......... |
| 41 | 25.0 | —15.3 | 23 | 30.78 | 30.30 | 30.13 | 4.67 | 0.0060 |
| 42 | ......... | ......... | ......... | 1.97 | 41.77 | 22.80 | 1.25 | ......... |
| 43 | ......... | ......... | ......... | 2.08 | 38.46 | 22.54 | 0.21 | ......... |
| 44 | 41.0 | —17.8 | 23 | 44.92 | 21.27 | 27.93 | 3.65 | 0.0640 |
| 45 | 59.1 | —21.0 | 23 | 61.26 | 1.16 | 34.60 | 0.15 | ......... |
| 46 | 29.2 | —17.0 | 23 | 35.29 | 25.00 | 30.05 | 5.90 | 0.0030 |
| 47 | 35.7 | —19.5 | 23 | 42.17 | 25.64 | 22.83 | 4.10 | 0.0000 |
| 48 | ......... | ......... | ......... | 41.67 | 18.02 | 0.08 | ......... |
| 49 | ......... | ......... | ......... | 35.24 | 16.66 | 20.58 | 0.10 | ......... |
| 50 | 60.0 | —22.2 | 23 | 62.79 | 1.44 | 34.47 | 0.53 | 0.0100 |

## ANALYSES BY H. A. WEBER.

*Description of samples.*

| No. | Bought from— | Remarks. |
|---|---|---|
| 1 | J. G. & L. Brown, Hunter street and 5th avenue, Columbus, Ohio. | New Orleans Molasses. |
| 2 | .....do ....................................:........... | Sugar-house Molasses. |
| 3 | Henry Thropp, 345 South High street, Columbus, Ohio. | New Orleans Molasses. |
| 4 | Esper & Sons, 403 South High street, Columbus, Ohio. | Do. |
| 5 | A. J. Evans, 236 and 238 East Long street, Columbus, Ohio. | Do. |
| 6 | Bowman Bros., corner Long street and Grant avenue, Columbus, Ohio. | Do. |
| 7 | M. A. Montgomery, 618 East Long street, Columbus, Ohio. | Do. |
| 8 | Atlantic Tea Company, 190 South 4th street, Columbus, Ohio. | 1 quart glass bottle Thurber's Maple Sirup; delicious flavor. |
| 9 | M. Theado & Co., 234 to 238 South 4th street, Columbus, Ohio. | Tin can labeled Williams Bros. & Charbonnean, Detroit, Mich. |
| 10 | Saul & Eberly, 74, 76, and 78 East Main street, Columbus, Ohio. | 1 glass bottle labeled California Nectarine Drips, National Sirup Company, Chicago and St. Paul. |
| 11 | .....do ............................................ | Tin can labeled Maple Honey Sirup, Bradshaw & Waite, Chicago, Ill. |
| 12 | ......do ........................................... | Rock Candy Drips, F. H. Leggett & Co., New York; glass bottle containing lump of rock candy. |
| 13 | Esper & Sons, 403 South High street, Columbus, Ohio. | Tin can labeled Pure Maple Sirup, Crane Bros., Garrettsville, Ohio. |
| 14 | .....do ............................................ | Tin can labeled Choice Table Maple Sirup, J. B. McNabb, Salem, Ohio. |
| 15 | .....do ......................................... | Corn Sirup. |
| 16 | ......do ........................................... | Glass bottle labeled Rock Candy Drips, F.H.Leggett's, New York, containing lump of candy. |
| 17 | March, Chestnut and High streets, Columbus, Ohio. | Can labeled Thurber's Mountain Sugar Maple Sirup. |
| 18 | Wachter, West 3d avenue, Columbus, Ohio .... | Can labeled Pure Maple Sirup, Williams Bros. & Charbonnean, Detroit, Mich; $100 reward for adulteration found. |
| 19 | F. R. Allen, Goodale and High streets, Columbus, Ohio. | Can labeled Pure Maple Sirup, L. G. Yoe & Co. |
| 20 | ......do ........................................... | New Orleans Molasses, second quality. |
| 21 | ......do ........................................... | New Orleans Molasses, first quality. |
| 22 | ......do ........................................... | Corn sirup. |
| 23 | A. Hawk, Goodale and High streets, Columbus, Ohio. | Rock Candy Drips, Bradshaw & Waite, Chicago, Ill. |
| 24 | ......do ........................................... | Bottle labeled Pure Maple Sirup, F. G. Strohmeyer & Co., New York. (Delicious flavor.) |
| 25 | ......do ........................................... | Central Park Drips, Thurber & Whyland, New York. |
| 26 | ......do ........................................... | New Orleans Molasses, second quality. |
| 27 | ......do ........................................... | New Orleans Molasses, firstquality. |
| 28 | J. C. March, 263 North High street, Columbus, Ohio. | New Orleans Molasses, 1 quart. |
| 29 | ......do ........................................... | Table Sirup. |

ANALYSES BY H. A. WEBER.

*Description of samples—Continued.*

| No. | Bought from— | Remarks. |
|---|---|---|
| 30 | Atlantic Tea Company, 240 North High street, Columbus, Ohio. | 1 jug maple sirup labeled Thurber's Maple Sirup. |
| 31 | Thos. Bergin, 51 North High street, Columbus, Ohio. | 1 bottle maple sirup labeled Thurber's Maple Sirup. |
| 32 | .....do ................................ | 1 can maple sirup labeled Donovan & Chrisman, Pure Maple Sirup, Cable, Ohio. |
| 33 | Henry Wachter, 3d and Harrison avenue, Columbus, Ohio. | 1 quart Golden Drips. |
| 34 | .....do ................................ | New Orleans Molasses (best). |
| 35 | A. B. Phelps, 3d and Harrison avenue, Columbus, Ohio. | New Orleans Molasses. |
| 36 | Solon Hyde, 5th avenue, Columbus, Ohio....... | Golden Drips. |
| 37 | J. G. & L. Brown, 5th avenue, Columbus, Ohio. | Fancy bottle labeled L. G. Yoe & Co.'s Pure Maple Sirup. |
| 38 | .....do ................................ | Golden Drips. |
| 39 | M. A. Stiling, 1416 North High street, Columbus, Ohio. | New Orleans Molasses. |
| 40 | .....do ................................ | Table Sirup. |
| 41 | R. H. Bobb, 297 South High street, Columbus, Ohio. | New Orleans Molasses. |
| 42 | .....do ................................ | Golden Sirup. |
| 43 | .....do ................................ | Rock Candy Drips. |
| 44 | Miln, Greenwood and High streets, Columbus, Ohio. | New Orleans Molasses. |
| 45 | .....do ................................ | Maple Molasses, sold in bulk. |
| 46 | H. K. Kaiser, 1520 North High street, Columbus, Ohio. | New Orleans Molasses. |
| 47 | Aug. Boesel, 1352 North High street, Columbus, Ohio. | Do. |
| 48 | .....do ................................ | Table Sirup. |
| 49 | J. M. Bell & Son, 1183 North High street, Columbus, Ohio. | 1 bottle labeled McMechen's Old Virginia Tree Maple Sirup, G. K. McMechen, Wheeling, W. Va. |
| 50 | Thos. Lacey, North High street, Columbus, Ohio. | 1 can Maple Sirup labeled Pure Maple Sirup, Elyria Canning Company, Elyria, Ohio. |

ANALYSES BY F. G. WIECHMANN.

*Description of samples.*

| No. | Price per pint. | Bought from. | Label. |
|---|---|---|---|
| 51 | $0.19 | H. M. Weyrauch, 805 3d avenue, New York.. | New Orleans Molasses. |
| 52 | .15 | ......do...................................... | Porto Rico Molasses. |
| 53 | .10 | H. Hahnenfeld, 767 3d avenue, New York.... | New Orleans Molasses. |
| 54 | .10 | H. Boeselager, 794 3d avenue, New York .... | Do. |
| 55 | .09 | J. H. Meyer & Bro., 341 East 23d st., New York. | Do. |
| 56 | .10 | C. W. Frieling, 397 2d avenue, New York.... | Do. |
| 57 | .07 | C. Tobaben, 379 2d avenue, New York ....... | Sirup. |
| 58 | .09 | ......do...................... .............. | Molasses. |
| 59 | .10 | J. Maatz, 361 2d avenue, New York.......... | New Orleans Molasses. |
| 60 | .10 | ......do........................... | Sirup. |
| 61 | .10 | D. Plumb, 282 3d avenue, New York......... | Do. |
| 62 | .10 | ......do............................... | Porto Rico Molasses. |
| 63 | .10 | ......do.. ..................................... | New Orleans Molasses. |
| 64 | .10 | D. Mehrtens, 280 3d avenue, New York...... | Sirup. |
| 65 | .10 | .....do ................................ | New Orleans Molasses. |
| 66 | .09 | J. Betzemann, 230 3d avenue, New York.... | Do. |
| 67 | .10 | H. Cordes, 1347 2d avenue, New York ...... | Molasses. |
| 68 | .09 | ......do ..............·....................... | Sirup. |
| 69 | .09 | L. Fette, 1333 2d avenue, New York ....... | New Orleans Molasses. |
| 70 | .08 | ......do .................................. | Sirup. |
| 71 | .10 | Ferris & Reehill, 442 4th avenue, New York. | New Orleans Molasses. |
| 72 | .10 | ......do ................................. | Porto Rico Molasses. |
| 73 | .10 | ......do ..................... ............... | Sirup. |
| 74 | .10 | E. Schmidt, 441 4th avenue, New York...... | Do. |
| 75 | .10 | ......do ...........·....................... | New Orleans Molasses. |
| 76 | .12 | J. Macaulay, 422 4th avenue, New York..... | Do. |
| 77 | .08 | J. A. Steinberg, Wythe avenue and South 5th street, Brooklyn, E. D. | Sirup. |
| 78 | .09 | ......do............................... | New Orleans Molasses. |
| 79 | .09 | P. John, Wythe avenue and South 4th street, Brooklyn, E. D. | Do. |
| 80 | .07 | ......do ... | Sirup. |
| 81 | .10 | F. H. Jaeger, 1033 3d avenue, New York.... | New Orleans Molasses. |
| 82 | .10 | .....do ..................................... | Sirup. |
| 83 | .08 | H. A. Butt, 3d avenue and 60th street, New York. | Do. |
| 84 | .10 | .....do ............................... | New Orleans Molasses. |
| 85 | .10 | .....do ..................................... | Porto Rico Molasses. |
| 86 | .09 | W. D. H. Jaeger, 1020 3d avenue, New York.. | New Orleans Molasses. |
| 87 | .09 | Schnakenberg & Kueck, Wythe avenue and South 6th street, Brooklyn, E. D. | Sirup. |
| 88 | .10 | ......do ............................... | New Orleans Molasses. |
| 89 | .09 | W. Gode, Wythe avenue and South 8th street, Brooklyn, E. D. | Do. |
| 90 | .08 | ......do ............................... | Sirup. |
| 91 | .10 | F. C. Hencken, 92 South 8th street, Brooklyn, E. D. | Do. |
| 92 | .10 | ......do ............................... | New Orleans Molasses. |
| 93 | .10 | F. Rippe, 919 3d avenue, New York......... | Golden Sirup. |
| 94 | .10 | Schroeder & Goldberger, 911 3d avenue, New York. | Sirup. |
| 95 | .09 | ......do ............................... | Porto Rico Molasses. |
| 96 | .10 | ......do ..................................; | New Orleans Molasses. |
| 97 | .09 | J. Möllers, 879 3d avenue, New York........ | Do. |
| 98 | .09 | ......do ............................... | Sirup. |
| 99 | .08 | Plumb & Evers, 311 1th avenue, New York. | Porto Rico Molasses. |
| 100 | .10 | ......do ............................... | New Orleans Molasses. |

*Analytical data.*

| No. | Polarization. Direct. | Polarization. Indirect. | Tempera- ture, °C. | Sucrose. | Reducing sugars. | Water. | Ash. | Tin or other metals. |
|---|---|---|---|---|---|---|---|---|
| | | | | Per cent. | Per cent. | Per cent. | Per cent. | |
| 51 | 46. 0 | — 2L 8 | .......... | 55. 2 | 15. 15 | 28. 25 | 2. 995 | Absent. |
| 52 | 38. 8 | — 16. 0 | .......... | 44. 6 | 21. 74 | 29. 85 | 3. 161 | Present. |
| 53 | 53. 0 | 24. 0 | .......... | 21. 8 | 38. 16 | 29. 05 | 2. 621 | Absent. |
| 54 | 118. 0 | 100. 0 | .......... | ......... | 34. 01 | 26. 05 | 2. 066 | Do. |
| 55 | 58. 0 | 5. 6 | .......... | 39. 5 | 18. 03 | 28. 88 | 3. 040 | Do. |
| 56 | 84. 0 | 57. 2 | .......... | 20. 2 | 32. 90 | 28. 10 | 2. 646 | Present. |
| 57 | 42. 0 | — 11. 6 | .......... | 43. 7 | 27. 47 | 22. 68 | 4. 428 | Do. |
| 58 | 124. 0 | 107. 4 | .......... | ......... | 30. 30 | 28. 00 | 2. 221 | Do. |
| 59 | 88. 4 | 77. 2 | .......... | 8. 4 | 40. 48 | 29. 18 | 2. 153 | Absent. |
| 60 | 36. 0 | — 14. 8 | .......... | 41. 4 | 26. 59 | 25. 80 | 4. 176 | Do. |
| 61 | 64. 8 | 28. 8 | .......... | 27. 1 | 30. 12 | 24. 45 | 3. 600 | Present. |
| 62° | 56. 0 | 19. 2 | .......... | 27. 7 | 28. 56 | 30. 02 | 4. 194 | Absent. |
| 63 | 44. 0 | — 15. 2 | .......... | 56. 4 | 19. 30 | 28. 93 | 3. 474 | Do. |
| 64 | 38. 4 | — 15. 2 | .......... | 43. 7 | 30. 46 | 23. 08 | 3. 755 | Present. |
| 65 | 45. 2 | — 13. 2 | .......... | 47. 6 | 19. 15 | 28. 93 | 3. 802 | Absent. |
| 66 | 80. 0 | 30. 8 | .......... | 37. 1 | 21. 83 | 26. 72 | 2. 545 | Do. |
| 67 | 47. 2 | — 18. 4 | .......... | 53. 4 | 14. 28 | 30. 38 | 2. 952 | Do. |
| 68 | 40. 8 | — 15. 6 | .......... | 45. 0 | 21. 27 | 23. 55 | 5. 934 | Do. |
| 69 | 68. 0 | 11. 6 | .......... | 42. 5 | 24. 51 | 26. 08 | 1. 742 | Do. |
| 70 | 38. 4 | — 15. 6 | .......... | 44. 0 | 32. 26 | 21. 84 | 2. 898 | Do. |
| 71 | 80. 0 | 35. 2 | .......... | 33. 8 | 22. 98 | 27. 38 | 2. 646 | Do. |
| 72 | 37. 6 | — 11. 6 | .......... | 37. 1 | 21. 46 | 29. 48 | 5. 332 | Present. |
| 73 | 37. 0 | — 15. 6 | .......... | 39. 6 | 29. 76 | 24. 75 | 3. 798 | Absent. |
| 74 | 38. 0 | — 16. 0 | .......... | 40. 7 | 24. 75 | 22. 40 | 5. 688 | Do. |
| 75 | 36. 4 | — 19. 6 | .......... | 42. 2 | 24. 15 | 27. 65 | 3. 096 | Present. |
| 76 | 46. 0 | — 19. 2 | .......... | 49. 1 | 14. 00 | 30. 35 | 3. 330 | Absent. |
| 77 | 105. 2 | 84. 4 | .......... | ......... | 32. 26 | 26. 70 | 2. 423 | Do. |
| 78 | 62. 8 | 7. 2 | .......... | 41. 9 | 21. 10 | 25. 55 | 2. 016 | Present. |
| 79 | 58. 4 | 5. 6 | .......... | 39. 8 | 25. 71 | 26. 83 | 2. 082 | Absent. |
| 80 | 39. 6 | — 9. 2 | .......... | 36. 8 | 28. 40 | 25. 95 | 3. 924 | Present. |
| 81 | 47. 6 | — 20. 4 | .......... | 51. 3 | 19. 15 | 24. 28 | 2. 484 | Absent. |
| 82 | 102. 0 | · 80. 0 | .......... | ......... | 35. 46 | 23. 58 | 2. 405 | Do. |
| 83 | 37. 2 | — 16. 0 | .......... | 40. 1 | 28. 90 | 23. 30 | 4. 428 | Do. |
| 84 | 44. 4 | — 17. 2 | .......... | 46. 4 | 16. 94 | 28. 68 | 3. 179 | Present. |
| 85 | 38. 0 | — 5. 2 | .......... | 32. 6 | 25. 77 | 28. 05 | 4. 331 | Do. |
| 86 | 82. 8 | 42. 0 | .......... | 30. 7 | 25. 77 | 26. 80 | 2. 124 | Do. |
| 87 | 39. 6 | — 14. 4 | .......... | 40. 7 | 27. 47 | 20. 43 | 4. 223 | Absent. |
| 88 | 115. 6 | 100. 0 | .......... | ......... | 30. 30 | 28. 60 | 2. 045 | Do. |
| 89 | 42. 8 | — 17. 6 | .......... | 45. 5 | 18. 08 | 28. 33 | 3. 690 | Present. |
| 90 | 39. 6 | — 14. 4 | .......... | 40. 7 | 22. 42 | 20. 80 | 7. 114 | Absent. |
| 91 | 37. 6 | — 13. 2 | .......... | 38. 3 | 23. 15 | 26. 70 | 4. 961 | Do. |
| 92 | 93. 6 | 70. 4 | .......... | 17. 5 | 28. 73 | 28. 30 | 3. 006 | Present. |
| 93 | 38. 4 | — 14. 0 | .......... | 39. 5 | 29. 58 | 20. 43 | 4. 428 | Absent. |
| 94 | 36. 8 | — 12. 8 | .......... | 37. 4 | 27. 93 | 24. 85 | 3. 787 | Do. |
| 95 | 48. 4 | — 15. 2 | .......... | 47. 9 | 14. 36 | 27. 58 | 3. 686 | Do. |
| 96 | 40. 0 | — 18. 8 | .......... | 44. 3 | 22. 42 | 25. 95 | 2. 646 | Present. |
| 97 | 36. 4 | — 19. 6 | .......... | 42. 2 | 25. 77 | 25. 53 | 2. 862 | Absent. |
| 98 | 38. 0 | — 16. 0 | .......... | 40. 7 | 31. 64 | 19. 88 | 3. 150 | Do. |
| 99 | 9L 2 | 70. 8 | .......... | †15. 4 | 33. 55 | 20. 55 | 2. 722 | Present. |
| 100 | 118. 0 | 107. 6 | .......... | ......... | 33. 38 | 27. 65 | 1. 242 | Do. |

ANALYSES BY CHEMICAL LABORATORY, U. S. DEPARTMENT OF AGRICULTURE.

| No. | Where bought. | Description. | Price per pint. |
|---|---|---|---|
| 8560 | A. A. Winfield, 215 13½ street SW......... | Porto Rico Molasses... .................... | $0.08 |
| 8561 | ......do ...................................... | New Orleans Molasses ..................... | .10 |
| 8562 | ......do ...................................... | Vanilla Sirup......................... | .10 |
| 8566 | 324 13th street NW...................... | Golden Drip Sirup (graining) ............ | .10 |
| 8568 | 1219 E street.. ...................... | Golden Drip Sirup...................... | .10 |
| 8569 | Waple & Co., corner E and 11th streets... | Honey Sirup........................... | .10 |
| 8572 | W. E. Abbott, 11th and H streets NW .... | Bulk Maple Sirup ..................... | .18 |
| 8573 | J. H. Seromes, 740 12th street........... ... | Maple Sirup (a)................... | .25 |
| 8575 | ......do ...................... | Golden Eagle Sirup...................... | .10 |
| 8576 | Franklin Barrott, New York avenue and 12th street. | Dark New Orleans Molasses.............. | .08 |
| 8579 | ......do ..................................... | Bottled Maple Sirup (b) .................... | .25 |
| 8580 | Hart and Higgins...................... | Bottled Maple Sirup (c)................. | .20 |
| 8582 | ......do ...................... | Pure Sugar Sirup...................... | .10 |
| 8585 | W. H. Combs, 934 9th street ............. | Golden Sirup... ................... | .10 |
| 8588 | Wilson & Schultz, I and 7th streets....... | New Orleans molasses.................. | .10 |
| 8592 | M. Oppenheimer, 823 7th street ........... | Golden Drip Sirup...................... | .10 |
| 8597 | H. Q. Keyworth, 531 7th street........... | New Orleans Molasses............... | .13 |
| 8611 | 1367 C street SW ..................... | Bright Sirup ...................... | .10 |
| 8612 | Estler Bros. & Co.,13½ and C streets SW .. | .....do ....................... | .10 |
| 8613 | J. W. Brewer, 13½ and C streets SW ...... | Now Orleans Molasses................. | .10 |
| 8614 | H. H. Bowie, 237 12th street SW........... | Porto Rico Molasses.................. | .08 |
| 8615 | J. F. Harvey, 400 11th street SW ...... ... | Black Molasses ................... | .08 |
| 8616 | J. O. Vermillion, 333 11th street SW....... | Strawberry Sirup (for flavoring only) (d) . | .25 |
| 8617 | ......do ...................... ...... | Crystal Sirup...................... | .10 |
| 8618 | ......do ...................... | New Orleans Molasses................. | .10 |
| 8645 | A. Katzenberg, 222 North Eutaw street, Baltimore, Md. | Maple Sirup (e) .................... | .20 |
| 8646 | Greene, 412 Baltimore street, Baltimore, Md. | ......do (f)................................ | .23 |
| 8647 | T. A. Agnew, corner Eutaw and Pratt streets, Baltimore, Md. | ......do (g) .................... | .25 |
| 8648 | J. F. Webster, 893 Howard street, Baltimore, Md. | Golden Sirup ...................... | .08 |
| 8649 | Corner Linden and Rose streets, Baltimore, Md. | ......do .................... | .08 |
| 8650 | J. T. Johnson, 300 Biddle street, Baltimore, Md. | Second Grade Sugar Sirup ............. | .07 |
| 8651 | Randall, 410 Baltimore street, Baltimore, Md. | Best Sirup...................... | .10 |
| 8652 | Mrs. Troll, 13 Pearl street, Baltimore, Md. | ......do .................... | .07 |
| 8653 | Ed. Reese & Son, 412 Baltimore street, Baltimore, Md. | New Orleans Molasses................. | .06 |

a Labeled: Vermont Maple Sirup. Put up by J. H. Barker & Sons, Rutland, Vt. New York office, 328 Cherry street. Picture with "We be maple sugar and sirup makers" as legend.

b Quart bottle labeled: Hazen's Vermont Maple Sirup, Warranted Pure.

c Quart bottle labeled: McMechen's Old Virginia Tree Maple Sirup, Absolutely Pure. Geo. K. McMechen & Son, Wheeling, W. Va.

d Labeled: Githens & Rexsamer Philadelphia. Trade-mark, X G & R X.

e Quart bottle, labeled: Vermont Maple Sirup from Austin, Nichols & Co., New York.

f Fancy quart bottle, labeled Strictly Pure; Natural Flavor; Pure Maple Sirup. Curtice Brothers, Rochester, N. Y., Packers of canned fruits and vegetables, pickles, preserves, sauces, etc.

g Glass-stoppered quart decanter, labeled: Thurber's Maple Sirup; delicious flavor; Thurber Whyland & Co., manufacturers.

ANALYSES BY CHEMICAL LABORATORY, U. S. DEPARTMENT OF AGRICUL-
TURE—Continued.

| No | Where bought. | Description. | Price per pint. |
|---|---|---|---|
| 8654 | Simms & Co., 116 Eutaw stroet, Baltimore, Md. | No. 6 Sirup | $0.06 |
| 8655 | Rider & Co., 709 Baltimore street, Baltimore, Md. | No. 3 Sirup | .06 |
| 8656 | J. Cowman & Bros., 254 Biddle street, Baltimore, Md. | New Orleans Pure Sugar Sirup | .07 |
| 8657 | E. T. Carter, 120 Camden street, Baltimore, Md. | Golden Drip Sirup | .06 |
| 8658 | 861 Howard street, Baltimore, Md | New Orleans Sirup | .07 |
| 8659 | R. F. H. Lawson, corner Charles and Hamilton streets, Baltimore, Md. | Maple Sirup (a). | .20 |
| 8660 | Reed, corner Charles and Franklin street, Baltimore, Md. | Bottled Sirup (b) | .20 |
| 8661 | Hopper, McGaw & Co., 222 Charles street, Baltimore, Md. | Rock-candy Sirup | .20 |
| 8662 | Rider & Co., 709 Baltimore street, Baltimore, Md. | Corn Sirup | .06 |
| 8663 | J. F. Johnson, 300 Biddle street, Baltimore, Md. | Sugar Sirup | .06 |
| 8665 | Jordan Stabler, corner Eutaw, Madison, and Garden, Baltimore, Md. | Bottled Maple Sirup (graining) (c) | .25 |
| 8666 | L. Pfefferkorn, 206 Camden street, Baltimore, Md. | Sirup | .08 |
| 8667 | L. Strauss, 226 North Eutaw street, Baltimore, Md. | Bulk Maple Sirup | .18 |
| 8668 | J. Cowman & Bros., 254 Biddle street, Baltimore, Md. | Black-strap | .05 |
| 8669 | J. F. O'Hara, corner Biddle and Virginia streets, Baltimore, Md. | Revere Sirup | .06 |
| 8670 | Greene, 412 Baltimore street, Baltimore, Md. | Sugar Drip Sirup | .08 |
| 8671 | Greene, 412 Baltimore street, Baltimore, Md. | Second Grade Sirup | .06 |
| 8672 | Bryant & Clarvoe, Baltimore, Md. | Sugar-house Sirup | .10 |
| 8673 | S. Beernstein, 312 Camden street, Baltimore, Md. | Sugar Sirup | .10 |
| 8674 | E. T. Carter, 120 Camden street, Baltimore, Md. | do | .08 |
| 8675 | Rider & Co., 709 Baltimore street, Baltimore, Md. | No. 1 Sirup | .06 |
| 8676 | G. E. French, corner Paca and Lexington streets, Baltimore, Md. | Bottled Sirup; (contained a piece of rock candy) (d). | .25 |
| 8677 | T. M. Reese & Sons, 347 Charles street, Baltimore, Md. | Maple Sirup (e) | 25 |

a Quart bottle labled: "Hampshire County Maple Sirup, choice quality, put up by Leslie, Dunham & Co., Pittsfield, Mass."

b Quart bottle labeled: "Queen Table Sirup, George Boyd & Sons, Philadelphia, Pa.

c Quart bottle labeled: "Maple Sirup. Having purchased this sirup from the owners of the trees, who shipped it direct to us from the forest in Vermont, I can guarantee its purity. Jordan Stabler, Eutaw, Madison and Garden streets."

d Pint bottle labeled: "Rock Candy Drips. Francis H. Leggett & Co., New York. To avoid spoiling, this bottle should be kept in a cool place."

e Quart bottle labeled: "Green Mountain Maple, Delicious Flavor. Austin, Nichols & Co., sole agents, New York." Sketch labeled "Sugar-making in Vermont."

*Analytical data.*

| No. | Polarization. Direct. | Indirect. | Temperature, °C. | Sucrose. | Reducing sugars. | Water. | Ash. | Tin or other metals. |
|---|---|---|---|---|---|---|---|---|
| | | | | Per cent. | Per cent. | Per cent. | Per cent. | |
| 8560 | 41. 9 | 6. 6 | 17. 6 | 26. 1 | 22. 03 | 32. 84 | 4. 90 | Tin. |
| 8561 | 98. 7 | 71. 9 | 18. 0 | 19. 9 | 27. 62 | 27. 98 | 3. 53 | Do. |
| 8562 | 97. 2 | 68. 4 | 18. 0 | 21. 3 | 33. 33 | 21. 14 | 3. 63 | Do. |
| 8566 | 40. 5 | — 17. 7 | 18. 0 | 43. 1 | 29. 58 | 17. 05 | 5. 00 | Tin and copper. |
| 8568 | 109. 4 | 87. 6 | 17. 0 | 16. 9 | 33. 44 | 24. 48 | 2. 51 | Copper. |
| 8569 | 141. 8 | 133. 8 | 17. 0 | 6. 0 | 38. 46 | 22. 63 | 1. 50 | Tin. |
| 8572 | 62. 2 | — 23. 7 | 17. 0 | 63. 4 | 4. 81 | 30. 04 | 0. 37 | Neither. |
| 8573 | 53. 4 | — 23. 1 | 17. 0 | 56. 5 | 11. 36 | 31. 02 | .......... | Not examined. |
| 8575 | 101. 1 | 75. 5 | 17. 2 | 18. 9 | 32. 05 | 27. 77 | 1. 80 | Neither. |
| 8576 | 30. 0 | — 21. 3 | 17. 8 | 37. 9 | 25. 91 | 23. 60 | 0. 10 | Copper. |
| 8579 | 63. 3 | — 24. 2 | 17. 0 | 64. 6 | Trace. | 33. 29 | 0. 57 | Tin. |
| 8580 | 60. 3 | — 23. 2 | 17. 0 | 61. 6 | 2. 86 | 32. 62 | 0. 97 | Do. |
| 8582 | 117. 9 | 100. 7 | 17. 0 | 12. 6 | 33. 78 | 26. 51 | 0. 77 | Tin and copper. |
| 8585 | 44. 6 | — 2. 3 | 18. 0 | 34. 7 | 31. 25 | 23. 72 | 3. 43 | Copper. |
| 8588 | 34. 5 | — 20. 9 | 18. 0 | 41. 0 | 27. 47 | 24. 92 | 4. 02 | Do. |
| 8592 | 37. 4 | — 17. 1 | 18. 0 | 40. 4 | 31. 75 | 19. 99 | 3. 74 | Tin. |
| 8597 | 45. 0 | — 15. 9 | 18. 0 | 45. 1 | 19. 68 | 27. 99 | 2. 07 | Copper. |
| 8611 | 40. 2 | — 9. 9 | 17. 6 | 37. 1 | 18. 38 | 27. 35 | 7. 76 | Do. |
| 8612 | 73. 5 | 39. 8 | 18. 0 | 25. 0 | 31. 61 | 23. 67 | 3. 94 | Tin. |
| 8613 | 93. 8 | 66. 4 | 18. 0 | 10. 3 | 27. 17 | 27. 78 | 3. 83 | Do. |
| 8614 | 62. 0 | 36. 3 | 18. 0 | 19. 0 | 30. 03 | 29. 36 | 3. 83 | Copper. |
| 8615 | 37. 4 | — 12. 3 | 17. 0 | 36. 8 | 20. 00 | 29. 14 | 5. 13 | Tin and copper. |
| 8616 | 34. 6 | 33. 7 | 17. 2 | .......... | 5. 15 | 31. 06 | 0. 20 | Not examined. |
| 8617 | 123. 2 | 108. 5 | 17. 0 | .......... | 34. 62 | 24. 28 | 2. 96 | Copper. |
| 8618 | 109. 7 | 90. 0 | 17. 0 | 14. 5 | 33. 11 | 22. 02 | 2. 67 | Tin and copper. |
| 8645 | 60. 6 | — 17. 6 | 22. 0 | 58. 9 | 7. 94 | 30. 43 | 3. 80 | Do. |
| 8646 | 87. 0 | 30. 6 | 22. 4 | 43. 5 | 16. 90 | 28. 80 | 1. 08 | Tin. |
| 8647 | 56. 0 | — 21. 1 | 22. 4 | 58. 5 | 7. 87 | 31. 54 | 0. 37 | Tin and copper. |
| 8648 | 36. 8 | — 12. 6 | 19. 2 | 36. 8 | 34. 24 | 20. 50 | 2. 64 | Do. |
| 8649 | 143. 6 | 136. 0 | 18. 4 | .......... | 38. 17 | 21. 52 | 1. 00 | Copper. |
| 8650 | 37. 8 | — 13. 4 | 21. 2 | 38. 4 | 24. 40 | 24. 52 | 5. 40 | Do.; |
| 8651 | 34. 6 | — 12. 0 | 20. 8 | 34. 9 | 36. 23 | 20. 03 | 3. 57 | Tin. |
| 8652 | 87. 1 | 51. 0 | 20. 8 | 27. 0 | 26. 18 | 20. 92 | 4. 73 | Do. |
| 8653 | 38. 2 | — 16. 4 | 20. 8 | 40. 8 | 31. 25 | 20. 84 | 4. 33 | Copper. |
| 8654 | 149. 6 | 138. 8 | 22. 4 | 8. 1 | 39. 21 | 16. 15 | 1. 18 | Tin. |
| 8655 | 137. 8 | 125. 6 | 20. 2 | 8. 8 | 34. 01 | 25. 55 | 1. 59 | Do. |
| 8656 | 40. 0 | — 14. 1 | 21. 0 | 40. 5 | 29. 32 | 22. 97 | 4. 13 | Neither. |
| 8657 | 37. 6 | — 13. 0 | 21. 0 | 38. 0 | 31. 85 | 25. 29 | 6. 65 | Copper. |
| 8658 | 40. 5 | -- 14. 8 | 19. 8 | 41. 2 | 16. 13 | 25. 88 | 9. 29 | Do. |
| 8659 | 76. 3 | 7. 6 | 18. 6 | 51. 0 | 10. 55 | 31. 91 | 0. 65 | Tin. |
| 8660 | 80. 1 | 51. 3 | 21. 4 | 21. 6 | 41. 32 | 21. 03 | 2. 86 | Copper. |
| 8661 | 61. 7 | — 22. 2 | 30. 2 | 62. 6 | 3. 11 | 33. 18 | 0. 10 | Neither. |
| 8662 | 143. 0 | 134. 2 | 20. 6 | .......... | 41. 15 | 19. 97 | .......... | Tin. |
| 8663 | 40. 0 | — 14. 3 | 20. 8 | 40. 6 | 29. 76 | 18. 66 | 3. 60 | Do. |
| 8665 | 65. 4 | — 21. 4 | 22. 6 | 65. 4 | Trace. | 32. 28 | 2. 06 | Tin. |
| 8666 | 39. 9 | — 14. 2 | 19. 0 | 40. 2 | 27. 85 | 20. 64 | 4. 39 | Tin and copper. |
| 8667 | 82. 6 | 45. 0 | 22. 8 | 28. 3 | 26. 00 | 32. 36 | 4. 44 | Neither. |
| 8668 | 22. 2 | — 21. 2 | 20. 8 | 32. 6 | 23. 50 | 24. 78 | 9. 98 | Tin and copper. |
| 8669 | 36. 6 | — 14. 2 | 19. 2 | 37. 7 | 28. 57 | 23. 63 | 3. 44 | Neither. |
| 8670 | 135. 5 | 124. 5 | 19. 0 | 8. 2 | 35. 46 | 26. 66 | 1. 76 | Do. |
| 8671 | 109. 2 | 87. 4 | 23. 0 | 16. 4 | 35. 70 | 24. 32 | 1. 91 | Tin. |
| 8672 | 38. 3 | — 14. 0 | 20. 0 | 39. 0 | 31. 44 | 18. 44 | 18. 70 | Copper. |
| 8673 | 41. 6 | — 10. 4 | 19. 2 | 38. 7 | 32. 78 | 15. 06 | 3. 00 | Do. |
| 8674 | 41. 2 | — 13. 7 | 19. 0 | 40. 9 | 18. 57 | 23. 59 | 5. 66 | Tin. |
| 8675 | 46. 8 | — 5. 4 | 19. 6 | 38. 9 | 17. 35 | 24. 70 | 6. 70 | Do. |
| 8676 | 50. 4 | — 19. 5 | 21. 8 | 59. 2 | .......... | 32. 83 | .......... | Not examined. |
| 8677 | 77. 9 | 24. 0 | 19. 0 | 40. 1 | .......... | 23. 44 | ...,...... | Tin. |

## REMARKS ON ANALYSES OF MOLASSES AND SIRUPS.

The general remarks which have been made concerning the purchase of samples in the case of sugars apply also to the molasses and sirups. The importance of the examination, however, in the case of molasses and sirups is much greater than with sugars. While it was expected that no adulteration would be found with sugars, it was known that adulteration is largely practiced in the case of molasses; that is, adulteration is practiced if the idea of molasses which is generally entertained is a correct one.

The common notion of molasses or sirup is a product derived wholly from sorghum, sugar cane, or maple sap. The popular idea of an adulterated molasses or sirup would be one made from other materials or compounds than those mentioned. It is true that the word molasses, in a more limited and technical sense, should be applied only to the liquid material draining from granulated cane sugar made from sugar cane, either by natural percolation or by·being treated in centrifugal machines. The commercial term molasses, however, applies to a larger number of products. It includes the molasses made from sorghum, and this is no mean product when the whole country is considered. It is difficult to get accurate estimates of the amount of sorghum molasses made. This product is made chiefly in small one-horse or two-horse mills, with simple evaporating apparatus, and no account of it is taken in commercial transactions. The farmer makes his own molasses from his small plot of sorghum and works up the plots of his neighbors, either on shares or for a certain price per gallon. The uncrystallizable portion of the product of maple orchards is also recognized in the trade as mo· lasses and known as maple molasses or maple sirup.

Perhaps the best distinction to be made between the term molasses and the term sirup is this:

Molasses is the natural product of the manufacture of sugar cane, sorghum, or maple sap, or any product from which a part of the sugar has been removed. Sirup is the product of the refining of these articles or the mixing of various other articles together.

It has long been known that a large part of the maple sirup sold in the market is made from glucose, understanding by this term the liquid product of the conversion of starch into sugar. It is also well known that large quantities of maple sirups are sold on the market which are fabrications made up of other sweets, to which a little maple molasses is added for the purpose of giving it flavor, or, as is often the case, being entirely free from any addition of maple product whatever. The maple flavor is imparted to sirups by mixing with them an extract of hickory bark, and this product has been made and sold under the term of "mapleine." It is safe to say that perhaps the greater quantity of maple molasses or sirup sold on the market is an adulteration in the true sense of the word. These definitions, however, are only of a popular nature, and a sirup could not be said to be adulterated, legally, unless some statute is enacted establishing a standard by which these products could be judged.

For the purposes of this report a molasses or sirup is adulterated whenever it contains glucose or any other substance which would not be a natural product of sorghum, sugar cane, or the maple tree. Molasses or sirups which are made exclusively of the products of sorghum, sugar cane, and maple sap can not be said to be adulterated in the strict sense of the term, no matter what the method of their preparation may be.

The sugar beet, as is noticed, is excluded from the above list because, in so far as I know, no table sirups of any kind are ever made from the product of the beet. On the other hand, a sirup made from a refined beet sugar could not properly be said to be adulterated. Sirups made from unrefined beet sugar, however, or the molasses resulting from the manufacture of beet sugar, would contain so large a quantity of alkaline materials as to be unfit for the table or for culinary purposes.

It has already been noticed under the head of sugars that a certain brand of sugar placed upon the market, viz, "yellow clarified," is washed in the centrifugal machine with a solution of chloride of tin. This tin would naturally find its way into the molasses, and being of a poisonous nature, its presence in the molasses in any large quantity would be highly objectionable. Molasses, therefore, which is the natural product of the sugar cane, but which contains tin as a result of washing the crystals in the centrifugal with that substance, should be considered adulterated. In looking for tin in a number of instances copper also was found in the molasses. This copper doubtless comes from the copper pans and copper coils used in evaporating the juices and sirups. Its presence being merely accidental it could not be considered as an adulteration. Copper salts are, however, not palatable, and their presence in a molasses or sirup is highly objectionable.

In regard to glucose it may be said that its presence in molasses or sirup is an adulteration unless the article containing it is distinctly so marked. A few years ago, when sugars and molasses were higher priced than they are now, the manufacture of sirups from glucose was very profitable. The price of genuine molasses, however, has at the present day fallen so low as to make the manufacture of glucose for the above purpose much less profitable than before. The advantage of using glucose, nevertheless, is very great aside from its cheapness. It gives to a sirup a fine body and a light color. A molasses or sirup, therefore, made chiefly of glucose and flavored with the refuse molasses of a refinery, makes a very attractive article for table use, in so far as appearance goes. In regard to wholesomeness also it is not possible to condemn glucose. When properly made it is apparently as wholesome an article of diet as cane sugar. In fact the starches which are consumed in our foods are all converted into glucose during the process of digestion. A glucose food, therefore, is a starch food already partially digested. The use of acids in converting the starch into glucose would prove detrimental to health unless they were carefully removed. Glucoses are, therefore, often made with ferments for the purpose of converting the starch into sugar rather than by the use of acids. Diastase is sometimes used for this purpose and other ferments are also employed. At the present time the use of glucose in the manufacture of molasses and sirups can not be said to be a fraud, from a financial point of view, inasmuch as the glucose costs quite as much as the other materials of which the molasses and sirups are made.

By glancing at the tables of analyses it is easy to pick out all those samples of molasses which contain glucose. They are recognized at once by their high right-handed polarization, both before and after inversion. They are also distinguished by the comparatively low quantity of sucrose which they contain.

In regard to the adulteration of maple sirup, large quantities of the sophisticated article have been sold, both under the name of maple sirup and mapleine. This product is manufactured under a patent issued to Josiah Daily, of Madison, Ind., dated July 18, 1882, and reissued February 13, 1883. This process is best described in the words of the patent itself, which follow:

*To all whom it may concern:*

Be it known that I, Josiah Daily, of Madison, in the county of Jefferson and State of Indiana, have invented a new and useful method of flavoring sirups and sugars and other saccharine matter, of which the following is a full, clear, and exact specification:

The object of my invention is to impart to saccharine matter the flavor of maple sirup; and the invention consists in the use of an extract of hickory for giving the desired flavor.

The extract is to be obtained in any convenient manner, such as making a decoction of the hickory bark or wood, or percolating liquid through the same, or drawing off the sap from the tree. The bark or wood of the hickory tree may be ground to facilitate the extraction of its principle and the extract may be made more or less strong by increasing or diminishing the quantity of bark or wood, or by boiling the extract for a longer or shorter time.

In preparing sirups I ordinarily add about three tablespoonfuls of the decoction to a gallon of heated or boiling sirup. Of course, the stronger the extract the less the quantity required for flavoring a given amount of sirup. The sirup may be manufactured from any kind of saccharine matter, or mixture of saccharine matters, or the sirups ordinarily found in the markets may be used. The effect of the extract or decoction is to give to the sirup the flavor of the maple, producing a sirup which can not be distinguished from genuine maple sirup.

The high price of maple sirup, as well as its scarcity throughout the country, renders this improved sirup of great value, since a good substitute for maple sirup is thus produced, which comes within the reach of all.

It is evident that the flavored sirup may be boiled down and a sugar resembling maple sugar in taste may be produced.

In defining the limits of my invention, I would state that I do not claim broadly the use of extracts of the wood or bark of trees for flavoring sirups or sugars, as I am aware that a decoction made from the wood of the maple has been used for the same purpose. The maple, however, belongs to a different genus of tree from that of the hickory, and it is well known that extracts of wood as a rule differ from each other in taste, according to the nature of the tree. I have discovered that the hickory tree will produce the flavor of the maple, and I therefore claim as my invention the use of the hickory extract wherever it may be employed to impart an agreeable flavor.

Having thus described my invention, what I claim, and desire to secure by letters patent, is—

1. The method herein described of flavoring saccharine matter, including sirup and sugar, which consists in treating or impregnating the same with the principle or extract of hickory, as specified.

2. An improved sirup or sugar, consisting of any suitable saccharine matter flavored with an extract of hickory, substantially as described.

JOSIAH DAILY.

Witnesses:
A. G. LYNE,
SOLON C. KEMON.

*Bleaching agents.*—There is a public demand which requires molasses and sirups exposed for sale to be of a light color. This bleaching is accomplished by the use of bone-black, or other agents, which will oxidize and destroy the coloring matters. Among such agents may be mentioned ozone, peroxide of hydrogen, sulphurous acid, metallic sulphites, and sulphuric acid, and other similar agents. The various processes which are offered the public for bleaching purposes, and which are held to be of secret composition, depend for their efficiency on some of the chemicals mentioned above.

From the information which has been received, it is fair to presume that a great deal of the dark centrifugal molasses of Louisiana is subjected to bleaching before mixing or placing on the market. This is well set forth in the letter from Dr. Stubbs, page 640.

In a letter from a large dealer in molasses in Boston, dated March 14, 1892, occurs the following:

We find it very hard work to sell our pure molasses in competition with the stuff that is shipped here by the New Orleans bleachers. The bleaching business is now being tried by parties in New York on foreign molasses. I can readily detect the bleached from the unbleached molasses by the taste; and always after tasting the bleached goods I find the roof of my mouth will begin to peel.

It is claimed by the bleachers that even if the agent used is deleterious to health, it is employed in such small quantities as to be practically harmless. Nevertheless such additions should be prohibited. We did not succeed in getting samples of the bleaching agents for analysis. The secret of their preparation and the method of their use are carefully guarded by the makers and users. Following is a list of the bleaching agents supposed to be most commonly used:

(1) Sulphur fumes; (2) chloride of tin, about 1 ounce of a saturated solution to each barrel of molasses; (3) sulphites and sulphuric acid; (4) sulphite of soda and zinc dust, afterwards oxalic acid to precipitate the zinc.

### NOTES ON THE SEVERAL ANALYSES.

### ANALYSES BY MR. HUSTON.

In the analysis of No. 54, labeled "Pure Vermont Maple Sirup," there is one remarkable fact, viz, that tin is present. The analysis shows only a trace of reducing sugar. A maple sirup should have a considerable quantity of reducing sugar on account of the fact that it is boiled in open pans for a long while, and this tends to convert some of the sucrose into reducing sugar. The high price charged for this sample, however, seems to preclude the possibility of its being an adulterated article. The presence of the green color in its ash is also a troublesome fact. Numbers 59, 60, and 61 are also maple sirups, but, it will be noticed, differ very materially in composition from No. 54. The remark made of No. 60 by Mr. Huston that it was made up from maple sugar and glucose does not seem to be properly borne out by the data given. Mr. Huston, however, failed to report his polarizations, and this makes it difficult to judge in all cases of the nature of the product.

No. 64 is rather a peculiar product claimed to be made from fruit and sugar. The sugar was evidently invert sugar, or else the natural acids of the fruit had almost completely inverted the cane sugar, which might originally have been present in it. The small amount of ash which was present would show that no molasses of any kind had been added to it.

The other samples examined by Mr. Huston are sufficiently described in the analytical data.

### ANALYSES BY MR. NICHOLSON.

The samples were purchased in Lincoln and Omaha. They comprised 9 samples of maple, 18 samples New Orleans, 5 samples of sorghum, and the rest of miscellaneous labels. No. 1706 is labeled " sorghum," but it could not have been a pure sorghum, on account of its low reducing sugar content. It is the custom of certain manufacturers to mix sorghum largely with glucose and sell the product as sorghum or under some other name. In this case, however, such a mixture could not have been made since the polarization before and after inversion shows that no admixture of glucose, which is always strongly dextrogyratory could have been practiced. The analytical data point to an admixture of sugar; but such a compounding would not be practical for commercial purposes. The nature of this sample, therefore, is undetermined by the analysis.

The number of samples containing glucose is 35 or 70 per cent of the total number examined. The glucose used in most instances consisted largely of dextrin, as is shown by the high polarization.

Take for instance No. 1724, labeled golden drip. This sirup is made almost wholly of a glucose exceedingly rich in dextrin. Nos. 1711, 1712, 1720, 1731, 1733, 1738, 1842, and 1746, sold as New Orleans molasses, are all largely adulterated with glucose.

Of the maple sirup, No. 1710 contains no maple product, except a little for flavoring purposes. It is made of a glucose rich in dextrose. Nos. 1743, 1751, 1752, 1753, and 1754, are almost pure glucose, although sold as high-grade maple sirups.

In No. 1745 the analytical data are of little worth on account of the impossibility of securing a sufficient clarification to permit of the polariscopic reading.

In No. 1750 is found almost pure glucose, sold as sorghum.
In the whole series of analyses the reducing sugars appear remarkably low.

ANALYSES BY MR. RISING.

The samples were purchased in Oakland and San Francisco. Of the total number 11 contained glucose or 22 per cent. Fifteen of the samples were labeled "New Orleans molasses." There were no samples of maple sirup.

Of the 15 samples of New Orleans molasses 7 are largely adulterated with glucose. No. 56, labeled extra New Orleans clarified, contains about 50 per cent of glucose.

No. 43, labeled golden sirup, California refinery, shows an anomalous composition. It contains of reducing sugar, sucrose, water, and ash only 57.45 per cent, leaving 42.55 per cent unaccounted for.

No. 46, on the other hand, has 103.67 per cent of the above constituents showing a peculiar composition. On account of the disturbing influence of other bodies present on the rotation produced by the sucrose of the samples the data afforded by the polariscope are not always indicative of the exact quantity of sucrose present. In molasses and sirup it can not be expected that the sum of the other constituents + the sucrose by polarization shall equal 100. It is only where there is a considerable variation, amounting to from 3 to 5 per cent that we are justified in suspecting the addition of some adulterating substance like glucose or invert sugar.

No. 63 shows an abnormal percentage of ash and yet is a sample not highly colored and gives no indication of adulteration. The consumption of large quantities of such a sirup, however, might prove prejudicial to health by reason of the introduction into the stomach of such large quantities of mineral matters.

Nos. 80 and 120 are other samples where a large deficit of solid matter is noticed.

ANALYSES BY M. A. SCOVELL.

Of the whole number of samples examined 19 or 38 per cent were adulterated with glucose. Fifteen of the samples were labeled "New Orleans." None of these were adulterated with glucose but 7 of them contained tin.

No. 41, labeled "New Orleans reboiled," shows an almost perfect inversion of the sucrose either by reboiling or by subsequent fermentation. It gives a left-handed solution in direct polarization.

There are 10 samples of maple sirup. Of these 7 are adulterated with glucose.

Five of the samples are marked sorghum. Of these 3 are adulterated with glucose.

Eighteen of the samples contained tin and one copper.

In all samples containing glucose, its presence is revealed by the high right-handed polarization and by the large quantity of undetermined matter. Glucose has a low factor for the sugars which reduce copper—and nevertheless all reducing sugars are entered as dextrose in the tables. There arises, therefore, a large deficit in total solids when this method of calculation is pursued.

## ANALYSES BY S. P. SHARPLES.

Of the whole number of samples only 8 contained glucose or 16 per cent. This freedom from glucose is doubtless due to the careful food-inspection laws of Massachusetts, the samples having been all bought in Boston and vicinity.

The number of samples labeled New Orleans is 12.

Of the 18 samples of maple sirup only 2 were adulterated with glucose.

Tin was found in only 7 of the samples.

The greater number of the samples appear to be made up of sirups and molasses without adulteration, or else to be made from cane sugar in such a way as to closely resemble the legitimate products.

NOTE BY MR. SHARPLES.—This is a very poor time of year (January, 1891) to get molasses other than New Orleans, as the maple is all last year's and largely made by dissolving maple sugar. The new crop West India molasses has not come into the market yet. New maple and West India will commence to come in in the course of a week or two, now. At present the market is supplied largely from New York.

## ANALYSES BY W. C. STUBBS.

It might be supposed that in New Orleans the practice of adding glucose to molasses would not be followed. The results of the analyses, however, show that this species of adulteration is more largely practiced there than in Boston. Sixteen samples were found mixed with glucose, or 32 per cent. No examination of the samples was made for tin.

Three kinds of molasses made from sugar cane are sold on the New Orleans market. The first of these is the open-kettle sugar molasses, usually of fine color and flavor and rich in sugar. The quantity of this molasses offered on the market diminishes from year to year as the more modern methods of manufacture supplant those heretofore in use. The second and rapidly increasing kind is centrifugal molasses. This product is much inferior in quality to the open-kettle molasses, and when two crops of sugar have been taken from it is little better than "black strap." It is largely used for mixing with glucose. There may be found a very limited supply of a kind of molasses known as *sirop de batterie*, made by boiling the clarified juice almost to the crystallizing point. This kind of molasses is esteemed as a delicacy. It should be made from rather green or inferior canes, so that the sugar it contains will not crystallize. Several samples of this kind of molasses may be found in the table of analyses.

The sugar plantations in Louisiana usually have a special name, and the sirups and sugars coming therefrom bear the name of the planta- tion. The names of many of these plantations will be found in the description of samples.

### ANALYSES BY SHIPPEN WALLACE.

A general description of the samples will be found in Mr. Wallace's letter of transmittal. It is a matter of regret that a fuller description of the samples was not furnished. The failure to detect tin in any of the samples suggests the remark that much depends on the delicacy of the tests applied. In the samples, for instance, examined in the De- partment laboratory, a trace of copper or tin was found in almost every instance, but in such minute quantities as to have easily escaped any quantitative determinations.

Of the whole number 31 were adulterated with glucose, being 62 per cent.

No samples of maple molasses were purchased. In the number of adulterated samples the contrast between Boston and Philadelphia is quite striking.

### ANALYSES BY H. A. WEBER.

Of the whole number of samples 23 contained glucose. These are indicated in the table of analyses by the percentage of dextrin which they contain. No molasses made from sugar cane would contain more than a trace of dextrin.

There are 15 samples of New Orleans molasses, only 4 of which are adulterated with glucose.

In 15 samples of maple sirup are found 4 adulterated with glucose.

Twenty-six of the samples were found to contain tin, and in most cases a quantitative determination of it was made. The detection of small quantities of metallic oxides in the ash of molasses by Mr. Weber quite corroborates our own experience.

### ANALYSES BY F. G. WIECHMANN.

Of the 50 samples of molasses and sirups analyzed, 20 consist of or unquestionably contain starch sirup (glucose), viz, Nos. 53, 54, 55, 56, 58, 59, 61, 62, 66, 69, 71, 77, 78, 79, 82, 86, 88, 92, 99, and 100; that is to say, 40 per cent of the samples analyzed are adulterated with glucose.

Tin was found in 18 of the 50 samples; in Nos. 52, 56, 57, 58, 61, 64, 72, 75, 78, 80, 84, 85, 86, 89, 92, 96, 99, and 100. This corresponds to 36 per cent.

Samples Nos. 51, 69, 75, 96, and 97 give a purple-red color on addi- tion of concentrated hydrochloric acid. This color is turned into a green on adding ammonia to alkalinity.

With basic acetate of lead the precipitate obtained is of a "Nile- green" color.

Press of work has prevented my isolating and positively identifying this coloring matter or matters.

Charles E. Cassal, in a paper on "Dyed sugars," read before the Society of Public Analysts in July, 1890,* states that certain sugars examined by him were dyed with tropæolin dyes—phosphine or chrysaniline. As the reactions with acid and alkalis which he there describes are identical with those which I obtained in the samples enumerated above, it seems most probable that these samples also have been treated with these dyestuffs, or that at least the sugars from which they are derived received such treatment.

Twenty-four of the samples were sold as "New Orleans molasses." Of this number 16, or 66.7 per cent, were adulterated with glucose. This shows the enormous extent to which mixing is practiced. One barrel of genuine open-kettle molasses may be made to do duty as 5 or 6 barrels of best New Orleans sirup.

## ANALYSES BY CHEMICAL DIVISION, U. S. DEPARTMENT OF AGRICULTURE.

Low-grade bulk molasses and sirups comprised most of the samples bought, but a few maple and other bottled sirups were procured. Polarizations were made as indicated under sugars. Boneblack was of necessity occasionally used, especially with invert solutions. A small pinch of the moist black was placed in the point of a small filter and about 50 per cent of the filtered solutions poured through in small portions and then thrown away. The residue was then passed through. This second filtrate was then used for polarization. Glucose was determined by titration, using Violette's solution.

To determine water a flat platinum dish, containing a little glass stirring rod, was tared, a portion of the molasses weighed in, and 2 or 3 cc of alcohol added and rubbed up to a paste with it. About a gram of acid-washed ignited kieselguhr was then weighed in from a weighing bottle, and the whole put to dry in a steam-heated bath, kept at a temperature of 100° for three hours, then into an air bath heated to 105° till constant weight was attained.

Ash was determined in another portion, using a porcelain crucible. For the detection of heavy metals about 50 grams of molasses were placed in a porcelain crucible, covered with sulphuric acid, and burned to whiteness in a muffle. The ash was dissolved in hot hydrochloric acid, the solution diluted, filtered, and hydrogen sulphide passed through. Any precipitate formed was collected on a paper filter, which was dried and burned in a porcelain crucible. The ash was fused with potassic cyanide, the melt rubbed up in an agate mortar, and examined with a lens for indications of metals. Such beads as were found were extremely minute.

---

Thirty-two of the samples contained traces of tin, 19 traces of copper, and 3 were not tested for these metals. In most cases only a small quantity of the metals was found; not enough to threaten the health of the consumer.

Many of the samples contained large quantities of ash, in one instance reaching 9.29 per cent for the sulphated ash.

Twenty-five samples of sirup were bought in Washington and 32 in Baltimore. Of these, 14 of the Washington samples (Nos. 8560, 8561, 8562, 8568, 8569, 8575, 8582, 8585, 8612, 8613, 8614, 8616, 8617, and 8618) gave evidence of the presence of commercial glucose or starch sugar. Of the 32 Baltimore samples, 13 contained glucose (Nos. 8646, 8649, 8652, 8654, 8655, 8659, 8660, 8662, 8667, 8670, 8671, 8675, and 8677.) Of the 57 samples examined, 27, or 47.3 per cent, showed the presence of glucose.

Eleven of these samples were sold as maple sirups (Nos. 8572, 8573, 8579, 8580, 8645, 8646, 8647, 8559, 8665, 8667, and 8677). Four showed evidence of glucose (Nos. 8646, 8650, 8659, and 8667). Nine samples were sold as New Orleans molasses or sirup (Nos. 8561, 8576, 8588. 8597, 8613, 8618, 8653, 8656, and 8658). Three of these (Nos. 8561, 8613, and 8618) had been let down with starch sirup. Two samples were sold as Porto Rico (Nos. 8560 and 8614); both contained glucose, Two samples (Nos. 8615 and 8668) were sold as "black strap." Neither contained glucose. A sample called "vanilla sirup" (No. 8562), 1 of "Golden Eagle" (No. 8545), 1 of "honey sirup" (No. 8569), 1 of "crystal sirup" (No. 8617), and 1 of "strawberry sirup" (No. 8616) were found to contain glucose. Seven samples called "golden drips" and "golden sirup" (Nos. 8566, 8568, 8585, 8592, 8648, 8649, and 8657) were tried and 3 (Nos. 8568, 8585, and 8649) were found to contain glucose. Two samples of "bright sirup" (Nos. 8611 and 8612) both contained glucose. A sample called "sugar-house sirup" (No. 8672) contained no starch sugar. Two samples (Nos. 8650 and 8671) were called "second-grade sirup." One (No. 8671) contained starch sirup. A sample of "best sirup" (No. 8651) contained none. A sample called "No. 3 sirup" (No. 8655), 1 called "No. 6 sirup" (No. 8654), 1 put up in a fancy bottle and called "queen sirup" (No. 8660), and a sample called "corn sirup" (No. 8662) consisted almost entirely of starch sirup. A sample of "No. 1 sirup" (No. 8675) contained a slight admixture, Two samples of "rock-candy sirup" (Nos. 8661 and 8676) were free from starch sugar. Three samples of "sugar sirup" (Nos. 8663, 8673, and 8674) were free from admixture. One sample (No. 8582), containing starch sugar, was called "sugar sirup," and another (No. 8570), likewise containing glucose, was called "sugar drips." Two samples (Nos. 8652 and 8666) were called simply sirups, one of which (No. 8652) contained glucose. "Revere sirup" (No. 8669) contained no starch sugar.

# CONFECTIONS.

## ANALYSES BY H. A. HUSTON.

### Description of samples.

| No. | Bought of— | Price per pound. | Manufacturer. | Remarks. | Name. | Color. |
|---|---|---|---|---|---|---|
| 151 | Chas. H. Slack, Chicago, Ill. | $0.15 | Chas. H. Slack. | ................... | Lime drops ... | Light greenish. |
| 152 | ....do ........... | .15 | ....do ....... | ................... | Iceland moss . | Light red. |
| 153 | ....do ........... | .15 | ....do ......... | Contains ultramarine. | Ribbon candy. | Green and red |
| 154 | ...:do ........... | .15 | ....do ........ | ................... | White candy.. | None. |
| 155 | ....do ........... | .15 | ... do ......... | ................... | Red candy.... | Reddish brown. |
| 156 | J. S. Ewry & Co., La Fayette. | (*) | ................ | In sticks of different colors. | Boston bean blowers. | Brown yellow. |
| 157 | ....do ........... | .125 | ................ | This grade candy is usually made by reboiling stale candy. | Horehound ... | Brown. |
| 158 | ....do ........... | (*) | ................ | Sample dry and stale; insoluble matter mostly starch and flour. | Marshmallow jelly roll. | Yellow. |
| 159 | ....do ........... | (*) | ................ | Sample dry and stale. | Marshmallow banana. | Pink. |
| 160 | ...do ........... | .125 | ................ | ................... | Broken taffy.. | Pink yellow. |
| 161 | Fred. Hetz, Indianapolis. | .30 | Fred. Hetz..... | ................... | Butter cups... | Red yellow. |
| 162 | Daggett & Co., Indianapolis. | .15 | Daggett & Co.. | .......... ......... | Derby candy.. | Pink and yellow, blue violet. |
| 163 | ....do ........... | .20 | . do ....... | ................... | Creams ....... | White, violet, pink. |
| 164 | Fred. Hetz, Indianapolis. | .30 | Fred. Hetz..... | ................... | Cherry creams | White. |
| 165 | Carter, Indianapolis. | .40 | Carter ......... | ................... | Peppermint creams. | Do. |
| 166 | ....do ........... | .20 | ................ | ................... | Clear candy... | Transparent. |
| 167 | G. R. Wysong. & Co., Indianapolis. | .30 | G. R. Wysong & Co. | ................... | Superior mix . | Pink, yellow, brown red. |
| 168 | Craig, Indianapolis. | .50 | Craig ......... | ................... | Pistach dips . | Pale green. |
| 169 | ....do ........... | .50 | ....do ........ | ................... | Raspberry dips. | Pink. |
| 170 | ...do ........... | .50 | ....do ......... | ................... | Violet dips ... | Violet. |
| 171 | Mnssick, Maxwell & Co., Indianapolis. | .15 | M. M. & Co.... | Offensive odor .... | Machine cuts. | Red and yellow. |
| 172 | ....do ........... | .30 | ....do ......... | ................... | Conversation lozenges. | Pink, yellow, salmon, white. |
| 173 | J. S. Ewry & Co., La Fayette. | (*) | ................ | ................... | Stick candy... | Red. |
| 174 | ....do ........... | .20 | ................ | ................... | Mint lozenges | White. |
| 175 | ...do ........... | .40 | ................ | ................... | Musk lozenges | Pink. |
| 176 | ....do ........... | .30 | ................ | Contains ultramarine. | Blue sugar sand. | Blue. |

* Penny goods.

720

*Analytical data.*

| No. | Polarization. Direct. | In-direct. | Temperature °C. | Sucrose. | Reducing sugars. | Water. | Ash. | Insoluble in cold water. | Coloring matter. |
|---|---|---|---|---|---|---|---|---|---|
|  |  |  |  | Per ct. | Per cent. | Per ct. | Per ct. | Per cent. |  |
| 151 |  |  |  | 80.11 | 19.13 | 0.32 | 0.04 | 0.11 | Organic. |
| 152 |  |  |  | 87.40 | 10.25 | 0.45 | 0.10 | 0.14 | Do. |
| 153 |  |  |  | 84.61 | 13.84 | 0.60 | 0.14 | .0.33 | Mineral and organic. |
| 154 |  |  |  | 81.46 | 13.00 | 0.64 | 0.31 | 2.34 | Organic. |
| 155 |  |  |  | 81.06 | 16.23 | 0.53 | 0.38 | 1.20 | Do. |
| 156 |  |  |  | 93.24 | 6.91 | 0.14 | 0.11 | 0.98 | Do. |
| 157 |  |  |  | 80.91 | 14.33 | 0.84 | 0.66 | 2.10 | Do. |
| 158 |  |  |  | 11.94 | 20.31 | 2.11 | 2.44 | 44.84 | Do. |
| 159 |  |  |  | 68.10 | 12.44 | 3.64 | 0.28 | 16.29 | Do. |
| 160 |  |  |  | 77.08 | 17.38 | 2.44 | 0.25 | 0.46 | Do. |
| 161 |  |  |  | 74.04 | 19.04 | 4.22 | 0.21 | 0.59 | Do. |
| 162 |  |  |  | 79.75 | 18.28 | 0.47 | 0.12 | Trace. | Do. |
| 163 |  |  |  | 75.52 | 17.08 | 8.06 | 0.35 | Trace. | Do. |
| 164 |  |  |  | 82.33 | 8.88 | 5.11 | Trace. | 2.00 | Do. |
| 165 |  |  |  | 92.20 | Trace. | 8.08 | 0.02 | Trace. | None. |
| 166 |  |  |  | 88.58 | 10.52 | 0.05 | 0.04 | Trace. | Do. |
| 167 |  |  |  | 80.44 | 11.54 | 6.03 | 0.01 | Trace. | Do. |
| 168 |  |  |  | 90.68 | 2.54 | 7.11 | 0.21 | 0.00 | Organic. |
| 169 |  |  |  | 91.97 | 0.83 | 6.62 | 0.13 | 0.00 | Do. |
| 170 |  |  |  | 85.76 | 3.97 | 10.28 | 0.07 | 0.00 | Do. |
| 171 |  |  |  | 88.56 | 10.52 | 1.93 | 0.04 | 0.00 | Do. |
| 172 |  |  |  | 80.14 | 8.69 | 0.08 | 0.03 | 12.44 | Do. |
| 173 |  |  |  | 68.79 | 26.49 | 0.18 | 1.64 | 2.38 | Do. |
| 174 |  |  |  | 44.49 | 13.08 | 0.84 | 1.41 | 21.44 | Do. |
| 175 |  |  |  | 8.34 | 44.23 | 0.49 | 2.10 | 34.40 | Do. |
| 176 |  |  |  | 92.10 | 00.00 | 0.04 | 6.99 | 7.44 | Mineral. |

ANALYSES BY H. H. NICHOLSON.

*Description of samples.*

| No. | Bought of— | Manufacturer. | Label. |
|---|---|---|---|
| 1806 | J. J. Miller, Omaha | | Stick Candy. |
| 1807 | ......do | | Rock Candy. |
| 1808 | Dalzells, Omaha | | Do. |
| 1809 | ......do | | Musk Candy. |
| 1810 | Anderson & Co., Beatrice | | Cream Drops (pink). |
| 1811 | William Fleming & Co., Omaha | | Vanilla Drops. |
| 1812 | ......do | | Cream Hearts. |
| 1813 | H. Schonberger, Omaha *a* | | White Candy. |
| 1814 | Reynolds & Grant, Omaha *b* | | Gum Drops. |
| 1815 | ......do | | Red Candy. |
| 1816 | ......do *c* | | |
| 1817 | D. A. Williams, Lincoln | | Jelly Beans, red. |
| 1818 | E. H, Jenkins, Lincoln | | Strawberry Cream. |

*a* Nothing could be done with sample.
*b* Gum coated with sugar; no results.
*c* Sample gave out; no inversion possible.

*Description of samples—Continued.*

| No. | Bought of— | Manufacturer. | Label. |
|---|---|---|---|
| 1819 | William Hotaling, Lincoln *a* | | Apricot Slices. |
| 1820 | G. H. Poehler, Lincoln | | Red Jelly Beans. |
| 1821 | ......do | | Green Jelly Beans. |
| 1822 | C. H. Rohman, Lincoln | | Red Wintergreen Drops. |
| 1823 | O. J. King, Lincoln | | Dewdrops, orange flavor. |
| 1824 | ......do | | Wintergreen. |
| 1825 | F. P. Folsom, Lincoln | F. P. Folsom | Stock Candy. |
| 1826 | ......do | ......do | Letters. |
| 1827 | ......do | ......do | Royal Wintergreen. |
| 1828 | ......do *b* | ......do | Banana. |
| 1829 | ......do | ......do | Tropic Fruit (green). |
| 1830 | ......do | ......do | Tropic Fruit (red). |

*a* Gum coated with sugar; no results.
*b* Nothing could be done with sample.

*Analytical data.*

| No. | Polarization. | | Tem-pera-ture °C. | Su-crose. | Reducing sugars. | Water. | Ash. | Insoluble in cold water. | Coloring matter. |
|---|---|---|---|---|---|---|---|---|---|
| | Direct. | In-direct. | | | | | | | |
| | | | | Per ct. | Per cent. | Per ct. | Per ct. | Per cent. | |
| 1806 | 10.4 | — 4.3 | 11 | 10.6 | 9.56 | 2.33 | 0.62 | No residue.. | Organic. |
| 1807 | 12.9 | 19.4 | 14 | | 7.54 | 8.12 | 0.14 | .. do ....... | Do. |
| 1808 | 101.7 | —38.4 | 13 | 101.9 | Traces. | 8.06 | 0.10 | ....do ....... | Do. |
| 1809 | 111.6 | — 5.8 | 13 | 85.4 | 6.16 | 1.25 | 0.16 | Starch and gum. | Do. |
| 1810 | 111.6 | — 4.8 | 14.5 | 85.1 | 5.76 | 3.38 | 0.19 | ....do ....... | Do. |
| 1811 | 111.9 | — 7.5 | 14 | 87.2 | 5.79 | 1.55 | 0.24 | No residue . | Do. |
| 1812 | 101.4 | —11.3 | 12.5 | 81.8 | 5.81 | 8.55 | 0.15 | Starch ...... | Do. |
| 1813 | 107.0 | | | | | 8.37 | 0.48 | ....do ....... | Do. |
| 1814 | | | | | | 22.78 | 0.30 | Starch and gum. | Do. |
| 1815 | 119.1 | 15.9 | 13 | 75.1 | 11.50 | 3.95 | 0.27 | No residue . | Do. |
| 1816 | 84.6 | | | | | 4.06 | 1.07 | ....do ....... | Do. |
| 1817 | 114.5 | 1.6 | 12 | 81.8 | 7.62 | 2.01 | 0.14 | ....do ....... | Organic and fluorescent. |
| 1818 | 104.3 | — 6.5 | 16 | 81.4 | 5.73 | 12.70 | 0.20 | ....do ....... | Organic. |
| 1819 | | | | | | 13.66 | 0.48 | Starch and gum. | Do. |
| 1820 | 102.0 | 18.1 | 11 | 60.5 | 7.24 | 7.52 | 0.14 | Starch ...... | Do. |
| 1821 | 103.5 | 4.6 | 11 | 71.4 | 8.16 | 4.76 | 0.30 | ....do ....... | Do. |
| 1822 | 109.1 | — 5.3 | 12 | 82.0 | 11.42 | 3.51 | 0.11 | No residue . | Do. |
| 1823 | 74.0 | —34.3 | 12 | 79.8 | 7.06 | 6.42 | 0.34 | ....do ....... | Do. |
| 1824 | 80.1 | —35.3 | 14 | 84.3 | 14.70 | 10.78 | 0.15 | ....do ....... | Do. |
| 1825 | 109.3 | — 7.0 | 11 | 84.0 | 8.06 | 13.85 | 0.30 | ... do ....... | Organic and fluorescent. |
| 1826 | 101.4 | —37.4 | 13 | 100.0 | Traces. | 0.73 | 0.14 | ....do ....... | Organic. |
| 1827 | 100.5 | 7.3 | 13 | 67.7 | 8.40 | 11.98 | 0.17 | Starch ...... | Do. |
| 1828 | | | | | 8.22 | 3.47 | 0.50 | ...do ....... | Do. |
| 1829 | 94.0 | — 0.8 | 11 | 69.7 | 10.52 | 3.28 | 0.12 | ....do ....... | Do. |
| 1830 | 109.2 | 3.1 | 11.5 | 76.7 | 11.42 | 6.04 | 0.10 | No residue . | Do. |

## ANALYSES BY W. B. RISING.

### Description of samples.

| No. | Label. | Where bought. | Price per pound. |
|---|---|---|---|
| 108 | Broken, mixed.............. | Bruning Bros., 7th and Washington, Oakland........... | $0.25 |
| 109 | Peppermint Drops.......... | Pacific Candy Factory, Oakland........................ | .25 |
| 110 | Stick candy........:........ | W. Braetle, 970 Washington street, Oakland............ | .20 |
| 111 | Wintergreen Drops......... | ......do ............................................... | .20 |
| 112 | Gum Drops................. | Anderson & Co., 467 7th street, Oakland ................ | .10 |
| 113 | Flat stick ................... | Pacific Candy Factory, Oakland ...................... | .20 |
| 114 | Broken, mixed.............. | Standeford & Co., 458 7th street, Oakland.............. | .12½ |
| 115 | ......do ...................... | Anderson & Co., 467 7th street, Oakland .............. | .12½ |
| 116 | Stick ...................... | Standeford & Co., 7th street, Oakland ................ | .20 |
| 117 | Chips....................... | Bruning Bros., 7th street, Oakland...................... | .25 |
| 118 | Molasses................... | Bacon & Co., Broadway and 10th, Oakland .............. | .20 |
| 177 | Stick ...................... | San Francisco Candy Factory, East street.............. | .20 |
| 178 | ......do .................... | San Francisco Candy Factory, East street .............. | .20 |
| 179 | Jelly Beans .................. | ......do .............................................. | .15 |
| 180 | Lemon Drops................. | ......do .............................................. | .20 |
| 181 | Stick molasses.............. | Peratta and 16th streets, Oakland ...................... | .15 |
| 182 | Mixed ..................... | Schaefer's, Mission, near 18th street, San Francisco .... | .20 |
| 183 | Marbles ..................... | ......do ..................................... .......... | .15 |
| 184 | Mixed ..................... | J. N. Postag, 2122 Mission street, San Francisco ......... | .20 |
| 185 | Lemon Drops ................. | ......do .............................................. | .20 |
| 186 | Mixed ...................... | Jessie and 19th streets, San Francisco ................... | .15 |
| 187 | Mixed broken ....:.......... | Schaefer's, Mission, near 18th street, San Francisco..... | .15 |
| 188 | Chewing Candy.............. | ......do .............................................. | .15 |
| 189 | Hoarhound.................. | Mission and 17th streets, San Francisco................. | .15 |
| 190 | Cinnamon Chewing.......... | ......do .............................................. | .15 |

### Analytical data.

| No. | Polarization. | | Tempera-ture° C. | Sucrose. | Reducing sugars. | Water. | Ash. | Insoluble in cold water. | Coloring matter. |
|---|---|---|---|---|---|---|---|---|---|
| | Direct. | Indirect. | | | | | | | |
| | | | | Per cent. | Per cent. | Per cent. | Per ct. | Per cent. | |
| 108 | 97.8 | 24.53 | ........ | 39.00 | 17.24 | 7.10 | 1.24 | 0.90 | White, brown. |
| 109 | 107.4 | 49.28 | ........ | 71.90 | 17.20 | 4.13 | 0.48 | 5.63 | White. |
| 110 | 105.5 | — 4.40 | ........ | 80.50 | 8.70 | 2:71 | 0.48 | 13.80 | Red. |
| 111 | 94.4 | — 23.50 | ........ | 86.30 | 2.70 | 2.07 | 0.11 | 0.29 | White. |
| 112 | 133.0 | 114.80 | ........ | 13.30 | 19.60 | 5.53 | 0.28 | 3.80 | White, red. |
| 113 | 105.8 | 0.00 | ........ | 77.20 | 9.20 | 3.79 | 0.20 | 0.29 | Yellow, white. |
| 114 | 85.0 | — 31.30 | ........ | 85.20 | 10.10 | 3.92 | 0.16 | 0.05 | Various, red, yellow, green. |
| 115 | 83.0 | — 28.60 | ........ | 82.20 | 11.50 | 2.63 | 0.15 | 0.30 | Do. |
| 116 | 98.0 | — 4.40 | ........ | 75.00 | 14.10 | 3.51 | 0.15 | 0.10 | Do. |
| 117 | 80.4 | — 12.30 | ........ | 68.00 | 3.00 | 3.77 | 0.32 | 1.40 | Brown. |
| 118 | 105.8 | 20.30 | ........ | 62.50 | 11.40 | 2.87 | 0.12 | 2.60 | Do. |
| 177 | 99.1 | — 4.84 | ........ | 76.10 | 5.49 | 1.66 | 0.09 | 0.003 | Yellow. |
| 178 | 101.4 | 0.70 | ........ | 73.70 | 9.40 | 3.85 | 0.06 | 0.01 | Red. |
| 179 | 107.9 | 25.00 | ........ | 59.00 | 11.90 | 2.55 | 0.22 | 4.56 | Green. |
| 180 | 77.8 | — 30.58 | ........ | 79.20 | 10.70 | 3.59 | 0.07 | 0.21 | Yellow. |
| 181 | 95.0 | — 18.48 | ........ | 56.10 | 19.60 | 3.14 | 0.72 | 0.02 | Various. |
| 182 | 100.4 | — 1.54 | ........ | 74.60 | 10.50 | 3.04 | 0.14 | 0.53 | Do. |
| 183 | 91.2 | — 27.94 | ........ | 87.30 | 0.18 | 0.84 | 0.21 | 3.22 | White. |

*Analytical data—Continued.*

| No. | Polarization. Direct. | Polarization. Indirect. | Tem- pera- ture° C | Sucrose. | Reducing sugars. | Water. | Ash. | Insoluble in cold water. | Coloring matter. |
|---|---|---|---|---|---|---|---|---|---|
| | | | | Per cent. | Per cent. | Per cent. | Per ct. | Per cent. | |
| 184 | 107.6 | 4.73 | ........ | 75.00 | 7.94 | 3.48 | 0.20 | 0.00 | Various. |
| 185 | 76.0 | — 30.14 | ........ | 77.40 | 13.17 | 3.70 | 0.06 | 0.01 | Yellow. |
| 186 | 105.5 | — 6.80 | ........ | 82.00 | 7.52 | 3.84 | 0.15 | 6.64 | Various. |
| 187 | 74.8 | — 35.14 | ........ | 78.20 | 12.00 | 4.52 | 0.05 | 0.03 | Do. |
| 188 | 102.8 | 35.20 | ........ | 49.50 | 4.52 | 6.12 | 1.28 | 7.50 | Red. |
| 189 | 94.1 | — 29.70 | ........ | 90.00 | 5.49 | 1.20 | 0.04 | 0.52 | Brown. |
| 190 | 87.3 | 18.70 | ........ | 50.40 | 10.16 | 5.52 | 0.10 | 0.58 | Yellow. |

*Composition of insoluble residue.*

| No. | Organic portion. | Inorganic portion. |
|---|---|---|
| 108 | Grease, starch ..................................... | Sodium chloride. |
| 109 | ......do ............................................... | |
| 110 | Starch ................................................ | |
| 111 | ......do ............................................... | |
| 112 | Gelatin ............................................... | |
| 113 | Coloring matter, nuts .............................. | |
| 114 | Coloring matter, starch ........................... | |
| 115 | Grease, starch ...................................... | |
| 116 | Grease, coloring matter............................ | |
| 117 | Grease, starch ...................................... | |
| 118 | ......do ............................................... | |
| 177 | Grease................................................ | |
| 178 | Grease, starch ...................................... | |
| 179 | Gelatin ............................................... | |
| 180 | Grease ............................................... | |
| 181 | Grease, starch ...................................... | |
| 182 | Coloring matter, starch ........................... | |
| 183 | Starch ................................................ | |
| 184 | ......do............................................... | |
| 185 | Grease............ .................................. | |
| 186 | Grease, starch ...................................... | |
| 187 | ......do ............................................... | |
| 188 | ......do ............................................... | Calcium carbonate. |
| 189 | ......do ............................................... | |
| 190 | ......do............................................... | |

## ANALYSES BY M. A. SCOVELL.

*Description of candies.*

Sample 151. Mint Lozenges, white; made by John Perkins, Cincinnati, Ohio. Sold by Henry Huneke & Co., Cincinnati, Ohio.

Sample 152. Mixed Creams, pink, red, white, and yellow; made by John Perkins, Cincinnati, Ohio. Sold by Henry Huneke & Co., Cincinnati, Ohio.

Sample 153. Stick Candy, striped with red, not colored on inside of stick; made by J. W. Lell, Lexington, Ky. Sold by Norris & Son, Lexington, Ky.

Sample 154. Cinnamon Stick, solid red on outside of stick, not colored inside; made by J. W. Lell, Lexington, Ky. Sold by Henry Vogt, Lexington, Ky.

Sample 155. Peppermint, red; made by J. W. Lell. Sold by Henry Vogt, Lexington, Ky.

Sample 156. Decorated Creams, yellow, blue, pink, red, purple, brown, and white. Bought by Norris & Son, of Thurber, Whyland & Co., New York. Bought of Norris & Son, Lexington, Ky.

Sample 157. Pink Lozenges; made by G. G. Ehrman & Sons, Louisville, Ky. Sold by T. N. McClelland, Lexington, Ky.

Sample 158. Cinnamon Drops, red; made by Rheinhart, Newton & Co., Cincinnati. Sold by Norris & Son, Lexington, Ky.

Sample 159. Peppermint Rings, red; made by G. G. Ehrman & Sons, Louisville, Ky. Sold by T. N. McClelland, Lexington, Ky.

Sample 160. Lemon Drops, straw color; made and sold by Beehive Candy Kitchen, Lexington, Ky.

Sample 161. Lemon Drops; made by G. G. Ehrman & Sons, Louisville, Ky. Sold by by T. N. McClelland, Lexington, Ky.

Sample 162. Fine Candy, bright and dull greens; made by G. G. Ehrman & Sons, Louisville, Ky. Sold by T. N. McClelland, Lexington, Ky.

Sample 163. French Kisses, light red; made and sold by Montgomery & Bailey, Louisville, Ky.

Sample 164. Verdant Squares, light-green and white; made by Hall, Hayward & Co., Louisville, Ky. Sold by Hall, Hayward & Co., Louisville, Ky.

Sample 165. Clove Drops, white, with red center; made and sold by Montgomery & Bailey, Lonisville, Ky.

Sample 166. White Creams; made by Hawley & Hoopes, New York. Sold by Montgomery & Bailey, Louisville, Ky.

Sample 167. Plain mixed, red, yellow, pink, white, straw color; made and sold by Hall, Hayward & Co., Louisville, Ky.

Sample 168. Light-pink Creams; made by Hawley & Hoopes, New York. Sold by Montgomery & Bailey, Louisville, Ky.

Sample 169. Dull-yellow Creams; made by Hawley & Hoopes, New York. Sold by Montgomery & Bailey, Louisville, Ky.

Sample 170. Gem Mixed, white, red-printed; made and sold by Hall, Hayward & Co., Louisville, Ky.

Sample 171. Mixed Creams, purple, red and straw color, and pink; made and sold by Hall, Hayward & Co., Lonisville, Ky.

Sample 172. Gem Creams, white; made and sold by Hall, Hayward & Co., Louisville, Ky.

Sample 173. Maple Caramels; made and sold by Beehive Candy Kitchen, Lexington, Ky.

Sample 174. Strawberry Creams; made by Hawley & Hoopes, New York, and sold by Montgomery & Bailey, Louisville, Ky.

Sample 175. Yellow Creams; made by Hawley & Hoopes, New York, and sold by Montgomery & Bailey, Louisville, Ky.

*Analytical data.*

| No. | Polarization. | | Tempera-ture °C. | Sucrose. | Reducing sugars. | Water. | Ash. | Insoluble in cold water. | Coloring matter. |
|---|---|---|---|---|---|---|---|---|---|
| | Direct. | Indirect. | | | | | | | |
| | | | | Per cent. | Per cent. | Per cent. | Per ct. | Per cent. | |
| 151 | 109.1 | 2.0 | 25.5 | 82.60 | 6.99 | 2.66 | 0.11 | .......... | None. |
| 152 | 103.6 | 1.6 | 25.2 | 80.98 | 6.02 | 3.50 | 0.08 | 0.91 | Organic. |
| 153 | 106.1 | 1.5 | 25.0 | 80.52 | 10.53 | 0.40 | 0.22 | 0.06 | Do. |
| 154 | 107.4 | 4.0 | 25.0 | 80.21 | 10.76 | 3.30 | 0.30 | .......... | Do. |
| 155 | 112.0 | 3.8 | 24.5 | 83.59 | 11.91 | 3.64 | 0.25 | .......... | Do. |

*Analytical data—Continued.*

| No. | Polarization. Direct | Polarization. Indirect. | Temperature °C. | Sacrose. | Reducing sugars. | Water. | Ash. | Insoluble in cold water. | Coloring matter. |
|---|---|---|---|---|---|---|---|---|---|
| | | | | *Per cent.* | *Per cent.* | *Per cent.* | *Per ct.* | *Per cent.* | |
| 156 | 106.4 | — 4.6 | 25.0 | 85.51 | 9.09 | 1.58 | 0.05 | .......... | Organic. |
| 157 | { 81.6 | — 29.5 | 24.0 | 87.65 | 10.42 | 4.42 | 0.15 | .......... | }Cochineal. |
| | { 85.0 | — 29.3 | 25.0 | 87.99 | 10.53 | 4.72 | 0.15 | .......... | |
| 158 | 110.4 | 0.7 | 25.4 | 84.28 | 8.20 | 1.46 | 0.15 | ........ .. | Eosin. |
| 159 | 96.4 | — 11.9 | 25.1 | 83.37 | 11.75 | 3.93 | 0.09 | .......... | Cochineal. |
| 160 | 73.2 | — 20.0 | 25.0 | 78.67 | 22.22 | 0.39 | 0.15 | .......... | None. |
| 161 | 91.0 | — 15.8 | 25.8 | 82.47 | 13.16 | 3.15 | 0.07 | .......... | Do. |
| 162 | 80.8 | — 15.2 | 21.8 | 78.47 | 11.36 | 2.64 | 0.11 | .......... | Organic. |
| 163 | 110.4 | 8.6 | 25.2 | 78.42 | 11.49 | 2.71 | 0.13 | .......... | Cochineal. |
| 164 | 100.8 | — 0.2 | 23.0 | 77.74 | 9.43 | 2.88 | 0.06 | .......... | Organic. |
| 165 | 103.8 | — 4.5 | 24.8 | 83.31 | 8.93 | 4.00 | 0.12 | .......... | Cochineal. |
| 166 | 107.4 | 7.0 | 25.6 | 77.40 | 8.69 | 2.50 | 0.11 | 0.10 | None. |
| 167 | 111.4 | 8.2 | 25.2 | 79.51 | 10.00 | 2.89 | 0.18 | .......... | Organic. |
| 168 | 100.4 | 5.9 | 25.2 | 77.43 | 9.80 | 2.41 | 0.12 | .......... | Cochineal. |
| 169 | 106.0 | 4.0 | 25.2 | 78.58 | 8.85 | 2.70 | 0.15 | ........ | Organic. |
| 170 | 100.0 | 1.7 | 26.0 | 75.96 | 6.25 | 3.49 | 0.14 | 12.40 | Do. |
| 171 | 98.4 | — 1.5 | 24.4 | 76.73 | 10.10 | 3.05 | 0.07 | .......... | Organic; some eosin. |
| 172 | 101.0 | 0.8 | 25.0 | 77.13 | 9.80 | 2.56 | 0.05 | .......... | None. |
| 173 | 91.2 | 12.1 | 24.0 | 60.66 | 11.60 | 3.85 | 0.88 | 13.57 | Do. |
| 174 | 104.6 | — 2.7 | 24.2 | 82.35 | 7.14 | 0.94 | 0.12 | .......... | Organic. |
| 175 | 107.6 | 6.0 | 25.2 | 77.81 | 9.60 | . 2.56 | 0.12 | .......... | Do. |

## ANALYSES BY S. P. SHARPLES.

*Description of sample.*

| No. | Price per pound. | Bought of— | Character. |
|---|---|---|---|
| 9551 | $0.16 | Cobb, Bates & Yerxa, Dock square, Boston, Mass. | Colored sugar. Colored with a red coal-tar color. |
| 9552 | .25 | M. A. Williams, Tremont street, Boston, Mass. | Molasses chips; of a bright-yellow color and very crisp. |
| 9553 | .10 | Italian street stand, Winter street, Boston, Mass. | Molasses candy. This candy was purchased of a fakir on the street. It looked well when first bought, but in the room softened and ran into a solid mass. It had a light-yellow color and contained a little flour and some grease. |
| 9554 | .20 | Wm. West, Washington street, Boston, Mass. | Stick candy. This was a white stick candy with a bright-red covering, which appeared to be colored with a coal-tar color. |
| 9555 | .20 | Hausman & Cook, 2167 Washington street, Roxbury, Mass. | Pipe candy. Colored with vegetable colors. |
| 9556 | .20 | C. F. Belcher, Cambridge, Mass. | Broken candy. Colored with vegetable colors. |
| 9557 | .15 | Egerton, Bowdoin square, Boston, Mass. | Broken candy. This candy was strongly flavored with peppermint and other oils. These oils seem to have a decided influence on the polarization; they are not removed by the acetate of lead, |

*Description of sample—*Continued.

| No. | Price per pound | Bought of— | Character. |
|---|---|---|---|
| 9558 | $0.13 | Yerxa & Yerxa, Cambridgeport, Mass. | Broken candy. |
| 0559 | ........ | Cobb Bros., Hanover street, Boston, Mass. | Mixed candy |
| 9560 | .20 | C. F. Belcher, Cambridge, Mass. | Do. |
| 9561 | .25 | J. Savezzo, 91 Warren street, Roxbury, Mass. | Red cinnamon drops. Colored a bright crimson with cochineal or carmine. |
| 9562 | .20 | C. D. Cobb & Bros., Hanover street, Boston, Mass. | Mixed candy. |
| 9563 | .12 | J. S. Bampton, 2271 Washington street, Boston, Mass. | Mixed soft candy; some starch. |
| 9564 | .10 | Italian street-stand, Winter street, Boston, Mass. | Do. |
| 9565 | .35 | Cobb Brothers, Boston, Mass ..... | Soft candy; yellow, vegetable color. |
| 9563 | .20 | E. S. Gilmore, 29 Main street, Charlestown, Mass. | Mixed candy. |
| 9567 | .12 | C. D. Cobb & Bros., Hanover street, Boston, Mass. | Mixed motto candy. The above were cheap loz- enges; they contained some gum and starch. |
| 9568 | .20 | M. Cashin, Clark street, Boston, Mass. | Lozenges; these contained considerable starch; they were not very soluble in water, and the so- lution after the addition of acetate of lead was very difficult to filter. |
| 0569 | .25 | J. Savezzo, 91 Warren street, Roxbury, Mass. | Lozenges; contained starch. |
| 9570 | .15 | M. M. Hirsche, 2019 Washington street, Boston, Mass. | Motto Lozenges. |
| 9571 | .40 | E. Babb, 97 Warren street, Roxbury, Mass. | Tablets marked "Cream;" contained some starch. |
| 9572 | .20 | J. M. Sond, 2334 Washington street, Roxbury, Mass. | Motto Hearts; contained starch. |
| 9573 | .35 | M. Cashin, Clark street, Boston, Mass. | Pink Lozenges; these were colored with eosin. The color was not removed by lead acetate, but readily yielded to bone char. It gave the pink color and fluorescence of eosin. |
| 0574 | .40 | Car station, Bartlett and Washington streets, Roxbury, Mass. | Pink Tablets marked "Musk;" contained consid- erable starch; colored with cochineal and fla- vored with musk. |
| 9575 | .40 | Wm. Schrafft, Elm street, Boston, Mass. | Lozenges; colored yellow with a vegetable color; flavored with lemon. |

*Analytical data.*

| No. | Polarization. | | Temperature, °C. | Sucrose. | Reducing sugars. | Water. | Ash. | Insoluble in cold water. | Coloring matter. |
|---|---|---|---|---|---|---|---|---|---|
| | Direct. | Indirect. | | | | | | | |
| | | | | *Per cent.* | *Per cent.* | *Per cent.* | *Per ct.* | *Per cent.* | |
| 9551 | 100.3 | −33.0 | 18 | 99.07 | Traces. | 0.00 | 0.04 | ..... | ..... |
| 9552 | 07.5 | 14.0 | 18 | 62.63 | 27.00 | 0.50 | 0.45 | ..... | ..... |
| 9553 | 118.0 | 57.0 | 17 | 45.46 | 23.12 | 1.63 | 2.01 | ..... | ..... |
| 9554 | 100.0 | −44.0 | 18 | 78.10 | 14.28 | 0.74 | 0.28 | ..... | ..... |
| 9555 | 81.3 | −30.4 | ..... | 83.78 | 14.74 | 0.68 | 0.17 | ..... | ..... |
| 9556 | 107.8 | 2.0 | 16 | 78.71 | 11.56 | 3.98 | 0.12 | ..... | ..... |
| 9557 | 87.5 | −27.0 | 15 | 85.18 | 9.02 | 6.31 | 0.05 | ..... | ..... |
| 9558 | 81.5 | −34.4 | 16 | 84.02 | 12.76 | 3.72 | 0.08 | ..... | ..... |
| 9559 | 83.4 | −31.2 | 16 | 86.16 | 12.48 | 2.98 | 0.07 | ..... | ..... |
| 9560 | 106.0 | − 4.0 | 16 | 81.88 | 9.72 | 3.54 | 0.18 | ..... | ..... |
| 9561 | 100.2 | 23.6 | ..... | 92.10 | 5.04 | 1.50 | 0.22 | ..... | ..... |
| 9562 | 99.9 | −17.0 | 16 | 86.07 | 4.96 | 2.24 | 0.14 | ..... | ..... |
| 9563 | 103.8 | 1.8 | 17 | 76.19 | 10.56 | 3.32 | 0.14 | ..... | ..... |
| 9564 | 06.7 | −11.6 | 17 | 80.90 | 7.96 | 4.62 | 0.16 | ..... | ..... |
| 9565 | 93.3 | − 9.0 | 18 | 76.73 | 11.82 | 3.50 | 0.08 | ..... | ..... |
| 9566 | 102.5 | − 8.4 | 17 | 82.84 | 7.96 | 2.60 | 0.20 | ..... | ..... |
| 9567 | 104.2 | 9.7 | 19 | 85.83 | 4.96 | 2.50 | 0.14 | ..... | ..... |
| 9568 | 90.8 | −18.9 | 18 | 82.28 | 2.43 | 2.51 | 0.15 | ..... | ..... |
| 9569 | 102.4 | 17.0 | 19 | 89.87 | 3.58 | 1.82 | 0.06 | ..... | ..... |
| 9570 | 166.8 | −17.2 | 18 | 93.00 | 3.79 | 1.54 | 0.07 | ..... | ..... |
| 9571 | 103.0 | 4.2 | 17 | 80.73 | 5.92 | 3.06 | 0.11 | ..... | ..... |
| 9572 | 104.2 | −10.0 | 18 | 85.65 | 4.86 | 1.49 | 0.02 | ..... | ..... |
| 9573 | 07.5 | −18.7 | 17 | 86.70 | 8.56 | 1.60 | 0.13 | ..... | ..... |
| 9574 | 106.7 | − 0.4 | 17 | 80.00 | 6.47 | 1.62 | 0.12 | ..... | ..... |
| 9575 | 95.6 | 31.2 | ..... | 94.87 | Trace. | 1.26 | 0.16 | ..... | ..... |

ANALYSES BY W. C. STUBBS.

*Description of samples.*

| No. | Bought of— | Manufacturer. | Remarks. |
|---|---|---|---|
| 1 | Bernard Klotz & Co., 75 North Peters street, New Orleans, La. | Bernard Klotz & Co., 75 North Peters street, New Orleans, La. | |
| 2 | .....do ............................ | .....do ....................... | Starch present. |
| 3 | .....do ............................ | .....do ....................... | |
| 4 | .....do ............................ | .....do ....................... | Copper present. |
| 5 | P.W. Dielmann & Co., Tchoupitoulas street, New Orleans, La. | P. W. Dielmann & Co., Tchoupitoulas street, New Orleans, La. | |
| 6 | .....do ............................ | .....do ....................... | |
| 7 | Marchel, Dauphine and St. Ann street, New Orleans, La. | Jaeger & De Pass, Common and Tchoupitoulas streets, New Orleans, La. | Do. |
| 8 | .....do ............................ | .....do ....................... | Starch present. |
| 9 | A. J. Kenner, Bienville and Burgundy streets, New Orleans, La. | Bernard Klotz & Co., 75 North Peters street, New Orleans, La. | Copper present. |
| 10 | P. W. Dielmann & Co., Tchoupitoulas street, New Orleans, La. | P. W. Dielmann & Co., Tchoupitoulas street, New Orleans, La. | |
| 11 | .....do ............................ | .....do ....................... | |
| 12 | Jas. J. Reiss & Co., 95 Decatur street, New Orleans, La. | Jas. J. Reiss & Co., 95 Decatur street, New Orleans, La. | |

*Description of samples*—Continued.

| No. | Bought of— | Manufacturer. | Remarks. |
|---|---|---|---|
| 13 | Domego, 165 Canal street, New Orleans, La. | James J. Reiss & Co., 95 Decatur street, New Orleans, La. | |
| 14 | J. Sambola, 269 Decatur street, New Orleans, La. | J. Sambola, 269 Decatur street, New Orleans, La. | |
| 15 | ......do ............................... | ......do ............................... | |
| 16 | ......do ............................... | ......do ............................... | |
| 17 | ......do ..............:............... | ......do ............................... | |
| 18 | Jaeger & De Pass, Common and Tchoupitonlas streets, New Orleans, La. | Jaeger & De Pass, Common and Tchoupitoulas streets, New Orleans, La. | |
| 19 | ......do ............................... | ......do ............................... | |
| 20 | ......do ............................... | ......do ............................... | Ultramarine present. |
| 21 | ......do ............................... | ......do ............................... | |
| 22 | ......do ............................... | ......do ............................... | |
| 23 | ......do ............................... | ......do ............................... | Large amount of starch. |
| 24 | Da Monte, grocery............... | Unknown........................... | Copper present. |
| 25 | Mrs. Du Val's, 1127 Magazine street, New Orleans, La. | ......do ............... ............... | |

*Analytical data.*

| No. | Polarization. | | Tempera-ture, °C. | Sucrose. | Reducing sugars. | Water. | Ash. | Insoluble in cold water. | Coloring matter. |
|---|---|---|---|---|---|---|---|---|---|
| | Direct. | Indirect. | | | | | | | |
| | | | | *Per cent.* | *Per cent.* | *Per cent.* | *Per ct.* | *Per cent.* | |
| 1 | 130.00 | 49.50 | 18 | 59.62 | 25.58 | 5.68 | 0.19 | 1.02 | ............ |
| 2 | 130.20 | 49.92 | 18 | 59.46 | 25.84 | 5.14 | 0.27 | 1.79 | ............ |
| 3 | 132.00 | 49.20 | 19 | 61.56 | 17.31 | 4.34 | 0.19 | 0.97 | ............ |
| 4 | 108.80 | 51.70 | 18 | 42.29 | 18.52 | 5.35 | 0.20 | 1.14 | ............ |
| 5 | 105.00 | 7.70 | 18 | 72.07 | 15.31 | 6.67 | 0.09 | 0.61 | ............ |
| 6 | 88.50 | −21.23 | 20 | 81.88 | 11.07 | 5.85 | 0.16 | 1.10 | ............ |
| 7 | 89.20 | −11.00 | 21 | 75.05 | 10.80 | 5.68 | 0.18 | 1.20 | ............ |
| 8 | 93.00 | −25.85 | 20 | 80.67 | 7.97 | 4.34 | 0.11 | 0.95 | ............ |
| 9 | 125.20 | 46.20 | 20 | 58.95 | 21.03 | 6.44 | 0.20 | 1.74 | ............ |
| 10 | 91.80 | −13.20 | 21 | 78.65 | 11.97 | 6.50 | 0.04 | 1.29 | ............ |
| 11 | 95.60 | − 8.58 | 20 | 77.74 | 4.77 | 7.35 | 0.01 | 0.43 | ............ |
| 12 | 87.60 | −27.50 | 20 | 85.89 | 9.01 | 6.34 | 0.12 | 0.83 | ............ |
| 13 | 89.50 | −24.75 | 22 | 85.90 | 8.75 | 6.39 | 0.12 | 0.75 | ............ |
| 14 | 97.00 | −19.36 | 21 | 87.10 | 3.48 | 2.83 | 0.04 | 0.44 | ............ |
| 15 | 97.40 | −11.55 | 22 | 81.91 | 10.05 | 4.34 | 0.07 | 0.55 | ............ |
| 16 | 88.55 | −25.08 | 22 | 85.43 | 9.37 | 4.53 | 0.05 | 0.50 | ............ |
| 17 | 88.40 | −26.40 | 21 | 85.99 | 7.93 | 4.32 | 0.06 | 1.31 | ............ |
| 18 | 90.20 | −25.19 | 21 | 86.43 | 8.16 | 4.25 | 0.15 | 1.40 | ............ |
| 19 | 87.55 | −23.10 | 21 | 82.88 | 10.18 | 4.77 | 0.11 | 1.52 | ............ |
| 20 | 90.40 | −22.88 | 21 | 84.85 | 8.80 | 4.24 | 0.18 | 0.80 | ............ |
| 21 | 85.15 | −31.02 | 14 | 84.79 | 9.33 | 2.26 | 0.00 | 0.00 | ............ |
| 22 | 89.00 | −25.08 | 14 | 83.27 | 9.69 | 4.18 | 0.13 | 0.31 | ............ |
| 23 | 105.00 | 24.53 | 13 | 58.52 | 14.50 | 4.97 | 0.11 | 12.61 | ............ |
| 24 | 61.50 | 49.72 | 17 | 10.90 | 21.22 | 2.65 | 0.53 | 1.67 | ............ |
| 25 | 90.20 | −23.32 | 23 | 85.67 | 8.92 | 4.77 | 0.07 | 0.00 | ............ |

## ANALYSES BY SHIPPEN WALLACE.

### Description of samples.

| No. | Kind. | No. | Kind. |
|---|---|---|---|
| 1 | Stick, red and yellow stripes. | 14 | Mixture. |
| 2 | Stick, red stripes. | 15 | Lozenges, pink. . |
| 3 | Do. | 16 | Drops, yellow, violet, brown, green. |
| 4 | Stick, red and brown. | 17 | Broken Candy. |
| 5 | Stick, black. | 18 | Fruit Caramels. |
| 6 | Stick, red, black, and yellow. | 19 | Gum Drops. |
| 7 | Stick, red. | 20 | Cocoanut Balls, red. |
| 8 | Candy Cakes, red and white. | 21 | Drops, green. |
| 9 | Sour Balls, red and yellow. | 22 | Mixtures, various colors. |
| 10 | Caramel, pink. | 23 | Do. |
| 11 | Taffy, red and pink. | 24 | Do. |
| 12 | Cream Candy. | 25 | Do. |
| 13 | Sour Balls, red, green, pink. | | |

### Analytical data.

| No. | Polarization. Direct. | Polarization. Indirect. | Tempera- ture° C. | Sucrose. | Reducing sugars. | Water. | Ash. | Insoluble in cold water. | Coloring matter. |
|---|---|---|---|---|---|---|---|---|---|
| | | | | Per cent. | Per cent. | Per cent. | Per ct. | Per cent. | |
| 1 | 106.5 | 8.0 | ....... | 73.5 | 16.33 | .......... | 0.100 | .......... | .......... |
| 2 | 85.0 | — 20.0 | ....... | 78.3 | 12.78 | .......... | 0.155 | .......... | .......... |
| 3 | 97.0 | — 11.0 | ....... | 80.5 | 15.50 | .......... | 0.098 | .......... | .......... |
| 4 | 99.0 | 0.0 | ....... | 73.8 | 18.32 | .......... | 0.090 | .......... | .......... |
| 5 | 102.0 | — 2.0 | ...... | 77.6 | 19.88 | .......... | 0.172 | .......... | .......... |
| 6 | 80.0 | — 20.0 | ....... | 74.6 | 24.62 | .......... | 0.200 | .......... | .......... |
| 7 | 80.5 | — 19.0 | ........ | 75.0 | 24.48 | .......... | 0.120 | .......... | .......... |
| 8 | 103.5 | 1.0 | ....... | 76.4 | 20.50 | .......... | 0.142 | .......... | .......... |
| 9 | 100.0 | — 6.0 | ....... | 79.1 | 17.80 | .......... | 0.105 | .......... | .......... |
| 10 | 98.0 | — 7.0 | ........ | 78.3 | 17.50 | .......... | 0.210 | .......... | .......... |
| 11 | 117.0 | 43.0 | ........ | 55.2 | 38.90 | .......... | 0.180 | .......... | .......... |
| 12 | 104.0 | 3.6 | ....... | 74.9 | 23.25 | .......... | 0.100 | .......... | .......... |
| 13 | 110.0 | 13.0 | ....... | 72.3 | 22.55 | .......... | 0.090 | .......... | .......... |
| 14 | 77.0 | — 7.0 | ...... | 62.6 | 24.75 | ......... | 0.310 | 10.22 | .......... |
| 15 | 104.0 | — 7.0 | ........ | 82.8 | 33.33 | .......... | 0.150 | .......... | .......... |
| 16 | 101.0 | — 20.0 | ...... | 90.3 | 6.85 | .......... | 0.050 | .......... | .......... |
| 17 | 124.0 | 30.0 | ... .... | 70.1 | 27.30 | ......... | 0.150 | .......... | .......... |
| 18 | 36.5 | 0.0 | ........ | 27.2 | 4.78 | .......... | 2.250 | 66.25 | .......... |
| 19 | 127.0 | 44.0 | ........ | 61.9 | 35.80 | .......... | 0.361 | .......... | .......... |
| 20 | 103.0 | — 5.0 | ........ | 65.6 | 8.77 | .......... | 0.734 | 20.52 | .......... |
| 21 | 96.0 | 14.0 | ...... | 61.1 | 37.22 | .......... | 0.100 | .......... | .......... |
| 22 | 110.0 | 5.0 | ...... | 78.3 | 10.10 | .......... | 0.225 | 5.92 | .......... |
| 23 | 90.0 | — 15.0 | ........ | 78.3 | 10.80 | .......... | 0.415 | 6.25 | .......... |
| 24 | 98.0 | — 12.0 | ...... | 82.0 | 10.50 | .......... | 0.205 | 6.58 | .......... |
| 25 | 100.0 | — 4.0 | ....... | 82.0 | 10.68 | .......... | 0.175 | 5.28 | .......... |

## ANALYSES BY H. A. WEBER.

*Description of samples.*

| No. | Coloring matter. | Other sub-stances. | Bought from— | Description. |
|---|---|---|---|---|
| 1 | ........................... | Dextrine . | J. G. & L. Brown, Hunter street and 5th avenue, Columbus. | White Stick Candy, Snyder & Chaffee, Columbus, Ohio. |
| 2 | Red, cochineal ............. | Dextrine, starch.' | ......do ................... | Do. |
| 3 | Pink, corallin; cream, methyl orange. | Dextrine . | Henry Thropp, 345 South High street, Columbus. | Cream Bonbons, Craft & Allen, Philadelphia. |
| 4 | Red, aniline red (Bengal red). | ....do ..... | Esper & Sons, 403 South High street, Columbus. | Red and White Taffy, Leggett, New York. |
| 5 | Red, corallin ; yellow, turmeric ; pink, corallin ; salmon pink, e o s i n ; green, aniline green ; lemou yellow, Victoria yellow. | ....do ..... | ......do ................... | Cream Candy, Leggett, New York. |
| 6 | ........................... | Starch .... | George Babb, 32 East Main street, Columbus. | Peppermint Lozenges, white, Wallace, New York. |
| 7 | Red, cochineal ............. | Dextrine, starch. | ......do ................... | Wintergreen Lozenges, red. |
| 8 | Pink, magenta.............. | ....do .... | ......do ................. | Cinnamon Drops, pink. |
| 9 | Red, eosin; black, lamp-black. | Starch.... | F. R. Allen, Goodale and High streets, Columbus. | Candy, red and white marbles. |
| 10 | Pink, eosin ............... | Dextrine, starch. | Thomas Bergen, 51 West High street, Columbus. | Barber-pole Candy, pink and white. |
| 11 | Red, Bengal red; yellow, chrysolin ; pink, eosin; orange red, fluorescein ; brown, Bismarck brown. | ...do ..... | H. K. Kaiser, 1520 North High street, Columbus. | Imitation Almond Candy, assorted colors. |
| 12 | Red, eosin ; pink, corallin ; brown, aniline brown. | Starch.... | Aug. Boesel, 1352 North High street, Columbus. | Candy Marbles. |
| 13 | Pink, eosin ............... | Dextrine, starch. | ......do ................... | Candy Colored Eggs. |
| 14 | Pink, corallin.............. | ....do ..... | M. Ferree, Herman street near Neil avenue, Columbus. | Pink Flat Stick Candy. |
| 15 | ........................... | ....do ..... | ......do ................... | White Flat Stick Candy. |
| 16 | Orange red, fluorescein ... | ....do ..... | ......do ................... | Imitation Almonds, white with a few orange and red. |
| 17 | Pink, corallin ; red, Bengal red. | ... do ..... | L. F. Clevenger, 187 South High street, Columbus. | Candied cloves. |
| 18 | Red, cochineal ............ | Dextrine . | Forrest, 252 South High street, Columbus. | Red Kisses. |
| 19 | Green, aniline green; cream, methyl orange; pink, corallin; red, Bengal red. | Dextrine, starch. | ......do ................... | Cream Candy. |
| 20 | Pink, cochineal......... .. | ....do ... . | R. H. Babb, corner Main and High streets, Columbus. | Cream Candy, made in Philadelphia. |
| 21 | Green, aniline green; cream, fluorescein; pink, corallin. | Starch .... | M. A. Sterling, 1416 North High street, Columbus. | Animal Candy. |

*Description of samples*—Continued.

| No. | Coloring matter. | Other substances. | Bought from— | Description. |
|---|---|---|---|---|
| 22 | Black, nigrosin; r e d, cochineal, and Bengal red; orange yellow, turmeric. | Starch .... | J. C. Dent, State street, Columbus. | Crimp Candy, Henry Hyde, Philadelphia, Pa. |
| 23 | .......................... | Dextrine . | .......do .................. | Peppermint Creams, white, H. Hyde, Philadelphia, Pa. |
| 24 | Pink, corallin.............. | ....do ..... | .......do .................. | Wintergreen Creams, pink, H. Hyde, Philadelphia, Pa. |
| 25 | .......................... | ....do ..... | .......do .................. | Maple-sugar Creams, H. Hyde, Philadelphia, Pa. |

*Analytical data.*

| No. | Polarization. Direct. | Polarization. Indirect. | Temperature °C. | Sucrose. | Reducing sugars. | Water. | Ash. | Insoluble in cold water. | Coloring matter. |
|---|---|---|---|---|---|---|---|---|---|
| | | | | *Per cent.* | *Per cent.* | *Per cent.* | *Per.ct.* | *Per cent.* | |
| 1 | ........ | ............ | ........ | 62.51 | 11.11 | 1.88 | 0.09 | 0.18 | .............. |
| 2 | ........ | ............ | ........ | 57.99 | 15.87 | 0.43 | 0.11 | 0.25 | .............. |
| 3 | ........ | ............ | ........ | 65.98 | 9.90 | 6.20 | 0.08 | 0.01 | .............. |
| 4 | ........ | ............ | ........ | 69.64 | 11.43 | 1.97 | 0.10 | 0.08 | .............. |
| 5 | ........ | ............ | ........ | 72.13 | 7.41 | 5.45 | 0.09 | 0.07 | .............. |
| 6 | ........ | ............ | ........ | 72.57 | 4.30 | 0.68 | 0.07 | 2.15 | .............. |
| 7 | ........ | ............ | ........ | 80.47 | 6.25 | 1.24 | 0.01 | 0.49 | .............. |
| 8 | ........ | ............ | ........ | 71.18 | 5.71 | 1.30 | 0.08 | 1.57 | .............. |
| 9 | ........ | ............ | ........ | 81.53 | 1.85 | 0.45 | 0.02 | 0.23 | .............. |
| 10 | .. .... | ............ | ........ | 64.73 | 12.50 | 3.06 | 0.10 | 0.27 | .............. |
| 11 | ........ | ............ | ........ | 55.19 | 13.33 | 2.31 | 0.14 | 9.96 | .............. |
| 12 | ........ | ............ | ........ | 81.63 | 1.69 | 0.79 | 0.10 | 0.66 | .............. |
| 23 | ........ | ............ | ........ | 78.01 | 4.09 | 2.91 | 0.15 | 2.94 | .............. |
| 14 | ........ | ............ | ........ | 73.09 | 12.34 | 3.19 | 0.09 | 0.45 | .............. |
| 15 | ........ | ............ | ........ | 71.20 | 12.73 | 3.30 | 0.10 | 0.34 | .............. |
| 16 | ... .... | ............ | ........ | 62.96 | 11.84 | 2.75 | 0.14 | 9.93 | .............. |
| 17 | ........ | ............ | ........ | 85.27 | 1.11 | 0.23 | 0.13 | 0.48 | .............. |
| 18 | ........ | ............ | ........ | 68.78 | 10.93 | 0.07 | 0.16 | 0.47 | .............. |
| 19 | ........ | ............ | ........ | 63.93 | 9.62 | 5.64 | 0.12 | 0.29 | .............. |
| 20 | ........ | ............ | ........ | 53.79 | 14.81 | 3.54 | 0.25 | 0.20 | .............. |
| 21 | ........ | ............ | ........ | 55.97 | 5.71 | 1.67 | 0.14 | 4.94 | .............. |
| 22 | ........ | ............ | ........ | 50.32 | 10.98 | 3.24 | 0.04 | 0.32 | .............. |
| 23 | ........ | ............ | ........ | 64.68 | 5.33 | 8.80 | 0.09 | ............ | |
| 24 | ........ | ............ | ........ | 62.89 | 6.25 | 8.73 | 0.09 | ............ | .............. |
| 25 | ........ | ............ | ........ | 65.91 | 7.54 | 7.96 | 0.13 | ............ | |

## ANALYSES BY F. G. WIECHMANN.

### Description of samples.

| No. | Price per pound. | Bought of— | Remarks. |
|---|---|---|---|
| 151 | $0.15 | Fajens, manufacturer, 1637 Columbus avenue, New York. | Selected from broken candy. Color. red and white. Translucent. |
| 152 | .15 | Bosch, 770 3d avenue, New York ......... | Cinnamon Candy. Color, red. |
| 153 | .13 | A. Jewell, manufacturer, 262 Grand street, New York. | Peppermint Cane. Color, white and red. Opaque. |
| 154 | (*) | 322 avenue A, New York................. | Musk Lozenges. Color, pink. |
| 155 | .15 | Fajens, manufacturer, 1637 Columbus avenue, New York. | Selected pieces from broken candy. Color, yellow and white. |
| 156 | .15 | .....do ...................................... | Selected pieces from broken candy. Color, red and white. Opaque. |
| 157 | .20 | H. Buckwalter, manufacturer, 437 6th avenue, New York. | Do. |
| 158 | .30 | .....do ...................................... | Lime-juice Bonbons. Color, green. Translucent. |
| 159 | .60 | .....do ...................................... | Violet Tablets. Color, lilac. Opaque. |
| 160 | .30 | J. Ahrens, manufacturer, 393 6th avenue, New York. | Cinnamon Drops. Color, red. |
| 161 | .40 | .....do ....................,......... | Lime-juice Bonbons. Color, green. |
| 162 | (†) | A. Carson, 223 West 27th street, New York | Musk Lozenges. Color, pink. |
| 163 | .13 | 231 West 27th street, New York........... | Selected piece from mixed candy. Color, red, with small white stripes. Translucent. Some of the candies bear the name Gray. |
| 164 | .13 | .....do ...................................... | Selected pieces from mixed candy. Color, yellow and white. Translucent. Candies marked Gray. |
| 165 | .13 | ..:....do .................................... | Selected pieces from mixed candy. Color, yellow and red. Opaque. Candies marked Gray. |
| 166 | .40 | Stern & Saalberg, manufacturers, wholesale confectioners, 489 8th avenue, New York. | Musk Lozenges. Color, pink. |
| 167 | .15 | .....do ...................................... | Selected pieces from mixed candy. Color, white and red. Opaque. |
| 168 | .15 | .....do ...................................... | Selected pieces from mixed candy; color, yellow, with red and white stripes. Translucent. |
| 169 | .40 | J. H. Simpson, 54 West 23d street, New York. | Lemon Tablets. Color, light yellow. Translucent. |
| 170 | .20 | H. Buckwalter, manufacturer, 437 6th avenue, New York. | Selected pieces from broken candy. Color, crushed strawberry. Opaque. |
| 171 | .15 | Weidmann, manufacturer, 1211 Broadway, New York. | Selected pieces from broken candy. Color, red and white. Opaque. |
| 172 | .20 | H. Willenbrok, manufacturer, 158 8th avenue, New York. | Cinnamon Candy. Color, red and white stripes. Translucent. |
| 173 | .20 | .....do .................................... | Cloves Candy. Color, yellow, with white and pink stripes. Translucent. |
| 174 | .30 | Dairy kitchen manufacture, 44 East 14th street, New York. | Wintergreen Tablets. Color, lilac. Opaque. |
| 175 | :.10 | Tifft's manufacture, 471 Fulton street, Brooklyn. Bought at branch store, 273 6th avenue, New York. | Pistachio Cachous. Color, green. Opaque. |

* Ten for 1 cent.　　† Eight for 1 cent.　　: Sample box.

*Analytical data.*

| No. | Polarization. Direct. | Polarization. Indirect. | Temperature °C. | Sucrose. | Reducing sugars. | Water. | Ash. | Insoluble in cold water. | Coloring matter.* |
|---|---|---|---|---|---|---|---|---|---|
| | | | | Per cent. | Per cent. | Per cent. | Per ct. | Per cent. | |
| 151 | 114.0 | 18.0 | ........ | .......... | 13.88 | 2.75 | 0.104 | 0.29 | Starch. |
| 152 | 72.0 | —31.0 | ........ | 77.6 | 19.61 | 2.75 | 0.029 | Trace. | |
| 153 | 86.5 | —29.8 | ........ | 87.6 | 7.84 | 3.54 | 0.115 | 1.03 | Do. |
| 154 | 108.0 | — 6.6 | ........ | .......... | 5.55 | 1.67 | 0.155 | 2.88 | Do. |
| 155 | 114.8 | 18.4 | ........ | .......... | 14.70 | 2.47 | 0.097 | Trace. | |
| 156 | 113.0 | 17.2 | ........ | .......... | 14.49 | 2.81 | 0.108 | 0.39 | Do. |
| 157 | 108.0 | 3 6 | ........ | .......... | 11.96 | 3.60 | 0.122 | Trace. | |
| 158 | 116.2 | 32.4 | ........ | .......... | 22.23 | 0.97 | 0.173 | Trace. | |
| 159 | 101.6 | —20.0 | ........ | .......... | 3.72 | 0.80 | 0.184 | 0.000 | Starch and violet color. |
| 160 | 80.2 | —31.2 | ........ | 83.9 | 13.70 | 2.24 | 0.036 | Trace. | |
| 161 | 73.0 | —28.6 | ........ | 76.6 | 16.45 | 3.62 | 0.043 | 0.40 | |
| 162 | 107.4 | — 5.4 | ........ | .......... | 5.49 | 1.71 | 0.148 | 0.000 | Starch. |
| 163 | 114.0 | 16.8 | ........ | .......... | 11.68 | 3.72 | 0.209 | 0.41 | Organic impurities not starch. |
| 164 | 114.0 | 14.4 | ........ | .......... | 10.71 | 3.77 | 0.108 | 0.38 | Do. |
| 165 | 118 6 | 26.2 | ........ | .......... | 13.05 | 4.60 | 0.208 | 0.43 | Do. |
| 166 | 108.0 | — 6.0 | ........ | ..... ... | 5.49 | 1.51 | 0.144 | 0.000 | Starch. |
| 167 | 82.0 | —32.0 | ........ | 85.9 | 10.18 | 3.65 | 0.036 | 0.34 | Organic impurities not starch. |
| 168 | 84.1 | —31.8 | ........ | 87.3 | 9.92 | 2.92 | 0.025 | 0.49 | Do. |
| 169 | 79.8 | —31.4 | ........ | 83.7 | 12.92 | 1.58 | 0 070 | Trace. | ............. |
| 170 | 110.8 | 22.8 | ........ | .......... | 17.01 | 4.12 | 0.155 | 0.29 | Coloring matter. |
| 171 | 84.0 | --32.1 | ........ | 87.5 | 9.86 | 3.59 | 0.090 | Trace. | ............. |
| 172 | 74.0 | —32 0 | ........ | 79.8 | 18.25 | 1.11 | 0.032 | Trace. | ............. |
| 173 | 78.6 | —32.4 | ........ | 83.6 | 15.02 | 2.39 | 0.025 | Trace. | ..... ..... |
| 174 | 88.0 | —29.6 | ........ | 83.6 | 0.25 | 7.34 | 0.014 | 0.000 | None. |
| 175 | 102.6 | —21.6 | ........ | .......... | 2.28 | 0.53 | 0.072 | 0.000 | None. |

* Destroyed by ignition.

## ANALYSES BY DEPARTMENT OF AGRICULTURE.

*Description of samples.*

| No. | Where bought. | Price per pound. | Labels, etc. |
|---|---|---|---|
| 8725 | R. P. White, corner 12th and M ........... | $0.13 | French Mixture. Soft candy of fancy shapes. |
| 8726 | ......do .............. .................. | .40 | Chocolate Creams. |
| 8727 | Gamble Market, corner 13th ............. | .20 | Stick Candy. |
| 8728 | J. S. Crocker, Riggs Market ............. | .20 | Molasses Caramel. Brown, paper covered cubes of a soft and sticky consistence. |
| 8731 | S. I. Bradley, 1315 14th street NW ........ | .50 | Gibson's Lime Fruit drops. Light green in color. Taste of spoiled limes. Contain tartaric acid. |
| 8732 | ......do ................................. | .20 | Marshmallows. |
| 8733 | A. Gutekunst, 1324 14th street NW ....... | .50 | Sugar-coated Almonds. Almonds = 20.58. |

*Description of samples*—Continued.

| No. | Where bought. | Price per pound. | Labels, etc. |
|---|---|---|---|
| 8734 | A. Gutekunst, 1324 14th street, NW...... | $0.25 | Lemon drops. |
| 8735 | Birch & Co., 1414 14th street N W ........ | .15 | Gum Drops. |
| 8736 | ......do .................................... | .20 | Jelly Beans. Bean-shaped and containing gelatinous core. |
| 8737 | —— ——, 324 13th street N W............. | .20 | Rock Candy. Rather dirty. |
| 8738 | —— ——, 327 13th street N W............. | .20 | Stick Candy. |
| 8739 | —— ——, 1309 E street N W ............. | .20 | Jaw Breakers. Large rounding pieces. |
| 8740 | Waple & Co., corner 11th and E .......... | .10 | Gum Drops. |
| 8741 | ......do .................................... | .20 | Peppermint Drops. |
| 8742 | Huyler's, 1103 Pennsylvania avenue ...... | .50 | Lemon Cups. |
| 8743 | Witthaft, 1219 E street.................... | .15 | Florence Orange Drops. Bright yellow balls. |
| 8744 | F. Candiote, 1116 I street ................ | .40 | Cinnamon Drops. Colored with carmine. |
| 8745 | G. W. Weidmann, stand 54 Center Market | .20 | Taffy. |
| 8746 | Vonieff, stand 538 Center Market ........ | .15 | Lemon Drops. Very slightly acid. |
| 8747 | G. J. Mueller, 314 Pennsylvania avenue... | .20 | Taffy. |
| 8748 | ......do .................................... | .40 | Wintergreen Wafers. |
| 8749 | J. F. Owens, 1363 C street S W............. | .30 | Marbles. |
| 8750 | Daly, 1309 C street S W.................... | .15 | Horehound Stick Candy. |
| 8751 | Alliss, corner C and 13th street S W ...... | .18 | Rock and Rye Balls. |

*Analytical data.*

| No. | Polarization. Direct. | Polarization. Indirect. | Temperature, °C. | Sucrose. | Reducing sugars. | Water. | Ash. | Insoluble in cold water. | Coloring matter. |
|---|---|---|---|---|---|---|---|---|---|
| | | | | Per cent. | Per cent. | Per cent. | Per ct. | Per cent. | |
| 8725 | 112.8 | 12.7 | 19.0 | 74.3 | 10.33 | 5.69 | .13 | .16 | .............. |
| 8726 | 102.8 | 24.4 | 19.0 | 58.3 | 13.81 | 3.78 | .48 | 15.43 | .............. |
| 8727 | 111.8 | 9.9 | 19.0 | 75.8 | 17.54 | 3.24 | .12 | .15 | .............. |
| 8728 | 128.6 | 95.6 | 21.4 | 24.7 | 29.24 | 5.96 | 1.12 | 17.10 | .............. |
| 8731 | 27.3 | —30.1 | 19.2 | 42.7 | 13.59 | 6.01 | .08 | .17 | .............. |
| 8732 | 109.4 | 93.2 | ........ | 20.0 | 39.68 | 11.09 | .70 | 12.81 | .............. |
| 8733 | 79.6 | —26.1 | 19.0 | 78.6 | 0.00 | .21 | .04 | .56 | .............. |
| 8734 | 35.9 | 7.1 | 21.0 | 21.6 | 10.59 | 4.15 | .10 | .33 | .............. |
| 8735 | 65.6 | 103.2 | 19.4 | .......... | 15.34 | 6.02 | .62 | 9.42 | .............. |
| 8736 | 104.0 | 24.4 | 19.0 | 59.2 | 8.47 | 3.72 | .22 | 6.20 | .............. |
| 8737 | 99.8 | —35.1 | 17.0 | 99.5 | 0.00 | .36 | .03 | .03 | .............. |
| 8738 | 109.6 | 3.3 | 18.6 | 78.0 | 10.25 | 3.75 | .13 | .07 | .............. |
| 8739 | 112.2 | 6.9 | 18.8 | 78.2 | 9.36 | 3.47 | .13 | .21 | .............. |
| 8740 | 62.1 | 103.6 | 18.4 | .......... | 28.74 | 7.81 | .56 | 9.09 | .............. |
| 8741 | 101.0 | —3.5 | 21.0 | 78.3 | 5.87 | 3.15 | .16 | 10.66 | .............. |
| 8742 | 80.8 | 6.6 | 18.2 | 55.3 | 27.47 | 2.18 | .31 | 5.41 | .............. |
| 8743 | 51.8 | —.2 | 21.4 | 38.8 | 12.68 | 7.32 | .11 | .13 | .............. |
| 8744 | 112.2 | 16.6 | 19.4 | 71.1 | 14.05 | 4.01 | .09 | 4.39 | .............. |
| 8745 | 109.2 | 33.1 | 19.0 | 56.5 | 14.88 | 8.20 | .72 | 5.37 | .............. |
| 8746 | 101.0 | —8.6 | 19.2 | 81.5 | 10.68 | 4.02 | .12 | 3.82 | .............. |
| 8747 | 105.0 | 11.0 | 18.2 | 69.7 | 16.13 | 5.51 | .67 | .25 | .............. |
| 8748 | 101.2 | —18.4 | 18.8 | 88.8 | 3.39 | 2.45 | .05 | 4.33 | .............. |
| 8749 | 104.2 | —18.6 | 19.0 | 91.3 | Trace. | 1.22 | .13 | .21 | .............. |
| 8750 | 99.4 | —8.9 | 20.0 | 80.8 | 10.73 | .68 | .18 | .31 | .............. |
| 8751 | 97.4 | —8.7 | 18.6 | 78.8 | 16.61 | .64 | .07 | .08 | .............. |

## REMARKS ON ANALYSIS OF CONFECTIONS.

The question of the adulteration of candies and confections is hardly debatable. The general conception of a pure confection is one that contains saccharine flavoring and coloring matters, so mixed and adjusted as to be attractive both to taste and sight. As long as these ingredients are not harmful to the health they can scarcely be regarded as adulterations.

Harmful ingredients and the admixture in confections of terra alba, kaolin, or other mineral substance calculated to give weight and volume to the mass must be regarded as adulterations.

Starches and gums, although insoluble in cold water, are not of themselves hurtful to the health, and their presence in certain kinds of confections may be regarded as necessary. Coloring matters are divided first of all into organic and inorganic classes. The metallic oxides comprising the latter class should never be used as pigments for confections. It has been claimed that lead compounds have been used for coloring candy, especially lead chromate, but our investigations have shown that inorganic colors are not used to any very great extent in this country. Were it otherwise more samples of it would have been found in the 250 samples, mostly colored, bought in open market in different parts of the country. The organic colors may be divided into innocuous and hurtful, but it is difficult to say where the line should be drawn. Harmless vegetable pigments, it may be said, can be used without endangering the health of the consumer. The same is true of the like compounds of insect origin like cochineal. Some of the coal tar colors are also said to be without injurious effect, but this statement can not be made to apply to the whole family of aniline dyes, perhaps the most frequent colors in candies. Among the colors found in the samples examined may be mentioned cochineal, eosin, and other aniline dyes, and ultramarine.

### ANALYSES BY MR. HUSTON.

Mineral coloring matter was found in Nos. 153 and 176. The nature of the base is not stated, but it is noted that both these samples contain ultramarine. Organic coloring matters were found in 20 of the samples equivalent to 80 per cent.

One of the samples had an offensive odor. Sample No. 158 had nearly 45 per cent of flour, which accounts in part, also, for its large percentage of ash. Eleven samples contain notable quantities of glucose. Other samples containing large quantities of starch and gum are 159, 172, 174, 175, and 176. This latter sample contains nearly 7 per cent of ash, which is almost high enough to point to the use of terra alba. This idea is corroborated by the fact that the insoluble portion and the ash are almost identical in amount. On the contrary, it can be urged with better reason that the adulteration with so small a portion of an inert earth would not prove financially profitable. The weight of the evidence is against the theory of such an admixture. Inasmuch as a mineral coloring matter was found in this sample, it may be that the high percentage of ash can be traced to this source.

In nearly all the samples it is noticed that sucrose forms the bulk of the saccharine matter. In such a sample as No. 158 there is apparently a mixture of a gum with a small quantity of sucrose and a large quantity of flour.

In No. 175 there is probably a mixture of starch with dextrose or milk sugar and a little sucrose.

In only one other case, No. 174, does the percentage of sucrose drop below 50. In all the other cases the chief part of the substance is sucrose, with the additions of small portions of glucose starch or flour, coloring and flavoring extracts.

NOTE BY MR. HUSTON.—Samples of red and yellow coloring for candies were obtained. The red was a preparation of cochineal, and the yellow was a sirup saturated with a fluorescent coal-tar product. Many of the pink and yellow candies gave fluorescent solutions. No indication of lead was found in any of the yellow candies.

### ANALYSES BY H. H. NICHOLSON.

All the samples contained organic coloring matter. Two of them contained a fluorescent pigment. Seven of them had large quantities of starch, four contained starch and gum, and fourteen were entirely soluble in cold water. Eighteen of the samples were mixed with glucose, or some similarly polarizing sugar.

Samples 1813, 1814, 1816, 1819, and 1828 were composed chiefly of gums. The composition of Nos. 1806 and 1807 is not sufficiently indicated by the analytical data. The principal part of all the other samples is sucrose.

Some of the samples contained large quantities of water, notably Nos. 1814, 1822, 1824, 1829, and 1830. Only one appears with ash above 1 per cent, viz, No. 1816, and the amount in this sample is too small to suggest any adulteration with an inert earth.

The percentages of reducing sugars were doubtless chiefly derived from the glucose used in the process of manufacture, or partly from the low-grade sugars employed.

### ANALYSES BY W. B. RISING.

Nine of the samples contain notable quantities of starch and gum insoluble in cold water, the largest quantity being in No. 110, a stick candy colored red, and selling for 20 cents a pound.

The smaller quantities of starch found in many of the other samples doubtless is incorporated there from the starch or flour used to prevent sticking during the process of manufacture. One sample, No. 112, labeled "gum drops," is almost pure confectioners' glucose, containing only 13.3 per cent of added sugar,

Seventeen of the samples contain glucose. In only one instance does the ash rise above 1 per cent, viz, No. 108.

Water is not present in excessive quantities in any of the samples.

Fourteen of the samples contain glucose and two contain gelatin.

SUMMARY.

|  | Samples. |
|---|---|
| Starch .......................................:............................. | ⎱ 9 |
| Starch and gum................................................ | ⎰ |
| Glucose...................................................... | 17 |
| Organic coloring matter....................................... | 25 |
| Mineral coloring matter ...................................... | 0 |
| Glucose.......................................:............... | 14 |
| Gelatin....................................................... | 2 |

ANALYSES BY M. A. SCOVELL.

All of the samples except one, viz, No. 157, contained glucose.

Only two contained notable quantities of starch and gum, viz, Nos. 170 and 173.

Nineteen of the samples had organic coloring matter added.

In no case did the percentage of ash reach .90, showing the entire absence of added earthy or mineral matter.

Sucrose was the chief constituent of all the samples examined.

SUMMARY.

|  | Samples. |
|---|---|
| Glucose ....................................................... | 24 |
| Organic coloring ............................................. | 19 |
| Of which— |  |
|     Cochineal.............................................. | 5 |
|     Eosin ................................................. | 2 |
| Starch and gum............................................... | 2 |

ANALYSES BY S. P. SHARPLES.

Sixteen samples contained glucose and two or three others possibly a small quantity.

Nearly all the samples (exact number not to be stated from data) contained organic colors, both vegetable and cochineal, and also many of them coal-tar colors.

Six of the samples contained considerable quantities of starch and gums. In only one case was there an excess of ash, No. 9553 having 2.01 per cent thereof.

As in the other sets, the chief constituent of all the samples is sucrose. In only one case, No. 9553, does this quantity fall below 50 per cent.

SUMMARY.

|  | Samples. |
|---|---|
| Glucose....................................................... | 16 |
| Coloring matter............................................... | Nearly all. |
| Coal-tar colors............................................... | 3 |
| Starch and gum............................................... | 6 |

NOTES BY MR. SHARPLES.—I have been unable to find a sample of candy colored or adulterated with a mineral substance. The use of a small quantity of glucose seems to be quite general even in candies that do not indicate it by their appearance.

The starch found in almost all the samples is used to prevent the candy sticking to the hands and tools during the manufacture; as in no case it exceeded a few per cent, no attempt was made to estimate it.

We did not succeed in finding a single bright yellow candy. The yellows obtained were colored with vegetable colors.

## ANALYSES BY W. C. STUBBS.

Eleven samples contained glucose, with two or three doubtful.

Sample No. 24 has a peculiar composition. It contains apparently, judged by the analytical data, dextrose or lactose. In no case is there any considerable amount of ash present.

In only two instances does the sucrose fall below 50 per cent. Unfortunately no description is given of the coloring matters present.

Copper was noticed in a number of samples, but the origin of the metal is not discussed. It comes probably from the copper vessels used in manufacture.

### SUMMARY.

|  | Samples. |
| --- | --- |
| Glucose | 11 |
| Starch | 3 |
| Copper | 4 |
| Ultramarine | 1 |

### ANALYSES BY SHIPPEN WALLACE.

Twenty-one of the samples examined contained glucose, but a few of them only small quantities.

In only one instance did the percentage of sucrose fall below 50.

One sample, No. 17, fruit caramels, had more than 2 per cent of ash. This ash was probably derived chiefly from the fruit. The presence of the fruit also accounts for the large percentage of this sample (66.25) which was insoluble in cold water.

Five samples had considerable quantities of starch and gum.

No mineral pigment was discovered.

### SUMMARY.

|  | Samples. |
| --- | --- |
| Glucose | 21 |
| Starch and gum | 5 |
| Coloring matter (organic in all cases). |  |

NOTES BY MR. WALLACE—Nos. 14, 15, 16, 18, 19, 20, 22, 23, 24, and 25 yield a reaction for starch, the remaining numbers do not.

The amount insoluble in water was so slight that I have only noted in cases where it was large.

The coloring agent was, as stated, an aniline color or cochineal. No mineral colors used and no arsenic detected.

The small amount of ash shows that no adulterant in the form of terra alba was used.

## ANALYSES BY H. A. WEBER.

Twenty-one of the samples contained glucose. It is assumed that all samples containing dextrin were mixed with glucose. Twenty-one samples contained coloring matter, in every case of an organic nature. The particular color was determined in each case, making the observations of Mr. Weber on this point of great value.

Seventeen of the samples contained starch, but only three any notable quantities, viz : Nos. 11, 16, and 21. Soluble starch was found in samples Nos. 5, 8, 11, and 20.

### SUMMARY.

|  | Samples. |
|---|---|
| Glucose | 21 |
| Insoluble starch, etc | 3 |
| Soluble starch | 4 |
| Coloring matters | 21 |
| Of which— | |
|     Cochineal | 5 |
|     Corallin | 8 |
|     Eosin | 6 |
|     Bengal red | 5 |

## ANALYSES BY F. G. WIECHMAN.

Of the 25 samples examined, 14, or 56 per cent, contain starch or glucose (starch sirup).

Eleven samples contain more than 0.25 per cent of matter insoluble in water; this ranges in amount from 0.29 to 2.88 per cent, and with but few exceptions consisted of starch.

The coloring matters were in all cases destroyed by ignition, and were with but two or three exceptions wholly soluble in water, which would class them as of vegetable or animal origin or as coal-tar colors.

NOTES BY MR. WIECHMANN.—Nos. 154, 162, and 166 contain a fluorescent coloring matter—pink and yellowish green—probably eosin.

Nos. 158 and 161 were tested for copper and iron, but with negative result.

No. 165 was examined for lead, also with a negative result.

The red coloring matter in No. 70 is partially insoluble in water and in alcohol. It turns purple with caustic potash and pink with acetic and with hydrochloric acids, and is most probably a lake of some vegetable color or cochineal.

The violet coloring matter in No. 159 is insoluble in water. Tests made prove that it is not indigo, Prussian blue, Antwerp blue, smalt, or ultramarine. It is either cyanin, the natural coloring matter of the violet, or else a coal-tar product.

RESUMÉ.

Out of the 175 samples analyzed there were adulterated—

|                                   | Per cent. |
| Out of 50 sugars ................................................................................................. | None = 00 |
| Out of 50 sirups and molasses : | |
|   With glucose ........................................................................... | 30 |
|   With tin............................................................................ | 18 |
|   With organic colors.................................................................... | 5 |
| | 53 |
| Allowing for repetition.............................................................. | 11 |
| | 32 = 64 |
| Out of 50 honeys................................................................... | 24 = 48 |
| Out of 25 confections ................................................................... | 14 = 56 |

These figures need no comment, they tell their own story.

In conclusion I would express my indebtedness to Messrs. E. G. Brainerd and R. Ziebolz for the valuable assistance they have given me in the execution of the analytical work here recorded.

## ANALYSES BY CHEMICAL DIVISION, U. S. DEPARTMENT OF AGRICULTURE.

But 3 samples of high-priced candies were bought. The others were cheap kinds bought at the small groceries. Polarization and glucose determinations were done in the main in the same way as for the other classes of samples. The gum drops and marshmallow samples presented great difficulties in polarization, owing to the presence of the gum, presumably gum tragacanth. For these the method used was to place 13.024 grams of the minced sample in a 100 cc flask, soften in about 50 cc of warm water, add about 40 cc of alcohol, mix, add lead acetate, cool, make up to the mark and filter enough for polarization, an operation attended with great difficulty.

For the inversion, a portion of the original unfiltered mixture was poured in a 50 cc flask up to the mark, 5 cc of acid added and the whole inverted as usual. Duplicates gave agreeing results, but of course the inversion numbers for such samples are practically worthless.

For the determination of insoluble matter a weighed portion of powdered candy was placed in a beaker, covered with cold distilled water and stirred vigorously, allowed to settle, the supernatant liquid poured into a Gooch crucible, and the treatment repeated till all soluble matter was washed out.

Finally the residue was transferred to the crucible and the whole dried and weighed. Drying was done either at 100° in an air bath, or at ordinary temperatures over sulphuric acid, according to the nature of the sample. After weighing it was ignited to get ash. Practically no ash was obtained from the portion of the candies insoluble in water, demonstrating the absence of mineral filling, such as terra alba, kaolin, etc., which are reputed to be often used. Total ash was in no instance high. No mineral colors could be found, although bright-colored and suspicious looking samples were bought in preference. Carmine was found in a sample of cinnamon drops, No. 8744. The acid drops, except in the case of "Gibson's lime fruit drops," were soured with citric acid. That sample contained a small amount of tartaric acid. The gum drops contained no nitrogen and consequently no gelatine.

Water in the hard samples was determined after powdering by drying in a platinum dish at 100°; in soft samples by first mincing the sample and then drying.

The sucrose in the samples was determined from the inversion data, using the factor 144.

$$S = \frac{a-a'}{144 - \dfrac{t}{2}}$$

S=sucrose.

$a$=polarization of normal sugar weight in 200 mm tube before inversion.

$a'$=polarization of normal sugar weight in 220 mm tube after inversion with 10 per cent by volume strong HCl.

$t$=temperature at which polarizations were made in degrees C.

Twenty of the samples contained glucose.

Twelve of these contained notable quantities of starch or glucose.

No mineral coloring matters were found.

SUMMARY.

|  | Samples. |
|---|---|
| Glucose | 20 |
| Starch and gum | 12 |

GENERAL SUMMARY.

| | Samples. |
|---|---|
| Total number of samples examined | 250 |
| Contained glucose | 173 |
| Contained starch and gum | 72 |
| Contained organic colors | 218 |
| Contained mineral colors | 2 |
| Contained grease | 14 |
| Contained copper | 4 |
| Contained gelatine | 2 |

In so far as the coloring matter was examined, the following table shows the character of the pigments used and the relative number of times they respectively were found:

| | Samples. | | Samples. | | Samples. |
|---|---|---|---|---|---|
| Cochineal | 14 | Ultramarine | 3 | Lamp black | 1 |
| Eosin | 12 | Turmeric | 2 | Victoria yellow | 1 |
| Corallin | 6 | Methyl orange | 2 | Magenta | 1 |
| Bengal red | 5 | Coal-tar colors | 2 | Orange red | 1 |
| Fluorescien | 3 | Carmin | 2 | Aniline brown | 1 |
| Fluorescent color | 3 | Cyanin | 1 | Bismarck brown | 1 |

In connection with the coloring matters, however, it should be remembered that in the great majority of cases no attempt was made to distinguish them further than to determine whether they were of an organic or inorganic nature.   Only one analyst (Weber) determined the nature of the coloring matter in each instance.   Two of the number (Stubbs, Wallace) did not report the number of samples colored.   In the general summary, this number was taken at 20 in each case.

The following substances were found in the 250 samples submitted to examination:

| | | |
|---|---|---|
| 1. Sucrose. | 17. Musk. | 33. Corallin. |
| 2. Dextrose. | 18. Marsh mallow. | 34. Bengal red. |
| 3. Maltose. | 19. Raspberry flavor. | 35. Fluorescein. |
| 4. Dextrin. | 20. Vanilla. | 36. Fluorescent color. |
| 5. Starch. | 21. Pistachio. | 37. Ultramarine. |
| 6. Soluble starch. | 22. Almonds. | 38. Turmeric. |
| 7. Gum. | 23. Apricot. | 39. Methyl orange. |
| 8. Gelatin. | 24. Strawberry. | 40. Coal-tar colors. |
| 9. Grease. | 25. Oil of wintergreen. | 41. Carmine. |
| 10. Flour. | 26. Banana flavor. | 42. Cyanin. |
| 11. Copper. | 27. Lemon flavor. | 43. Lampblack. |
| 12. Mineral colors. | 28. Cinnamon. | 44. Victoria yellow. |
| 13. Citric acid. | 29. Cloves. | 45. Magenta. |
| 14. Tartaric acid. | 30. Cocoanut. | 46. Orange red. |
| 15. Peppermint. | 31. Cochineal. | 47. Aniline brown. |
| 16. Horehound. | 32. Eosin. | 48. Bismarck brown. |

The above list does not, by any means, pretend to be a complete catalogue of the materials found in the confections of commerce.   It represents only the substances incidentally found in the 250 samples purchased in open market to supply the material for the examinations made.

# HONEY AND ITS ADULTERATIONS.

The samples of honey described in the report were liquid or strained honey or comb honey packed in glass jars. The examination did not extend to comb honey in frames.

Perhaps there is no other article of food which has been so generally adulterated in the United States, during the last twenty years, as honey. The ease with which sophistication could be practiced, the cheapness of the material used, and the high price of the genuine product have presented temptations which the manufacturer, producer, and dealer have not been able to withstand.

As long as honey was sold wholly in the comb, the difficulties in the way of successful sophistication were so great as to practically preclude its practice. The popular impression to the effect that comb honeys are adulterated was probably produced rather by ingenious attempts to manufacture the spurious article than by the commercial success of the enterprise. Artificial comb honey has been regarded as a possible article of commerce by many scientific men.

Many samples of comb honey containing only glucose have come under my observation, but in all these cases the comb, presumably after the separation of the honey by a centrifugal machine, had been placed in glass bottles and the glucose then added. I have never yet found a sample of comb honey, sold in the frame, which was artificial, except in the use of comb foundation.

Mr. C. O. Perrine secured letters patent, No. 176347, issued April 18, 1876, for a device for storing comb honey in glass jars. His idea was to have these vessels made a part of the hive and to be filled by the bees. Cylindrical comb foundations are to be inserted in the jar in its central portion so that the cells may have equal depth on all sides. The packages are to be placed in the hives over suitable openings to allow the bees to enter.

The true friend of the apiary interests of the country is not he who shuts his eyes to patent adulterations, but rather he who recognizes facts, even if unpleasant, and who, having seen the enormity of the extent of honey adulteration, supports the labors of those who seek to detect and prevent it.

In this connection, it is only just to say that the fact of the extensive adulteration of honey in the last four or five years has not been sufficiently recognized by that part of the agricultural press devoted to

744

apiary interests. In an editorial in the American Bee Journal, of July 25, 1888, the following language occurs :

We are *not* ignorant of the fact that extracted honey *was* quite generally adulterated when it brought higher prices, but now its price is so low that it will not pay to adulterate it, and it is, in consequence, hardly ever done. Persons will not adulterate any article when it will not pay them to do so. Adulteration of honey (now a thing of the past) we fought with all our energies until it ceased to exist.

This also appears to be the opinion of Mr. C. O. Perrine, expressed in a letter found on another page. Evidently, however, it still pays to adulterate honey, as the data obtained in the following tables clearly indicate.

## METHODS OF JUDGING OF THE PURITY OF HONEY.

Although not a matter of national legislation, the standard of pure honey is not hard to fix. By universal consent it may be stated that a pure honey is the nectar of flowers and other saccharine exudations of plants, gathered by bees and stored in cells built at least in part by the bees themselves. Honey made by feeding bees glucose, sugar, invert sugar, or other saccharine substances is not pure honey. Nor is that pure honey which is made by adding to an empty or partially filled honeycomb glucose or any other saccharine substance.

Strained honey, that is, honey separated from the comb, is pure when it contains only the materials of a liquid nature mentioned in the definition of pure honey given above, with such accidental solid particles, such as pollen, parts of bees, fragments of comb, etc., as would naturally be found therein.

### PROPERTIES OF PURE HONEY.

*Polarization.*—A pure honey has, with rare exceptions, at ordinary temperatures, a slight left-handed rotary effect on a plane of polarized light. This lævo-rotatory power is less than that produced by pure invert cane sugar. Measured as degrees on a cane-sugar scale, with normal sugar weight, a pure honey will rarely show more than − 20° at 20° C. A greater number than this may not be conclusive of adulteration, but may well be looked on with suspicion.

*Water.*—The content of water in a pure honey may vary from 12 to 20 per cent. It is rarely as low as 12 and does not frequently exceed 20 per cent.

*Color.*—The color of pure honey may vary from almost a water white through various shades of amber to deep brown or black. The source from which the honey is taken, the manner in which it is stored, and the length of time it has been kept are the chief factors in determining variations in color. White clover gives almost a colorless honey, while golden rod and other highly colored flowers produce a deeper-colored article.

*Ash.*—The content of ash is very small, varying from a mere trace to 0.30 per cent. A higher content of ash than this will be due to dust sifting over the flowers while the bees are at work, or to some tampering with the product after the bees have finished with it.

*Sucrose.*—The amount of cane sugar varies from nothing to 8 to 10 per cent, according to quantity of cane sugar in the nectar and the extent of inversion to which it is subjected in passing the organism of the bee.

*Reducing sugar.*—In a pure honey there should be a large percentage of reducing sugar measured as dextrose. This reducing sugar should consist of dextrose and levulose naturally existing in the nectar. Whenever the dextrose is in excess of the levulose it points to its artificial addition in the form of the glucose or grape sugar of commerce. The total quantity of reducing sugar, measured as dextrose, should generally fall between the limits of 60 and 75 per cent, although there are many cases where these limits may be transgressed.

*Pollen.*—Some idea of the purity and source of honey may be derived from a microscopic examination of the pollen grains which it contains.

### HISTORY OF ADULTERATION.

Some points in the early history of honey adulteration may not be inappropriate in this connection.

#### HISTORY AND RESULTS OF THE ADULTERATION OF HONEY.*

About twenty years ago I sent 6 or 7 barrels of extracted honey to Mr. Perrine, a dealer of Chicago, at 17 cents a pound, and some time after saw at a grocery in Hamilton 1 or 2 dozen small glasses containing liquid honey, sent by the same firm, at 16 cents a pound. This adulterating business was a paying one, the glucose added being sold at 16 cents a pound, with a profit of about 11 cents per pound.

Nine or ten years later, in St. Louis, I saw comb honey in small glass jars filled with liquid glucose, sold by Messrs. Thurber & Co., of New York, cheaper than I asked for my extracted. I bought one of these bottles and exhibited it at a meeting of beekeepers held at Burlington.

It was at about the same time that Mr. A. D. Root invented his comb-foundation machine. The announcement of this new step in bee culture gave to many people the idea that it produced comb and we could dispense altogether with bees, especially when it was hinted that paraffin could be used instead of wax. Yet paraffin was soon discarded by those who used it, not only because the bees objected to it, but on account of its low melting point, for the smallest addition increased the ductility of the wax and the comb dropped in a mess to the bottom of the hive.

Having obtained Mr. Perrine's present address from Mr. H. C. Bannard of Chicago, I wrote him for information on this subject, and received the following courteous reply:

RIVERSIDE, CAL., *August* 26, 1890.

DEAR SIR: Your esteemed favor of June 3, inclosing letter of introduction from my friend, Mr. H. C. Bannard, is at hand.

In regard to the adulteration of honey as practiced in the United States, all I know is what I did myself.

---

* Charles Dadant, American Bee Journal, August 15, 1888, p. 537.

During the year 1865 I received the idea from a friend that the common dark honey then on the market could be much improved by the addition of a large per cent (sometimes 75 per cent) of good white sugar. I took the idea up, and after making some experiments I worked up quite a large trade among families by selling from house to house; in fact I bought all the cheap honey I could find in the neighborhood (Cincinnati, Ohio), and finally I had to send East and South for supplies of honey. Where 1 pound was used before I commenced, I afterwards sold 100 pounds, as it was much more palatable.

After a few years I introduced my goods into several of the larger western cities, and still later on I opened business in Philadelphia and Brooklyn, N. Y. During all this time I handled large quantities of comb honey, giving customers their choice.

This peddling business was done in wagons, two men to each wagon; each man selling 50 to 100 pounds per day, 90 per cent of which was the mixed article generally.

I have met hundreds of persons who could eat the sugared article, but to whom pure honey was almost a rank poison. I suppose it is like strong black coffee, compared with a milder decoction, with plenty of cream and sugar.

About the year 1870 I tried some French and German glucose, using it as a part substitute for sugar, and when good glucose was made in this country I became patriotic and used only goods of home manufacture.

There were two objects in view in the mixing business; one was cheapness, the other was the production of a more popular grade of goods; for it was a fact that if I made the mixture too strong of honey objection was made.

I have known of many recipes for making imitation honey; one was, slippery elm bark with some sugar, flavored with one or more of the flavoring extracts; but I never knew of any quantity being sold.

While honey was an expensive luxury there was a profit in mixing, but now that comb honey at wholesale is worth but 10 to 15 cents and liquid honey 4 to 6 cents per pound, there can be but little profit in mixing.

I think that the most of the mixing is done in the larger business centers.

I know of no successful experiment in feeding bees a mixture to be filled into combs; pure liquid honey is sometimes fed to complete unfinished combs after the flow of honey has ceased in the flowers.

Respectfully,

C. O. PERRINE.

Prof. H. W. WILEY,
*Washington, D. C.*

---

## NOTES RELATING TO HONEYS OF DIFFERENT ORIGIN AND TO ARTIFICIAL HONEYS.

### ON THE PRODUCTION OF ARTIFICIAL HONEY.[*]

About 1870 the author made the observation that the action of the mineral acids on starch was somewhat different from that of the stronger organic acids. By the action of oxalic acid on wheat, maize, buckwheat, and other cereal starches, he obtained sugary products, which, after two or three weeks standing, were exactly like an old honey in appearance and taste. In order to avoid giving any assistance to adulteration, he refrained from publishing the results of his observations, communicating them only to a few friends. For some years, however, honey, especially American, has been exposed to the risk of adulteration with the sugar from corn starch. About a year previously, the author obtained information that in North America a maize starch sirup was made and much used as a substitute for honey. A periodical that he had lately read gave a review of the situation of the condition

---

[*] H. Hager, Pharm. Centralhalle, 26, 303; Chem. Centralblatt, 1885, 655.

of the maize glucose industry, and made the statement that the sirup in question resembled honey. It was stated that a mixture of this sirup with an equal amount of honey was exported to Europe as American honey. Furthermore, the method of manufacture of the sirup was stated to be a secret. The author therefore thought it his duty to explain this secret, and to publish the fact that by using oxalic acid instead of sulphuric acid a honey-like glucose was obtainable. Potato starch could not be used. It is well to be on the watch for adulteration in American honey.

MANUFACTURE OF ARTIFICIAL HONEY.*

An English patent, No. 8863, July 22, 1885, prescribes the mixture of 35 parts of dextrose and 40 parts of levulose, a fruit ether, and enough cane sugar to make a 10 per cent solution and give a rotation of 1° on a Soleil Ventzke polariscope. The mixture may be crystallized by adding some granulated honey.

SUGAR HONEY. †

At the tenth annual meeting of the Independent Association of Bavarian Representatives of Applied Chemistry, held at Augsburg on July 17, Theodore Weigle reported on sugar honey. This material has lately been brought to the notice of the public as a cheap substitute for genuine honey. It consists of water, invert sugar, traces of mineral matter, and free acid, flavored so as to imitate the odor and taste of genuine honey. Dextrine, sucrose, or other bodies foreign to genuine honey could not be found in the artificial product and it is apparent that both chemically and physically the substitute so closely approximates honey that it can not be distinguished from it. R. Kayser, of Nuremberg, substantiated the above and claimed that if the manufacture of sugar honey remains in the hands of reliable men, it would soon reduce the production of genuine honey materially.‡

HONEY ANALYSIS.§

An English firm, A. Lyle & Co., has put on the market a so-called "artificial honey" made from cane sugar, and consisting of levulose and dextrose like the natural honey, which it closely resembles in every respect except as to taste and smell. To differentiate between this substance and honey, can be used the total lack of phosphoric acid in the former. Natural honey contains between 0.014 and 0.035 per cent phosphoric acid. On the other hand the starch sirup, also used as an adulterant, contains from 0.01 to 0.107 per cent. The ash of pure honey and that of Lyle's substitute are heavily alkaline ; that from glucose or glucose mixtures is always neutral.

EUCALYPTUS HONEY AND ITS EXPOSÉ. ‖

In 1887, Dr. Thomas Caraman, communicated to the Paris Académie de Médecine an account of finding a giant colony of hitherto undescribed bees (named by him *Apis nigra mellifica*) in eucalyptus trees in Tasmania. In one instance a hive was said to contain 11,000 pounds of honey. This honey was described as a thick, transparent

---

* Pharm. Centralhalle, 28, 92.

† Deutsche Znckerindustrie, 16, 1043.

‡ Experiments in the manufacture of sugar honey on a large scale were made as early as 1885 by Dr. A. Herzfeld and were reported in Deutsche Zuckerindustrie, 1885, No. 33, p. 1120.

§ O. Hebner, Analyst, 1885, 217; Report. anal. Chem., 6, 41 ; abs. Chem. Central-blatt, 1885, 204.

‖ Pharm. Era, Feb. 15, 1891, p. 107.

sirup of a deep orange color, smelling like eucalyptus oil.  Analysis by Ch. Hori-
son gave—

| | |
|---|---|
| Sugar (mostly levulose) | 61. 16 |
| Ash | . 18 |
| Moisture | 21. 66 |
| Active principles (eucalyptol, eucalyptene, cymol, etc) | 17. 10 |
| | 100. 00 |

Rotatory power, 22° [direction not given]; sp. g., 1.44.

Doubt was at the time expressed that a honey gathered from the blossoms should
contain principles peculiar to the leaf of the eucalyptus, and in Australia there was
an opinion that eucalyptus honey was a mixture of ordinary honey and eucalyptus
oil.  Prof. T. P. A. Stuart (University of Sydney, New South Wales) investigated the
matter and found that, while honey was really collected from eucalypti, such stu-
pendous hives had not been heard of.  The native bee (*Trigona carbonaria*) collects
not above an average of 5 pounds of honey per hive.  The comb presents an inter-
laced looking structure, not resembling the hexagonal structure of comb made by our
hive bees.  Analysis gave:

| | |
|---|---|
| Water | 13. 63 |
| Levulose, dextrose, etc | 78. 98 |
| Cane sugar | 0. 00 |
| Wax, pollen, and inorganic matter | 2. 15 |
| Ash | . 31 |
| Undetermined | 4. 93 |
| | 100. 00 |

The specimen was clear, homogeneous, dark red, and semifluid.  No trace of essential oil, terpene, rosin, or similar substances could be found.

### DATE HONEY (DATE SIRUP).[*]

Date honey was on exhibition at the last Parisian World's Fair among the productions of Algeria.  In Algeria it is used largely for medicinal purposes, mostly as
a specific for pulmonary troubles.  It has an unpleasant smell and taste, the latter at
first reminding one of "syrupus Hollandicus," afterwards of the date.  The usual
aroma of honey is absent.  The color is brownish yellow.  On long keeping it gradually candies.  It feebly reddens blue litmus.  In a 1 to 2 solution it rotates the
polarized ray 20° to the left.  It contains traces of dextrin; chlorine in tolerable
quantity, 0.95 per cent (calculated as NaCl, 1.53 per cent); sulphuric acid, 0.19 per
cent.  The product though called "date honey" appears to be the exuded sap of the
date tree and is therefore a sirup, and not a honey.

### POISONOUS HONEY. [†]

That the poisonous honey which Xenophon mentions in his Anabasis is collected
by bees from the blossoms of the *Rhododendron ponticum* or the *Azalea pontica* was
pretty generally recognized even before the poisonous ingredient of this plant was
known.  Plugge has demonstrated from investigation with honey collected from these
flowers that the honey is really poisonous and that its poisonous quality is due to
andromedotoxin.

---

* Karl Gaab, Chem. Zeit., Jan. 28, 1891, p. 118.

† P. C. Plugge.  Arch. Pharm., 1891, 229, 554; abs. Chem. Zeit., 1891, No. 28, 310.

## POISONOUS HONEY.[*]

A case was reported from Branchville, S. C. A number of people ate honey gathered from gelsemium flowers. Three died and 20 were rendered ill. Analysis of the honey showed large quantities of gelsemin.

## FENNEL HONEY.[†]

Fennel honey consists of 500 grams purified honey; malt sugar, 1,000 grams; fennel oil, 5 drops, and a little glycerin.

## TINTED HONEY.[‡]

Tinted honey of great beauty and delicacy has been produced. The comb is virgin, the wax almost white, the honey limpid, pure, and of the color of pale red currant jelly. The secret of its production is not revealed, except that it is the result of artificial feeding.

## ANALYSIS OF ETHIOPIAN HONEY.[§]

This honey is the product of an insect resembling a large fly and is deposited underground. No wax is secreted. The honey gave on analysis: Water, 25.50 per cent; fermentable sugar (levulose with one-sixth dextrose, but no cane sugar), 32; mannite, 3; dextrin, 27.90; ash, 2.50; and other substances and loss, 9.10.

## HONEY FROM SUMATRA. ||

This sample was the product of *Apis indica* and was gathered during the rainy season. When it came into the author's hands half a year later it was fermenting, but was nevertheless analyzed. It contained 26.6 per cent of water; levulose and dextrose in the ratio of 5.92 to 7.41, and traces of wax, starch, and pollen grains. Neither cane sugar nor dextrin could be detected. The ash amounted to 0.23 per cent.

---

* Chem. Zeit, 1886, 27.

† Pharm. Zeit., 1879, 719; Am. Jour. Pharm., March, 1880, 132; Proc. Amer. Pharm. Assoc., 1880, 60.

‡ Pharm. Jour. Lond., Dec., 1–70; Abs. in Proc. Amer. Pharm. Assoc., 1871, 313.

§ A. Villiers, Comptes rendu, 88, 292; abs. Chem. Centralblatt, 1879, 229.

|| A. P. N. Franchimont, Chem. Centralblatt, 1883, 138.

# HONEYS.

ANALYSES BY MR. H. A. HUSTON.

*Description of samples.*

| No. | Bought of. | Price per pound. | Source. | Description. | Remarks. |
|---|---|---|---|---|---|
| 1 | Hogan & Johnson, La Fayette, Ind. | $0.15 | Fuller & Fuller, Chicago, Ill. | Strained Indiana Honey. | |
| 2 | David Hill, La Fayette, Ind. | .30 | ...................... | Pure Strained Honey | |
| 3 | Longgear & Co., La Fayette, Ind. | .25 | Dan. Stuart, Indianapolis, Ind. | Strained Buckwheat Honey. | |
| 4 | W. G. Brown, La Fayette, Ind. | .15 | ...................... | California Honey ... | |
| 5 | The Fair, Chicago, Ill. | .18 | Apiary of A. Christie, Smithland, Iowa. | Honey (strained) ... | |
| 6 | ....do ............... | .18 | Apiary of J. S. Crnch. | Pure Honey gathered from white clover. | |
| 7 | Chas. H. Slack, Chicago, Ill. | .25 | Put up by Chas. H. Slack. | Strained Honey .... | |
| 8 | L. M. Brown & Sons, La Fayette. | .25 | Guest & Beever, Cheneysville, Ill. | ....do ............... | |
| 9 | ....do ............... | .25 | Los Angeles, Cal ... | Henderson's Pure White Clover Honey. | Bad odor; ash brown. |
| 10 | Schwarm & Heinmiller, LaFayette. | .25 | F. G. Strohmeyer & Co., New York. | Pure Orange Blossom Honey. | |
| 11 | Pottlitzer Bros., La Fayette, | .25 | Packed by Hildreth Bros., & Logelken, New York. | Choice Extracted Honey. | |
| 12 | Bodeman & Conrad, Chicago, Ill. | .35 | ...................... | Strained Honey..... | |
| 13 | C. Jevno & Co., Chicago, Ill. | .30 | ...................... | Absolutely Pure "June" strained honey. | |
| 14 | H. C. Honerlah, Chicago, Ill. | .15 | Jno. K. McAllister, Chicago, Ill. | Honey (strained).... | |
| 15 | Hassett's, Chicago, Ill. | .20 | ...................... | Strained Honey..... | |
| 16 | Joyce & Co., Chicago, Ill. | .20 | ...................... | Honey (strained).... | Heavy precipitate of dextrin. |
| 17 | J. H. Wells & Co, Chicago, Ill. | .30 | ...................... | Pure Strained Honey | |
| 18 | Deutsch Apotheke, Chicago, Ill. | .28 | ...................... | Pure Honey (strained). | |

751

*Description of samples* —Continued.

| No. | Bought of. | Price per pound. | Source. | Description. | Remarks. |
|---|---|---|---|---|---|
| 19 | Sprague Warner & Co., Chicago. | ........ | .................... | California Honey ... | Sprague Warner & Co. stated that the sample contained glucose; heavy precipitate of dextrin. |
| 20 | F. Prussing, Chicago, Ill. | 0.25 | Put up by F. Prussing. | Pure Strained Honey | Stated to be country honey. |
| 21 | Ordway & Wallace, Chicago, Ill. | .15 | .................... | California Strained Honey. | Stated to be pure goods. |
| 22 | D. B. Scully, Chicago | .15 | .. .................. | ....do ................ | |
| 23 | Rockwood Bros., Chicago, Ill. | .30 | G. K. McMechen & Son, Wheeling. W. Va. | Old Virginia Pure Honey. | Sign around neck of bottle, "Those goods are absolutely pure." Heavy precipitate of dextrin. |
| 24 | A. R. Bremer & Co , Chicago, Ill. | ........ | .................... | Pure California Honey. | |
| 25 | ....do ............ ...... | | .................... | Mixed Honey (Glucose). | Bremer & Co. stated that this sample was mixed goods. Contain dextrin. |
| 26 | P. J. Ryan, Indianapolis, Ind. | .25 | F. H. Leggett & Co., New York. | Strained Honey..... | |
| 27 | Sockwell, Indianapolis, Ind. | .25 | Bradshaw & Wait. Chicago. | White Clover Honey, California. | Contains some comb. Fluid clear. |
| 28 | N. A. Moon & Co., Indianapolis. | .25 | ....do ............... | ....do ............... | Contains some comb. Fluid not clear. |
| 29 | C. W. Coulter, Indianapolis, Ind. | .20 | Refined and packed by Dobson & Hils. | Mississippi Valley White Clover Honey. | Contains some comb. |
| 30 | Indianapolis Market, House. | .20 | ....do ............... | ....do ............... | Contains no comb. |
| 31 | Harwick Indianapolis Market House. | .20 | Portland, Ind ....... | White Clover Honey. | Stated to be pure. |
| 32 | .. do ............... | .125 | Vincennes, Ind ..... | Spanish Needle Honey. | Do. |
| 33 | ....do ............... | .125 | Phœnix, Ariz. ...... | Sagebush Honey.... | Do. |
| 34 | ... do ............... | .15 | California ... ...... | White Sagebush Honey. | Stated to be pure and extra fine. |
| 35 | .. do ............... | .125 | Phœnix, Ariz ....... | Alfalfa Honey ...... | Stated to be pure. |
| 36 | ...do ............... | .15 | .................... | Golden Rod Honey.. | Stated to contain glucose and withdrawn from sale. Gives heavy precipitate of dextrin. |
| 37 | Geo. F. Traub, Indianapolis, Ind. | .40 | .................... | Strained Honey..... | Sample put up behind prescription case; contained two distinct layers, top one apparently water. |

## Description of samples.—Continued.

| No. | Bought of | Price per pound. | Source. | Description. | Remarks. |
|---|---|---|---|---|---|
| 38 | C.T.Bedford, Indianapolis, Ind. | $0.40 | ..................... | PureStrained Honey | |
| 39 | P. H. Kelley, Indianapolis, Ind. | .50 | ..................... | Strained Honey...... | |
| 40 | Remedy Drug Store, Indianapolis, Ind. | .20 | Hamilton Co., Ind .. | ....do ............... | |
| 41 | H. H. Loe & Co., Indianapolis, Ind. | .25 | ..................... | XG and RX White Clover Honey XX. | Gave no test for dextrin. |
| 42 | J. M. Balfour, Indianapolis, Ind. | .15 | Near Wellington, Ohio. | Pure White Clover Honey. | |
| 43 | E. Pasquier, Indianapolis, Ind. | .20 | ....;................. | California Honey ... | |
| 44 | A. J. Ferrell, Indianapolis, Ind. | .15 | Illinois............. | Illinois Honey ...... | |
| 45 | W. F. Clem, Indianapolis, Ind. | .15 | ..................... | Pure White Comb Honey. | Contains some comb. |
| 46 | John Honk & Son, Indianapolis, Ind. | .15 | Walter S. Prouder, Indianapolis, Ind. | Pure Extracted Honey. | Sample fluid. |
| 47 | J. B. Hoover, Indianapolis, Ind. | .15 | ....do ............... | ....do .... .......... | Sample solid. |
| 48 | Edward Meeker, Indianapolis, Ind. | .15 | ....do ............... | ....do ............... | Do. |
| 49 | Jamison Brothers, La Fayette, Ind. | .20 | ..................... | California Honey.... | Odor bad; heavy prec. of dextrin. |
| 50 | Louis Schism, La Fayette, Ind. | .15 | From mountains, California. | ....do ............... | Stated to be pure honey. |

*Analytical data.*

| No. | Polarization. | | Tempera-ture, °C. | Sucrose. | Reducing sugars. | Water. | Ash. |
|---|---|---|---|---|---|---|---|
| | Direct. | Indirect. | | | | | |
| | | | | *Per cent.* | *Per cent.* | *Per cent.* | *Per cent.* |
| 1 | .......... | .......... | .......... | 1.910 | 81.800 | 13.56 | 0.126 |
| 2 | .......... | .......... | .......... | 2.560 | 76.056 | 21.59 | 0.073 |
| 3 | .......... | .......... | .......... | 0.617 | 76.056 | 18.80 | 0.141 |
| 4 | .......... | .......... | .......... | 8.100 | 65.425 | 16.60 | 0.230 |
| 5 | .......... | .......... | .......... | 3.210 | 75.380 | 14.77 | 0.209 |
| 6 | .......... | .......... | .......... | 3.600 | 77.140 | 14.66 | 0.150 |
| 7 | .......... | .......... | .......... | 8.640 | 78.260 | 14.04 | 0.063 |
| 8 | .......... | .......... | .......... | 1.330 | 77.140 | 15.15 | 0.167 |
| 0 | .......... | .......... | .......... | 2 940 | 65.850 | 21.46 | 0.363 |
| 10 | .......... | .......... | .......... | 0.153 | 72.970 | 18 97 | 0.082 |
| 11 | .......... | .......... | .......... | 0.020 | 72.000 | 17.95 | 0.152 |
| 12 | .......... | .......... | .......... | 10.240 | 67.500 | 17.50 | 0.063 |
| 13 | .......... | .......... | .......... | 0.020 | 70.410 | 16.16 | 0.030 |
| 14 | .......... | .......... | .......... | 4.090 | 65.850 | 16.54 | 0.146 |
| 15 | .......... | .......... | .......... | 2.560 | 63.529 | 16.40 | 0.191 |
| 16 | .......... | .......... | .......... | 1.470 | 66.840 | 16.24 | 0.225 |
| 17 | .......... | .......... | .......... | 0.344 | 77.140 | 16.88 | 0.075 |
| 18 | .......... | .......... | .......... | 0.210 | 72.970 | 16.11 | 0.069 |
| 10 | .......... | .......... | .......... | 9.710 | 61.430 | 14.93 | 0.156 |
| 20 | .......... | .......... | .......... | 2.660 | 78.260 | 14.77 | 0.063 |
| 21 | .......... | .......... | .......... | 3.190 | 72.000 | 14.46 | 0.099 |
| 22 | .......... | .......... | .......... | trace | 70.410 | 14.97 | 0.063 |
| 23 | .......... | .......... | .......... | 11.380 | 62.790 | 14.18 | 0.100 |
| 24 | ...,..... | .......... | .......... | 4.450 | 81.370 | 12.10 | 0.040 |
| 25 | .......... | .......... | .......... | 11.400 | 60.000 | 15.32 | 0.340 |
| 26 | .......... | .......... | .......... | 3.610 | 80.507 | 15.85 | 0.070 |
| 27 | .......... | .......... | .......... | 3.750 | 60.230 | 21.06 | 0.233 |
| 28 | .......... | .......... | .......... | 7.610 | 67.500 | 19.25 | 0.225 |
| 20 | .......... | .......... | .......... | 5.080 | 65.060 | 16.80 | 0.136 |
| 30 | .......... | .......... | .......... | 3.800 | 65.060 | 18.85 | 0.281 |
| 31 | .......... | .......... | .......... | 4.210 | 82 375 | 16.34 | 0.075 |
| 32 | .......... | .......... | .......... | 1.470 | 79.410 | 16.01 | 0.205 |
| 33 | .......... | .......... | .......... | 0.683 | 76.056 | 14.20 | 0.057 |
| 31 | .......... | .......... | .......... | 2.290 | 79.410 | 14.63 | 0.058 |
| 35 | .......... | .......... | .......... | trace | 80.507 | 11.21 | 0.072 |
| 36 | .......... | .......... | .......... | 9.030 | 61.360 | 16.30 | 0.205 |
| 37 | .......... | .......... | .......... | 1.210 | 70.986 | 21.73 | 0.041 |
| 38 | .......... | .......... | .......... | 2.560 | 76.056 | 14.57 | 0.201 |
| 30 | .......... | .......... | .......... | 2.420 | 75.380 | 20.51 | 0.027 |
| 40 | .......... | .......... | .......... | 0.830 | 70.410 | 13.54 | 0.064 |
| 41 | .......... | .......... | .......... | 16.760 | 62.068 | 15.05 | 0.004 |
| 42 | .......... | .......... | .......... | 7.600 | 65.850 | 16.49 | 0.143 |
| 43 | .......... | .......... | .......... | 9.570 | 63.529 | 17.30 | 0.138 |
| 44 | .......... | .......... | .......... | 3.840 | 60.000 | 13.12 | 0.061 |
| 45 | .......... | .......... | .......... | 1.380 | 79.410 | 15.83 | 0.073 |
| 46 | .......... | .......... | .......... | 10.290 | 60.000 | 15.36 | 0.070 |
| 47 | .......... | .......... | .......... | 1.290 | 81.810 | 14.60 | 0.208 |
| 48 | .......... | .......... | .......... | 2.050 | 81.810 | 16.09 | 0.103 |
| 40 | .......... | .......... | .......... | 3.840 | 66.640 | 20.25 | 0.253 |
| 50 | .......... | .......... | .......... | 1.830 | 70.410 | 21.48 | 0.057 |

## ANALYSES BY H. H. NICHOLSON.

### Description of samples.

| No. | Bought of. | Wholesaler or manufacturer. | Label. |
|---|---|---|---|
| 1756 | Stevens, Lincoln.................. | Ritter Conserve Co., Philadelphia | Pure Honey, Cal. |
| 1757 | Starrett Bros., Lincoln ............ | ................................... | No label. |
| 1758 | Clark & Son, Lincoln ............. | McMechen......................... | Old Virginia. |
| 1759 | .....do ......................... | .................................. | Pure Honey. |
| 1760 | Jas. Miller, Lincoln.............. | .................................. | Do. |
| 1761 | O. J. King, Lincoln .............. | .................................. | Do. |
| 1762 | W. A. Klock, Lincoln ............. | McMechen......................... | Old Virginia. |
| 1763 | J. D. Johnson, Lincoln............ | .................................. | Pure Honey. |
| 1764 | Wm. Hotaling, Lincoln .......... | MoMcchen.............. ......... | Old Virginia. |
| 1765 | Jno. Nightengale, Lincoln ........ | N. E. Melick, Davey, Nebr ........ | Pure Honey. |
| 1766 | J. D. Garner, Lincoln ............. | .................................. | No label. |
| 1767 | ......do ......................... | .................................. | Pure Honey. |
| 1768 | Fullerton Bros., Lincoln .......... | N. E. Melick, Davey, Nebr ........ | Do. |
| 1769 | C. M. Seitz, Lincoln.............. | .................................. | No label. |
| 1770 | A. C. Schuler, Lincoln ........... | .................................. | Do. |
| 1771 | John Nightengale, Lincoln ...... | .................................. | Do. |
| 1772 | J. D. Garner, Lincoln ............ | McMechen......................... | Pure Honey. |
| 1773 | Fullerton Bros., Lincoln .......... | ......do ......................... | Do. |
| 1774 | A. C. Schuler, Lincoln ........... | .................................. | Do. |
| 1775 | J. C. McCargar, Lincoln .......... | .................................. | No label. |
| 1776 | Arenson Bros., Lincoln .......... | .................................. | Do. |
| 1777 | L. E. Johnson & Co , Lincoln ...... | .................................. | Do. |
| 1778 | Ell S. Vose, Crete ................ | Chas. Fisher...................... | Do. |
| 1779 | ......do ......................... | .................................. | Do. |
| 1780 | C F. A. Bartling, Beatrice ........ | Henderson, Los Angeles........... | White Clover. |
| 1781 | Koss & Hackman, Beatrice ....... | .................................. | No label. |
| 1782 | I. L. Fisk, Beatrice ............. | .................................. | California honey. |
| 1783 | Anderson & Co., Beatrice ........ | .................................. | Do. |
| 1784 | Pettinger & Co., Beatrice......... | .................................. | No label. |
| 1785 | Lang & Moschel, Beatrice ....... | .................................. | Do. |
| 1786 | Robertson & McCallum, Beatrice. | .................................. | Do. |
| 1787 | Wm. Fleming & Co., Omaha ...... | Virginia ......................... | Pure Honey. |
| 1788 | Little & Williams, Omaha......... | McMechen......................... | Do. |
| 1789 | C. B. Moore & Co., Omaha......... | Ritter, California ................. | White Clover. |
| 1790 | Henry Pundt, Omaha.............. | ......do ......................... | Do. |
| 1791 | Heimrod & Co., Omaha ........... | ......do ......................... | Do. |
| 1792 | J. D. Wilde, Omaha ............... | A. C. Davidson, Omaha........... | Pure Honey. |
| 1793 | D. L. Carpenter, Omaha........... | .................................. | No label. |
| 1794 | Fred. K. Babcock, Omaha ......... | Ritter Conserve Co .............. | White Clover. |
| 1795 | D. L. Carpenter, Omaha .......... | .................................. | No label. |
| 1796 | Fred. K. Babcock, Omaha......... | .................................. | Do. |
| 1797 | P. M. Back, Omaha .............. | .................................. | Do. |
| 1798 | A. Bennecker, Omaha............. | .................................. | Pure Honey. |
| 1799 | C. F. Evans, Omaha .............. | Wiehert ......................... | Do. |
| 1800 | Thos. Catlin, Omaha ............. | .................................. | No label. |
| 1801 | M. H. Gross, Omaha.............. | .................................. | Do. |
| 1802 | Jens. Jensen, Omaha ............. | .................................. | Do. |
| 1803 | King Bros., Omaha............... | .................................. | Pure Honey. |
| 1804 | McShane & Benner, Lincoln .... | .................................. | Do. |
| 1805 | Clark & Son, Lincoln . .......... | .................................. | Do. |

*Analytical data.*

| No. | Polarization. | | Tempera- | Sucrose. | Reducing | Water. | Ash. |
|-----|---------------|------|----------|----------|----------|-------|------|
|     | Direct. | Indirect. | ture, °C. | | sugars. | | |
|     | | | | Per cent. | Per cent. | Per cent. | Per cent. |
| 1756 | 20.8 | —12.5 | | | 57.16 | 19.06 | 0.24 |
| 1757 | 46.1 | 36.2 | | | 66.64 | 18.07 | 0.10 |
| 1758 | —23.0 | —28.5 | | | 71.60 | 23.39 | 0.16 |
| 1759 | —23.5 | —29.2 | | | 72.80 | 20.93 | 0.12 |
| 1760 | —24.9 | —29.3 | | | 72.80 | 20.38 | 0.14 |
| 1761 | 42.4 | 36.9 | | | 57.16 | 16.00 | 0.14 |
| 1762 | —21.0 | —28.6 | | | 70.50 | 20.10 | 0.14 |
| 1763 | —24.8 | —28.8 | | | 80.00 | 22.71 | 0.17 |
| 1764 | 61.2 | 52.0 | | | 60.40 | 14.81 | 0.14 |
| 1765 | —23.5 | —28.1 | | | 76.80 | 17.79 | 0.08 |
| 1766 | 57.5 | 56.5 | | | 62.40 | 32.78 | 0.56 |
| 1767 | —24.8 | —28.4 | | | 70.00 | 19.27 | 0.19 |
| 1768 | —23.7 | —28.1 | | | 70.00 | 14.56 | 0.14 |
| 1769 | 72.3 | 66.6 | | | 50.20 | 19.98 | 0.24 |
| 1770 | —23.5 | —25.3 | | | 71.90 | 15.81 | 0.19 |
| 1771 | —23.3 | —28.8 | | | 59.90 | 22.12 | 0.10 |
| 1772 | 43.2 | 33.7 | | | 61.60 | 20.27 | 0.17 |
| 1773 | 42.4 | 34.4 | | | 62.40 | 23.10 | 0.08 |
| 1774 | —23.3 | —28.3 | | | 71.60 | 22.36 | 0.07 |
| 1775 | —12.5 | —20.7 | | | 74.20 | 22.74 | 0.02 |
| 1776 | —26.8 | —29.1 | | | 71.90 | 27.59 | 0.00 |
| 1777 | —23.0 | —28.8 | | | 78.10 | 16.11 | 0.13 |
| 1778 | —19.8 | —26.3 | | | 77.50 | 22.12 | 0.12 |
| 1779 | 76.0 | 70.3 | | | 56.50 | 20.62 | 0.32 |
| 1780 | 75.5 | 70.4 | | | 55.90 | 29.17 | 0.23 |
| 1781 | —19.9 | —28.1 | | | 69.90 | 34.99 | 0.16 |
| 1782 | 82.0 | 77.4 | | | 54.30 | 29.43 | 0.21 |
| 1783 | 83.8 | 79.0 | | | 52.30 | 26.81 | 0.21 |
| 1784 | —16.4 | —26.8 | | | 66.20 | 36.70 | 0.07 |
| 1785 | — 7.4 | —29.3 | | | 74.10 | 30.35 | 0.06 |
| 1786 | 82.8 | 77.1 | | | 51.70 | 28.46 | 0.22 |
| 1787 | 61.9 | 52.8 | | | 59.50 | 27.39 | 0.15 |
| 1788 | 30.9 | 12.2 | | | 51.50 | 17.31 | 0.16 |
| 1789 | 31.6 | 12.0 | | | 59.50 | 30.64 | 0.06 |
| 1790 | —12.6 | —20.2 | | | 69.40 | 30.26 | 0.21 |
| 1791 | —17.1 | —27.3 | | | 60.60 | 23.01 | 0.10 |
| 1792 | —15.6 | —20.8 | | | 77.90 | 32.67 | 0.20 |
| 1793 | 116.2 | 102.0 | | | 51.00 | 23.83 | 0.25 |
| 1794 | 12.9 | —21.0 | | | 68.50 | 29.62 | 0.08 |
| 1795 | 63.8 | 57.7 | | | 56.80 | 21.03 | 0.25 |
| 1796 | 28.1 | 11.4 | | | 61.00 | 22.07 | 0.21 |
| 1797 | —23.2 | —29.0 | | | 73.50 | 32.20 | 0.08 |
| 1798 | 61.6 | 52.6 | | | 55.00 | 28.77 | 0.18 |
| 1799 | 72.6 | 66.0 | | | 55.00 | 33.90 | 0.19 |
| 1800 | 31.1 | 22.7 | | | 64.50 | 25.98 | 0.06 |
| 1801 | 43.7 | 34.5 | | | 62.50 | 22.92 | 0.13 |
| 1802 | —20.4 | —28.7 | | | 74.10 | 27.38 | 0.15 |
| 1803 | 82.9 | 76.5 | | | 53.20 | 19.17 | 0.26 |
| 1804 | 47.2 | 38.5 | | | 61.30 | 19.35 | 0.09 |
| 1805 | —23.0 | —28.7 | | | 67.60 | 30.40 | 0.12 |

## ANALYSES BY W. B. RISING.

*Description of samples.*

| No. | Label. | Where bought. | Price. | Color, etc. |
|---|---|---|---|---|
| 1 | Fine Extra White San Diego Honey ; bottled by Philadelphia Manufacturing Company, 110 Ellis street, San Francisco. | Eichwede, Muhr & Co., Adeline and 7th, Oakland. | $0.25 pint......... | Brown liquid. |
| 2 | Los Angeles Honey, in cans. | Congdon & Co., Berkeley. | $0.10 pint......... | Light yellow. |
| 11 | Pure California Honey, Tillman & Bendel, San Francisco. | Hadler Bros.,16th and Mission, San Francisco. | $0.20 ½ pint ....... | Pale yellow liquid. |
| 12 | Orange Blossom Honey, San Jose Fruit Packing Company, San Jose, Cal., (Trade-mark, eagle and two bears.) | ......do ..................... | ....do ............. | Dark amber liquid. |
| 14 | Los Angeles Honey, in cans. | Stewart Bros., Berkeley.. | $0.15 pint......... | Yellow. |
| 15 | Pure Extracted Honey, put up by Risdon, Cahn & Co., San Francisco. | Ainsworth Bros., Market and 14th, Oakland. | $0.20 pint......... $0.25 pint......... | Pale yellow. Pale yellow liquid. |
| 16 | Schacht & Lemke,San Francisco, Monarch Brand. | Palmer & Co., Market and 14th, Oakland. | $0.10 per pint..... | Do. |
| 17 | No label ..................... | A. Wallman, Adeline and 14th, Oakland. | | |
| 18 | No label. | M. Walsh, Peralta and 14th, Oakland. | $0.10 ½ pint ....... | Very pale. |
| 19 | Same label as No. 12......... | 5th and Kirkham, Oakland | $0.25 ½ pint ....... | Dark yellow. |
| 20 | Pure Extracted Honey, Castle Bros., San Francisco. | Northeast corner Cypress and 16th, Oakland. | $0.15 ½ pint......... | Yellow. |
| 21 | Honey, bottled by Philadelphia Manufacturing Company, 118 Ellis street, San Francisco. | Northwest corner 18th and Valencia, San Francisco. | $0.25 pint ......... | Do. |
| 22 | Extra White Los Angeles Honey ; bottled by Philadelphia Manufacturing Company, San Francisco. | Southwest corner 18th and Mission, San Francisco. | ....do ............. | Do. |
| 23 | No label; said to be from Sonoma County. | C. Butt, corner 19th and Stevenson, San Francisco. | $0.10 ½ pint......... | Pale yellow. |
| 24 | No label. ................. | Southwest corner 19th and Mission, San Francisco. | ....do ......... .... | Pale yellow, semi solid. |
| 25 | No label; said to be from San Diego. | Southwest corner 18th and Valencia, San Francisco. | $0.20 pint.......... | Pale yellow. |
| 26 | No label................... | Southwest corner 19th and Mission, San Francisco. | $0.25 pint.......... | Brown. |
| 27 | ......do ................... | C. Dellwigg, Valencia, near 18th, San Francisco. | $0.20 pint ......... | Light yellow; crystallized. |
| 28 | As in No. 12 ........... .... | Southwest corner 19th and Mission, San Francisco. | ....do ............. | Brown, part crystallized. |
| 29 | No label ................. | F. Paulsen, Valencia and | ....do ............. | Very pale yellow. |

*Description of samples—*Continued.

| No. | Label. | Where bought. | Price. | Color, etc. |
|---|---|---|---|---|
| 35 | Orange Grove, Los Angeles, guaranteed to be pure. | A. Aldrich, 16th, near Valencia, San Francisco. | $0.25 per pint ..... | Yellow. |
| 36 | No label; said to be from Los Angeles; in tins. | ......do ................... | ....do ............. | Yellow, turbid |
| 37 | No label .................... | H. Roessel, 16th and Rondel, San Francisco. | $0.10 per ¼ pint ... | Yellow. |
| 38 | ......do .................... | A. Bly, 16th and Hoff avenue, San Francisco. | ....do ............. | Light yellow. |
| 39 | .....do .................... | 17th and Valencia, San Francisco. | ....do ............. | Do. |
| 64 | No label; in 5-gallon tins; said to be from Los Angeles. | E. G. Sim, 18th and Mission, San Francisco. | $0.10 per pound... | Golden yellow. |
| 65 | Pure San Diego Honey; bottled expressly for family use by C. Q. Williams & Co., 417 Washington street, San Francisco. | 2d and Mission, San Francisco. | $0.15 per ¼ pint ... | Pale yellow. |
| 80 | No label ................... | R. V. Mehden, 4th and Mission, San Francisco. | .................... | Do. |
| 128 | Schacht & Lemcke; Monarch brand. | Schacht & Lemcke, Sacramento and Drumm, San Francisco. | .................... | Do. |
| 129 | No label ................... | ......do ................... | .................... | Brown yellow. |
| 130 | In pint cans labeled Pure, Extracted Queen Bee Honey, put up by Russ, Sanders, & Co., San Francisco. (Red can.) | Russ, Sanders & Co...... | .................... | Yellow. |
| 131 | Same as No. 130. (Green can) | .................... | .................... | Golden yellow. |
| 132 | Same as No. 128............ | Schacht & Lemcke, San Francisco. | .................... | Yellow. |
| 133 | Strictly Pure Extracted Honey, Sullivan Bros., San Francisco. Trade-mark, R. ✦ C. | Sullivan Bros............. | .................... | Reddish. |
| 134 | Same as label No. 133 ....... | ......do ................... | .................... | Yellow. |
| 135 | ......do ................... | ......do ................... | .................... | Red. |
| 136 | ......do ................... | ......do ................... | .................... | Yellow. |
| 137 | Pure Los Angeles honey, F. Marten's, 56 Washington Market. | Frist & Geslin, Washington Market. | $0.25 per pint..... | Reddish candied. |
| 138 | No label, in cans............ | Goldberg, Bowon & Co., Pine, near Kearney, San Francisco. | $0.65 per quart ... | Yellow. |
| 139 | No label; said to be from Los Angeles; in fruit jar. | A. W. Fink, Washington Market, San Francisco. | $0.45 per quart ... | Pale yellow. |
| 140 | No label; in 5 gallon cans; said to be from Los Angeles. | Newlott & Graber, California Market. | $0.50 per quart ... | Dark yellow. |
| 141 | No label; in fruit jars...... | Bennett, California Market | $9.45 per quart ... | Pale yellow. |
| 142 | No label ................... | Asmann & Oesting, California Market. | .................... | Yellow. |
| 143 | ......do ................... | Lebenbaum & Co., 215 Sutter, San Francisco. | .................... | Pale yellow. |
| 102 | Los Angeles honey ..... ... | California Market, San Francisco. | $0.30 per pint..... | Yellow. |

*Analytical data.*

| No. | Polarization. Direct. | Indirect. | Tempera-ture °C. | Sucrose. | Reducing sugars. | Water. | Ash. |
|---|---|---|---|---|---|---|---|
|  |  |  |  | *Per cent.* | *Per cent.* | *Per cent.* | *Per cent.* |
| 1 | — 13.75 | — 17.25 | ......... | 2.50 | 66.7 | 15.34 | 0.800 |
| 2 | — 21.00 | — 24.97 | ......... | 2.35 | 68.5 | 17.83 | 0.103 |
| 11 | — 15.20 | — 21.34 | ......... | 4.49 | 68.5 | 14.95 | 0.110 |
| 12 | 30.60 | 19.80 | ......... | 8.00 | 64.1 | 17.66 | 0.290 |
| 14 | — 18.50 | — 24.75 | ......... | 4.28 | 67.6 | 14.00 | 0.080 |
| 16 | 9.40 | 3.30 | ......... | 4.49 | 61.0 | 21.05 | 0.090 |
| 15 | 32.50 | 24.75 | ......... | 5.71 | 62.5 | 14.30 | 0.320 |
| 17 | — 20.00 | — 20.90 | ......... | 0.72 | 78.1 | 17.97 | 0.140 |
| 18 | 46.40 | 41.47 | ........ . | 3.57 | 53.8 | 17.25 | 0.230 |
| 10 | — 16.20 | — 20.02 | ......... | 2.86 | 69.0 | 16.45 | 0.140 |
| 20 | 18.00 | 14.70 | ......... | 1.30 | 64.8 | 17.40 | 0.130 |
| 21 | — 17.60 | — 18.32 | ......... | 0.93 | 65.8 | 21.75 | 3.800 |
| 22 | — 12.80 | — 27.28 | ......... | 10.77 | 64.1 | 16.72 | 0.070 |
| 23 | 58.80 | 52.03 | ......... | 3.40 | 58.1 | 14.66 | 0.210 |
| 24 | — 18.90 | — 18.90 | ......... | 0.00 | 68.5 | 16.41 | 0.160 |
| 25 | — 16.50 | — 27.50 | ......... | 8.14 | 67.6 | 15.56 | 0.080 |
| 26 | — 22.50 | — 22.50 | ......... | 0.00 | 67.5 | 17.08 | 0.820 |
| 27 | 68.10 | 63.30 | ......... | 3.42 | 64.9 | 15.51 | 0.510 |
| 28 | — 16.20 | — 19.58 | ......... | 2.42 | 69.1 | 15.22 | 0.110 |
| 29 | — 16.40 | — 24.09 | ......... | 5.64 | 64.1 | 14.39 | 0.060 |
| 30 | — 12.30 | — 23.54 | ......... | 8.30 | 64.9 | 14.20 | 0.080 |
| 31 | — 22.40 | — 24.64 | ......... | 1.80 | 70.4 | 12.80 | 0.090 |
| 32 | — 19.60 | — 23.65 | ......... | 3.00 | 71.0 | 13.07 | 0.100 |
| 33 | — 21.10 | — 23.54 | ......... | 2.44 | 71.4 | 15.58 | 0.050 |
| 34 | — 21.50 | — 23.60 | ......... | 1.70 | 73.5 | 14.96 | 0.060 |
| 35 | — 16.40 | — 21.80 | ......... | 4.00 | 69.4 | 15.22 | 0.110 |
| 36 | — 18.90 | — 23.65 | ......... | 3.49 | 64.4 | 16.25 | 1.420 |
| 37 | — 16.90 | — 20.35 | ......... | 2.49 | 63.7 | 15.15 | 0.090 |
| 38 | — 18.20 | — 23.76 | ......... | 4.00 | 71.4 | 13.33 | 0.040 |
| 30 | — 16.00 | — 25.19 | ......... | 6.77 | 65.4 | 15.42 | 0.080 |
| 64 | — 20.60 | — 25.19 | ......... | 8.35 | 66.2 | 13.03 | 0.080 |
| 65 | 87.00 | 87.10 | ......... | 0.00 | 32.9 | 22.09 | 0.200 |
| 80 | — 21.60 | — 23.60 | ......... | 1.42 | 66.2 | 16.35 | 0.090 |
| 128 | — 17.90 | — 23.65 | ......... | 3.86 | 52.6 | 15.00 | 0.840 |
| 129 | — 19.50 | — 21.12 | ......... | 1.14 | 64.9 | 14.39 | 0.060 |
| 130 | — 17.60 | — 22.11 | ......... | 3.28 | 64.1 | 20.66 | 0.118 |
| 131 | — 18.50 | — 22.83 | ......... | 2.80 | 65.8 | 14.37 | 0.120 |
| 132 | — 19.10 | — 21.67 | ......... | 1.86 | 65.7 | 15.78 | 0.100 |
| 133 | — 18.50 | — 23.40 | ......... | 3.57 | 67.1 | 17.17 | 0.270 |
| 134 | — 20.00 | — 23.10 | ......... | 2.14 | 64.5 | 15.58 | 0.950 |
| 135 | — 18.00 | — 23.10 | ......... | 3.79 | 64.1 | 17.16 | 0.250 |
| 136 | — 17.90 | — 23.30 | ......... | 3.93 | 61.9 | 14.46 | 0.060 |
| 137 | — 20.40 | — 28.10 | ......... | 1.93 | 67.2 | 21.35 | 0.340 |
| 138 | — 18.90 | — 23.40 | ......... | 3.28 | 69.4 | 18.24 | 0.050 |
| 139 | — 18.40 | — 28.60 | ......... | 3.83 | 64.6 | 18.92 | 0.030 |
| 140 | 119.20 | 112.80 | ......... | 4.65 | 43.5 | 19.08 | 0.200 |
| 141 | — 16.00 | — 25.70 | ......... | 7.15 | 61.0 | 17.17 | 0.144 |
| 142 | — 17.50 | — 23.60 | ......... | 3.00 | 62.4 | 16.97 | 0.120 |
| 143 | — 14.90 | — 23.10 | ......... | 6.00 | 62.8 | 19.56 | 0.060 |
| 102 | — 18.50 | — 23.40 | ......... | 3.57 | 63.0 | 17.21 | 0.100 |

## ANALYSES BY M. A. SCOVELL.

*Description of samples.*

**Sample 101.** McMechen's Old Virginia Pure Honey, prepared by Geo. K. McMechen & Son, Wheeling, W.Va. In bottle. Label around neck reads, "These goods are absolutely pure." Signed, Geo. K. McMechen & Son. Sold by Joseph R. Peeble's Son's Co., Cincinnati, Ohio.

**Sample 102.** Pure California Honey, from Los Angeles, Cal. Sold in bulk by Hamilton, Cincinnati, Ohio.

**Sample 103.** Choice Comb Honey; made by Githens & Reamer, Philadelphia, Pa. In glass jar. Sold by R. J. McCombs, Cincinnati, Ohio. There is some comb in the bottle, but the greater portion is liquid. The liquid only was taken for analysis.

**Sample 104.** Pure Machine-Extracted Honey, from the Italian apiary of Chas. F. Muth, 976 and 978 Central avenue, Cincinnati, Ohio. Sold in bottle by Joseph Peeble's Son's Co., Cincinnati, Ohio.

**Sample 105.** Pure California Honey, from Los Angeles, Cal. Sold in bulk by R. Schudeldecker, 230 Elm street, Cincinnati, Ohio.

**Sample 106.** Bought of Stephens W. Hollen, commission merchant, Cincinnati, Ohio. Country honey in tin buckets.

**Sample 107.** Pure honey, prepared by Dickerson & Tyler, Bowling Green, Ky. Sold in bulk by John Edwell, Bowling Green, Ky.

**Sample 108.** California honey. Sold in bulk by E. T. Poynter, Bowling Green, Ky.

**Sample 109.** Honey prepared by Hanna, Lexington, Ky. Sold in bulk by W. H. May, Lexington, Ky.

**Sample 110.** California Strained Honey, product of the San Diego apiary. Sold in tin cans by L. G. Yoe, Chicago, Ill.

**Sample 111.** Honey, sold by Arthur Peter & Co., Louisville, Ky.

**Sample 112.** Honey, prepared by James Downing, Lexington, Ky. Sold at market house, Lexington, Ky.

**Sample 113.** Pure Machine-Extracted Honey, from the Italian apiary of Chas. F. Muth & Son, corner of Freeman and Central avenues, Cincinnati, Ohio. Sold in bottle by H. Wedekind & Co., Louisville, Ky.

**Sample 114.** Pure California White Sage Honey. Thurber & Whyland, New York City. In bottle ; label around neck reads, "This honey is absolutely pure and unlike liquid honey that has been mixed with glucose to keep it from granulating. It will naturally candy or granulate and become a solid mass in course of time. If preferred in its liquid state, remove the cork and place the bottle in hot water until the honey is melted." Sold by Schnabacher, Cincinnati, Ohio.

**Sample 115.** Buckwheat Honey, from New York. Sold by J. B. Wnrach, Louisville, Ky.

**Sample 116.** Pure Sage California Honey. Sold by Gooch & Edwards, Franklin, Ky. Bought of H. C. Armstrong, Louisville, Ky.

**Sample 117.** Linn California Honey. Through Castner & Gage, Louisville, Ky. Retailed by L. Goose, Louisville, Ky.

**Sample 118.** California White Clover. Through Castner & Gage. Retailed by S. Scholtz, Louisville, Ky.

**Sample 119.** Honey, prepared by Graham. Sold by J. I. Younglove & Bro., druggist, Bowling Green, Ky.

**Sample 120.** California Honey. Sold by T. H. Watkins, Louisville, Ky.

**Sample 121.** Honey, prepared by Campbell. Sold by J. I. Younglove & Bro., Bowling Green, Ky.

**Sample 122.** Pure honey, from Dr. R. J. Spurr, Greendale, Ky,

Sample 123. Almond Blossom Honey, from Los Angeles, Cal., in bulk, by J. B. Wurach, Louisville, Ky.

Sample 124. Honey, from Mrs. Read, Montgomery, Ohio. Sold in bulk by L. T. Griffiths, northwest corner Sixth and Central avenues, Cincinnati, Ohio.

Sample 125. McMechen's Old Virginia Pure Honey. Prepared by George K. McMechen & Son, Wheeling, W. Va. Sold by H. Huneke, Cincinnati, Ohio, in bottle with label around neck;[that reads, "These goods are absolutely pure." Signed, Geo. K. McMechen.

Sample 126. Muth's California Honey. Sold in bulk by S. Scholtz, Cincinnati, Ohio.

Sample 127. Honey, put up by Charles F. Muth & Son, Cincinnati, Ohio, in bottles. Label on neck of bottle reads "Warranted pure;" red label on stopper says, "Warranted pure honey." Sold by Sterritt, Cincinnati, Ohio. Light straw color.

Sample 128. Pure Orange Blossom Eagle Brand Honey, put up by Strohmeyers, New York. Sold by E. W. James, Louisville, Ky., in pear-shaped bottles. Label around neck reads, "Pure extracted honey; all pure honey will congeal, especially when exposed to light and cold; in such cases remove cork, place bottle in cold water and let it boil ten minutes and the honey will regain its liquid state."

Sample 129. Pure Extracted White Clover Honey, from the apiary of Charles Hill, Mount Healthy, Ohio. Sold by the Peebles' Son's Company, Cincinnati, Ohio. Put up in glass jelly jars; light colored.

Sample 130. Honey, put up by James Hanna, Lexington, Ky. Sold by S. K. Coxine, Lexington, Ky., in bottles. Light color.

Sample 131. Honey, put up by J. R. Vanmeter, near Lexington, Ky. Sold by John Hutchinson, Ky. Light colored, beginning to candy.

Sample 132. Honey, put up by Dr. B. L. Price, near Lexington, Ky. Sold by Scully & Yates, Lexington, Ky. Light colored; sold in bulk; candied.

Sample 133. Honey, put up by Brown Vanmeter, Fayette County, Ky. Sold by G. H. Kinnear, Lexington, Ky. Light colored, somewhat candied.

Sample 134. Honey, put up by Brown Vanmeter, Fayette County, Ky. Sold by Henry Vogt, Lexington, Ky.

Sample 135. Comb Honey, put up in glass jars by Githens & Rexsamer, Philadelphia, Pa. Sold by Henry Huneke, Cincinnati, Ohio. Light colored, some comb in it and filled with strained honey. Liquid only taken for analysis.

Sample 136. McMechens Comb Honey, Old Virginia. Sold by G. W. Jefferson, Louisville, Ky. Sold in glass jars; light colored.

Sample 137. California Water White Honey. Sold by J. B. Wurach, Louisville, Ky. Brought in bulk from Los Angeles, Cal.

Sample 138. Honey, put up by Joe Downing, near Lexington, Ky. Sold by Henry Vogt, Lexington, Ky. Light colored. For analysis liquid only was taken.

Sample 139. California Clover Honey. Bought in 50-pound cans; said to come from Los Angeles, Cal. Sold by George Collet & Bro., Bowling Green, Ky.

Sample 140. Choice Comb Honey. Githens & Rexsamer, in quart jars with glass covers. Some comb, and jar filled up with strained honey.

Sample 141. Pure machine-extracted Honey, from the Italian apiary of Charles F. Muth, corner Freeman and Central avenues, Cincinnati, Ohio. Sold in 1-pound bottle by Hamberger & Newburgh, Cincinnati, Ohio.

Sample 142. Alfalfa Honey, from Arizona. Sold by J. J. Hunt, Lexington, Ky.

Sample 143. Pure California Honey, from Los Angeles, Cal. Put up in 50-pound packages, and sold by Colter & Co., Cincinnati, Ohio.

Sample 144. McMechen's Comb Honey, Old Virginia. Put up in glass jars. Sold by Henry Huneke, Cincinnati.

Sample 145. Honey, put up in bottles, with label around the neck which reads, "Warranted pure," signed by Charles F. Muth & Son.   Sold by B. H. Kroger, Cincinnati, Ohio.

Sample 146. Honey, put up by J. Hanna, near Lexington, Ky.   Sold in bulk; retailed by McClelland, Lexington, Ky.

Sample 147. Honey, put up by A. C. Kumman.   Sold by Louis Roessler, Cincinnati, Ohio.   Light colored.

Sample 148. White Clover Honey, put up by Thomas Austin, Nichols & Co., Albany, N. Y.   Sold by George Gelfins, Louisville, Ky.

Sample 149. Honey, put up by Charles F. Muth & Son, in bottle.   The label on neck reads, "Warranted pure."   Sold by A. Barnes, northwest corner Sixth and Elm streets, Cincinnati, Ohio.   Light colored. [Beginning to candy.

Sample 150. California Honey.   Sold in bulk by M. J. Doyle, Louisville.   Dark colored.

*Analytical data.*

| No. | Polarization. | | Tempera-ture ° C. | Sucrose. | Reducing sugars. | Water. | Ash. |
|---|---|---|---|---|---|---|---|
| | Direct. | Indirect. | | | | | |
| | | | | *Per cent.* | *Per cent.* | *Per cent.* | *Per cent.* |
| 101 | 54. 0 | 46. 5 | 24. 0 | 5. 75 | 62. 50 | 9. 86 | 0. 08 |
| 102 | —17. 4 | —22. 7 | 24. 8 | 4. 07 | 75. 47 | 14. 36 | 0. 06 |
| 103 | 92. 8 | 89. 0 | 24. 8 | 3. 08 | 52. 63 | *16. 09 | 0. 21 |
| 104 | 51. 0 | 45. 3 | 24. 8 | 4. 38 | 61. 54 | 13. 99 | 0. 11 |
| 105 | —15. 6 | —18. 3 | 25. 0 | 2. 08 | 73. 39 | 14. 88 | 0. 12 |
| 106 | —13. 1 | —16. 8 | 25. 2 | 2. 85 | 75. 47 | 13. 83 | 0. 07 |
| 107 | —12. 2 | —14. 8 | 24. 8 | 2. 60 | 74. 07 | 13. 15 | 0. 05 |
| 108 | —15. 2 | —20. 8 | 24. 8 | 4. 31 | 72. 73 | 13. 77 | 0. 08 |
| 109 | —16. 8 | —18. 4 | 24. 2 | 1. 23 | 75. 47 | 14. 31 | 0. 06 |
| 110 | 72. 6 | 67. 9 | 24. 8 | 3. 62 | 56. 34 | 18. 54 | 0. 16 |
| 111 | —18. 0 | —21. 6 | 24. 5 | 2. 77 | 73. 39 | 13. 97 | 0. 04 |
| 112 | —13. 2 | —16. 4 | 25. 2 | 2. 46 | 74. 76 | 15. 77 | 0. 03 |
| 113 | —11. 2 | —18. 5 | 24. 8 | 5. 61 | 74. 07 | 16. 21 | 0. 19 |
| 114 | — 7. 2 | —15. 1 | 24. 8 | 6. 08 | 75. 47 | 11. 76 | 0. 20 |
| 115 | — 3. 4 | —18. 1 | 24. 4 | 11. 29 | 65. 57 | 13. 95 | 0. 12 |
| 116 | 75. 2 | 71. 1 | 25. 2 | 3. 16 | 57. 97 | 13. 81 | 9. 19 |
| 117 | —19. 6 | —22. 5 | 24. 6 | 2. 23 | 72. 73 | 17. 78 | 0. 07 |
| 118 | —15. 6 | —21. 7 | 24. 8 | 4. 69 | 74. 07 | 15. 08 | 0. 08 |
| 119 | — 1. 2 | — 7. 0 | 24. 4 | 4. 45 | 72. 07 | 15. 64 | 0. 08 |
| 120 | —17. 0 | —21. 6 | 24. 8 | 3. 54 | 71. 43 | 19. 28 | 0. 07 |
| 121 | —13. 6 | —15. 3 | 24. 6 | 1. 31 | 72. 73 | 17. 37 | 0. 08 |
| 122 | —11. 0 | —14. 4 | 24. 8 | 2. 62 | 65. 57 | 22. 57 | 0. 04 |
| 123 | —14. 8 | —16. 7 | 24. 8 | 1. 46 | 71. 43 | 16. 00 | 0. 13 |
| 124 | —15. 8 | —19. 3 | 24. 0 | 2. 68 | 81. 63 | 13. 51 | 0. 07 |
| 125 | — 9. 2 | —12. 4 | 24. 0 | 2. 45 | 65. 04 | 26. 90 | 0. 19 |
| 126 | 93. 4 | 89. 5 | 24. 8 | 3. 00 | 56. 34 | 13. 01 | 0. 25 |
| 127 | 41. 0 | 37. 7 | 24. 2 | 2. 53 | 64. 51 | 13. 87 | 0. 12 |
| 128 | — 14. 8 | —18. 8 | 24. 2 | 3. 07 | 74. 07 | 13. 35 | 0. 08 |
| 129 | — 14. 0 | —16. 7 | 24. 8 | 2. 08 | 75. 47 | 13. 31 | 0. 06 |
| 130 | — 13. 2 | —16. 4 | 24. 2 | 2. 45 | 72. 73 | 14. 28 | 0. 02 |
| 131 | — 10. 4 | —15. 0 | 24. 8 | 3. 54 | 74. 08 | 14. 65 | 0. 02 |
| 132 | — 14. 2 | —16. 9 | 24. 4 | 2. 07 | 73. 39 | 16. 86 | 0. 02 |
| 133 | — 10. 4 | —14. 6 | 24. 0 | 3. 22 | 72. 73 | 14. 30 | 0. 03 |
| 134 | — 11. 2 | —16. 4 | 24. 0 | 3. 99 | 73. 39 | 14. 15 | 0. 01 |
| 135 | 92. 4 | 88. 0 | 24. 6 | 3. 38 | 56. 34 | 13. 94 | 0. 27 |
| 136 | 103. 8 | 97. 6 | 24. 8 | 4. 77 | 50. 63 | 16. 42 | 0. 36 |
| 137 | 1. 8 | —19. 7 | 24. 8 | 16. 54 | 60. 61 | 15. 88 | 0. 05 |
| 138 | — 12. 2 | —15. 2 | 24. 0 | 2. 30 | 75. 47 | 12. 15 | 0. 03 |
| 139 | — 18. 2 | —21 5 | 24. 6 | 2. 53 | 72. 73 | 13. 96 | 0. 08 |
| 140 | 84. 4 | 80. 1 | 24. 6 | 3. 31 | 54. 78 | 15. 48 | 0. 18 |
| 141 | 46. 4 | 40. 2 | 24. 8 | 4. 77 | 64. 51 | 13. 11 | 0. 07 |
| 142 | — 12. 4 | —19. 8 | 24. 2 | 5. 67 | 76. 91 | 15. 68 | 0. 10 |
| 143 | — 17. 2 | —23. 2 | 24. 8 | 4. 61 | 75. 47 | 12. 83 | 0. 01 |
| 144 | 117. 4 | 113. 5 | 24. 6 | 3. 00 | 50. 00 | 11. 96 | 0. 18 |
| 145 | — 12. 0 | —17. 2 | 24. 0 | 3 98 | 74. 07 | 14. 68 | 0. 05 |
| 146 | — 14. 8 | —17. 4 | 24. 2 | 2. 00 | 74. 07 | 16. 80 | 0. 04 |
| 147 | — 10. 6 | —15. 4 | 24. 8 | 3. 69 | 74. 76 | 15. 52 | 0. 19 |
| 148 | — 14. 8 | —19. 0 | 24. 8 | 3. 23 | 72. 73 | 13. 20 | 0. 06 |
| 149 | 40. 0 | 35. 2 | 24. 6 | 3. 69 | 66. 67 | 14. 30 | 0. 14 |
| 150 | — 15. 8 | —17. 5 | 24. 8 | 1. 31 | 73. 39 | 16. 53 | 0. 16 |

ANALYSES BY S. P. SHARPLES.

*Description of samples.*

| No. | Bought from— | Label. | Price. | Remarks. |
|---|---|---|---|---|
| 9501 | Richard Tubman & Co , Roxbury, Mass. | F. P. Adams & Co., 230 Dover street, Boston, Mass. Warranted Pure Florida Honey. | $0.15 | In tumbler, candied. |
| 9502 | J. F. Johnson, 256 Shawmut avenue, Boston, Mass. | Sold as Pure California Honey. No label. | .10 | In tumbler, not candied. |
| 9503 | A. N. Swallow & Co., 12 City square, Charlestown, Mass. | No label. Sold as California Honey. | .10 | Do. |
| 9504 | Broadway Market, 30 Broadway, South Boston, Mass. | No label .................... | .15 | Piece of comb in honey. In tumbler. |
| 9505 | E. W. Favor, 150 Cambridge street, Boston, Mass. | E. W. Favor, groceries, teas, coffees, and flour a specialty, 150 Cambridge street, Boston, Mass. | .18 | In tumbler. Comb in honey and candied. |
| 9506 | Ware, Eliot square, Boston, Mass. | No label ...................... | .15 | In tumbler with comb; clear and thin. |
| 9507 | C. P. Cobb & Bros., Union street, Boston, Mass. | ......do ...................... | .10 | In tumbler; clear and dark-colored. |
| 9508 | J. F. Johnson, 256 Shawmut avenue, Boston, Mass. | ......do ...................... | .10 | In tumbler, clear. |
| 9509 | Chas. Smith, Cambridge street, Boston, Mass. | ......do ...................... | .10 | In tumbler; clear, good flavor. |
| 9510 | J. R. Bampton, 2271 Washington street, Roxbury, Mass. | ......do ...................... | .10 | In tumbler, clear. |
| 9511 | Ballard's grocery, Broadway, South Boston, Mass. | ......do ...................... | .10 | Do. |
| 9512 | J. R. Bampton, Washington street, Roxbury, Mass. | ......do ...................... | .23 | Comb honey in pound box. Candied after extraction. |
| 9513 | Cobb, Aldrich & Co., 2233 Washington street, Roxbury, Mass. | ......do ...................... | .22 | Do. |
| 9514 | C. D. Swain & Co., Roxbury, Mass. | Choice Comb Honey from E. J. Smith, Grand View Apiary, Addison, Vt. | .25 | Comb honey in pound box. Candied nearly solid after extraction. |
| 9515 | F. O. White & Co., Dudley street, Boston, Mass. | White Clover Honey from the apiary of V. V. Blackmer, Orwell, Vt. | .25 | Comb honey in wooden box; candied nearly solid after extraction. |
| 9516 | W. S. Melcher & Co., Roxbury, Mass. | Choice Comb Honey from Buck Mountain Apiary, Sturtevant & Thompson, Weybridge, Vt. | .25 | Comb honey in pound box; slightly candied. |
| 9517 | Cobb, Bates & Yerxa, Dock square, Boston, Mass. | White label printed in red. Comb Honey from the apiary of H. D. Spencer, Coventryville, N. Y. | .25 | Comb honey in box; clear. |

*Description of samples—Continued.*

| No. | Bought from— | Label. | Price. | Remarks. |
|---|---|---|---|---|
| 9518 | Robert McCullagh, Roxbury, Mass. | White label printed in red. Comb Honey from the apiary of Ward Lankin, Goodyears, Cayuga County, N.Y. | $0.25 | Comb honey in blue pasteboard pound box; clear. |
| 9519 | J. H. Wythe & Co., Cambridge, Mass. | No label .............................. | .30 | In Mason jar, pint; clear. |
| 9520 | Tisdale, Washington street, Roxbury, Mass. | Gilt Edge Brand Pure Honey. State assayer's office, 297 Franklin street. Boston, Mass., Oct. 24, 1890. To J.G. Turner, Medford, Mass. The sample of honey submitted for analysis has been carefully examined with the following results: It gives all the tests of pure honey. We find no traces of any foreign substance in it whatever. The sample is also fresh and has a very fine odor. H. S. Bowker, State assayer. Put up by J. G. Turner, Medford, Mass. | .16 | Put up in small wide-mouthed bottle; clear. |
| 9521 | J. Dana Hovey, Cambridge, Mass. | Pure Houey, J. G. Turner, Medford, Mass. | .17 | Do. |
| 9522 | J. A. Holmes, Cambridge, Mass. | Warranted Pure. Pure Honey, J. G. Turner, Medford Mass. | .17 | In medium-mouthed bottle. |
| 9523 | H. D. Gloyd, 395 Rutherford avenue, Charlestown, Mass. | Pure Strained Honey, put up by H. D. Gloyd, 395 Rutherford avenue, Charlestown, Mass. | .18 | In medium - mouthed bottle; clear. |
| 9524 | S. S. Pierce & Co., Boston, Mass. | Miel de Table Suisse, from J. J. Hurlimann, Rapperswyl, Switzerland. Purveyor to hotels throughout Switzerland. S. S. Pierce & Co., sole agents for the United States. | .40 | Wide-mouthed bottle; clear. |
| 9525 | F. O. White & Co., Dudley street, Roxbury, Mass. | ......do .............................. | .40 | Clear, and working slightly when opened. |
| 9526 | Tighe & Burke, 11 Charles street, Boston, Mass. | This honey is absolutely pure and unlike liquid honey that has been mixed with glucose to keep it from granulating, it will naturally candy or granulate and become a solid mass in course of time. If preferred in its liquid state, remove the cork and place the bottle in hot water until the honey is melted. Pure California White Sage Honey, Thurber, Whyland & Co., New York. | .25 | In wide-mouthed bottle; clear and dark colored. |
| 9527 | J. Sullivan, 1490 Tremont street, Boston, Mass. | Extracted California Honey, warranted pure, by E. T. Cowdrey Co., manufacturers of pickles, preserves, and canned goods, 80 Broad street, Boston, Mass. | .20 | In wide-mouthed bottle. |
| 9528 | Cobb, Bates & Yerxa, Court street, Boston, Mass. | ......do .............................. | .25 | Do. |

*Description of samples—Continued.*

| No. | Bought from— | Label. | Price. | Remarks. |
|---|---|---|---|---|
| 9529 | Mendum, 141 Hampden street, Boston, Mass. | (Warranted Pure Honey, B. Otis Hoge, Brooklyn, N. Y.) on cork. On neck of bottle: B. Otis Hoge, 264 Willoughby avenue, Brooklyn, N. Y. On side of bottle: Pure Extracted Honey. This honey is obtained by shaving off the delicate capping of the cells, putting the combs into the little wire baskets illustrated above and revolving by means of a crank. The honey thus thrown out by centrifugal force runs down the sides of the can and is put into jars. We guarantee it absolutely pure. Once tried always used. This honey is the pure liquid minus the wax comb. B. Otis Hoge, 264 Willoughby avenue, Brooklyn, N. Y. | $0.17 | One-half pound bottle; clear. |
| 9530 | Robert McCullagh, corner Dale and Washington streets, Boston, Mass. | ......do ....... ..................... | .10 | Quarter-pound bottle; clear. |
| 9531 | John Gilbert, Tremont Row, Boston, Mass. | Pure Honey. Should this honey granulate, set the bottle in hot water until liquefied. A. J. Raymond, Everett, Mass. | .25 | Wide-mouthed bottle; clear. |
| 9532 | Haynes & Murphey, corner Mount Vernon and Charles streets, Boston, Mass. | ......do .................. | .25 | Do. |
| 9533 | A. J. Lovell, Cambridge street, Boston, Mass. | Label same as sample No. 9531........ | $0.15 | Wide-mouthed bottle; clear. |
| 9534 | W. S. Melcher, 65 Warren street, Boston, Mass. | ......do ................. | .18 | ..................... |
| 9535 | B. F. Jerome & Co., 1447 Tremont street, Roxbury, Mass. | Vermont Honey. Particularly for medicinal use. David Holland, Peacham, Vt. | .18 | In wide-mouthed bottle; clear. |
| 9536 | W. A. Holmes, Causeway street, Boston, Mass. | Strained Honey, warranted pure. Reid & Co., Boston, Mass. | .35 | In fancy bottle with screw top; clear. |
| 9537 | Richard Tubman, Roxbury, Mass. | ......do .................. | .30 | In fancy bottle with screw top; granulated. |
| 9538 | C. A. Adams, Berkeley street, Boston, Mass. | ......do .................. | .15 | Small, wide-mouthed bottle; granulated. |
| 9539 | Benny, Eliot square, Roxbury, Mass. | White Clover Honey from W. J. Lamb | .20 | In wide-mouthed bottle; clear. |
| 9540 | H. A. Davenport, Warren street, Roxbury, Mass. | Pure Honeysuckle Honey from W. J. Lamb. | .25 | In screw-top bottle; slightly cloudy. |

*Description by samples*—Continued.

| No. | Bought from— | Label. | Price. | Remarks. |
|---|---|---|---|---|
| 9541 | Sibley, 1339 Tremont street, Boston, Mass. | Pure White California Honey, extracted and bottled expressly for family use. F. P. Adams & Co., Boston, Mass. | $0.25 | In screw-top bottle; clear. |
| 9542 | F. S. Plateen, 529 Tremont street, Boston, Mass. | Pure California Honey................ | .30 | In wide-mouthed bottle; slightly candied. |
| 9543 | Winthrop Market, Roxbury, Mass. | Guaranteed Strictly Pure White Honey from the celebrated Monte Blanco apiaries of Wm. T. Richardson & Co., Santa Barbara, Cal., Jno. A. Andrews & Co., Agents, Boston, Mass. Should this honey granulate set the bottle in water and heat gradually until liquefied. | .35 | In wide-mouthed bottle, screw top; clear. |
| 9544 | C. D. Swain & Co., 2364 Washington street, Boston, Mass. | Pure Honey, put up by C. D. Swain & Co., grocers, 2364 Washington street, Boston, Mass. | .15 | Wide-mouthed bottle; dark-colored and clear. |
| 9545 | Cobb, Aldrich & Co., 2233 Washington street, Roxbury, Mass. | Pure Strained Honey, put up by H. D. Gloyd, 395 Rutherford avenue, Charlestown, Mass. | .18 | In wide-mouthed bottle; candied. |
| 9546 | A. W. Peabody, 112 F. H. Market, Boston, Mass. | No label .................... | .25 | In wide-mouthed bottle; clear. |
| 9547 | Fessenden, Court street, Boston, Mass. | These goods are absolutely pure. George K. McMechen & Son. Mincemeat, jellies, preserves, ketchups, pickles, hyden salad. McMechen's Old Virginia Pure Honey. Prepared by George K. McMechen & Son, Wheeling, W. Va. | .25 | Wide-mouthed bottle; clear. |
| 9548 | C. D. Cobb, Thompson square, Charlestown, Mass. | Strained Honey, warranted pure by the packers, Colgate & Co., Boston, Mass. | .10 | Wide-mouthed bottle; candied. |
| 9549 | F. P. Merrill, Cambridge, Mass. | Warranted Pure Honey. Analysis: Stoneham, Mass., Aug. 28, 1890. New England Sauce Co., 36 Beach street, Boston, Mass. Gentlemen: We have examined a sample of your pure extracted honey and found it to be absolutely pure, and a very superior article. Assayed at the laboratory of the E. S. Patch Co., put up by the New England Sauce Co., Boston, Mass. | .25 | In wide-mouthed bottle; candied. |
| 9550 | Worcester County Creamery, Berkeley street, Boston, Mass. | Label same as sample No. 9549........ | .18 | Small bottle; clear. |

FOODS AND FOOD ADULTERANTS.

*Analytical data.*

| No. | Polarization. Direct. | Polarization. Indirect. | Tempera- ture ° C. | Sucrose. | Reducing sugars. | Water. | Ash. |
|---|---|---|---|---|---|---|---|
| | | | | Per cent. | Per cent. | Per cent. | Per cent. |
| 9501 | — 6.70 | —12.50 | 18 | .......... | 73.36 | 16.02 | 0.06 |
| 9502 | — 17.20 | —20.10 | 21 | .......... | 74.77 | 16.12 | 0.04 |
| 9503 | — 20.30 | —24.50 | 20 | .......... | 76.23 | 16.12 | 0.10 |
| 9504 | 68.20 | 64.20 | .......... | .......... | 58.91 | 21.34 | 0.11 |
| 9505 | — 16.60 | —21.50 | 20 | .......... | 74.77 | 14.66 | 0.20 |
| 9506 | 60.50 | 58.40 | 20 | .......... | 58.91 | 23.52 | 0.00 |
| 9507 | — 11.00 | —12.00 | 20 | .......... | 74.77 | 16.80 | 0.13 |
| 9508 | — 19.00 | —20.60 | 20 | .......... | 74.77 | 17.32 | 0.09 |
| 9509 | — 18.40 | — 22.60 | 20 | .......... | 75.06 | 15.62 | 0.08 |
| 9510 | — 17.30 | —21.80 | 18 | .......... | 76.08 | 16.38 | 0.08 |
| 9511 | — 17.40 | —23.00 | 19 | .......... | 76.08 | 14.94 | 0.07 |
| 9512 | — 16.00 | —20.40 | 19 | .......... | 76.23 | 14.72 | 0.08 |
| 9513 | — 13.10 | —21.80 | .......... | .......... | 76.38 | 13.57 | 0.06 |
| 9514 | — 7.80 | —14.60 | 20 | .......... | 72.00 | 20.60 | 0.15 |
| 9515 | — 15.10 | —18.60 | 19 | .......... | 77.45 | 17.00 | 0.07 |
| 9516 | — 13.20 | —15.60 | 20 | .......... | 76.23 | 14.92 | 0.07 |
| 9517 | — 16.30 | —18.00 | 20 | .......... | 76.08 | 16.09 | 0.06 |
| 9518 | — 13.90 | —14.00 | 20 | .......... | 79.55 | 16.18 | 0.16 |
| 9519 | — 16.60 | —20.20 | 22 | .......... | 73.22 | 14.08 | 0.07 |
| 9520 | — 18.30 | —24.20 | 19 | .......... | 76.23 | 16.68 | 0.07 |
| 9521 | — 18.80 | —24.20 | 24 | .......... | 75.06 | 18.46 | 0.10 |
| 9522 | — 19.80 | —23.20 | 24 | .......... | 77.45 | 17.32 | 0.10 |
| 9523 | — 14.10 | —17.60 | 21 | .......... | 74.48 | 20.68 | 0.13 |
| 9524 | 113.00 | 92.00 | 20 | .......... | 40.50 | 16.54 | 0.26 |
| 9525 | 109.50 | 90.20 | .......... | .......... | 30.83 | 20.94 | 0.26 |
| 9526 | 42.00 | 40.00 | 22 | .......... | 67.03 | 15.39 | 0.24 |
| 9527 | — 21.30 | —22.00 | 16 | .......... | 77.47 | 18.09 | 0.08 |
| 9528 | — 12.80 | —14.60 | 22 | .......... | 73.50 | 18.56 | 0.20 |
| 9529 | — 13.80 | —16.20 | 22 | .......... | 72.26 | 15.82 | 0.24 |
| 9530 | — 16.50 | — 18.00 | 22 | .......... | 75.06 | 16.32 | 0.10 |
| 9531 | — 17.60 | —22.00 | 22 | .......... | 79.23 | 15.60 | 0.07 |
| 9532 | — 17.80 | —21.60 | 22 | .......... | 79.30 | 13.90 | 0.09 |
| 9533 | — 15.30 | —21.60 | 22 | .......... | 74.77 | 15.64 | 0.06 |
| 9534 | — 15.60 | —20.40 | 22 | .......... | 76.08 | 16.48 | 0.07 |
| 9535 | — 13.40 | —17.60 | 22 | .......... | 72.00 | 19.14 | 0.00 |
| 9536 | — 18.10 | —20.60 | 21 | .......... | 78.07 | 14.76 | 0.07 |
| 9537 | — 21.80 | —25.20 | 21 | .......... | 81.00 | 18.14 | 0.13 |
| 9538 | — 19.80 | —20.00 | 21 | .......... | 75.06 | 17.40 | 0.12 |
| 9539 | — 16.10 | —21.60 | 21 | .......... | 79.23 | 20.04 | 0.13 |
| 9540 | — 2.30 | — 6.00 | 21 | .......... | 71.73 | 21.70 | 0.20 |
| 9541 | — 16.00 | —21.60 | 20 | .......... | 74.77 | 19.18 | 0.06 |
| 9542 | — 12.80 | —14.60 | 20 | .......... | 74.94 | 15.28 | 0.16 |
| 9543 | — 16.30 | —20.60 | 20 | .......... | 70.69 | 15.32 | 0.08 |
| 9544 | — 0.80 | —12.00 | 21 | .......... | 77.76 | 18.98 | 0.13 |
| 9545 | — 16.80 | —17.60 | 20 | .......... | 72.00 | 14.88 | 0.09 |
| 9546 | — 14.80 | —15.60 | 21 | .......... | 74.77 | 17.12 | 0.14 |
| 9547 | 50.50 | 52.00 | 20 | .......... | 62.71 | 16.05 | 0.11 |
| 9548 | — 11.80 | —16.00 | ... | .......... | 74.77 | 15.50 | 0.18 |
| 9549 | — 17.80 | —21.60 | 20 | .......... | 70.39 | 18.32 | 0.10 |
| 9550 | — 15.90 | —20.00 | 20 | .......... | 77.76 | 14.90 | 0.10 |

## ANALYSES BY W. C. STUBBS.

*Description of samples.*

| No. | Bought from— | No. | Bought from— |
|---|---|---|---|
| 1 | A. S. Field & Bro., Rampart & DeLord streets, New Orleans, La. | 26 | McDuff's Pharmacy, Annunciation street New Orleans, La. |
| 2 | B. Fehnbacher, Dryades street, New Orleans, La. | 27 | H. Homberg, 859 Magazine street, New Orleans, La. |
| 3 | John Lagan, 191 Orleans street, New Orleans, La. | 28 | George F. Brown, Magazine street, New Orleans, La. |
| 4 | Southern Drug Company, New Orleans, La. | 29 | Mrs. F. Stunger, Seventh street, New Orleans, La. |
| 5 | Alfred Levy, Saint Charles street, New Orleans, La. | 30 | E. Sauter, 913 Magazine street, New Orleans, La. |
| 6 | Leon C. Peres, Magazine street, New Orleans, La. | 31 | Eugene May, Canal and Exchange streets, New Orleans, La. |
| 7 | I. L. Lyons & Co., Camp Street, New Orleans, La. | 32 | Bogh Drug Company, 111 Canal street, New Orleans, La. |
| 8 | D. M. Holders, Canal street, New Orleans, La. | 33 | St. Cry. Fourdade, 215 Canal street, New Orleans, La. |
| 9 | J. F. Seekman, 75 South Rampart street, New Orleans, La. | 34 | American Drug Store, Canal street, New Orleans, La. |
| 10 | J. M. W. Otto, Gravier street, New Orleans, La. | 35 | L. C. Peres, 238 Canal street, New Orleans, La. |
| 11 | Joseph Taber, 198 Rampart street, New Orleans, La. | 36 | L. C. Cusachs, Canal and Baronne streets, New Orleans, La. |
| 12 | J. A. Florat, 12 New Basin street, New Orleans, La. | 37 | A. Griffs, 299 Royal street, New Orleans, La. |
| 13 | William Graner, Baronne street, New Orleans, La. | 38 | Marcel Magean, Du Maine and Bourbon streets, New Orleans, La. |
| 14 | F. C. Godbold, 361 Magazine street, New Orleans, La. | 39 | M. T. Breslin, Dauphine and St. Peters streets, New Orleans, La. |
| 15 | William C. Harrison, Thalia street, New Orleans, La. | 40 | Legendre & Co., Dauphine and Custom-House streets, New Orleans, La. |
| 16 | William M. Levy, 420 Magazine street, New Orleans, La. | 41 | P. H. Jansen, St. Charles and Girod streets, New Orleans, La. |
| 17 | J. D. Browlee, Felicity street, New Orleans, La. | 42 | James Wilson & Co., Prytania and Felicity streets, New Orleans, La. |
| 18 | A. J. Keenan, 580 Magazine street, New Orleans, La. | 43 | Lawrence's Pharmacy, Jackson and Prytania streets, New Orleans, La. |
| 19 | H. E. Grice & Co., 613 Magazine street, New Orleans, La. | 44 | Wright's Pharmacy, 111 Prytania street, New Orleans, La. |
| 20 | C. J. Mattingly, Napoleon avenue, New Orleans, La. | 45 | E. Turpin, New Orleans, La. |
| 21 | E. H. Rosenfeld, 1148 Magazine street, New Orleans, La. | 46 | H. C. Ahlers, 339 Mississippi street, New Orleans, La. |
| 22 | J. B. Schmidt, Magazine street, New Orleans, La. | 47 | J. F. Christine, Du Maine and Galoez streets, New Orleans, La. |
| 23 | L. B. Diez, Perriston street, New Orleans, La. | 48 | L. J. Cousin, Du Maine and Claiborne streets, New Orleans, La. |
| 24 | G. D. Feldner, 366 Magazine street, New Orleans, La. | 49 | Marcel Magean, Bourbon and Du Maine streets, New Orleans, La. |
| 25 | H. Dannemann, Chippewa street, New Orleans, La. | 50 | J. Laddo, New Orleans, La. |

*Analytical data.*

| No. | Polarization. Direct. | Polarization. Indirect. | Tempera- ture °C. | Sucrose. | Reducing sugars. | Water. | Ash. |
|---|---|---|---|---|---|---|---|
| | | | | *Per cent.* | *Per cent.* | *Per cent.* | *Per cent.* |
| 1 | — 6.40 | — 8.25 | 19 | 1.38 | 69.00 | 24.14 | 0.12 |
| 2 | 65.80 | 21.85 | 20 | 32.05 | 33.30 | 24.02 | 0.17 |
| 3 | — 5.30 | — 9.40 | 20 | 2.94 | 64.60 | 29.26 | 0.61 |
| 4 | — 2.51 | —26.10 | 20 | 0.97 | 74.00 | 24.19 | 0.35 |
| 5 | 53.80 | 51.26 | 20 | 1.14 | 62.40 | 29.74 | 0.29 |
| 6 | 55.00 | 51.70 | 20 | 2.47 | 64.60 | 25.46 | 0.15 |
| 7 | — 1.50 | — 4.40 | 10 | 2.16 | 63.24 | 21.31 | 0.24 |
| 8 | 6.40 | —15.29 | 20 | 12.33 | 56.20 | 22.40 | 0.08 |
| 9 | —17.00 | —20.20 | 12 | 2.18 | 73.30 | 22.00 | 0.21 |
| 10 | —25.20 | —27.83 | 12 | 1.90 | 71.72 | 22.64 | 0.28 |
| 11 | 52.20 | 49.94 | 21 | 1.60 | 67.09 | 22.43 | 0.22 |
| 12 | — 4.00 | — 6.82 | 21 | 2.11 | 74.74 | 26.27 | 0.08 |
| 13 | 4.00 | 1.65 | 23 | 1.77 | 71.72 | 24.44 | 0.43 |
| 14 | — 9.40 | —10.07 | 26 | 0.96 | 74.23 | 21.62 | 0.24 |
| 15 | 3.20 | 1.65 | 23 | 1.09 | 72.98 | 24.27 | 0.36 |
| 16 | —11.30 | —13.31 | 26 | 1.56 | 74.66 | 23.17 | 0.11 |
| 17 | —12.90 | —13.86 | 26 | 0.73 | 76.36 | 22.69 | 0.02 |
| 18 | 79.60 | 77.00 | 26 | 1.90 | 64.00 | 23.93 | 0.09 |
| 19 | —15.50 | —17.82 | 25 | 1.76 | 72.90 | 22.25 | 0.05 |
| 20 | —11.30 | —13.09 | 26 | 1.36 | 74.37 | 23.92 | 0.09 |
| 21 | 64.70 | 61.82 | 26 | 2.19 | 63.03 | 24.17 | 0.23 |
| 22 | —14.40 | —15.40 | 26 | 0.76 | 70.50 | 25.76 | 0.35 |
| 23 | 3.60 | 0.70 | 26 | 2.16 | 67.20 | 25.30 | 0.07 |
| 24 | 63.40 | 61.05 | 25 | 1.78 | 59.29 | 25.45 | 0.38 |
| 25 | 64.50 | 56.80 | 25 | 1.53 | 61.09 | 27.25 | 0.65 |
| 26 | 54.80 | 48.10 | 10 | 1.36 | 52.63 | 31.82 | 0.27 |
| 27 | 49.60 | 13.75 | 25 | 29.31 | 37.33 | 31.77 | 0.16 |
| 28 | —16.00 | —13.94 | 25 | 0.53 | 73.30 | 22.91 | 0.06 |
| 29 | — 1.50 | — 6.38 | 10 | 3.51 | 64.00 | 24.74 | 0.22 |
| 30 | 44.30 | 38.30 | 25 | 1.65 | 57.60 | 29.95 | 0.25 |
| 31 | —12.00 | —13.97 | 18 | 1.46 | 75.22 | 22.93 | 0.16 |
| 32 | —11.30 | —12.65 | 17 | 0.99 | 70.48 | 27.19 | 0.08 |
| 33 | 59.90 | 57.97 | 17 | 1.42 | 53.05 | 23.84 | 0.11 |
| 34 | —12.60 | —14.30 | 17 | 1.25 | 74.09 | 23.25 | 0.05 |
| 35 | 54.40 | 52.80 | 20 | 1.19 | 58.43 | 27.55 | 0.20 |
| 36 | —13.00 | —15.40 | 25 | 1.82 | 55.08 | 21.63 | 0.24 |
| 37 | 43.30 | 41.09 | 25 | 1.22 | 51.09 | 27.34 | 0.31 |
| 38 | 43.80 | 42.02 | 20 | 1.32 | 59.29 | 29.40 | 0.19 |
| 39 | — 8.50 | —12.19 | 15 | 2.70 | 72.51 | 24.91 | 0.08 |
| 40 | —24.00 | —20.95 | 15 | 2.16 | 73.07 | 22.56 | 0.31 |
| 41 | 2.30 | — 0.55 | 20 | 2.12 | 65.45 | 28.42 | 0.17 |
| 42 | —13.50 | —15.05 | 20 | 1.82 | 69.04 | 24.47 | 0.14 |
| 43 | — 8.00 | — 9.35 | 20 | 1.00 | 73.04 | 23.87 | 0.11 |
| 44 | —11.50 | —12.65 | 20 | 0.85 | 70.48 | 27.53 | 0.11 |
| 45 | 127.20 | 124.85 | 20 | 1.75 | 48.00 | 27.60 | 0.25 |
| 46 | 71.65 | 58.58 | 16 | 0.61 | 57.27 | 27.43 | 0.42 |
| 47 | —11.60 | —13.42 | 15 | 1.33 | 72.52 | 25.23 | 0.03 |
| 48 | —10.87 | —12.87 | 16 | 1.47 | 70.48 | 26.25 | 0.08 |
| 49 | 43.07 | 40.53 | 15 | 2.52 | 65.03 | 32.82 | 0.19 |
| 50 | 1.00 | — 2.20 | 16 | 2.35 | 72.51 | 26.43 | 0.36 |

## ANALYSES BY SHIPPEN WALLACE.

*Description of samples.*

| No. | Label. | Bought from— | Price. |
|---|---|---|---|
| 1 | Pure California Honey........................ | P. J. Ritter Company, Philadelphia....... | $0.25 |
| 2 | XXX California Honey................:........ | No maker .................................. | .25 |
| 3 | White Clover Honey......................... | Sleeper, Wells & Aldrich ................. | .25 |
| 4 | Honey ...................................... | Arthur Todd, Philadelphia................ | .25 |
| 5 | Virginia Honey.........................'.... | Philadelphia Pickling Company .......... | .15 |
| 6 | Pure Extracted Honey ......... ...... .... | T. S. Borden, Burlington, N. J............. | .25 |
| 7 | Honey ...................................... | No maker................................. | . .10 |
| 8 | ......do ................................... | Philadelphia Pickling Company .......... | .10 |
| 9 | White Clover XXX Honey .................. | Sleeper, Wells & Aldrich ................. | .25 |
| 10 | White Clover Honey........................ | W. G. Griffiths, Philadelphia ............. | .25 |
| 11 | Pure Honey ................................ | Anderson & Co., Camden, N. J........... | .15 |
| 12 | ......do ................................... | No maker................................. | .20 |
| 13 | California Honey ........................... | ......do.................................... | .20 |
| 14 | White Rose Honey ......................... | New Jersey Preserving Co., Camden...... | .20 |
| 15 | Choice Extra Northern Honey.............. | Geo. D. Powell, New York ................. | .25 |
| 16 | Superior Extracted Honey.................. | Walker, McCord & Co., Philadelphia ..... | .25 |
| 17 | XXX White Clover California.............. | J.O.Schimmel Preserving Co.,Philadelphia | .25 |
| 18 | Strictly Pure Extracted Honey............. | Austin, Nichols & Co., New York......... | .25 |
| 19 | Pure Honey ................................ | Stevenson & Co., Burlington, N.J ....... | .25 |
| 20 | California Honey .......................... | E. T. Coudrey & Co., Boston ............. | .25 |
| 21 | Choice Northern Honey..............:...... | Geo. D. Powell, New York... ............. | .25 |
| 22 | Choice Honey............................... | Wm. Collins, New York.................... | .25 |
| 23 | Choice Los Angeles Honey.................. | John Long, New York...................... | .25 |
| 24 | California Honey........................... | No maker................................. | .15 |
| 25 | Choice California Honey.................... | P. J. Ritter Co ...... ,.................... | .25 |
| 26 | Pure Old Virginia Honey .....'............ | Geo.K. McMechen & Son,Wheeling,W.Va. | .25 |
| 27 | Pure Clover Honey ......................... | No maker................................. | .15 |
| 28 | XX White Clover Honey ................... | G. & R., Philadelphia...................... | .25 |
| 29 | Honey...................................... | Chas. G. F. Denk, Philadelphia .......... | . .10 |
| 30 | Golden Rod Honey ......................... | Wm. Thompson, New York ............... | .20 |
| 31 | Wittman's Superior Honey ................. | Philadelphia .............................. | .10 |
| 32 | Pure California Honey...................... | Thos. Martingdale, Philadelphia .......... | .25 |
| 33 | Extracted Honey ........................... | C. H. Luttgers, Hammonton, N. J......... | .25 |
| 34 | Pure Honey ............................... | P. A. Garrettson, Hillsboro, N. J.......... | .25 |
| 35 | California Honey .......................... | No maker................................. | .10 |
| 36 | Absolutely Pure Virginia Honey ........... | Geo. K. McMechen & Son ................. | .25 |
| 37 | Strained Honey............................. | Max Ams, New York ..................... | .20 |
| 38 | California Honey .......................... | In glass tumblers, no maker .............. | .10 |
| 39 | Pure Honey................................ | ......do.................................... | .10 |
| 40 | White Clover Honey ....................... | ......do.................................... | .10 |
| 41 | Honey ..................................... | ......do.................................... | .15 |
| 42 | Golden Rod Honey......................... | ......do.... ............................... | .10 |
| 43 | Strained Honey............................. | ......do.................................... | .10 |
| 44 | Honey ..................................... | ......do.................................... | .10 |
| 45 | ......do ................................... | ......do.................................... | .10 |
| 46 | Pure Honey ............................... | ......do.................................... | .10 |
| 47 | Extracted Honey .......................... | ......do.................................... | .10 |
| 48 | California Honey .......................... | ......do.................................... | .10 |
| 49 | Clover Honey.............................. | ......do ................... ...........| .10 |
| 50 | Pure Honey ............................... | Henry Bassett, Salem, N. J ............... | .25 |

*Analytical data.*

| No. | Polarization. | | Tempera-ture,°C. | Sucrose. | Reducing sugars. | Water. | Ash. |
|---|---|---|---|---|---|---|---|
| | Direct. | Indirect. | | | | | |
| | | | | *Per cent.* | *Per cent.* | *Per cent.* | *Per cent.* |
| 1 | 29.0 | — 13.0 | .......... | 31.3 | 38.50 | .......... | 5.21 |
| 2 | 66.0 | 61.0 | .......... | 3.7 | 51.20 | .......... | 0.17 |
| 3 | 9.0 | — 10.0 | .......... | 14.1 | 47.54 | .......... | 0.15 |
| 4 | — 4.0 | — 6.0 | .......... | 1.4 | 62.60 | .......... | 0.09 |
| 5 | 110.0 | 27.0 | .......... | 61.9 | 41.38 | .......... | 0.12 |
| 6 | — 10.0 | — 16.0 | .......... | 4.4 | 69.85 | .......... | 0.15 |
| 7 | — 19.5 | — 19.0 | .......... | (?) | 70.10 | .......... | 0.27 |
| 8 | 102.0 | 92.6 | .......... | 7.0 | 44.20 | .......... | 0.10 |
| 9 | — 3.5 | — 16.0 | .......... | 9.4 | 72.30 | .......... | 0.08 |
| 10 | — 8.0 | — 12.0 | .......... | 2.9 | 69.85 | .......... | 0.05 |
| 11 | — 13.5 | — 14.0 | .......... | 0.3 | 71.50 | .......... | 0.20 |
| 12 | — 13.0 | — 13.0 | .......... | .......... | 71.50 | .......... | 0.22 |
| 13 | — 18.5 | — 20.0 | .......... | 1.1 | 72.75 | .......... | 0.27 |
| 14 | 78.0 | 72.0 | .......... | 4.5 | 35.50 | .......... | 0.08 |
| 15 | 83.5 | 70.0 | .......... | 10.0 | 31.50 | .......... | 0.15 |
| 16 | 51.0 | 47.0 | .......... | 2.9 | 29.85 | .......... | 0.10 |
| 17 | 19.0 | 16.0 | .......... | 2.2 | 45.78 | .......... | 0.18 |
| 18 | — 7.5 | — 9.0 | .......... | 1.1 | 65.70 | .......... | 0.07 |
| 19 | 41.0 | 31.0 | .......... | 7.4 | 40.25 | .......... | 0.09 |
| 20 | — 9.5 | — 10.0 | .......... | 0.3 | 67.22 | .......... | 0.20 |
| 21 | 92.5 | 58.0 | .......... | 25.7 | 38.80 | .......... | 0.12 |
| 22 | 53.5 | 41.0 | .......... | 9.3 | 29.65 | .......... | 0.18 |
| 23 | 10.5 | — 8.0 | .......... | 13.8 | 45.92 | .......... | 0.09 |
| 24 | — 11.0 | — 12.0 | .......... | 0.7 | 72.50 | .......... | 0.28 |
| 25 | 30.5 | 13.0 | .......... | 13.0 | 51.65 | .......... | 0.18 |
| 26 | 52.0 | 32.0 | .......... | 14.9 | 27.60 | .......... | 0.21 |
| 27 | — 14.0 | — 14.0 | .......... | .......... | 71.95 | .......... | 0.25 |
| 28 | 7.5 | — 14.0 | .......... | 16.0 | 68.22 | .......... | 0.18 |
| 29 | — 19.0 | — 19.0 | .......... | .......... | 74.80 | .......... | 0.22 |
| 30 | 71.0 | 64.0 | .......... | 5.2 | 33.75 | .......... | 0.17 |
| 31 | — 17.0 | — 17.0 | .......... | .......... | 73.10 | .......... | 0.23 |
| 32 | — 15.0 | — 15.0 | .......... | .......... | 71.50 | .......... | 0.28 |
| 33 | — 12.0 | — 14.0 | .......... | 1.4 | 70.95 | .......... | 0.25 |
| 34 | — 10.0 | — 11.0 | .......... | 0.7 | 67.80 | .......... | 0.31 |
| 35 | 102.5 | 83.0 | .......... | 14.5 | 40.55 | .......... | 0.15 |
| 36 | 11.0 | — 15.0 | .......... | 19.4 | 64.30 | .......... | 0.19 |
| 37 | — 14.0 | — 14.0 | .......... | .......... | 71.75 | .......... | 0.32 |
| 38 | 57.5 | — 20.0 | .......... | 57.8 | 20.85 | .......... | 0.18 |
| 39 | 53.0 | 4.0 | .......... | 38.0 | 40.15 | .......... | 0.15 |
| 40 | 7.5 | — 16.0 | .......... | 17.5 | 68.50 | .......... | 0.20 |
| 41 | — 5.0 | — 17.0 | .......... | 8.0 | 65.20 | .......... | 0.27 |
| 42 | 8.3 | — 16.0 | .......... | 18.1 | 68.25 | .......... | 0.18 |
| 43 | 53.0 | 8.0 | .......... | 33.5 | 52.50 | .......... | 0.14 |
| 44 | 10.0 | 8.0 | .......... | 13.4 | 44.25 | .......... | 0.16 |
| 45 | — 5.0 | — 8.0 | .......... | 2.2 | 68.95 | .......... | 0.22 |
| 46 | 110.0 | 27.0 | .......... | 61.9 | 41.50 | .......... | 0.15 |
| 47 | 102.0 | 92.6 | .......... | 7.0 | 40.15 | .......... | 0.15 |
| 48 | 78.0 | 70.0 | .......... | 5.9 | 36.50 | .......... | 0.20 |
| 49 | 65.0 | 50.0 | .......... | 11.1 | 49.45 | .......... | 0.18 |
| 50 | — 11.0 | — 12.0 | .......... | 0.7 | 72.65 | .......... | 0.27 |

## ANALYSES BY H. A. WEBER.

*Description of samples.*

| No. | Bought from— | Label. | Remarks. |
|---|---|---|---|
| 1 | Procured by Dairy and Food Company, in Cleveland, Ohio. | California Honey, put up by Williams' Brothers, Cleveland, Ohio. | Dextrine reaction. |
| 2 | J. H. Haner, State and 4th street, Columbus, Ohio. | Warranted Pure Extracted Honey. Apiary of S. R. Morris, Bloomingburg, Ohio. | |
| 3 | J. G. & S. Brown, Hunter street and 5th avenue, Columbus, Ohio. | Pure California White Sage Honey, Thurber, Whyland & Co., New York. | Do. |
| 4 | ......do .................. .......... | Superior White Clover Honey ........ | |
| 5 | Henry Thropp,345 South High street, Columbus, Ohio. | Honey, Leggett's, New York.......... | |
| 6 | Esper & Sons, 403 South High street, Columbus, Ohio. | White Clover Honey, Warranted Strictly Pure, Leggett's, New York. | |
| 7 | J. M. Babb, 267 South High street, Columbus, Ohio. | McMechen's Old Virginia Pure Honey, Wheeling, W. Va. | Do. |
| 8 | A. J. Evans, 236-238 East Long street, Columbus, Ohio. | California Honey...................... | |
| 9 | A. M. Montgomery, 618 East Long street, Columbus, Ohio. | Strained Honey, Francis H. Leggett, New York. | |
| 10 | Atlantic Tea Company, 190 South 4th street, Columbus, Ohio. | Pure California White Sage Honey, Thurber, Whyland & Co.,New York. | |
| 11 | Saul & Eberly, 74, 76, 78 Main street, Columbus, Ohio. | Strictly Pure Extracted Honey, Austin, Nichols & Co., New York. (Old sample.) | Do. |
| 12 | Holden Brothers, North High street, Columbus, Ohio. | McMechen's Old Virginia Pure Honey, Wheeling, W. Va. (Old sample.) | |
| 13 | Aug. Boesel, 1352 North High street, Columbus, Ohio. | White Clover Honey. (Jar contained piece of comb honey.) | Do. |
| 14 | McDonald & Steube, South High street, Columbus, Ohio. | White Clover XX Honey............. | |
| 15 | F. R. Allen, Goodale and High street, Columbus, Ohio. | None. Said to be pure............... | |
| 16 | J. C. March, 263 North High street, Columbus, Ohio. | Strained Honey, F. H. Leggett's, New York (Bottle.) | |
| 17 | Thos. Bergin, 51 North High street, Columbus, Ohio. | White Clover Honey. (Jar).......... | Do. |
| 18 | H. J. Woodworth, Nelsonville, Ohio. | Lutz Brothers' Pure Honey. (Jar.) (Dark.) | Do. |
| 19 | ......do ............................ | Lutz Brothers' Pure Honey. (Jar.) (Light.) | Do. |
| 20 | ......do ............................ | None. Said to be packed by farmer... | |
| 21 | M. A. Stirling, 1416 North High street, Columbus, Ohio. | White Clover Honey. (Jar).......... | Do. |
| 22 | J. M. Bell & Son, 1183 North High street, Columbus, Ohio. | Pure California White Sage Honey, Thurber, Whyland & Co., New York. | |
| 23 | R. J. McComb & Co., east corner Sycamore and 4th, Cincinnati, Ohio. | Pure Machine Extracted Honey, Italian Apiary, C. F. Muth & Son, Cincinnati, Ohio. | |
| 24 | ........do ...................... | Warranted Pure Honey, C. F. Muth & Son, Cincinnati, Ohio. | Do. |
| 25 | Joseph R. Peebles' Sons' Co., Pike Building, Cininnati, Ohio. | Pure Honey from the Italian Apiary, C. F. Muth & Son, Cincinnati, Ohio. | Do. |

*Description of samples—Continued.*

| No. | Bought from— | Label. | Remarks. |
|---|---|---|---|
| 26 | Joseph R. Peebles' Sons' Co., Pike Building, Cincinnati, Ohio. | Pure Extracted White Clover Honey, from the apiary of Charles Hill, Mount Healthy, Ohio. | |
| 27 | ......do .............................. | Absolutely Pure, McMechen's Old Virginia Pure Honey. | Dextrine reaction. |
| 28 | Chas. F. Muth & Son, Cincinnati, Ohio. | California Sage Honey. (Sample from original package.) | |
| 29 | ......do .............................. | White Clover Honey. (Sample from original package.) | |
| 30 | ......do .............................. | Orange Blossom Honey from California. (Sample from original package.) | |
| 31 | ......do .............................. | Mangrove Honey. (Sample from original package.) | |
| 32 | ......do .............................. | Aster Honey. (Sample from original package.) | |
| 33 | Smith Brothers, Newark. Ohio...... | Pure California White Sage Honey, Thurber & Whyland, New York. | Do. |
| 34 | W. L. Danner, Newark, Ohio........ | None. Called Licking County Honey. | Do. |
| 35 | ......do .............................. | Pure Honey, Lutz Brothers .......... | Do. |
| 36 | Black & Roe, Newark, Ohio.......... | White Clover Honey. (Chicago)..... | Do. |
| 37 | T. H. Sites, Newark, Ohio............ | Strained Honey, Francis H. Leggett's, New York. | |
| 38 | George P. Herman, Woodland and Wilson avenues, Cleveland, Ohio. | Pure Honey ......................... | |
| 39 | Euclid Station Grocery, Euclid and Wilson avenues, Cleveland, Ohio. | Pure California White Sage Honey, Thurber, Whyland & Co., New York. | |
| 40 | Fred. Valentine, 366 Central avenue, Cleveland, Ohio. | Warranted Pure Honey, Geo. C. Willard, Cleveland, Ohio. | |
| 41 | Chandler & Co., Euclid avenue, Cleveland, Ohio. | Warranted Pure Honey, from Apiary of L. H. Brown, Bissell, Ohio. | |
| 42 | Woolverton & Schaeffer, Prospect and Perry streets, Cleveland, Ohio. | White Clover Honey, Moore Brothers, Rockaway, Ohio. | |
| 43 | P. O'Brien, Case Building, Cleveland, Ohio. | Pure Extracted Honey, J. B. Haines, Bradford, Ohio. | |
| 44 | ......do .............................. | G. and R. White Clover Honey........ | |
| 45 | Klaustermyer, Prospect and Brownell streets, Cleveland, Ohio. | Warranted Pure Honey, Evergreen Apiary, H. Bosworth & Sons, Ford, Ohio. | |
| 46 | W. H. Graham, 114 Main street, Zanesville, Ohio. | Purified Honey.......... ............ | Do. |
| 47 | Bailey Brothers, 172 Main street, Zanesville, Ohio. | Pure Honey ......................... | Do. |
| 48 | G. R. Clements, Zanesville, Ohio .... | White Clover Honey, XX ............ | Do. |
| 49 | W. T. Gray & Co., Zanesville, Ohio.. | Pure Machine Extracted Honey, Italian Apiary, Chas. F. Muth & Son, Cincinnati, Ohio. | |
| 50 | Conners Brothers, Cumberland, Ohio | McMechen's Old Virginia Honey. These goods are absolutely pure. (Thin, fermenting). | |

*Analytical data.*

| No. | Polarization Direct. | Indirect. | Temperature, °C. | Sucrose. | Reducing sugars. | Water. | Ash. |
|---|---|---|---|---|---|---|---|
| | | | | Per cent. | Per cent. | Per cent. | Per cent. |
| 1 | | | | 2.79 | 48.08 | 21.16 | 0.05 |
| 2 | | | | 0.00 | 76.92 | 17.42 | 0.01 |
| 3 | | | | | 70.42 | 21.19 | 0.26 |
| 4 | | | | ?.48 | 50.00 | 24.16 | 0.23 |
| 5 | | | | | 73.52 | 16.95 | 0.05 |
| 6 | | | | 3.34 | 71.11 | 18.56 | 0.06 |
| 7 | | | | 2.09 | 50.52 | 17.12 | 0.11 |
| 8 | | | | | 74.62 | 20.67 | 0.08 |
| 9 | | | | | 74.62 | 18.02 | 0.04 |
| 10 | | | | 3.04 | 71.42 | 18.06 | 0.08 |
| 11 | | | | 2.89 | 60.24 | 23.39 | 0.21 |
| 12 | | | | 1.57 | 65.78 | 27.93 | 0.11 |
| 13 | | | | | 49.50 | 22.23 | 0.13 |
| 14 | | | | 18.77 | 53.76 | 18.11 | 0.05 |
| 15 | | | | 5.22 | 71.42 | 20.37 | 0.04 |
| 16 | | | | 3.12 | 72.46 | 20.28 | 0.04 |
| 17 | | | | | 49.05 | 23.76 | 0.17 |
| 18 | | | | 4.78 | 50.51 | 20.13 | 0.15 |
| 19 | | | | | 52.08 | 20.51 | 0.26 |
| 20 | | | | | 74.62 | 16.55 | 0.10 |
| 21 | | | | .88 | 47.61 | 22.08 | 0.17 |
| 22 | | | | 4.23 | (†) | 18.64 | 0.11 |
| 23 | | | | | 64.93 | 18.61 | 0.10 |
| 24 | | | | | 64.93 | 18.74 | 0.11 |
| 25 | | | | 2.20 | 60.97 | 16.95 | 0.08 |
| 26 | | | | | 75.75 | 18.23 | 0.02 |
| 27 | | | | 1.49 | 61.72 | 16.37 | 0.06 |
| 28 | | | | 3.04 | 71.42 | 17.80 | 0.07 |
| 29 | | | | 3.12 | 72.46 | 18.30 | 0.06 |
| 30 | | | | | 72.46 | 17.79 | 0.05 |
| 31 | | | | 2.18 | 74.62 | 20.96 | 0.16 |
| 32 | | | | | 73.52 | 22.83 | 0.35 |
| 33 | | | | | 62.50 | 18.14 | 0.25 |
| 34 | | | | 2.97 | 60.97 | 18.23 | 0.11 |
| 35 | | | | 2.64 | 50.51 | 17.08 | 0.45 |
| 36 | | | | | 37.79 | 26.75 | 0.22 |
| 37 | | | | 1.04 | 73.52 | 19.21 | 0.16 |
| 38 | | | | | 75.75 | 17.74 | 0.22 |
| 39 | | | | | 74.62 | 17.17 | 0.08 |
| 40 | | | | 2.11 | 73.52 | 20.39 | 0.09 |
| 41 | | | | | 75.75 | 18.47 | 0.20 |
| 42 | | | | 3.04 | 71.42 | 20.95 | 0.13 |
| 43 | | | | | 72.46 | 18.51 | 0.23 |
| 44 | | | | 2.26 | 61.72 | 18.21 | 0.22 |
| 45 | | | | | 74.62 | 17.40 | 0.41 |
| 46 | | | | 2.30 | 62.50 | 16.66 | 0.19 |
| 47 | | | | 3.04 | 71.42 | 16.37 | 0.15 |
| 48 | | | | 11.93 | 51.54 | 18.26 | 0.17 |
| 49 | | | | | 74.62 | 21.05 | 0.23 |
| 50 | | | | | 60.97 | 32.64 | 0.29 |

## ANALYSES BY F. G. WIECHMANN.

*Description of samples..*

| No. | Price. | Bought from— | Manufacturer, etc. |
|---|---|---|---|
| 101 | $0.20 | A. Brasch, 1632 Columbus avenue, New York. | Basswood Pure Extracted Honey ; B. Otis Hoge, 264 Willoughby avenue, Brooklyn, N. Y. |
| 102 | .20 | ......do................... | Choice Extracted Northern Honey ; put up by George D. Powell. |
| 103 | .25 | H. Boeselager, 794 3d avenue, New York. | Turpin's Genuine Strained Honey ; manufactured expressly for family use. New York. |
| 104 | .35 | Ahrens, 784 3d avenue, New York. | Choice Extracted Clover Honey ; put up expressly for table use. Leslie, Dunham & Co., Pittsfield, Mass. |
| 105 | .20 | L. Eicke, 4th avenue and 11th street, New York. | Choice Honey ; E. A. & P. Walker, 137–141 Oakland avenue, Brooklyn, N. Y. |
| 106 | .25 | F. C. Rahe, Broome & Forsyth streets, New York. | Turpin's Genuine Strained Honey ; manufactured expressly for family use. New York ; Ernest Turpin. |
| 107 | .20 | L. Gieseler, Wythe avenue and South- 1st street, Brooklyn, E. D. | XXX Pure Honey ; put up by Charles Israel & Bro., New York. |
| 108 | .30 | P. U. Montorsi, 60 South 5th avenue, New York | Strained Honey ; Francis H. Leggett & Co., New York. "Should this honey become candied, it will be restored to its natural state if immersed in warm water." |
| 109 | .15 | Tompkins, 70 Son th avenue, New York | White Clover Honey. (No name of manufacturer given.) |
| 110 | .20 | Bergonzi Bros., 58 Grand street, New York. | Pure Honey ; Max Ams, New York. |
| 111 | .25 | R. C. Hewitt, 201 3d avenue, New York. | Choice Extracted Clover Honey ; put up expressly for Robert C. Hewitt, by Leslie, Dunham & Co. |
| 112 | .18 | A. Becker, 283 Avenue A, New York. | Choice Honey ; E. A. Walker & Bro., 135 Oakland street, Brooklyn, N. Y. |
| 113 | .25 | Junghertchen, 310 Avenue A, New York. | White Clover Honey ; E. A. Walker, New York. |
| 114 | .25 | Charles & Co., 50 East 43d street, New York. | Choice Extracted Clover Honey ; put up expressly for Charles & Co., by Leslie, Dunham & Co. |
| 115 | .25 | H. Middendorf, 415 3d avenue, New York. | Strained Honey ; Francis H. Leggett & Co., New York. |
| 116 | .25 | Vermilya, 1598 Columbus avenue, New York. | Leslie, Dunham & Co., Orange Blossom Honey ; warranted strictly pure. |
| 117 | .25 | H. Riechers, 243 7th avenue, New York. | California White Sage Honey; E. Brommond. |
| 118 | .18 | Bock & Spreen, 275 7th avenue, New York. | California White Sage Honey ; E. Brommond. This honey is absolutely pure, and, unlike liquid honey that has been mixed with glucose to keep it from granulating, it will naturally candy or granulate and become a solid mass in course of time. If preferred in its liquid state, remove the cork and place the bottle in hot water until the honey is melted. |
| 119 | .20 | A. Bollenbacher, 293 7th avenue, New York. | Choice Honey ; put up by G. A. & J. Distler, 226 and 228 Java Street, Brooklyn. Choice extracted honey from New York State. |
| 120 | .25 | F. Dannemann & Co., 930 6th avenue, New York. | Strained Honey ; Francis H. Leggett & Co., New York. |
| 121 | .20 | C. Elfers, 109 West 53d street, New York. | Choice California Honey. E. L. Johnston & Co., New York. "This honey is of an excellent flavor and put up expressly for the best trade." |
| 122 | .20 | Fayen & Brockmeyer, 100 West 53d street, New York. | Choice Extracted Clover Honey ; put up expressly for table use. Leslie, Dunham & Co., Pittsfield, Mass. |
| 123 | .25 | D. W. C. Ward, 938 6th avenue, New York. | One pound Pure Honey ; put up expressly for table use. A. & E. Thomson, New Canaan, Ct. "From Hive to Table." |
| 124 | .50 | Houston & Steinle, 771 6th avenue, New York. | L. J. Wyeth, Jr. Pure Extracted Honey ; G. S. Wyatt & Co., Agents, New York. |

*Description of samples—Continued.*

| No | Price. | Bought from— | Manufacturer, etc. |
|---|---|---|---|
| 125 | $0.20 | Perceval & Co., 769 6th avenue, New York. | Francis H. Leggett & Co., New York. Should this honey become candied it will be restored to its natural state if immersed in warm water. |
| 126 | 20 | W. Simpson, 757 6th avenue, New York. | Leslie, Dunham & Co., Pittsfield, Mass. Choice Extracted Clover Honey; put up expressly for table use. |
| 127 | .25 | J. W. Lohse, 752 6th avenue, New York. | Basswood; B. Otis Hoge, 264 Willoughby avenue, Brooklyn, N. Y.; warranted pure honey. |
| 128 | .25 | H. Diestel & Co.. Columbus avenue and 92d street, New York. | Basswood; Pure Extracted Honey; B. Otis Hoge, 264 Willoughby avenue, Brooklyn, N. Y.; warranted pure honey. |
| 129 | .25 | ......do...................... | Choice Extracted Clover Honey; put up expressly for table use; Leslie, Dunham & Co., Pittsfield, Mass. |
| 130 | .20 | C. Adam, 1563 Columbus avenue, New York. | Choice Extracted Northern Honey. Put up by Geo. D. Powell. |
| 131 | .23 | Mackenzie & Bobrick, 1559 Columbus avenue, New York. | Strained Honey. Francis H. Leggett & Co., New York. |
| 132 | .25 | J. C. Lilley & Co., 1542 Columbus avenue, New York. | Basswood; Extracted Honey; B. Otis Hoge, 264 Willoughby avenue, Brooklyn, N. Y.; warranted pure honey. |
| 133 | .25 | ......do...................... | Orange Blossom Honey; warranted strictly pure; Leslie, Dunham & Co. |
| 134 | .25 | W. Meyer, 1533 Columbus avenue, New York. | Pure Honey; G. A. & J. Distler, Brooklyn, N. Y.; choice extracted honey from New York State. |
| 135 | .25 | N. Schelling, 1528 Columbus avenue, New York. | Basswood; Pure Extracted Honey; B. Otis Hoge, 264 Willoughby avenue, Brooklyn, N. Y-; warranted pure honey. |
| 136 | .25 | Wiesner & Frese, 1482 Columbus avenue, New York. | Orange Blossom Honey; warranted strictly pure; Leslie Dunham & Co. |
| 137 | .24 | ......do...................... | Basswood; Pure Extracted Honey; B. Otis Hoge, 264 Willoughby avenue, Brooklyn, N. Y.; warranted pure honey. |
| 138 | .25 | H. J. Ohlckers, Columbus avenue and 86th street, New York. | Strained Honey; Francis H. Leggett & Co., New York. |
| 139 | .25 | ......do...................... | Orange Blossom Honey; warranted strictly pure; Leslie, Dunham & Co. |
| 140 | .25 | Müller, 1606 Columbus avenue, New York. | Choice Comb Honey; Chas. Israel & Bro., New York. |
| 141 | .25 | R. Kempe, 1608 Amsterdam avenue, New York. | Choice Extracted Northern Honey; put up by Geo. D. Powell. |
| 142 | .25 | H. Eitzen, 1392 Amsterdam avenue, New York. | Ritter's Pure California White Clover Honey; the P. J. Ritter Conserve Company, 2154-2158 East Dauphin street, Philadelphia. |
| 143 | .20 | ......do...................... | Pure Honey; G. A. & J. Distler, Brooklyn, N. Y,; choice extracted honey from New York State. |
| 144 | .20 | ......do...................... | No label; said by seller to be from G. A. & J. Distler, Brooklyn, N. Y. |
| 145 | .25 | Hohnhorst, 1413 Amsterdam avenue, New York. | Choice Golden Rod Honey; from Wm. Thompson, Wayne County, N. Y. |
| 146 | .25 | 1522 Amsterdam avenue, New York. | Pure Honey; Max Ams, New York. |
| 147 | .25 | H. Boeselager, 794 3d avenue, New York. | Pure Comb Honey; from the apiary of J. G. Whitten, Genoa, N. Y. |
| 148 | .17 | D. Brinkman, 753 3d avenue, New York. | No label; said by seller to be from G. A. & J. Distler, Brooklyn, N. Y. |
| 149 | .20 | H. Ahrens, 784 3d avenue, New York. | No label; said by seller to be from Leslie, Dunham & Co. |
| 150 | .35 | ......do...................... | From the apiary of Henry F. Dobson, manufacturer of Bee Hives, New Paltz, Ulster County, N. Y. |

*Analytical data.*

| No. | Polarization Direct. | Polarization Indirect. | Tempera-ture,° C. | Sucrose. | Reducing sugars. | Water. | Ash. |
|---|---|---|---|---|---|---|---|
| | | | | Per cent. | Per cent. | Per cent. | Per cent. |
| 101 | — 19.0 | — 23.6 | 20 | 3.46 | 71.93 | 20.58 | 0.104 |
| 102 | 104.2 | 100.4 | 20 | .......... | 52.08 | 20.57 | 0.313 |
| 103 | 96.3 | 92.2 | 20 | 3.09 | 50.00 | 24.22 | 0.324 |
| 104 | 84.2 | 81.2 | 20 | 2.26 | 54.35 | 22.65 | 0.277 |
| 105 | 108.9 | 105.2 | 20 | .......... | 50.00 | 20.60 | 0.648 |
| 106 | 103.2 | 99.4 | 20 | .......... | 49.50 | 23.35 | 0.292 |
| 107 | — 16.5 | — 20.6 | 20 | 3.09 | 72.46 | 21.35 | 0.090 |
| 108 | — 19.7 | — 24.6 | 20 | 3.69 | 72.99 | 20.20 | 0.050 |
| 109 | 122.6 | 119.4 | 20 | .......... | 44.64 | 21.82 | 0.220 |
| 110 | 71.2 | 69.4 | 20 | 1.35 | 56.82 | 23.00 | 0.245 |
| 111 | 8.4 | 5.6 | 20 | 2.11 | 66.66 | 19.76 | 0.137 |
| 112 | 92.4 | 89.0 | 20 | 2.56 | 52.63 | 22.27 | 0.238 |
| 113 | 96.5 | 93.8 | 20 | 2.03 | 52.08 | 21.65 | 0.385 |
| 114 | — 14.0 | — 18.4 | 20 | 3.31 | 69.93 | 21.78 | 0.144 |
| 115 | — 19.4 | — 25.0 | 20 | 4.22 | 72.46 | 20.22 | 0.065 |
| 116 | — 19.6 | — 23.0 | 20 | 2.56 | 70.42 | 21.78 | 0.140 |
| 117 | 43.6 | 28.2 | 20 | 11.61 | 53.76 | 23.60 | 0.205 |
| 118 | 63.3 | 52.0 | 20 | 8.51 | 55.87 | 20.78 | 0.220 |
| 119 | 107.6 | 104.4 | 20 | .......... | 50.00 | 20.60 | 0.205 |
| 120 | — 19.6 | — 24.2 | 20 | 3.47 | 72.99 | 20.15 | 0.065 |
| 121 | 12.0 | 7.0 | 20 | 3.76 | 67.56 | 22.35 | 0.097 |
| 122 | 91.0 | 88.4 | 20 | 1.95 | 50.00 | 23.13 | 0.277 |
| 123 | — 13.8 | — 18.0 | 20 | 3.16 | 72.46 | 24.75 | 0.268 |
| 124 | — 12.0 | — 17.2 | 20 | 3.92 | 71.94 | 23.53 | 0.090 |
| 125 | — 20.4 | — 23.0 | 20 | 1.95 | 73.53 | 23.09 | 0.083 |
| 126 | 88.2 | 86.2 | 20 | 1.51 | 51.81 | 23.13 | 0.288 |
| 127 | — 15.8 | — 18.4 | 20 | 1.94 | 71.94 | 22.13 | 0.198 |
| 128 | — 17.2 | — 21.0 | 20 | 2.86 | 71.43 | 22.98 | 0.122 |
| 129 | — 9.6 | — 14.0 | 20 | 3.31 | 68.50 | 23.65 | 0.097 |
| 130 | 106.2 | 104.0 | 20 | .......... | 51.54 | 22.10 | 0.288 |
| 131 | — 19.6 | — 24.6 | 20 | 3.76 | 71.94 | 22.00 | 0.043 |
| 132 | — 18.8 | — 23.6 | 20 | 3.62 | 73.53 | 22.10 | 0.101 |
| 133 | — 16.0 | — 19.4 | 20 | 2.56 | 68.50 | 23.98 | 0.108 |
| 134 | — 12.6 | — 17.6 | 20 | 3.76 | 73.53 | 21.38 | 0.104 |
| 135 | — 16.0 | — 20.0 | 20 | 3.01 | 72.46 | 21.53 | 0.115 |
| 136.. | — 11.8 | — 17.2 | 20 | 4.06 | 68.50 | 23.40 | 0.158 |
| 137.. | — 17.8 | — 21.0 | 20 | 2.41 | 71.94 | 20.82 | 0.126 |
| 138.. | — 19.6 | — 24.2 | 20 | 3.46 | 71.94 | 23.05 | 0.043 |
| 139.. | — 24.0 | — 29.6 | 20 | 4.22 | 73.53 | 20.55 | 0.061 |
| 140.. | 98.4 | 94.4 | 20 | 3.01 | 51.02 | 21.00 | 0.223 |
| 141.. | 92.6 | 89.4 | 20 | 2.41 | 54.65 | 21.50 | 0.234 |
| 142.. | 31.8 | 16.0 | 20 | 11.01 | 56.50 | 21.20 | 0.115 |
| 143.. | 115.4 | 112.2 | 20 | .......... | 44.64 | 24.53 | 0.198 |
| 144.. | 87.8 | 84.6 | 20 | 2.41 | 52.63 | 21.73 | 0.198 |
| 145.. | 46.0 | 42.6 | 20 | 2.56 | 60.61 | 22.15 | 0.158 |
| 146.. | 59.8 | 56.6 | 20 | 2.41 | 55.55 | 27.60 | 0.342 |
| 147.. | — 10.8 | — 13.2 | 20 | 1.81 | 72.46 | 21.75 | 0.198 |
| 148.. | 93.6 | 88.6 | 20 | 3.76 | 56.82 | 21.68 | 0.205 |
| 149.. | 26.8 | 24.0 | 20 | 2.11 | 63.68 | 24.24 | 0.259 |
| 150.. | — 15.2 | — 10.6 | 20 | 3.32 | 73.53 | 24.50 | 0.054 |

ANALYSES BY CHEMICAL DIVISION, UNITED STATES DEPARTMENT OF AGRICULTURE.

*Description of samples.*

| No. | Where bought. | Description. | Price per pack-age.* |
|---|---|---|---|
| 8515 | Waple & Co., E and 11th streets NW. | Made by W. O. Anderson, Lanham, Prince George County, Md. | $0.15 |
| 8516 | Elphonzo Youngs & Co., 428 9th street NW. | Orange Blossom Honey, warranted strictly pure; Leslie, Dunham & Co. | .25 |
| 8517 | ......do ............................... | Hoge's Horehound Honey, G. D. Powell, 81 3d street, Brooklyn, N. Y. | .25 |
| 8518 | F. Ritter, K Street Market............ | No label; made by W. O. Anderson, Lanham, Prince George County, Md. | .15 |
| 8519 | Stadelmann, K Street Market ........ | Grown by brother in Virginia and bottled by seller. | .20 |
| 8520 | Wilson & Schultz, 934 7th street NW. | Pure California White Sage Honey; Thurber, Whyland & Co., New York. | .25 |
| 8521 | Spignul & Co., corner New York avenue and 7th street. | Pure Orange Blossom Honey, Eagle brand.... | .25 |
| 8522 | M. & P. Metzger, 417 7th street....... | No label; said to be grown in Montgomery County, Md. | .25 |
| 8523 | ....do ............................... | Choice Extracted Northern Honey, put up by George D. Powell. | .25 |
| 8524 | Chas. I. Kellogg, 602 9th street NW... | Strained Honey; Francis H. Leggett & Co., New York. | .25 |
| 8525 | W. H. Coombs. 924 9th street NW..... | Choice Extracted Clover Honey, put up by Leslie Dunham & Co., Pittsfield, Mass. | .25 |
| 8526 | Dutton. 811 9th street NW............ | Old Virginia Pure Honey, put up by Geo. K. McMechen & Son, Wheeling, W. Va. | .25 |
| 8527 | T. H. Walker & Co., 946-950 Louisiana avenue. | Pure California Honey, from T. H. Walker & Co., Louisiana avenue. | .25 |
| 8528 | Benj. Pettit, stand No. 569, Center Market. | Strained by seller from Virginia comb honey.. | .15 |
| 8529 | Stand No. 63, Center Market.......... | Warranted Pure Honey, from E. M. Pitman, Centerville, Va. | .15 |
| 8530 | Joseph Fish, stand 465, Center Market. | Strained by seller from Virginia comb honey.. | .40 |
| 8531 | Stand 42, Center Market.............. | Strained by seller from Virginia comb honey. | .15 |
| 8532 | 502 14th street ...................... | Pure Honey; A. C. Hoopes................... | .15 |
| 8533 | A. Heitmüller & Co., 1333 14th street.. | Choice Clover Honey; Israel & Bros., New York | .25 |
| 8534 | Birch & Co., 1414 14th street ......... | No label; said to be bottled by sellers from California honey. | .12 |
| 8535 | Cottage Market, 818 14th street....... | Strictly Pure Honey; Thurber, Whyland & Co., New York. | .25 |
| 8536 | Alexander C. Clark, corner 7th street and Florida avenue. | Put up by W. O. Anderson, Lanham, Prince George County, Md. | .15 |
| 8538 | George F. Kennedy & Sons, 1209 F street NW. | Choice Extract Northern Honey, put up by George D. Powell. | .25 |
| 8539 | Matthew Goddard, corner H and 13th streets. | Ritter's Pure California White Clover Honey; The P. J. Ritter Conserve Co., Philadelphia, Pa. | .25 |
| 8540 | Willet & Gwynn, Circle Market, corner Vermont avenue and L street. | Choice Comb Honey; Chas. Israel & Bro., New York. | .25 |
| 8578 | Franklin Barret, corner New York avenue and 12th street. | California Honey............................. | .20 |

* For weight of each sample, exclusive of package, see following table.

*Description of sample—Continued.*

| No. | Where bought. | Description. | Price per pack-age.* |
|---|---|---|---|
| 8619 | Elphonzo Youngs, Washington, D. C. | Horehound Honey...... ...................... | $0.25 |
| 8678 | —— , Baltimore.................... | G. and R. White Clover Honey XX.......... | .25 |
| 8679 | Edmonston & Gosnell, 304 Biddle st., Baltimore, Md. | Choice Golden Rod Honey from Wm. Thompson, Wayne County, N. Y. | .20 |
| 8680 | P. A. Agnew, corner Eutaw and Pratt streets, Baltimore. | No label. ............... ................,...... | .15 |
| 8682 | Relter & Co., 709 Baltimore street, Baltimore. | California Pure Honey; Jas. Miles, Monroe street, San Francisco, Cal. | .10 |
| 8683 | Reitz Bros., 206 North Eutaw street, Baltimore. | Pure Orange Blossom Honey; F. G. Strohmeyer, New York. | .25 |
| 8684 | Wm. Preston, Lexington market, Baltimore. | Made in Reno County, Md., and bottled by seller. | .13 |
| 8685 | A. Katzenberg, 218 Eutaw street, Baltimore. | Choice Extracted Honey, strictly pure; E. G. Hazard, New York. | .25 |
| 8686 | L. Strauss, 226 Eutaw street, Baltimore. | Pure White Comb Honey; F.G.Strohmeyer & Co , New York. | .35 |
| 8687 | Hopper, McGaw & Co., 220 Charles street, Baltimore. | No label ; packed at Ellicott City, Md., for seller. | .25 |
| 8688 | Edmonds, corner Lexington and Pearl streets, Baltimore. | Orange Blossom, Eagle Brand. .............. | .25 |
| 8689 | T. Stabler, corner Eutaw, Madison and Garden, Baltimore. | No label ; California Honey.................... | .20 |
| 8690 | Stadelmann & Co., Lexington Market, Baltimore. | No label ; Maryland Honey............ ........ | .20 |
| 8691 | Hopper, McGaw & Co., 220 Charles street, Baltimore. | Pure Clover ; put up expressly for Hopper, McGaw & Co. | .25 |
| 8692 | ......do.................... | No label ; Maryland Honey...... ............ | .25 |
| 8693 | R. F. H. Lawson, corner Charles and Hamilton, Baltimore. | Orange Blossom Honey ; Leslie, Dunham & Co. | .25 |
| 8694 | L. H. Reitz, 227 Hanover street, Baltimore. | Bulk Honey, bought in Florida............ .... | .15 |
| 8695 | R. S. Shamburg, 613 Lexington, Baltimore. | Put up in Philadelphia ..............:...... | .25 |
| 8696 | A. O. Wright, 1632 14th street, Washington, D. C. | Strictly Pure Extracted Honey ; Austin Nichols & Co. | .25 |
| 8697 | J. P. Love, 1534 14th street, Washington, D. C. | Pure Extracted Honey; R. F. Weir, South River, Md. | .12 |
| 8698 | E. L. Yewell, 1141 9th street, Washington, D. C. | Ritter's Pure California White Clover Honey. | .25 |
| 8711 | Cox, O Street Market, Washington, D. C. | Comb Honey................................ | .18 |
| 8752 | Benjamin Pettit, Center Market, Washington, D. C. | ......do ..... ............................ | .25 |
| 8753 | Joseph Fish, stand 364, Center Market, Washington, D. C. | Bottled by seller from Virginia Honey........ | .20 |
| 8754 | P. Cannon, stand 42, Center Market, Washington, D. C. | ......do.................................... | .15 |

* For weight of each sample, exclusive of package, see following table.

COPIES OF LABELS ON HONEY SAMPLES.

No. 8515.  Honey bought from Waple & Co., corner E and Eleventh streets NW. Price, 15 cents.  Label: "Pure Extracted Honey.  Should this honey granulate, place the jar in hot water and it will liquefy.  If the honey in this jar be found impure, or in any manner adulterated, I will forfeit $10 to the one discovering it.  Bees and honey always for sale.  W. O. Anderson, Lanham's, Prince George County, Md."  Sample put up in Rumford's baking powder bottle.  Golden-yellow in color.

No. 8516.  Honey bought from Elphonzo Youngs & Co., 428 Ninth street.  Price 25 cents.  Label: "Orange Blossom Honey, strictly pure; Leslie, Dunham & Co."  Sample golden-yellow in color; put up in wide-mouthed pickle bottle.

No. 8517.  Honey bought from Elphonzo Youngs & Co., 428 Ninth street NW.  Price 25 cents.  Label: "Hoge's Horehound Honey; balsamic, expectorant, and soothing.  A speedy, effectual, and pleasant remedy for coughs, colds, asthma, bronchitis, consumption, hoarseness, and all affections of the throat, chest, and lungs.  A product of nature secreted in the petals of horehound blossoms and gathered by the honey bee.  Price 25 cents.  G. D. Powell, 81 and 83 Third street, Brooklyn, N. Y."  A circular inclosed contains among other things the following:

"HOGE'S HOREHOUND HONEY.—The story is rife that horehound honey is a myth, but we take the responsibility of assuring the world that pure horehound honey is a fact known to many of our citizens, and that it is produced in large quantities in several cañons in this county, where the horehound plants grow in such profusion as to entirely choke out anything else around them.  Mr. Hoge has gone to great pains and devoted several years to horehound honey, and has secured control of all that is produced in this country, and is creating a good demand for it.  We therefore feel that he is justly entitled to any advantage which may come from our indorsement of the fact that pure horehound honey is a bona fide production of this county.—Ventura County (Cal.) Republican.

"This is to certify that to my personal knowledge the locality referred to by Mr. Hoge is covered with flourishing growth of horehound, from which large quantities of pure horehound honey are gathered by his bees.  S. M. W. Easley, notary public, Ventura County, Cal.

"HOGE'S HOREHOUND HONEY.—Wherever a bee flies within the virgin wilderness of Hoge's Cañon, along the banks of the river, along the bluffs and headlands and deep leafy glens, the horehound plant blossoms in lavish abundance.  It is the work of the honeybee to gather the sweet treasure, horehound honey, so divinely prepared, and bear it off, saying to those suffering from coughs: 'Eat! It is the soul of the blossom.'"

This sample, as will be seen from the analysis, was composed of a solution of cane sugar and some alcohol.

No. 8518.  Honey bought from F. Bitter, K Street Market.  Price 15 cents.  No label; made by same man as 8515.  This man sells bottles labeled and unlabeled; says the honey is the same in each case, but that it is more expensive to label, consequently does not label all samples.  Color of sample golden yellow; contains slight light-colored precipitate.  Put up in Rumford's baking powder bottle.

No. 8519.  Honey bought from Stadelman, K Street Market.  Price 20 cents.  Grown by brother in Virginia and put up by seller in jars with tin cover.  Color, golden yellow; clear.

No. 8520.  Honey bought from Wilson & Schultz, 934 Seventh street.  Price 25 cents.  Label: "Pure California White Sage Honey.  This honey is absolutely pure and unlike liquid honey that has been mixed with glucose to keep it from granulating, it will naturally candy or granulate and become a solid mass in course of time.  If preferred in its liquid state, remove the cork and place the bottle in hot water until the honey is melted.  Thurber, Whyland & Co., manufacturers, New York."  Color, light brown; put up in pickle bottle; slightly fluorescent.

No. 8521.  Honey bought from Spignui & Co., corner New York avenue and Seventh street.  Price, 25 cents.  Label : "Pure Orange Blossom Honey, Eagle Brand." Neck label: "Pure Extracted Honey.  All pure honey will congeal, especially when exposed to light and cold.  In such cases remove cork, place bottle in cold water, let water boil ten minutes and honey will regain its liquid state."  Color, brownish yellow, clear.  Put up in pickle bottle.

No. 8522.  Honey bought from M. & P. Metzger, 417 Seventh street NW.  Said to be grown in Montgomery County, Md.  No label.  Price 25 cents.  Color, golden yellow.  Contained piece of honeycomb.  Put up in jar with tin cover.

No. 8523.  Honey bought from M. & P. Metzger, 417 Seventh street NW.  Price 25 cents.  Label: "Choice Extracted Northern Honey put up by Geo. D. Powell." Color, golden yellow, clear.  Put up in wide-mouthed bottle with metal cover.

No. 8524.  Honey bought from Chas. I. Kellogg, 602 Ninth street NW.  Price 25 cents.  Color, golden yellow.  Put up in wide-mouthed bottle.  Label : " Strained Honey.  Francis H. Leggett & Co., New York."  Neck label :. " Should this honey become candied, it will be restored to its natural state if immersed in warm water."

No. 8525.  Honey bought of W. H. Coombs, 924 Ninth street NW.  Price, 25 cents. Put up in wide-mouthed bottle.  Color, light brownish yellow.  Label : "Choice Extracted Clover Honey.  Put up expressly for table use.  Leslie, Dunham & Co., Pittsfield, Mass."

No. 8526.  Honey bought from —— Dutton, 816 Ninth street NW.  Price, 25 cents. Put up in wide-mouthed bottle.  Color, golden yellow ; clear.  Label : "McMechen's Old Virginia Pure Honey, prepared by George K. McMechen & Son, Wheeling, W. Va."  Neck label: "These goods are absolutely pure.  Geo. K. McMechen & Son." Sealed with plaster of Paris and tin foil.

No. 8527.  Honey bought from T. H. Walker & Co., 946-950 Louisiana avenue. Price, 25 cents.  Put up in wine bottle.  Color, pale yellow ; clear.  Label : "Pure California Honey, from T. H. Walker & Co., grocers, 946-950 Louisiana avenue, Washington, D. C."

No. 8528.  Honey bought from Benjamin Pettit, stand No. 569 Center Market ; price, 15 cents ; no label ; strained by himself from Virginia comb honey ; put up in wide-mouthed bottle ; color, golden yellow ; contains a few fine particles in suspension.

No. 8529.  Honey bought from Joseph Fish, stand No. 465 Center Market ; no label ; strained by himself from Virginia comb honey ; put up in pickle bottle ; color, brownish yellow ; slightly cloudy ; price, 40 cents.

No. 8531.  Honey bought from stand No. 42 Center Market ; price, 15 cents ; strained by seller from Virginia honey ; no label ; put up in small bottle with " Rumford " blown in glass ; color, very dark brown ; opaque.

No. 8532.  Honey bought from No. 502 Fourteenth street NW. ; price, 15 cents ; label, "Pure Honey, A. C. Hoopes."  Put up in small bottles ; color, dark brown ; translucent.

No. 8533.  Honey bought from A. Heitmuller, 1333 Fourteenth street.  Price, 25 cents.  Put up in wide-mouthed bottle.  Color, light yellow.  Sample has completely candied.  Label : "Choice Clover Honey packed by Chas. Israel & Bro., New York." Neck label : "Notice.—This honey being pure, is liable to granulate, particularly in cold weather.  If in said state place the bottle in cold water, set on hot stove, and allow the bottle to become hot with the water, and let boil for ten minutes, which will bring the honey to its liquid form.  Be sure to remove cork before placing in water."

No. 8534.  Honey bought from Birch & Co., 1414 Fourteenth street.  Price, 12 cents.  No label.  Said to be "bottled by ourselves from California honey."  Color, pale yellow ; clear.  Put up in bottle with " Rumford " blown in glass.

No. 8535.  Honey bought from Cottage Market, 818 Fourteenth street.  Price, 25 cents.  Color, golden yellow.  Granulated throughout.  Put up in bottle.  Label:

"Strictly Pure Honey. Thurber, Whyland & Co., New York." Neck label: This label is torn, but a fragment adhering shows, "Choice st——," and "from Los A——." Sealed with plaster of Paris, of which a little dropped in in opening.

No. 8536. Honey bought from Alexander C. Clark, corner Seventh and Florida avenue. Price 15 cents. Color golden yellow, clear; put up in bottle with "Rumford" blown in glass. Label: "Pure Extracted Honey. Should this honey granulate, place the jar in hot water and it will liquify. If the honey in this jar be found impure or in any manner adulterated, I will forfeit $10 to the one discovering it. Bees and honey always for sale. W. O. Anderson, Lanham's, Prince George County, Md." See serial No. 8515, same as this sample.

No. 8538. Honey bought from George E. Kennedy & Sons, 1209 F street. Label, "Choice Extracted Northern Honey, put up by George D. Powell." Color, golden yellow; clear. Put up in metal-capped wide-mouthed bottle. Price, 25 cents. (See No. 8523.) Retailer would not guarantee purity, as price was too low.

No. 8539. Honey bought from Matthew Goddard, corner H and Thirteenth streets. Price, 25 cents. Label: "Ritter's Pure California White Clover Honey. The R. G. Ritter Conserve Company, Philadelphia." Color, light brownish yellow; in square wide-mouthed bottle. Neck label: "Put up expressly for family use."

No. 8540. Honey bought from Willett & Gwynne, Circle Market, corner Vermont avenue and L street. Price, 25 cents. Label: "Choice Comb Honey from Chas. Israel & Bro., New York." In appearance the sample is opaque; looks like lard in a semifluid state. Contains piece of comb.

No. 8696. "Strictly Pure Extracted Honey, Austin, Nichols & Co., 61 Hudson street, New York. Choice extracted honey from New York State. All pure honey will congeal, especially when exposed to light or cold. In such cases remove cork, place bottle in cold water, let water boil for ten minutes, and honey will regain its liquid state." Clear red-brown.

No. 8797. "Pure Extracted Honey. Should this honey granulate place the jar in hot water and it will liquefy. If the honey in this jar be found impure or in any way adulterated, I will forfeit $10 to the one discovering it. Bees and honey always for sale. R. F. Wier, South River, Anne Arundel County, Maryland." "Dixon" jar. Granulated.

No. 8698. "Ritter's Pure California White Clover Honey. The P. J. Ritter Conserve Company, Philadelphia. Put up expressly for family use."

### BALTIMORE HONEY.

No. 8678. Trade mark "X G R X." "G & R White Clover Honey, XX." Slightly turbid brown solution. Honey bottle.

No. 8679. "Choice Golden Rod Honey from Wm. Thompson's, Wayne County, N. Y. This honey is of an excellent flavor, and put up expressly for best grocery trade and family use." Clear yellowish brown.

No. 8680. "Delicious White Sage Extracted California Honey, packed at the apiary of L. Lawrence, Linda Vista, San Diego County, Cal. Walden & Neale, selling agents for the East. California honey is considered the best for all medicinal and household uses, and for the convenience of the family a pure, wholesome, and nutritious white sage honey has been packed in this economical form (candied in a jar). If the extracted honey in this package becomes 'candied' place it in warm water until it dissolves. All pure honey will granulate."

No. 8681. Duplicate of 8679.

No. 8682. "California Pure Honey, James Miles, Monroe street, San Francisco, Cal." Jar. Looks like tallow.

No. 8683. "Pure Orange Blossom Honey, F. G. Strohmeyer & Co., New York. This honey is absolutely pure, and, unlike liquid honey that has been mixed with glucose to keep it from granulating, it will naturally candy or granulate and become a solid mass in course of time. If preferred in its liquid state remove the cork and place the bottle in hot water until the honey is melted." Completely candied; amber. Honey bottle.

No. 8684. No label. Stated by seller to have been made in Maryland, and bottled by him. Jar. Clear brownish yellow.

No. 8685. "Choice Extracted Honey. Strictly pure; E. G. Hazard & Co., New York. Pure Extracted Honey. All pure honey will congeal, especially when exposed to light and cold. In such cases remove cork, place bottle in cold water, let water boil ten minutes, and honey will regain its liquid state." Honey bottle; clear amber.

No. 8686. "Pure White Comb Honey, F. G. Strohmeyer, New York. This honey is strictly pure, and, unlike liquid honey that has been mixed with glucose to keep it from granulating, will naturally candy or granulate and become a solid mass in the course of time. If preferred in its liquid state, heat the bottle in warm water. F. G. Strohmeyer & Co., New York." Jar with bail; granulated.

No. 8687. Packed at Ellicott City, Md., for seller; no label.

No. 8688. "Pure Orange Blossom Honey, Eagle brand. Pure extracted honey. All pure honey will congeal, especially when exposed to light or cold. In all such cases remove cork, place bottle in cold water, let water boil ten minutes and honey will regain its liquid state." Clear red-brown; honey bottle.

No. 8689. No label. Said to be California honey. Preserve jar.

No. 8690. No label. Maryland honey. Clear when bought.

No. 8691. "Pure Clover Honey, put up expressly for Hopper, McGaw & Co., 220 and 222 North Charles street, Baltimore, Md." Said to be Maryland honey. Honey bottle.

No. 8692. No label. Maryland honey.

No. 8693. "Orange Blossom Honey, warranted strictly pure. We receive this honey direct from the best apiaries among the fine orange groves along the Indian River in Florida, and recommend it as the most delicious extracted honey in the market. Leslie, Dunham & Co., Brooklyn, N. Y."

No. 8694. Bulk honey, bought in barrels in Florida by retailer.

No. 8695. "Put up in Philadelphia." Jar.

WASHINGTON HONEYS.

*Analytical data.*

| No. | Polarization. | | Tempera-ture °C. | Sucrose. | Reducing sugars. | Water. | Ash. |
|---|---|---|---|---|---|---|---|
| | Direct. | Indirect. | | | | | |
| | | | | *Per cent.* | *Per cent.* | *Per cent.* | *Per cent.* |
| 8515 | — 10.56 | — 13.25 | 25.5 | .......... | 74.17 | 12.70 | 0.06 |
| 8516 | — 17.18 | — 19.00 | 24.7 | .......... | 73.64 | 15.89 | 0.08 |
| 8517 | 78.90 | 2.40 | 24.6 | 58.1 | 7.92 | 23.12 | 0.03 |
| 8518 | — 11.86 | — 13.85 | 24.8 | .......... | 75.26 | 14.55 | 0.07 |
| 8519 | — 14.27 | — 16.90 | 23.0 | .......... | 77.52 | 12.12 | 0.27 |
| 8520 | — 14.27 | — 19.18 | 24.6 | .......... | 74.71 | 12.05 | 0.18 |
| 8521 | — 12.20 | — 15.70 | 24.4 | .......... | 73.64 | 13.08 | 0.48 |
| 8522 | — 5.18 | — 11.84 | 24.2 | .......... | 66.10 | 16.94 | 0.17 |
| 8523 | 126.60 | 125.80 | 21.2 | .......... | 48.31 | 13.01 | 0.20 |
| 8524 | — 14.70 | — 19.35 | 22.0 | .......... | 72.35 | 14.91 | 0.06 |
| 8525 | 74.50 | 71.35 | 22.8 | .......... | 56.03 | 13.87 | 0.35 |
| 8526 | 58.00 | 54.85 | 17.0 | .......... | 63.64 | 12.54 | 0.23 |
| 8527 | — 17.15 | — 24.35 | 23.0 | .......... | 72.61 | 16.29 | 0.06 |
| 8528 | — 8.00 | — 12.60 | 24.9 | .......... | 71.61 | 15.62 | 0.27 |
| 8529 | — 8.50 | — 12.40 | 25.4 | .......... | 73.50 | 14.10 | 0.35 |
| 8530 | — 10.30 | — 15.20 | 25.4 | .......... | 72.61 | 20.10 | 0.08 |
| 8531 | — 12.20 | — 15.05 | 25.6 | .......... | 67.83 | 25.10 | 0.16 |
| 8532 | 6.35 | .60 | 25.4 | .......... | 62.87 | 18.54 | 0.82 |
| 8533 | 44.70 | 40.45 | 26.1 | .......... | 64.44 | 16.23 | 0.18 |
| 8534 | — 16.20 | — 22.45 | 26.8 | .......... | 71.61 | .. ....... | 0.05 |
| 8535 | 12.35 | 6.85 | 27.0 | .......... | 67.83 | 20.83 | 0.17 |
| 8536 | — 11.45 | — 15.35 | 27.4 | .......... | 74.71 | 16.09 | 0.06 |
| 8538 | 114.90 | 113.47 | 27.5 | .......... | 49.81 | 18.31 | 0.22 |
| 8539 | 28.90 | 15.15 | 27.8 | .......... | 61.01 | 15.17 | 0.15 |
| 8540 | 59.70 | 57.60 | 17.0 | .......... | 64.44 | 20.42 | 0.21 |
| 8578 | — 18.50 | — 20.70 | 24.1 | ........ | 72.47 | 20.29 | 0.34 |
| 8678 | 11.30 | — 19.90 | 25.4 | 23.8 | 53.76 | 17.77 | 0.14 |
| 8679 | 55.50 | 53.20 | 26.0 | .......... | 62.50 | 17.38 | 0.17 |
| 8680 | — 5.90 | —· 14.10 | 24.6 | .......... | 68.50 | 20.25 | 0.31 |
| 8682 | 40.70 | 38.30 | 24.4 | .......... | 65.80 | 18.99 | 0.34 |
| 8683 | 22.80 | 10.40 | 24.6 | .......... | 61.73 | 20.59 | 0.24 |
| 8684 | — 10.40 | — 12.80 | 24.8 | .......... | 71.43 | 23.42 | 0.34 |
| 8685 | — 17.60 | — 19.80 | 25.0 | .......... | 75.75 | 15.01 | 0.11 |
| 8686 | — 6.80 | — 8.40 | 24.0 | .......... | 74.62 | 18.87 | 0.15 |
| 8687 | 59.80 | 56.80 | 23.8 | .......... | 58.82 | 14.18 | 0.12 |
| 8688 | — 14.00 | — 18.30 | 24.4 | .......... | 75.75 | 14.18 | 0.09 |
| 8689 | — 14.40 | — 17.10 | 24.0 | .......... | 75.75 | 13.14 | 0.19 |
| 8690 | — 9.40 | — 10.40 | 24.0 | .......... | 75.75 | 18.32 | 0.15 |
| 8691 | 21.30 | 16.30 | 23.2 | .......... | 64.51 | 20.49 | 0.21 |
| 8692 | — 8.60 | — 10.00 | 22.0 | .......... | 66.67 | 25.82 | 0.23 |
| 8693 | — 15.70 | — 19.20 | 22.0 | ....... ... | 73.53 | 20.75 | 0.08 |
| 8694 | — 11.90 | — 13.70 | 22.0 | .......... | 70.43 | 21.60 | 0.20 |
| 8695 | — 16.40 | — 22.40 | 22.0 | .......... | 72.47 | 18.31 | 0.08 |
| 8696 | — 15.00 | — 18.20 | 22.2 | .......... | 73.53 | 20.01 | 0.02 |
| 8697 | — 7.20 | — 9.60 | 22.0 | .......... | 70.92 | 20 58 | 0.11 |
| 8698 | 29.90 | 14.40 | 21.0 | 11.6 | 61.35 | 16.00 | 0.12 |
| 8711 | — 10.40 | — 15.80 | 21.0 | .......... | 73.53 | 18.49 | 0.11 |
| 8752 | — 8.60 | — 13.00 | 19.0 | .......... | 70.43 | 19.73 | 0.31 |
| 8753 | — 8.40 | — 14.20 | 19.0 | .......... | 71.43 | 16.89 | 0.12 |
| 8754 | 7.10 | 6.50 | 21.2 | .......... | 73.53 | 20.85 | 0.15 |

## NOTES ON PRECEDING TABLES.

### ANALYSES BY H. A. HUSTON.

Four of the samples were sold as comb honey, being honeycomb in jars presumably filled with glucose or some honey substitute. It is to be regretted that Mr. Huston failed to report the polarizations obtained and also to note what samples were abnormal in their optical behavior. Repeated requests for this information have not succeeded in their object, and the other data therefore go to press without these important complements.

### ANALYSES BY H. H. NICHOLSON.

Of the 50 samples analyzed by Mr. Nicholson the following were adulterated with commercial glucose, viz: Nos. 1757, 1761, 1764, 1766, 1769, 1772, 1773, 1779, 1780, 1782, 1783, 1786, 1787, 1788, 1789, 1793, 1795, 1796, 1798, 1799, 1800, 1801, 1803, and 1804. In all, 26 samples, or 52 per cent of the whole number. Some of these appear to have had only from 25 to 50 per cent of glucose added, or else principally that form of starch sugar known as grape sugar. This product is chiefly dextrose and its presence is indicated by a rather low right-handed polarization which is not greatly changed on inversion unless cane sugar is also present in considerable quantities.

Illustrations of this kind of adulteration are more numerous in these samples than in any other set examined; in fact, their number is so large as to excite comment. Samples Nos. 1788, 1789, 1796, 1800, etc., are illustrations. The use of dextrose as a honey adulterant is not common, and its occurrence in so many of these samples is not probable. They are rather to be regarded as mixtures of honey and glucose in the proportions mentioned above.

Samples Nos. 1756 and 1794 clearly indicate the addition of consid. erable quantities of cane sugar.

In samples Nos. 1766, 1776, 1780, 1781, 1782, 1784, 1785, 1786, 1787, 1789, 1790, 1792, 1794, 1797, 1798, 1799, 1802, and 1805, the excessive quantities of water found show that the samples can not be genuine. Eight of these are included under those adulterated with glucose, leaving 10 to be added to the total of adulterated samples. These, in all make 38, samples certainly adulterated, giving to the unadulterated class all the doubtful samples.

The general result of the analyses is therefore 38 adulterated to 12 doubtful and genuine samples.

The percentage of adulteration is 76.

The labels on the packages of honey bought are very misleading. No. 1756, adulterated with cane sugar, is labeled "Pure California Honey;" 1761, "Pure Honey;" 1772, "Pure Honey;" 1773, "Pure Honey;" 1780, "White Clover Honey;" 1782, "California Honey;" 1783, "California Honey;" 1787, "Pure Honey;" 1788, "Pure Honey;" 1789,

"White Clover Honey;" 1798, "Pure Honey;" 1799, "Pure Honey;" 1803, "Pure Honey;" 1804, "Pure Honey," etc.

Many samples of spurious honey were provided with labels indicating that they come from California. The honeys delivered to commerce by the bee keepers of California have been found almost always pure. The very honesty of the California bee keeper is made a stock in trade for his less scrupulous cismontane factor.

### ANALYSES BY W. B. RISING.

The analyses of the samples of honey purchased in the markets of San Francisco and vicinity are of peculiar interest both on account of the magnitude of the bee industry in California and by reason of the fact that the low price of the honeys in the home markets of the State is a powerful safeguard against the practice of adulteration. It is a rule of universal application which forbids fabrication when the price of the genuine article approaches that of the constituents of the sophisticated article plus the cost of compounding.

In the whole number of samples purchased in open market by Mr. Rising only the following were found adulterated, viz: Nos. 12, 15, 16, 18, 20, 23, 27, 65, and 140; in all, 9 or 18 per cent. This is a good showing for California honeys in their own markets as compared with the extent of their adulteration in other parts of the country.

Sample No. 12 is included in the above list as an adulterated article, but in justice to the label which represents it as made from orange blossoms it is only fair to say that no comparative study of a certainly genuine honey from orange blossoms can be cited to show that sample in question is abnormal.

No. 19 had the same label as No. 12, yet the analysis of this sample is quite within the limits of a genuine article. These two cases show that a label is often used to catch the eye of the purchaser instead of to describe the character of the goods to be sold.

Sample No. 15 is quite without the limits of a genuine honey, but it is difficult to state the character of the adulteration. It is probably a starch sugar or glucose very rich in dextrose. Its label, "Pure Extracted Honey," has been used to cover a multitude of sins in the trade.

No. 16 is a puzzling sample. It may be a genuine sample of right-handed honey. The only authentic instances, however, of a genuine honey being right-handed are in cases where the bees have gathered their stores from the honey dew of pine trees. It is possible that there may be plants in California affording a saccharine exudation of a similar character. If not, the composition of the sample is peculiar. It should perhaps be taken out of the adulterated list and marked doubtful. Its label affords no clue to its origin.

No. 18, without any distinguishing label, appears to be adulterated with about 50 per cent of glucose.

No. 20, labeled "Pure Extracted Honey," contains apparently from 20 to 30 per cent of glucose.

No. 23 contains from 50 to 60 per cent of glucose.

No. 27 contains from 60 to 70 per cent of glucose.

No. 65, labeled "Pure San Diego Honey, bottled expressly for family use," contains from 75 to 85 per cent of glucose. It grew chiefly in the corn belt of the Northwest, and not in the flowers of southern California.

No. 140 is pure glucose, with probably only enough honey added to give it a little flavor.

The content of water in the samples is quite in contrast with the quantities found in the honeys purchased in the vicinity of Omaha. The latter, as has already been stated, contain water in abnormal quantities, while the California samples all fall within the limits set for pure honeys.

### ANALYSES BY M. A. SCOVELL.

Sample 101 is adulterated with a heavy confectioners' glucose about 40 per cent, or with glucose containing a large quantity of dextrose, about 60 to 70 per cent. Its low content of water would indicate the former method of adulteration.

The capacity of " Old Virginia" to produce honey would seem to be equal to that of California, judging from the frequency with which George K. McMechen & Son's goods are found on the market. Although warranted "absolutely pure," it is evident that this firm depend on the glucose factory rather than the petals of the flower for their chief stock in trade.

No. 103, labeled "Choice Comb Honey" is another instance of the sale of comb honey which is a mechanical mixture of the comb with glucose.

No. 104 " Pure Machine-Extracted Honey" from the Italian apiary of Charles F. Muth, contains fully 50 per cent of adulterant. The machine alluded to in the label is doubtless the converter in which corn starch is changed into glucose in Buffalo and other places.

No. 110 is a further proof of the freedom with which the good name of California is prostituted in the fabrication of false wares. It is at least two-thirds glucose.

No. 116 belongs in the same category as the foregoing.

No. 126, labeled " Muth's California Honey," is almost pure glucose.

No. 127 is "Warranted Pure Honey," put up by C. F. Muth & Son, is nearly half glucose.

No. 135 is another spurious comb honey, manufactured by Githens & Rexsamer, Philadelphia.

No. 136 is another of the fraudulent preparations of McMechen's Old Virginia brand.

No. 137 is a doubtful sample. Judged by the other samples of pure California honey, it is adulterated with cane sugar; the extent of the adulteration, however, is not great enough to permit its classification with the fraudulent samples without this word of explanation.

No. 140 shows that Githens & Rexsamer have worked the Cincinnati markets pretty thoroughly with their imitation comb honeys.

No. 141 is explained by note on 104.

No. 144 is another of McMechen's Old Virginia.

No. 149 is another illustration of an adulterated honey bearing the label of C. F. Muth & Son.

*Summary.*—Of the whole number 13 are certainly adulterated, 26 per cent and 1 other probably, 28 per cent in all. In the present state of our knowledge it is necessary to pass all moderately left-handed honeys as pure, although there may be a great percentage of adulteration in such samples. Methods are now perfecting which will enable us to detect an adulteration in a left-handed sugar with as great a degree of certainty as we are now able to do with a right-handed one.

ANALYSES BY S. P. SHARPLES.

In the case of the strained honeys on the market, the price seems to be governed entirely by the will of the retailer, the same-sized tumbler selling from 10 to 18 cents, according to the store.

The highest priced were the two samples of fraudulent Swiss honey, while the cheapest was the pint jar of pure honey from Cambridge.

The practical working of a good anti-adulteration law, properly enforced, is well illustrated in the samples of honey collected in and near Boston. Only 6 samples out of 50 were found to be adulterated with glucose, or 12 per cent. These are Nos. 9504, 9506, 9524, 9525, 9526, and 9547.

In Nos. 9504 and 9506 is seen the temerity of fraudulent comb honey seeking a market in the only city in the country where a serious attempt to prevent the sale of such sophisticated articles is made. The maker affixed no label, depending, evidently, on the presence of the comb to secure a ready sale and immunity from inspection.

In Nos. 9524 and 9525 samples of the breakfast honey so enjoyed by travelers in Switzerland are found. They are almost pure glucose, very possibly made in America. The label in this case commanded a high price, as indicated above.

No. 9526 has a label which is calculated to carry conviction to a hesitating heart. It is endowed with the natural granulating principle which pure honey has in a high degree, especially after extraction. The character of the adulteration is not clear, but it is apparently dextrose, probably the anhydrous variety. It is at least a right-handed sugar, whose rotatory power is not appreciably affected by heating with an acid during the process of inverting cane sugar.

As in the other cases, left-handed honeys have been passed without question as genuine. After more definite means have been devised to discriminate between pure honey and pure invert sugar it will be possible to pass judgment upon the purity of such samples.

### ANALYSES BY W. C. STUBBS.

Of the 50 samples examined the following were adulterated with glucose, viz : Nos. 2, 5, 6, 11, 18, 21, 24, 26, 27, 30, 33, 35, 37, 38, 45, 46, and 49, in all 17 samples, or 34 per cent.

The following were adulterated with sucrose, viz : Nos. 2, 8, 16, and 27. Of this list No. 2 is found in the first category, leaving 3 additional samples to be placed in the adulterated column, making a total of 20 samples, equivalent to 40 per cent.

The following samples would indicate that the honey was part obtained from the honeydew of pine forests, viz: Nos. 12, 13, 15, 23, 41, and 50. This statement rests upon the belief that there are no genuine right-handed honeys which do not have their origin in the honeydew mentioned, the properties of which are given in another part of this report.

The peculiarly favorable facilities which the bees in Louisiana have of access to cane sugar would probably explain the abnormally high percentage of this substance in some of the samples, leading to their classification with the adulterated articles.

The water, as in the case of the Omaha samples, is abnormally high, but this may be due to the fact that the humidity of the air in Louisiana is usually very high and the sweets to which the bees have access are consequently richer in water than in a dry climate, such as, for instance, that of California.

### ANALYSES BY SHIPPEN WALLACE.

Of the whole number examined Mr. Wallace only gives 10 as pure, equivalent to an adulteration of 80 per cent. I would, however, add to the list of honeys probably pure No. 9, which he regards as adulterated with glucose and cane sugar, and all of those classified by him as adulterated with inverted sucrose. The reasons for this transfer are those already stated, viz: The difficulty at the present time of deciding definitely in regard to added inverted sucrose. This emendation of the classification would add 11 samples to the list of probably pure honeys, and reduce the percentage of adulteration to 58.

Our old friends " Pure Honey," " Pure California Honey," and " Geo. K. McMechen & Son's Pure Old Virginia Honey," are found, as usual, decorating the adulterated columns.

Mr. Wallace classifies the honeys examined by him as follows :

### HONEY, PROBABLY PURE.

| No. | Polarization. | | Sucrose. | Reducing sugar. | Ash. |
|---|---|---|---|---|---|
| | Direct. | Invert. | | | |
| | | | Per cent. | Per cent. | Per cent. |
| 4 | — 4.0 | — 6.0 | 1.4 | 62.00 | 0.09 |
| 6 | —10.0 | —16.0 | 4.4 | 60.85 | .15 |
| 10 | — 8.5 | —12.0 | 2.9 | 60.85 | .05 |
| 18 | — 7.5 | — 9.0 | 1.1 | 65.70 | .07 |
| 20 | — 9.5 | —10.0 | 0.3 | 67.22 | .20 |
| 33 | —12.0 | —14.0 | 1.4 | 70.95 | .25 |
| 34 | —10.0 | —11.0 | 0.7 | 67.80 | .31 |
| 41 | — 5.0 | —17.0 | 8.9 | 65.20 | .27 |
| 45 | — 5.0 | — 8.0 | 2.2 | 68.95 | .22 |
| 50 | —11.0 | —12.0 | 0.7 | 72.65 | .27 |

### HONEY ADULTERATED WITH GLUCOSE OR GLUCOSE AND CANE SUGAR.

| | | | | | |
|---|---|---|---|---|---|
| 2 | 66.0 | 61.0 | 3.7 | 51.20 | 0.17 |
| 5 | 110.0 | 27.0 | 61.9 | 41.38 | .12 |
| 8 | 102.0 | 92.6 | 7.0 | 44.20 | .10 |
| 14 | 78.0 | 72.0 | 4.50 | 35.50 | .08 |
| 15 | 83.5 | 70.0 | 10.0 | 31.50 | .15 |
| 16 | 51.0 | 47.0 | 2.9 | 29.85 | .10 |
| 17 | 19.0 | 16.0 | 2.2 | 45.78 | .18 |
| 19 | 41.0 | 31.0 | 7.4 | 40.25 | .09 |
| 21 | 92.5 | 58.0 | 25.7 | 38.80 | .12 |
| 22 | 53.5 | 41.0 | 9.3 | 29.65 | .18 |
| 25 | 30.5 | 13.0 | 13.0 | 51.65 | .18 |
| 26 | 52.0 | 32.0 | 14.9 | 27.50 | .21 |
| 30 | 71.0 | 64.0 | 5.2 | 33.75 | .17 |
| 35 | 102.5 | 83.0 | 14.5 | 40.55 | .15 |
| 39 | 55.0 | 4.0 | 38.0 | 40.15 | .15 |
| 43 | 53.0 | 8.0 | 33.5 | 52.50 | .14 |
| 46 | 110.0 | 27.0 | 61.9 | 41.50 | .15 |
| 47 | 102.0 | 92.6 | 7.0 | 40.15 | .15 |
| 48 | 78.0 | 70.0 | 5.9 | 36.50 | .20 |
| 49 | 65.0 | 50.0 | 11.1 | 49.45 | .18 |
| 9 | — 3.5 | —16.0 | 9.4 | 72.30 | .08 |

### ADULTERATED WITH CANE SUGAR.

| | | | | | |
|---|---|---|---|---|---|
| 1 | 29.0 | —13.0 | 31.3 | 38.50 | 0.21 |
| 3 | 9.0 | —10.0 | 14.1 | 47.54 | .15 |
| 28 | 7.5 | —14.0 | 16.0 | 68.22 | .18 |
| 36 | 11.0 | —15.0 | 19.4 | 64.30 | .19 |
| 40 | 7.5 | —16.0 | 17.5 | 68.50 | .20 |
| 42 | 8.3 | —16.0 | 18.1 | 68.25 | .18 |
| 44 | 10.0 | — 8.0 | 13.4 | 44.25 | .16 |
| 23 | 10.5 | — 8.0 | 13.8 | 45.92 | .09 |
| 38 | 57.5 | —20.0 | 57.8 | 20.85 | .18 |

ADULTERATED WITH INVERTED SUCROSE.

| No. | Polarization. | | Sucrose. | Reducing sugar. | Ash. |
|---|---|---|---|---|---|
| | Direct. | Invert. | | | |
| | Per cent. | | Per cent. | Per cent. | Per cent. |
| 7 | —19.5 | —19.0 | .......... | 70.10 | 0.27 |
| 11 | —13.5 | —14.0 | .......... | 71.50 | .20 |
| 12 | —13.0 | —13.0 | .......... | 71.50 | .22 |
| 13 | —18.5 | —20.0 | 1.1 | 72.75 | .27 |
| 24 | —11.0 | —12.0 | 0.7 | 72.50 | .28 |
| 27 | —14.0 | —14.0 | .......... | 71.95 | .25 |
| 29 | —19.0 | —19.0 | .......... | 74.80 | .22 |
| 31 | —17.0 | —17.0 | .......... | 73.10 | .23 |
| 32 | —15.0 | —15.0 | .......... | 71.50 | .28 |
| 37 | —14.0 | —14.0 | .......... | 71.75 | .32 |

### ANALYSES BY H. A. WEBER.

The samples adulterated with glucose are the following, viz: Nos. 1, 4, 7, 11, 13, 17, 18, 19, 21, 23, 24, 25, 27, 33, 34, 35, 36, 44, 46, and 48. The labels characterizing the adulterated articles can be seen in the foregoing description. Some of them have grown to be quite familiar. No. 1 is " California Honey," No. 7 " McMechen's Old Virginia," etc.

No. 13 was a spurious comb honey in a jar.

No. 23 is labeled " Pure Machine-Extracted Honey from the Italian apiary of C. F. Muth & Son.

No. 33, labeled " Pure California White Sage Honey from Thurber & Whyland," shows an addition of a large quantity of dextrin, probably in the form of glucose.

It is to be regretted that Mr. Weber did not use the same methods of detecting glucose adulterations as was practiced by the other analysts engaged in the work. He has passed some samples as unadulterated in which we should have expected to find large quantities of glucose, from an inspection of the names and labels they bear.

### ANALYSES OF F. G. WIECHMANN.

#### NOTES BY MR. WIECHMANN.

The samples analyzed were liquid, " strained honey," excepting samples Nos. 140, 144, 148, 149, each of which had a piece of comb in the liquid, and No. 147, which was comb-honey.

In numerous samples a sediment appeared ; in sample No. 124 the contents of the bottle had separated into halves, the lower portion being filled with a yellowish gray solid, while above this stood a dark-brown solution. These were of course thoroughly mixed before analysis.

In No. 106 a brown flocculent precipitate appeared throughout sample.

All honeys having an ash of 0.30 and over were tested for calcium sulphate. These were the samples :

Per cent.

No. 102 ........................................................ 0.313
No. 103........................................................ .324
No. 105........................................................ .648
No. 113........................................................ .385
No. 146........................................................ .342

In all of these calcium and sulphuric acid were found.

Where the ash amounted to 0.20 and over, the color and appearance of the same were noted.

| No. | Color of ash. | Appearance of ash. | No. | Color of ash. | Appearance of ash. |
|-----|---------------|---------------------|-----|---------------|---------------------|
| 102 | White ............ | Fluffy. | 119 | White ............ | Fluffy. |
| 103 | ....do ............ | Scaly. | 122 | ....do ............ | Scaly. |
| 104 | ....do ............ | Fluffy. | 123 | ....do ............ | Very bulky and |
| 105 | Gray ............ | Scaly. | | | fluffy. |
| 106 | White ............ | Do. | 126 | ....do ............ | Fluffy. |
| 110 | Pink ............ | Fluffy. | 130 | ....do ............ | Do. |
| 112 | White ............ | Do. | 140 | ....do ............ | Do. |
| 113 | ....do ............ | Do. | 141 | Gray ............ | Do. |
| 117 | ....do ............ | Very bulky and | 146 | Pink............ | Do. |
| | | fluffy. | 149 | ....do ............ | Do. |
| 118 | White, with yellow tinge. | Fluffy. | | | |

Ashes Nos. 110, 146, and 149, pink in color, were tested for iron and were found to contain this metal.

In order to learn the composition of an undoubtedly pure honey, two samples of comb honey were obtained from Edmund Rose, Delhi, N. Y. These samples were purchased, the seller knowing that they would be analyzed for test purposes. The one sample (A) was made by bees that had fed on white clover and possibly a little milkweed; this was of a bright gold-yellow in color. The other sample (B) was obtained from bees that had fed principally on buckwheat. This was dark brown in color.

The capping was carefully removed by knife from both sides of the combs, the intermediate wax wall perforated, and the honey allowed to drain through a fine wire gauze into a porcelain dish. The combs were kept covered during the draining, and after a few hours, when this was completed, the strained honey was placed in airtight jars.

The analyses of these two samples resulted as follows:

| Sample. | Polarization of normal weight solution in 200 mm. tube at 20° C. | | Reducing sugars. | | Sucrose.* | Water. | Ash. |
|---------|------------------------------|-------------------|------|-------------------|---------|--------|------|
| | Before inversion. | After inversion. | Before inversion. | After inversion. | | | |
| A........ | —13.6 | —14.6 | 70.92 | 74.07 | 3.31 | 20.67 | 0.144 |
| B........ | —14.2 | —16.0 | 72.40 | 75.18 | 2.86 | 22.47 | 0.083 |

* Calculated from difference in amounts of reducing sugar, before and after inversion, a 1 per cent solution being used in both instances. Neutralization after inversion was effected by sodium carbonate.

The polarization before inversion corresponds to a specific rotatory power for sodium ray, in sample A = — 4.698, sample B = — 4.906.

On examining the analyses of the 50 samples of honey recorded above in order to determine which are genuine and which are not, one is confronted by a problem in many cases difficult, in others actually impossible of solution.

However, carefully studying the bearing of all of the different factors in the question, the following conclusions appear warranted by the data.*

* For contributions to this subject, see H. W. Wiley in The American Apiculturist, Vol. III, No. 12, 1885; the same, in American Chemical Journal, Vol. XIII, No. 1, 1891; A. H. Allen, Commercial Organic Analysis, Vol. I, 2d Ed., 1885; Hassall, Food and its Adulterations; E. Sieben, in Zeitschrift des Vereines für Rübenzucker-Industrie, Vol. 34, p. 837, 1884.

The samples may be divided into: Group I, presumably pure honeys. Group II, adulterated honeys.

In Group I must be placed Nos. 101, 107, 108, 111, 114, 115, 116, 120, 121, 123, 124, 125, 127, 128, 129, 131, 132, 133, 134, 135, 136, 137, 138, 139, 147, and 150.

Many of these samples have been placed in this group simply because it is impossible to prove their adulteration by analysis. Judging from the general appearance, color, taste, and fluidity of the samples, the writer feels morally certain that more than half of those enumerated above consist essentially of inverted sucrose. However, as it is practically impossible to demonstrate this claim, one is forced to class them with the genuine honeys, and this group has therefore advisedly been marked: "Presumably" genuine.

Group II is capable of subdivision into: II *a*. Unquestionably adulterated with starch sirup (glucose). II *b*. Adulterated with starch sirup (glucose), with sucrose, or with both.

Group II *a* embraces Nos. 102, 105, 106, 109, 119, 130, and 143.

Group II *b* embraces Nos. 103, 104, 110, 112, 113, 117, 118, 122, 126, 140, 141, 142, 144, 145, 146, 148, and 149.

This shows 24 out of 50 samples examined to be undoubtedly adulterated. This corresponds to 48 per cent, and of the remaining 26 samples, as already stated, more than one-half are in all probability also not pure.

## ANALYSES BY F. G. WIECHMANN.

Mr. Wiechmann has very satisfactorily discussed the data obtained by him, and I will add only a few notes.

No. 118 is evidently the same brand of honey as No. 114, examined by Mr. M. A. Scovell, and No. 9526, by Mr. S. P. Sharples. The label and description are identical, with the exception of the name of the wholesale dealer, which in two cases is Thurber & Whyland and in one case E. Brommond.

Mr. Wiechmann's data are compared with Mr. Scovell's below:

| | Before inversion. | After inversion. | Reducing sugars. | Water. | Ash. |
|---|---|---|---|---|---|
| | ° | ° | *Per cent.* | *Per cent.* | *Per cent.* |
| Wiechmann ........... | 63.3 | 52.0 | 55.87 | 20.78 | 0.22 |
| Scovell ............... | — 7.2 | —15.1 | 75.47 | 11.76 | 0.20 |
| Sharpless ............. | 42.00 | 40.0 | 67.03 | 15.39 | 0.24 |

Nothing could illustrate better than the above table the utter meaninglessness of labels. Here we find one label and description applied indiscriminately to three samples of honey totally different in their composition. The sample examined by Mr. Scovell is apparently genuine. Those examined by Messrs. Wiechmann and Sharples are undoubtedly adulterated, but not to the same extent.

It appears to be the habit of the enterprising dealer to arm himself with an assortment of altisonant labels and a pot of paste and then to make a descent on a helpless pile of genuine and spurious packages of honey, applying the labels indiscriminately.

Honeys were polarized as is described under molasses and sugars. Glucose was determined in a 1 per cent solution by titration, using Violette's solution. Water and ash were found in the same manner as with molasses, using kieselguhr in determining the former. In a few samples the degree Brix was determined after dilution. The process was:

Weigh a 50 cc flask, drop in 20 or 30 grams of honey, reweigh, fill up to the mark with water, again weigh, and shake violently. After stand. ing some time to allow bubbles to escape, take the apparent specific gravity of the mixture by means of a pyknometer. The corresponding degree Brix is found from Stammer's table and corrected for temperature. This is taken as representing the per cent of solids in the mixture of honey and water. The weight of the mixture multiplied by this per cent gives the total amount of solids in the weighed amount of honey placed in the flask.

The following samples were found to be adulterated with glucose, viz: Nos. 8517, 8523, 8525, 8526, 8533, 8538, 8539, 8540, 8679, 8682, 8683, 8687, 8691, and 8698, in all 14 samples, equivalent to 28 per cent.

Two samples, Nos. 8517 and 8678, contained some sugar as an adulterant.

Six samples, Nos. 8532, 8535, 8683, 8691, 8697, and 8754, are difficult to classify. They may contain small quantities, 15 to 30 per cent, of glucose, or they may belong to the natural right-handed honeys gathered from pine forests.

The percentage of samples certainly adulterated is therefore 32, and if the 6 doubtful samples are included, that number rises to 44, or since one sample has been counted twice as adulterated, 42.

No. 8517 should hardly be included in the list of honeys used for foods since it is clearly designed only for medical use.

No. 8525 comes under the attractive title of " Choice Extracted Clover Honey," and presumably all the way from Massachusetts. Such sophistications being prohibited in the home markets, they naturally seek an outlet where the laws are more lenient and consumers more indifferent. Nowhere else are these conditions so favorable as in the District of Columbia.

In 8526 we meet our old friend, " Pure Old Virginia Honey," put up by that enterprising firm of George K. McMechen & Son, who seem to have left very few of the markets of the country untried with their products.

In 8533 " Choice Clover Honey " is again made to do duty in securing favorable consideration for the inversion product of corn starch.

"Choice Extracted Northern Honey" is the label under which No. 8538 deceives the innocent purchaser.

" Pure California White Clover Honey" is the label applied to the glucose mixture No. 8539. Had a skilled botanist been doing this mixing he would not have located the origin of a white-clover sample in California. He would have stuck to wild sage or orange blossoms, as in 8683, and left the clovers for New England and New York, as was done by the more considerate mixer of No. 8540.

"Golden Rod Honey" is a most attractive name under which to sell starch sugar, and the vendor of No. 8679 has pressed that name into his service.

While the honeys exposed for sale in Baltimore and Washington are not so extensively adulterated as in a few other localities, yet it appears that nearly one-half of the samples of liquid honey which may be bought at random in these two cities is spurious.

In regard to the weight of honey in each package a number of experiments were made. The weights given below are seriatim, with the exception of number three, which is omitted.

Weight in grams :

308, 411, ——, 280, 308, 400, 422, 300, 345, 434, 386, 364, 543, 165, 255, 431, 285, 244, 393, 273, 391, 282, 301, 414.

It will be seen that except in one instance the amount of honey in a package does not reach one pound, viz, 454 grams. In one case there was less than half a pound in the package, while in a number of cases the actual weight of honey was only approximately three-quarters of a pound.

### AFFIDAVIT HONEYS.

Five of the 6 samples of honey of guaranteed purity (Nos. 9009, 9010, 9011, 9012, and 9014) were bought in Gaithersburg, Md., by a representative of the Department, July 20: The country round Gaithersburg is rather rolling, and is fairly well wooded with second growth pine and hard wood. At the time of buying there were few field flowers apparent, and the bees appeared to be at work mainly on the black cherry trees which are numerous in this piece of country. These cherries, which grew wild, were small and black, but very sweet. No attempt had evidently been made to gather them anywhere, and the ground underneath the trees was covered with decaying fruit. The sellers of the honey did not know whence the bees derived their honey, but thought it came from the woods. Sample No. 9014 came from a bee tree in the woods, and was evidently the accumulation of several years. It was black, dirty, and full of bee bread and dead bees.

By reason of the fact that these five samples were right-handed they have an unusual interest. They are the only samples of honey, known to be genuine, which have shown right-handed polarization which have been found in our investigations, now extending over a series of several years.

Does this dextro-rotation arise from the consumption by the bees of the honey dew of the neighboring pine forest, or is it due to the wild cherries? The true source of this phenomenon is at present unknown.

One sample, No. 9015, was bought in another locality, and showed the customary levorotation.

*Sample No. 9009.*

Personally appeared before me, Charles W. Crawford, justice of the peace in and for Montgomery County, State of Maryland, E. M. Thompson, who takes oath that the sample of honey forwarded by him to the Department of Agriculture is perfectly pure and free from adulteration, and that the bees preparing it have neither been fed nor allowed access to artificial saccharine substances, nor have they been given comb foundation, nor has wax in any form been given to the bees or introduced into the hive artificially.

In evidence whereof witness my hand and seal, this 18th day of July, 1891.

CHARLES W. CRAWFORD, *J. P.* [SEAL.]

*Sample No. 9010.*

Personally appeared before me, Charles W. Crawford, justice of the peace in and for Montgomery County, State of Maryland, V. P. Hinkley, who takes oath that the sample of honey forwarded by him to the Department of Agriculture is perfectly pure and free from adulteration, and that the bees preparing it have neither been fed nor allowed access to artificial saccharine substances, nor have they been given comb foundation, nor has wax in any form been given to the bees or introduced into the hive artificially.

In evidence whereof witness my hand and seal this 18th day of July, 1891.

CHARLES W. CRAWFORD, *J. P.* [SEAL.]

*Sample No. 9011.*

Personally appeared before me, Charles W. Crawford, notary public in and for State of Maryland, Montgomery County, Albert O. Appleby, who takes oath that the sample of honey forwarded by him to the Department of Agriculture is perfectly pure and free from adulteration, and that the bees preparing it have neither been fed nor allowed access to artificial saccharine substances, nor have they been given comb foundation, nor has wax in any form been given to the bees or introduced into the hive artificially.

In evidence whereof witness my hand and seal, this 18th day of July, 1891.

CHARLES W. CRAWFORD, *J. P.* [SEAL.]

*Sample No. 9012.*

Personally appeared before me, Charles W. Crawford, justice of the peace in and for Montgomery County, State of Maryland, Edmund Gloyd, who takes oath that the sample of honey forwarded by him to the Department of Agriculture is perfectly pure and free from adulteration, and that the bees preparing it have neither been fed nor allowed access to artificial saccharine substances, nor have they been been given comb foundation, nor has wax in any form been given to the bees or introduced into the hive artificially.

In evidence whereof witness my hand and seal this 18th day of July, 1891.

CHARLES W. CRAWFORD, *J. P.* [SEAL.]

*Sample No. 9015.*

VIRGINIA, *Loudoun County, to wit*:

Personally appeared before me, Jos. E. Wright, a notary public for Loudoun County, John W. Bauckman, who certifies that the 25 pounds of comb-honey sent by him this 23d day of July to the Chemical Division of the Department of Agriculture is pure honey, that the bees have not been artificially fed, and that no artificial comb foundation of any kind has been used.

Witness my hand and seal this 23d day of July, 1891.

JOS. E. WRIGHT,
*Notary Public.*

*Analyses of samples of honey obtained from localities near Washington, accompanied by affidavits.*

| No. | Polarization. | | Tempera-tnre °C. | Reducing sugar. | Water. | Sucrose. | Ash. |
|---|---|---|---|---|---|---|---|
| | Direct. | Invert. | | | | | |
| | | | | *Per cent.* | *Per cent.* | *Per cent.* | *Per cent.* |
| 9009 | 8.2 | 2.8 | 29 | 64.52 | 17.00 | 5.0 | .12 |
| 9010 | 7.2 | 3.3 | 29 | 66.45 | 18.33 | 3.1 | .10 |
| 9011 | 5.1 | 2.4 | 30 | 63.42 | 18.65 | 2.1 | .19 |
| 9012 | 7.3 | 2.6 | 29.5 | 58.42 | 16.72 | 3.6 | .20 |
| 9014 | .6 | — 2.2 | 29 | 64.10 | 19.00 | 2.2 | .25 |
| 9015 | —10.65 | —11.7 | 30 | 67.80 | 19.60 | .7 | .16 |

In connection with the analyses of the samples of honey certified by the producers to be pure and which, nevertheless, showed right-handed polarization, I beg to call attention to the character of a honey dew exuded by the pine tree, which, when used as food by bees, may give rise to the phenomenon mentioned.

### PINE-TREE HONEY DEW AND PINE-TREE HONEY.[*]

In March, 1890, I received from Mr. W. M. Evans, of Amherst, Va., a sample of pine-tree honey dew and of pine-tree honey.

The honey dew, according to the description sent by Mr. Evans, was collected drop by drop from the pine leaves. At the same time Mr. Evans sent me a sample of pine-tree honey, which he says was without doubt made by the bees from the pine leaves during the winter, since no other honey-producing plants were accessible to them. Having seen it stated in some of the foreign journals that honey made from pine forests gave a right-handed polarization, I thought it would be of interest to examine the two samples sent by Mr. Evans to determine, if possible, their nature. The small quantity of the honey dew which I had at my disposal made, of course, a thorough study impossible. So far as could be determined, however, it had the following characteristics:

It contained 54.41 per cent of water and 45.59 per cent of solid matters. Calculated as dextrose it contained 17.44 per cent of reducing sugar. After inversion it contained 26.03 per cent of reducing sugar, which would indicate a content of sucrose equivalent to 8.16 per cent. At 31° by direct polarization it gave an angular deviation equivalent to 36° 56 of the cane sugar scale (Ventzke). If we assume that the reducing sugar present was pure invert sugar, then the levogyrate influence of 17.44 per cent of invert sugar at 31° would be equal to — 4° 97 of the cane sugar scale. Adding this number to the direct polarization, it is seen that this would have amounted to 41.53 divisions of the scale. Deducting from this number the right-handed polarization due to the sucrose present, viz, 8.16, we have 33.37 divisions of right-handed rotation, due to bodies other than sucrose present in the dew. The sum of the rotations of the invert sugar, viz, 17.44 per cent, and the sucrose, 8.16 per cent, is 25.60 per cent of the total solid matter due to sucrose and invert sugar. Deducting this number from the total solids present, viz, 45.59, there is left 19.99 per cent solid matter, which has caused the right-handed deviation of 33.37 divisions. This substance, therefore, has a specific rotatory power fully one-half greater than sucrose. It is not, therefore, due to pinite, but to some body or mixture of bodies having a specific rotatory power of $(a)_d = 105$ (circa).[*] Having thus found that the pine tree exuda-

---

[*] Contributions from the Chemical Division, U. S. Department of Agriculture, published in American Chemical Journal, Vol. 13, pp. 24, et seq.

[†] This rotation would indicate that the body might be arabinose [ $(a)_d = 105$], but there was not a sufficient amount of it definitely to determine this point.

tion itself is a right-handed body, I naturally expected to find the honey made therefrom also right-handed; in this expectation, however, I was disappointed. The direct polarization of the honey, under normal conditions at 31°, was — 13 divisions of the cane sugar scale and the total reducing sugar which it contained, calculated as dextrose, was 70.42. Not only, therefore, was this sample of pine-tree honey left-handed, but it was also left-handed to a degree greater than that ordinarily exhibited by honeys. From this fact the inference is to be drawn either that in gathering the honey the bees exerted upon it an inverting effect which made it left-handed, or else Mr. Evans was mistaken in supposing that the bees had derived their stock of honey from the trees in question.

The peculiar climatic conditions of last winter presented, through the whole season, the mildness of spring, affording, perhaps, an exceptional opportunity for the development of the pine-tree honey-dew, and I am sorry that my attention was not called to the matter in time to have secured much larger quantities of this interesting substance.

The probable existence in honey of a right-handed body, not sucrose or dextrose, was indicated by me in a paper published in the American Apiculturist, Vol. 3, No. 12, 1885. In this paper it is shown that a varying amount of substance, which I supposed then to be pure dextrin, was found in honey, amounting in this case to as much as 4 per cent.

Amthor has found* that honey gathered from pine forests contains dextrin, as he supposed at that time, even in such quantities as to become dextro-rotatory.

Klinger claims that this phenomenon is not confined exclusively to honey of coniferous origin. At that time I was led to express, in the paper referred to, my doubt of the truth of Lenz's observation,† that after fermentation honey yields no optically active substance. This doubt of mine has been confirmed by subsequent investigations.

Raumer ‡ calls attention to the fact that the statement of Sieben, that the addition of starch sirup to honey could with certainty be detected by the residue of right-handed dextrin, is held to be unreliable. According to Sieben, 25 grams of honey dissolved in 150 cc of water and treated with 12 grams pressed yeast (starch-free) are completely fermented in two days. The residue, clarified with aluminium hydrate and filtered, is completely inactive optically and does not reduce Fehling solution. Even when treated with hydrochloric acid, to convert any starch or dextrin into dextrose, no reduction takes place. Raumer asserts that Sieben's observations must have been made on abnormal honeys.

Amthor has also called attention to the fact that honeys treated according to the method of Sieben, described above, showed right-handed polarization, and that this phenomenon was supposed to be due to the honey having been largely gathered from pine forests. Honeys of known purity were found to be uniformly right-handed after fermentation. In 3 samples the dextrogyratory power, after fermentation, was expressed by the following numbers respectively, 2.83, 1.58, 2.7. In 3 more samples of doubtful origin the numbers obtained were 2.13, 2.53, 3.23 respectively.

In the first three samples all possibility of adulteration is positively excluded. It was also established that the bees had not been fed with glucose. It is well known that feeding glucose or ordinary sugar causes foul brood. Only pure rock candy can be used for such purposes.

It was next deemed of interest to determine the nature of this dextrogyratory body. In order to purify the fermentation residue as completely as possible the method of Schmidt for obtaining the so-called gallisin was employed.§

---

* Report. anal. Chem., 1885, 163.
† Chem. Zeit., 8, 613.
‡ Zeit. f. angew. Chem., 1889, 607.
§ Ber. d. chem. Ges., 1884, 17, 1000 and 2456.

The honey in 10 per cent solution, after fermentation, was filtered and evaporated to a thin sirup and poured into absolute alcohol. The brownish precipitate thus obtained was rubbed with absolute alcohol, the liquid poured off and the residue rubbed twice with 96 per cent alcohol, separated on a filter, and treated three times with ether. The residue was next dissolved in a small quantity of water, treated with bone-black and filtered. If the water-clear solution is now poured into absolute alcohol, a snow-white precipitate is formed. When the precipitate has subsided the alcohol is removed with a siphon and the residue treated again with a mixture of water-free ether and absolute alcohol. After thirty-six hours it was found that the precipitate had settled well to the bottom. The liquid was poured off and the residue poured into a large asbestos filter previously weighed. The washing was performed three times with absolute alcohol and three times with ether, and a stream of dried hydrogen conducted over the residue which caused it to fall into a pulverulent mass. Finally it was dried in hydrogen at 60°. At this temperature the mass fell together into a lump. The filter was further dried forty-eight hours over sulphuric acid and weighed in a closed tube. The specific rotatory power for four samples of the substance, prepared as above, from four different kinds of honey, was as follows :

| | |
|---|---:|
| From Nuremberg honey | 64. 06 |
| Do. | 59. 30 |
| From honey from head gardener, Seyfferth | 58. 30 |
| From Nuremberg honey | 52. 60 |

The reducing power of the body for Fehling solution was determined for the first and second samples, both before and after inversion.

### No. 1.

| | g copper. |
|---|---:|
| Before inversion, 1 g substance reduced | .455 |
| After inversion, 1 g substance reduced | 1.200 |

### No. 2.

| | |
|---|---:|
| Before inversion, 1 g substance reduced | .3048 |
| After inversion, 1 g substance reduced . | .8450 |

It is evident from the foregoing that no single substance composes the unfermentable residue of honey and it is further evident that this substance is not largely composed of dextrin. It was further established that the substance, after inversion, was fully fermentable. Judged by its specific rotatory power above this substance resembles Schmidt's gallisin, but its reducing power is quite different. The researches show that the purity of a honey can not be safely determined by the fermentation process as practiced heretofore.

In regard to this right-handed body in honey, Amthor and Stern* have made some interesting investigations:

44.9655 grams of a sample of undoubtedly genuine honey were dissolved in 300 cc of water and allowed to ferment with yeast. After filtering and making up to 200 cc (?) the liquid was examined in a Laurent polariscope and gave 24.°09' in a 20 cm tube. The dextrin was then converted into dextrose by heating 100 cc with 10 cc hydrochloric acid for three hours in a water bath. After cooling and making up again to 100 cc, the polarization gave 9°.21', equal to 2.249 per cent dextrose. Allihn's gravimetric process gave 2.266 per cent. The formation of dextrose points to the honey having contained dextrin. The authors further confirmed this view by preparing phenylglucazone. A large quantity of honey was fermented in a weak solution ; the filtrate yielded on evaporation a brown, thickish sirup, which was

---

* Zeit. f. angew. Chem., 1889, 575.

really an impure dextrin. After dissolving in a little water, phosphotungstic acid, containing some sulphuric acid, was added, and the liquid filtered. The excess of reagent was removed by means of baryta water, and this in turn by the cautious addition of sulphuric acid. After concentrating a little *liquor plumbi* was added, the liquid filtered, and the excess of lead removed by means of hydrogen sulphide. The filtrate was evaporated in the water bath until it became a thin sirup, and 200 cc of 90 per cent alcohol were added, which were sufficient to keep the dextrin in solution. After filtering and evaporating, the dextrin was obtained as a brown sirup, which was purified with animal charcoal, until it was finally obtained as a yellowish, brittle, amorphous mass.

To obtain the related glucose, 5 grams of this dextrin were dissolved in 200 cc of water, mixed with 20 cc of 20 per cent sulphuric acid and heated for three hours on the water bath. The liquid was neutralized with barium carbonate, filtered and evaporated to a sirup, which was repeatedly exhausted with alcohol. After distilling off, a brownish sirup was obtained, which was purified by animal charcoal.

It crystallizes in granules, reduces Fehling's solution strongly, and the authors succeeded in forming phenylglucazone by warming 1 gram with two grams of phenylhydrazin, 3 grams of sodium acetate, and 20 cc of water. The crude product was recrystallized from alcohol and obtained in small yellow needles, fusing at 204° C. This removes all doubt about the original substance being dextrin, the presence of which in honey may perhaps be explained by the supposition of the bees feeding, when they get a chance, on malt in breweries.

From a careful study of the above data, it is shown that the honey-like exudation of the pine tree, without doubt, differs in a marked degree from that of the honeys of ordinary plants in being right-handed, from a polariscopic point of view, and containing bodies not sucrose nor invert sugar, with a specific rotatory power of about 105. It appears further that, according to the observations of some authors, honey made from the exudation of pines is naturally right-handed, though this observation is not confirmed by the single sample which I had at my disposal.

I should be glad hereafter to receive samples of honey of undoubted pine tree origin for the purpose of making a further study in regard to its nature, and I hope to take advantage of the next mild winter to obtain more extensive samples from the localities affording those samples already examined.

Up to the present time it must be confessed that no genuine sample of honey collected in this country has shown a right-handed rotation. Honey possessing this property therefore greatly excites suspicion and warrants an inquiry concerning its composition.

The status of honey adulteration in 1885 may be seen from a paper published at that time containing the results of some preliminary studies on the subject:

[From the American Apiculturist, Vol. III, No. 12, 1885.]

### HONEY AND ITS ADULTERATIONS, BY PROF. H. W. WILEY.

Pure honey is the nectar of flowers passed through the organism of the bee and stored in a comb. Adulterated honey is any compound or preparation known or sold as honey which has not been formed in the manner described. Chemically considered, therefore, pure honey consists of the substances gathered by the bee from flowers, subjected to such modifications as they may undergo in the insect laboratory through which they pass.

The saccharin exudation of flowers consists of a mixture of various sugars, containing, in the form of pollen, a small quantity of nitrogenous matter. The exact number and kind of sugars in the nectar of flowers has never been determined. Wilson* estimated the reducing sugar and sucrose in the nectar of certain flowers.

---

All the sugars, however, reducing copper were classed as glucose. In general, the total quantities of such sugars were greater than the sucrose present. In the flower of the red clover the glucose was three times as much as the sucrose. Since in pure honey there is very little sucrose, it follows that the chief change which the nectar undergoes before it appears as honey is in the inversion of sucrose.

During the last year I have had examined by the division of chemistry of the Department of Agriculture a large number of honeys, some of which were known to be genuine and others of unknown origin.

Following is a description of the various samples examined:

No. 1. Choice Golden-Rod Honey, from William Thompson, Wayne County, N. Y.; price, 25 cents per pound.

No. 2. Choice Comb Honey, from Githens & Rexmer, Philadelphia, Pa.; price, 25 cents per pound.

No. 3. Same as No. 2.

No. 4. Same as No. 2.

No. 5. Strained Honey; marked C. O. Perrine, Indiana; price, 20 cents per pound.

No. 6. A very Dark Honey ; exhibited at Indiana Beekeepers' Association.

No. 7. Choice Clover Honey, from Charles Israel, New York; 25 cents per pound.

No. 8. Pure White Clover Honey; 30 cents per pound; marked G. R. X. X., Pennsylvania.

No. 9. Honey in comb; 30 cents per pound; locality not given.

No. 10. California Comb Honey ; bought in La Fayette, Ind.; 20 cents per pound.

No. 11. Same as No. 5.

No. 12. Eagle Brand Honey (in comb); Cayuga, County, N. Y.; bought in open market, La Fayette Ind.; price, 25 cents per pound.

No. 13. White Clover Honey, from C. W. Hutchinson, Acton, Marion County, Ind.

No. 14. Sample from Louisiana; C. F. Muth, Cincinnati, Ohio.

No. 15. Basswood or Linn Honey, from Illinois; C. F. Muth, Cincinnati, Ohio.

No. 16. Mangrove Honey, from Florida; C. F. Muth, Cincinnati, Ohio.

No. 17. Mangrove Honey, from Florida; C. F. Muth, Cincinnati, Ohio.

No. 18. Pure White Clover Honey, apiary M. B. Shaw, 378 Union street, Indianapolis, Ind. ; price, 30 cents per pound.

No. 19. Strained Honey, from choice selected white clover; 40 cents per pound.

No. 20. Pure Extracted Honey (crystallized) ; 20 cents per pound; from R. F. Weir, South River, Md.

No. 21. Pure Extracted Honey (liquid); 20 cents per pound; from R. F. Weir, South River, Md.

No. 22. No brand, from J. Hepsberger, Maryland; 25 cents per pound.

No. 23. Comb Honey ; made in Tippecanoe County, Ind.; price, 20 cents per pound.

No. 24. Strained Honey ; bought in bulk; 20 cents per pound.

No. 25. Comb Honey; bought in open market, Indianapolis, Ind.; from H. K. Thurber, New York; 25 cents per pound.

No. 26. Pure Machine-Extracted Honey, Italian apiary, F. W. Abbott, Indianapolis, Ind.; 30 cents per pound.

No. 27. Sample marked B. F. Davis, North Salem, Hendricks County, Ind.

No. 28. White Clover and Basswood Honey (comb), Linden Place Apiary, Indianapolis, Ind., Pugh & Dougherty.

No. 29. Choice Extracted Honey; strictly pure; 25 cents per pound; from McCaul & Hildreth, New York.

No. 30. No brand, from Charles S. Duvall, Spencerville, Md.; 20 cents per pound.

No. 31. Comb Honey, made in Tippecanoe County, Ind.; 25 cents per pound.

No. 32. Comb Honey, from Chicago, Ill.; 20 cents per pound.

No. 33. Comb Honey, made in California; 20 cents per pound.

No. 34. Strained Honey, marked White Clover XXG & R, 30 cents per pound.

No. 35. Comb Honey; bought in open market, Indianapolis, Ind.; 25 cents per pound.

No. 36. Pure Extracted Honey, from F. S. Bull & Sons, Valparaiso, Ind.
No. 37. Pure Extracted Honey, from Dougherty & McKee, Indianapolis, Ind.
No. 38. Extracted Honey (dark); supposed to be from sunflowers.
No. 39. Sample, donated by C. F. Muth, Cincinnati, Ohio.
No. 40. Clover Honey, donated by C. F. Muth, Cincinnati, Ohio.
No. 41. White Sage Honey, J. E. Pleasants, Santa Ana, Los Angeles County, Cal.
No. 42. Sumac Honey, J. E. Pleasants, Santa Ana, Los Angeles County, Cal.
No. 43. Clover Honey, from near Cincinnati, C. F. Muth, Cincinnati, Ohio.

For convenience of study, I have arranged the analyses of the above samples in five groups:

In Table 1 are collected the analyses of those samples which were adulterated with starch sugar sirup.

In Table 2 are found those samples which apparently were adulterated with sucrose.

In Table No. 3 are grouped those samples to which it appears that invert sugar may have been added.

In Table No. 4 are found the analyses of those samples which appear to be genuine.

In Table No. 5 are collected the analyses of those specimens which were obtained from producers or dealers, and which I have every reason to believe to be genuine.

TABLE No. 1.—HONEYS ADULTERATED WITH STARCH SUGAR.

| No. of analysis. | Per cent of water. | Per cent of ash. | Per cent of albuminoids. | Per cent of reducing sugar. | Polarizations. | | | | Per cent of sucrose by polarization. | Per cent of reducing sugar after inversion. | Per cent of sucrose by reduction. | Per cent of total solids. | Per cent of solids not determined. | Per cent of reducing sugar before inversion to total solids. |
|---|---|---|---|---|---|---|---|---|---|---|---|---|---|---|
| | | | | | Direct. | Temperature °C. | Invert. | Temperature °C. | | | | | | |
| 1...... | 19.79 | 0.36 | .26 | 60.18 | 52.25 | 30.5 | ......... | ...... | 3.99 | 61.33 | 1.09 | 80.21 | 15.42 | 75.03 |
| 2...... | 16.93 | 0.21 | .07 | 57.40 | 74.50 | 21.5 | ......... | ...... | ...... | 59.85 | 2.33 | 83.07 | 25.39 | 69.09 |
| 3...... | ...... | ...... | ...... | 51.99 | 74.00 | 24.5 | 73.80 | 24.00 | ...... | ......... | ...... | ...... | ...... | ...... |
| 4...... | ...... | ...... | ...... | 60.91 | 9.50 | 25.0 | ......... | ...... | ...... | ......... | ...... | ...... | ...... | ...... |
| 5...... | 22.45 | 0.31 | .24 | 40.00 | 89.50 | 21.5 | 67.50 | 21.60 | 16.50 | 57.00 | 16.15 | 77.55 | 0.50 | 51.50 |
| 6...... | 15.41 | 1.27 | .35 | 57.60 | 24.65 | 23.0 | 16.90 | 22.60 | 5.84 | 64.35 | 6.43 | 84.59 | 19.53 | 68.09 |
| 7...... | 19.07 | 0.18 | .00 | 65.23 | 26.38 | 25.5 | 23.50 | 25.00 | 0.00 | 64.85 | 0.00 | 89.93 | 15.52 | 80.60 |
| Mean.. | 18.73 | 0.47 | .18 | 56.19 | ......... | ...... | ......... | ...... | 6.58 | 61.48 | 5.20 | 79.27 | 19.27 | 70.08 |

TABLE No. 2.—HONEYS APPARENTLY ADULTERATED WITH SUCROSE.

| | | | | | | | | | | | | | | |
|---|---|---|---|---|---|---|---|---|---|---|---|---|---|---|
| 8...... | 23.90 | .16 | .18 | 58.85 | 1.30 | 25.0 | —16.50 | 24.0 | 13.49 | 74.07 | 14.46 | 76.10 | 3.42 | 77.33 |
| 9...... | 16.09 | .12 | .18 | 69.64 | — 2.75 | 29.5 | —12.45 | 30.5 | 7.37 | 75.29 | 8.22 | 83.91 | 6.60 | 71.03 |
| 10...... | 15.01 | .01 | .24 | 69.75 | — 7.50 | 23.5 | —20.50 | 23.0 | •9.81 | 80.25 | 19.47 | 84.99 | 5.15 | 82.01 |
| 11...... | 22.45 | .31 | .24 | 40.00 | 89.50 | 21.5 | 67.50 | 21.6 | 16.50 | 57.00 | 16.15 | 77.55 | 20.50 | 51.58 |
| Mean.. | 19.46 | .16 | .21 | 58.81 | ......... | ...... | ......... | ...... | 11.79 | 71.65 | 14.58 | 80.64 | 8.92 | 70.49 |

**TABLE No. 3.—HONEYS APPARENTLY ADULTERATED WITH INVERTED SUCROSE.**

| No. of analysis. | Per cent of water. | Per cent of ash. | Per cent of albuminoids. | Per cent of reducing sugar. | Polarizations. | | | | Per cent of sucrose by polarization. | Per cent of reducing sugar after inversion. | Per cent of sucrose by reduction. | Per cent of total solids. | Per cent of solids not determined. | Per cent of reduction before inversion to total solids. |
|---|---|---|---|---|---|---|---|---|---|---|---|---|---|---|
| | | | | | Direct. | Temperature°C. | Invert. | Temperature°C. | | | | | | |
| 12 | 15.12 | .23 | .56 | 75.85 | −15.50 | 21.5 | −17.7 | 21.6 | 1.65 | 77.20 | 1.28 | 84.88 | 6.59 | 89.36 |
| 13 | 17.24 | .04 | .24 | 75.50 | −17.20 | 25.5 | −19.8 | 26.0 | 1.98 | 77.10 | 1.52 | 82.76 | 5.00 | 91.23 |
| 14 | 23.25 | .40 | .31 | 73.50 | −15.00 | 25.0 | −17.4 | 25.4 | 1.82 | 71.80 | 0.00 | 76.75 | 0.72 | 95.77 |
| 15 | 10.46 | .14 | .35 | 73.05 | −15.25 | 25.0 | −18.4 | 26.0 | 2.40 | 78.42 | 5.10 | 80.54 | 4.60 | 90.70 |
| 16 | 20.51 | .13 | .28 | 75.02 | −19.15 | 25.0 | −21.0 | 25.4 | 1.41 | 77.42 | 2.28 | 79.49 | 2.65 | 94.38 |
| 17 | 21.03 | .13 | .28 | 73.30 | −18.85 | 25.5 | −20.7 | 25.2 | 1.56 | 74.10 | 0.76 | 78.97 | 3.70 | 92.82 |
| 18 | 18.25 | .06 | .28 | 73.80 | −17.35 | 22.5 | −19.7 | 23.0 | 1.77 | 77.15 | 3.78 | 81.75 | 5.84 | 90.28 |
| 19 | 19.42 | .08 | .21 | 69.90 | −19.70 | 21.5 | −23.6 | 22.0 | 2.93 | 73.50 | 3.42 | 80.58 | 7.46 | 86.75 |
| 20 | 22.76 | .06 | .16 | 72.12 | −14.50 | 26.0 | −16.0 | 26.0 | 1.14 | 73.53 | 1.33 | 77.24 | 3.76 | 93.87 |
| 21 | 10.35 | .04 | .09 | 73.78 | −13.00 | 25.8 | −17.0 | 25.0 | 3.03 | 74.50 | 0.77 | 80.65 | 3.71 | 91.48 |
| 22 | 17.77 | .10 | .24 | 74.75 | −14.25 | 24.5 | −14.5 | 25.0 | 0.20 | 75.77 | 0.97 | 82.23 | 6.94 | 90.90 |
| 23 | 18.82 | .11 | .53 | 73.75 | −14.55 | 21.5 | −17.1 | 22.5 | 1.92 | 75.10 | 1.28 | 81.18 | 4.87 | 90.97 |
| 24 | 20.74 | .08 | .70 | 67.55 | −14.40 | 21.5 | −16.1 | 22.0 | 1.27 | 67.00 | 0.00 | 79.26 | 9.66 | 85.23 |
| 25 | 16.68 | .08 | .35 | 75.00 | −15.55 | 22.5 | −18.7 | 22.6 | 2.37 | 77.00 | 1.90 | 83.32 | 5.52 | 90.01 |
| 26 | 16.15 | .05 | .35 | 76.05 | −14.10 | 22.5 | −16.1 | 23.0 | 1.51 | 76.25 | 0.19 | 83.85 | 5.89 | 90.70 |
| 27 | 15.91 | .14 | .42 | 74.75 | −14.95 | 25.5 | −16.4 | 27.4 | 1.11 | 77.00 | 2.18 | 84.09 | 7.67 | 88.89 |
| 28 | 17.92 | .05 | .35 | 75.45 | −14.40 | 22.5 | −17.1 | 22.6 | 2.03 | 74.80 | 0.00 | 82.08 | 4.20 | 91.92 |
| Mean | 18.85 | .11 | .34 | 73.71 | −15.75 | ...... | −18.1 | ...... | 1.77 | 75.16 | 1.64 | 81.15 | 5.22 | 90.87 |

**TABLE No. 4.—HONEYS BOUGHT IN OPEN MARKET WHICH APPEAR TO BE GENUINE.**

| No. of analysis. | Per cent of water. | Per cent of ash. | Per cent of albuminoids. | Per cent of reducing sugar. | Direct. | Temperature°C. | Invert. | Temperature°C. | Per cent of sucrose by polarization. | Per cent of reducing sugar after inversion. | Per cent of sucrose by reduction. | Per cent of total solids. | Per cent of solids not determined. | Per cent of reduction before inversion to total solids. |
|---|---|---|---|---|---|---|---|---|---|---|---|---|---|---|
| 29 | 29.90 | .16 | .18 | 69.48 | − 2.50 | 25.0 | − 3.50 | 24.0 | 0.76 | 71.70 | 2.17 | 79.10 | 8.52 | 87.93 |
| 30 | 17.84 | .41 | .26 | 68.55 | − 1.95 | 25.0 | − 4.25 | 25.0 | 1.75 | 73.14 | 4.37 | 82.16 | 11.10 | 83.43 |
| 31 | 19.85 | .13 | .50 | 72.00 | −12.55 | 23.5 | −15.20 | 23.6 | 2.00 | 71.60 | 0.00 | 80.15 | 5.33 | 89.83 |
| 32 | 17.08 | .14 | .53 | 73.85 | −11.25 | 23.0 | −14.00 | 23.0 | 2.07 | 73.88 | 0.00 | 82.92 | 6.33 | 89.06 |
| 33 | 16.64 | .07 | .17 | 70.35 | − 0.40 | 21.5 | −18.50 | 22.0 | 6.84 | 75.75 | 5.13 | 83.36 | 5.93 | 84.39 |
| 34 | 17.79 | .22 | .39 | 68.80 | − 6.55 | 21.5 | −12.20 | 22.0 | 4.24 | 71.40 | 2.47 | 82.21 | 8.56 | 83.69 |
| 35 | 16.38 | .25 | .28 | 74.45 | − 8.05 | 23.5 | −10.10 | 23.0 | 1.55 | 75.70 | 1.19 | 83.62 | 7.09 | 80.03 |
| Mean | 18.00 | .20 | .34 | 71.09 | − 7.40 | ...... | −11.11 | ...... | 2.74 | 73.32 | 2.19 | 81.93 | 7.56 | 86.77 |

**TABLE No. 5.—HONEYS FURNISHED BY PRODUCERS AND DEALERS, APPARENTLY GENUINE.**

| No. of analysis. | Per cent of water. | Per cent of ash. | Per cent of albuminoids. | Per cent of reducing sugar. | Direct. | Temperature°C. | Invert. | Temperature°C. | Per cent of sucrose by polarization. | Per cent of reducing sugar after inversion. | Per cent of sucrose by reduction. | Per cent of total solids. | Per cent of solids not determined. | Per cent of reduction before inversion to total solids. |
|---|---|---|---|---|---|---|---|---|---|---|---|---|---|---|
| 36 | 14.97 | .14 | .24 | 74.70 | −11.55 | 22.5 | −14.1 | 23.0 | 1.92 | 76.60 | 1.81 | 85.03 | 8.03 | 87.85 |
| 37 | 21.75 | .03 | .21 | 68.75 | −12.15 | 22.5 | −13.7 | 23.0 | 1.17 | 71.00 | 1.16 | 78.25 | 7.00 | 88.83 |
| 38 | 18.75 | .27 | .39 | 69.65 | − 5.40 | 25.5 | − 8.0 | 25.6 | 1.98 | 73.25 | 3.42 | 81.25 | 8.96 | 85.72 |
| 39 | 21.32 | .77 | .59 | 66.10 | −10.50 | 25.5 | −12.0 | 27.0 | 1.15 | 69.05 | 2.70 | 78.66 | 10.07 | 84.01 |
| 40 | 18.35 | .08 | .31 | 72.50 | −11.88 | 25.5 | −13.8 | 25.2 | 1.62 | 74.35 | 1.78 | 81.65 | 7.14 | 88.79 |
| 41 | 14.62 | .05 | .21 | 71.25 | −11.50 | 25.5 | −20.5 | 26.5 | 6.88 | 75.35 | 3.90 | 85.38 | 6.96 | 83.42 |
| 42 | 14.32 | .06 | .24 | 71.10 | −12.10 | 25.5 | −20.0 | 26.5 | 6.04 | 73.85 | 2.61 | 85.67 | 8.23 | 82.95 |
| 43 | 19.60 | .07 | .31 | 73.50 | −12.85 | 25.0 | −15.7 | 25.4 | 2.17 | 74.55 | 1.02 | 80.40 | 4.35 | 91.40 |
| Mean | 17.96 | .18 | .31 | 71.07 | −10.09 | ...... | −14.7 | ...... | 2.87 | 73.50 | 2.30 | 82.04 | 7.66 | 86.64 |

*Remarks on tables.*—The temperature at which the direct polarization is taken is given, so that if any great difference in the two temperatures should occur it can be at once noted. Since the temperature has a marked influence on the levorotatory power of invert sugar, it should always be taken into account in expressing the data of the work. In order to secure results which are strictly comparable, some definite degree of temperature should be chosen, at which all the polarizations should be made, or to which they should be reduced. I am now having an instrument constructed which will enable me to make all such polarizations at any selected temperature.

The percentage of reducing sugar is calculated for dextrose, and the numbers, therefore, must be taken with this understanding. In the last column of each table are found the percentages of such sugars in terms of total solids. This gave a much better idea of their relative amount than if they were expressed in percentages of the weight of the substances examined.

In the polarizations the numbers given are divisions of the cane-sugar scale of a larger Laurent shadow polariscope in which 16.2 grams of pure sugar in a volume of 100 cc. will produce a right-handed rotation of 100. The sucrose was calculated from the two polariscopic readings (before and after inversion) by the usual formula.

Table No. 1. In all these samples as indicated by the analysis, starch sirup (glucose) was largely used as an adulterant. In sample No. 5, very little real honey could have been present, the sample was composed almost exclusively of starch sirup and of sucrose, which has been added to give it sweetness. In the other cases the sucrose which was found by analysis was probably originally present in the honey part of the mixture, since, had it been added as an adulterant, more of it would have been found. The characteristics of each sample, as well as of all of them collectively, can be seen by studying the table.

Table No. 2. The mean percentage of sucrose present in these samples as determined by double polarizations is 11.79, and by reduction 14.58. With the exception of No. 11, to which sucrose was undoubtedly added, I can not think that any sucrose was added by producer or dealer, on account of the small percentage of it found. In such cases it is proper to suppose that the bees had access to flowers whose nectar was rich in sucrose, or that they had been fed a solution of that substance. The use of solutions of sucrose as bee food is not unusual.

Table No. 3. These 16 samples I have grouped together on account of their great levorotatory power. For the first polarization this amounts to 16.75 divisions, and for the inverted liquids to 18.10. It is possible that this great deviation to the left may have been due to the entire absence of dextrine or sucrose in the honeys, or that it might have been produced by the bee food being rich in sucrose, which suffered a nearly complete inversion in the body of the insect.

It would be quite improper to definitely assert that invert sugar sirup had been added as an intended adulterant. I think it quite possible that bees having access to sucrose food might at one time produce a honey like that in Table No. 2, and at another like that in Table No. 3.

Table No. 4. These honeys all appear to be genuine although it is hard to draw the line between such samples as Nos. 31 and 32 and those found in Table No. 3. The mean reading to the left is 7.40 divisions before inversion and 11.11 afterwards. The mean of undetermined solids is 7.56, and the percentage of reducing sugar before inversion to total solids, 86.77. The means of sucrose as determined by both methods are low and fairly agree, although, as in the other table, they differ widely in single instances.

Table No. 5. These honeys, obtained directly or indirectly from well known apiarists, I have every reason to believe to be pure. If they contain any adulteration it has been added by artificial feeding and not intentionally. It will be observed that these honeys are strongly levorotatory, and indeed so much so, that some of them might have appeared in Table No. 3.

18808—No. 13——12

It will be instructive to compare the numbers in the above tables with those obtained by other analysts. Koenig* gives the following means of 17 analyses:

|                      | Per cent. |
|----------------------|-----------|
| Water                | 19.61     |
| Albuminoids          | 1.20      |
| Grape sugar          | 70.96     |
| Sucrose              | 2.76      |
| Pollen               | 0.17      |
| Ash                  | 0.19      |
| Phosphoric acid      | 0.03      |

O. Hehner † gives the following numbers as the mean of 25 samples:

|                 | Per cent. |
|-----------------|-----------|
| Glucose         | 67.2      |
| Water           | 19.2      |
| Not determined  | 13.5      |

According to Hehner the fluidity of the honey does not depend on the amount of water it contains. In 10 cases the quantity of glucose after inversion was less than before, in one instance 5.23 per cent less. The rotating power was generally zero, a condition which I have never found in American honeys, genuine or artificial. These conclusions are so at variance with ordinary experience as to indicate that the samples analyzed were anomalous, or the methods employed unreliable.

Sieben ‡ gives the mean composition of 60 samples of honey as follows:

|            | Per cent. |
|------------|-----------|
| Dextrose   | 34.71     |
| Levulose   | 39.24     |
| Sucrose    | 1.80      |
| Water      | 19.98     |
| Non-sugars | 5.02      |

The solids not determined, as will be seen by the analyses presented in this paper, are of considerable importance. In adulterations with the starch sugar sirup these undetermined solids consist chiefly of maltose and dextrine. In many other cases dextrine, as will be shown further on, is doubtless present.

Genuine honey has also a slightly acid reaction. This acidity is due either to certain organic acids derived from the plants or, more probably, to an acid furnished by the bee itself. The kind and quantity of acids in honey have not been accurately studied. I have found the total acidity measured as formic acid to be about 0.02 per cent. That the acid furnished by the bee is formic there is little doubt. Will § states that he has found the active principle of the poison of all hymenoptera to be formic acid. Carlet, || in a communication to the French Academy, shows that the poison of all the hymenoptera has an acid reaction, but that it contains also an active alkaline substance. The activity of the poison is conditioned on the presence of both the acid and alkali. The acid is always in large excess and each substance is furnished by a special gland. The inversion of the cane sugar in the organism of the bee may be due to the presence of these acids. On the other hand it is plain that certain species of pine and some other plants furnish formic acid, and therefore the detection of this acid in honey is not positive evidence that it is derived from the bee. In a recent article ¶ the author claims that the formic acid which honey contains tends to preserve it from fermentation. Honey sirup from which the greater

---

* Nahrungsmittel, p. 161.
† Analyst, Vol. 9, pp. 64 et seq.
‡ Zeitsch. d. Ver. f. d. Rübenzucker Industrie, Vol. 34, pp. 837 et seq.
§ Schleiden and Forops Not., September, 1848, p. 17.
|| Comptes Rendus, June 23, 1884, p. 1550.
¶ Deutsch Americanische Apotheker Zeit. 5, 21, p. 664.

part of the formic acid has been washed out or expelled by heat does not keep as well as the normal product. The latest researches show that this acid is deposited by the bees themselves by means of their stings. From time to time the bees apply to the walls of the cells of the comb the tiny drops of poison (formic acid), that gather on the ends of their stings. Sooner or later this remarkable antiseptic is incorporated with the honey. The preservative power of this acid is said to be greater even than that of phenol.[*]

A careful study of the results of these analyses shows the chief adulterants of honey are the following:

### 1. Commercial Glucose.

This substance, an account of its honey-like appearance and low price, has been one of the most common substitutes for honey. Mixed with enough of the genuine article to give it a flavor, it is sold extensively as pure extracted honey. A very frequent method of adulteration is to take a few ounces of genuine comb honey, place in a can holding one or two pounds, and then filling up with glucose. The real honey will gradually diffuse throughout the whole mass, giving the required flavor.

This, the most frequent sophistication of honey, is also the most readily detected. The high dextro rotatory power of commercial glucose renders its detection by optical methods extremely easy. Containing as it does a considerable percentage of dextrine and maltose, its percentage of reducing sugar is consequently small. In 10 samples purchased at random in the eastern markets three were adulterated in this way. In 11 samples purchased in the western market only 1 was glucose. This percentage, however, does not represent the actual extent of the adulteration. In making these purchases I endeavored to get a sample of each kind of honey on sale. It will be found that the strained honeys of commerce are quite generally adulterated with glucose.

*Detection of adulteration with glucose.*—I have never yet found a genuine honey which is not levorotatory. Nevertheless, the turning of the polarized plane to the right is not conclusive evidence of the presence of glucose, unless the amount of deflection is more than 100° of the cane sugar scale, when the amount of the substance taken for examination is the same in weight as that required by pure sucrose to read 100 divisions.

After treatment with 0.1 volume of hydrochloric acid and heating to 70° the solution is cooled and repolarized. If now it still reads to the right the presence of starch sugar sirup is established. In such cases, after inversion the free acid is neutralized and the reducing sugar determined by an alkaline copper solution. The percentage of this sugar will fall much below 70 unless a large part of the adulteration has been due to cane sugar.

### 2. Cane Sugar (Sucrose).

A thick sirup made of cane sugar is also used to adulterate honey. There is only one reason why it is not more extensively employed, viz, its tendency to crystallize. On this account it can only be used in small quantities. There would be no difficulty in detecting added cane sugar in honey were it not for the fact that we can not definitely say how much of this substance is present in the genuine article. In the analyses given by Sieben[†] the mean of sucrose in the 60 samples was 1.08 per cent; in one case, however, it amounted to 8 per cent. In the analyses given in this paper the mean percentage of sucrose in 8 samples of genuine honey was 2.87, and in 7 samples which appear to be genuine, 2.74; and in the samples contained in table No. 3, 16 in number, which may be genuine, 1.77 per cent. Judging from these analyses, I would say that it is a rare thing to find a genuine honey which contains more than 4

---

[*] Comptes rendus, Vol. LXI, p. 1179.
[†] Op. cit.

per cent sucrose. In the 2 samples of California honey, Nos. 41 and 42, the percentage of sucrose is very high. Doubtless the kind of flower and climate have much to do with this and it would not be strange if California honey, produced in the unique conditions of climate and flora which there obtain, should develop some constant difference from honeys produced in other parts of the world.

*Detection of cane sugar in honey.*—The presence of cane sugar in honey is easily detected by the process of double polarization. Illustration: Sample No. 14, weight of sample taken, 16.2 grams in 100 cc, length of observation tube; 400 mm; reading of scale, —15; divide this number by two gives —7.5 divisions, correct reading for a 200 mm tube. After inversion the reading in a 220 mm tube was —20.5 divisions, temperature, 23°; difference of the two readings 13 divided by 144 —11.5, equals 9.18 per cent; equals sucrose present.

The method of double reduction of Fehling's solution, once before and once after inversion of the cane sugar, can also be employed. The optical method is quicker and, when properly conducted, more reliable than the method by reduction. If the rotatory power of the sample is quite small, two or three times the normal quantity may be taken and the polarization conducted in a 400 or 500 mm tube.

### 3. Inverted Cane Sugar.

As an adulterant of honey the inverted cane sugar is much superior to the sucrose itself. It does not crystallize, and when properly made is palatable and wholesome. Sucrose is usually inverted by heating with an acid, and for commercial purposes sulphuric acid is the one generally employed. The difficulty of removing all traces of this acid renders the detection of inverted sugar somewhat easy by the presence of the traces of the sulphuric acid which still remains in the solution. It is now said, however, that inverted sugar is made in large quantities by treatment with brewer's yeast and without the use of acids of any kind. When added to honey in large quantities it can be detected by its great levorotatory power, which, however, decreases rapidly as the temperature rises. At 23° a pure invert sugar solution would mark —32.5 divisions. In the present state of our knowledge it would be difficult to detect the addition of a small quantity of invert sugar to honey. From the above studies it appears that pure honey is essentially composed of invert sugar, together with a certain portion of sugars optically inactive (anoptose), water, a small quantity of albuminous matter, ash, and solids not sugar, *i. e.*, those which, while resembling sugar in chemical composition, are yet not detected in the ordinary process of analysis.

In addition to the above it appears from the results of a large amount of work done at my suggestion by Mr. G. L. Spencer, that pure honey contains a varying amount of dextrin, which in some cases amounts to as much as 4 per cent.[*]

This investigation is still in progress, and therefore its result can not yet be announced. The presence of. dextrin in honey doubtless accounts for the phenomenon that in some samples of pure honey the levorotatory power is very small, or, according to some authors, entirely disappears, which would not be the case except for the presence of some highly dextrorotatory substance.

AGRICULTURAL DEPARTMENT, WASHINGTON, D. C.

---

[*] Since this investigation was undertaken Amthor (Report. anal. Chem., 1885, p. 163) had shown that honey gathered from pine forests contains dextrin, often in such quantities as to become dextrorotatory. Klinger claims that this phenomenon is not exclusively confined to honey of coniferous origin. According to our observations, even left-handed honey may contain marked quantities of dextrin. If this be so it can hardly be true, as W. Lenz (Chem. Zeit., 8, 613) affirms that after fermentation honey yields no optically active substance.

## NOTES RELATING TO RIGHT-HANDED ROTATION OF HONEYS.

### POLARIZATION OF HONEYS.[*]

The author separates natural honeys into two classes, flower and fir honeys. The former appear white to brown, contain no dextrin and are levorotatory. Fir honeys are all brown, smell of pine, contain dextrin, and turn the ray to the right. For adulteration of honey, starch sirup in generally used. A 10 per cent solution of this, in a 200 mm tube, gives a reading of 100 on a Soleil-Duboscq instrument. Solutions of pure honey mixed with starch sirup gave:

| Flower honey. | Starch sirup. | Rotation. | | Fir honey. | Starch sirup. | Rotation. |
|---|---|---|---|---|---|---|
| | | *Pr. ct.* | | | | *Pr. ct.* | |
| 100 | ........ | — 3 to — 10 | | 100 | ........ | 22 |
| 90 | 10 | 20 to 28 | | 90 | 10 | 62 |
| 80 | 20 | 50 to 65 | | 80 | 20 | 89 |
| 70 | 30 | 80 to 99 | | 70 | 30 | 119 |
| 60 | 40 | 117 to 133 | | 60 | 40 | 149 |
| 50 | 50 | 154 to 160 | | 50 | 50 | 170 |
| 40 | 60 | 194 to 200 | | 40 | 60 | 205 |

Traces of chlorine and sulphuric acid are no indication of adulteration.

### DEXTROROTARY HONEYS.[†]

A sample of honey described by the author, and which he regards as indubitably pure, showed a specific rotation to the right of 3.74° for sodium light. Its composition was: water, 22.61 per cent; ash, 0.09 ; levulose and dextrose, 64.33 ; and sucrose, 12.59. It was clear, transparent, almost colorless, very sweet, and only slightly aromatic. It showed no tendency to grain. Another sample showed a right rotation of 1.66. It consisted of 21.09 per cent water; 0.09, ash; levulose and dextrose, 69.41, and 8.41 sucrose. The author believes the abnormal rotation to be due to sucrose.

### RIGHT ROTARY HONEY.[‡]

Honey gathered by bees in the habit of resorting to sugar refineries is very clear and thin but almost without aroma. Four samples analyzed contained, respectively, 4.88, 16.38, and 9.93 per cent sucrose.

*Notes relating to the analyses of honey.*

### A NEW METHOD OF TESTING HONEY.[§]

About five years ago every expert would condemn any sample of honey as adulterated which turned the ray of polarized light to the right instead of the left, but at about that time Dr. Haenle succeeded in finding some natural (wild) honey which polarized to the right. This was subsequently ascertained to be due to the fact that it had been collected from coniferous products. The author has now ascertained that if the honey be dialyzed before polarization the result is a sure indication of its char-

---

[*] O. Haenle, abs. Chem. Centralblatt, 1888, 443.

[†] R. Bensemann, Zeit. f angew. Chem., 1888, 4, 117; abs. Chem. Centralblatt, 1888, 19, 479.

[‡] Von Lippman, Zeit. f. angew. Chem., 1888, No. 22 ; abs. Analyst, 1889, 14, 20.

[§] Dr. Oscar Haenle, Amer. Drug. and Pharm. Zeit.; Analyst, April, 1891, 79,

acter. A number of experiments are adduced to prove this position. A sample of pure Alsatian flower honey was dissolved in twice its weight of water. The solution polarized — 2ð. It was then subjected to dialysis for sixteen hours, after which the residue in the dialyzer was optically inactive (— 0). Thirty grams of a pure honey were dissolved in 150 grams of water, the solution decolorized and then dialyzed. After eighteen hours the residue was inactive. Fifty grams of a similar honey were dissolved in 250 grams of water. After sixteen hours' dialysis the residue was optically inactive. On further evaporating this residue and again dialyzing its inactivity remained unaltered. A 10 per cent solution of glucose sirup, which polarized 100, was decolorized and dialyzed. After sixteen hours it still polarized 5. The residue was then concentrated, and in proportion as this progressed so rose the angle of polarization. Forty grams of a pure honey, polarizing in a 1 in 2 solution, — 35, were mixed with 10 grams of glucose sirup. A 10 per cent solution of this mixture was subjected to dialysis, and the residue was found to remain dextrogyrate at 4. Thirty grams of a pure honey were mixed with 20 grams of glucose sirup dissolved in 250 parts of water and the solution decolorized by charcoal. It polarized + 65. After twenty-four hours' dialysis the residue retained a permanent polarization of 14 +. After concentrating this residue to half its weight its polarizing angle had increased to 60. Fifty grams of a glucose honey were dissolved in 250 grams of water. The solution polarized + 95. It was then dialyzed and the liquid on the dialyzer examined at intervals of two hours.

It polarized after—

| | | | |
|---|---|---|---|
| 2 hours | 45 | 9 hours | 12 |
| 4 hours | 33 | 10 hours | 11 |
| 6 hours | 18 | 11 hours | 10 |
| 8 hours | 15 | 12 hours | 10 |

Further dialysis did not change the angle (10).

General conclusion : Any honey which, after having been dialyzed, does not polarize to the right, is free from glucose. Any honey retaining a dextrogyration after this treatment is adulterated with glucose.

### EXAMINATION OF HONEY.*

Dr. Mansfeld made the statement that the greater part of commercial honey was adulterated, and that there was no short yet reliable method known for the examination of honey. The methods of Haenle and Dieterich can not be recommended. The best results are given by inversion and by fermentation with compressed yeast. Not beer or wine yeast. The optical examination is very reliable.

### CRYSTALLOIDS AND COLLOIDS OF HONEY.†

For diffusion of honey, a parchment paper tube of 25 mm diameter is used. This is filled with a solution of honey in three times its weight of water and hung in U form in a beaker of water. In Dieterich's experiments diffusion was carried on for seventy-two hours, at an average temperature of 17°. At the expiration of this time the surrounding water became colored a pale yellow, and on evaporation gave a sirup amounting to 50 per cent of the honey employed. This sirup could not be brought to crystallize, despite repeated solutions in alcohol. Flavor and odor were extraordinarily good; better, indeed, than those of any other honey Dieterich had ever handled. The fluid remaining in the tube contained slimy flocks, although the original honey solution had been filtered. After evaporation the residue possessed no odor of honey whatever. The taste was feebly sweet.

---

*Versammlung Nahrungsmittel Chemiker u. Mikroskopiker, Vienna, Oct. 13, 1891.
†E. Dieterich, Chem. Centralblatt, 1877, 318.

## ACTION OF PHENOLS ON HONEYS. *

If honey is covered with aqueous solution of phloroglucin and a large quantity of strong hydrochloric acid, a weak reddish coloration forms after some time, which on standing longer becomes more pronounced. Using resorcin in the same way a beautiful light-red color is formed. The other phenols act only after heating. A solution of aniline sulphate in water produces a yellow color in a honey solution after some time. These reactions the author regards as due to the presence in the honey of compounds of the aromatic series, such as appear in wood.

## NOTES RELATING TO THE FERMENTATION OF HONEY.†

According to R. Kayser ‡ the residue after the fermentation of honey is not usually optically active, and when heated with HCl only exceptionally gives any reducing sugar. The first two methods, therefore, proposed by Sieben § for investigating honey Kayser altered as follows: Twenty-five grams of honey are mixed with 12 grams starch-free yeast and enough water to make up to about 200 cc and the whole allowed to stand forty-eight hours. Alumina hydrate is next added, and the whole made up to 250 cc; 200 cc of clear filtrate are evaporated to 50 cc and polarized. A dextro-rotation of more than 1° (Wild) shows the presence of starch sugar. Twenty-five cc of the solution used for the polarization are then to be mixed with 25 cc water and 5 cc concentrated HCl, and the mixture heated in a boiling-water bath for an hour; neutralized, made up to 100 cc, and reducing sugar estimated in 25 cc by Allihn's method. The sugar content multiplied by 40 gives the sugar resulting from the fermentation residue of 100 grams of honey. If this is over 1 per cent it indicates adulteration with glucose.

E. Dieterich ‖ recommends the determination of the acidity of honey as affording valuable characteristics. Dissolve 10 grams of honey in 90 cc water, add 3 drops phenolphtalein solution and titrate with $\frac{n}{10}$ KHO.. Six samples of honey gave readings between 3.5 and 6.5 cc alkali (=19.6 to 36.4 mg KHO) for the acid of 10 grams honey. Hebner.(Analyst, 10, 217) recommends the estimation of $P_2O_5$ in honey ash. He found in five natural honeys per cents ranging between 0.013 and 0.035 per cent, $P_2O_5$. Reaction of ash strongly alkaline. Artificial honey made from glucose (made with mineral acids) gave a neutral ash containing $P_2O_5$, equivalent to 0.085 to 0.0108 per cent of the honey. Artificial honey made from cane sugar gave a slightly alkaline ash containing no trace of $P_2O_5$ even when 50 grams of sample were burnt.

## ALCOHOLIC FERMENTATION OF HONEY.¶

Honey, even under favorable conditions, undergoes the alcoholic fermentation with difficulty, the cause of which is probably due to its lack of sufficient quantity of ash ingredient and nitrogen. The author has experimented with additions of various nutrient substances and has finally adopted a mixture consisting of:

|  | Parts. |
|---|---|
| Diammonium phosphate | 100 |
| Neutral ammonium tartrate | 350 |
| Cream of tartar | 600 |
| Magnesia | 20 |
| Gypsum | 50 |
| Common salt | 3 |
| Sulphur | 1 |
| Tartaric acid | 250 |

---

* A. Ihle. Chem. Zeit. 14, 3.; abs. Chem. Centralblatt, 1890, 1, 390.

† Fres. Zeit. f. a. Chem., 1888, 231.

‡ Ber. über die Vte. Versamm. von bayr. Vertr. d. angew. Chemie,Berlin, 1886, 91.

§ Fres. Zeit. f. a. Chem., 24, 137.

‖ Geschäftsber. d. Papier und Chem. Fabrik in Helfenberg bei Dresden, 1885-'86; also, Helfenberger Annalen, 1886-'87.

¶ G. Gastine, Comptes rend., 109, 479.

Adding 5 to 7 grams of this substance to a liter of a 25 to 30 per cent solution of honey, together with some wine yeast, a practically complete fermentation can be obtained. A solution containing 230 grams of honey to the liter, fermented almost completely in 12 days, as completely at any rate as wine must.

### FERMENTATION.*

The author brings out the following points: (1) For the fermentation of honey, the addition of nutrient salts, which Gastine prescribes, is not necessary. Any noteworthy further fermentation of dextrin by injudicious selection of yeast is not possible. (2) For the fermentation test, it is not a matter of indifference which yeast is used. Wine yeast acts least upon the dextrin of honey. Beer yeast has more action, but not enough to produce complete fermentation. Using pressed yeast and working at proper temperatures, complete fermentation is usually obtained, so that the author suggests that it is desirable always to use pressed yeast in honey tests in order that comparative results may be obtained. At present great care is necessary in judging or condemning honey on analytical data. Hilger confirmed the ltatements in the paper of Raumer and expressed the hope that a yeast would be prepared possessing the qualities necessary in honey investigations. Will recalled the fact that Hansen, of Copenhagen, had investigated the action of different yeasts on the various sugars and dextrins, and proposed that, as far as possible, pure cultures only be used, inasmuch as the determination of the fermentative power of the yeast to be used is not sufficient.

### NOTES RELATING TO THE ADULTERATION OF HONEY WITH GLUCOSE OR STARCH SIRUP AND METHODS OF DETECTION. †

With regard to the adulteration of honey with starch sirup, v. Planta proposes to estimate the amount of grape sugar before and after inversion with a 2 per cent solution of sulphuric acid. Pure honey yields about 8 per cent of grape sugar while, that sophisticated with starch sirup shows an increase of as much as 45 per cent ; moreover, pure honey contains 63 to 71 per cent of reducing sugar already formed ; artificial honey only 29 to 37 per cent.

### DETECTION OF GLUCOSE IN HONEY.‡

A cheap and easy way to test for the presence of glucose in honey is to put some of it into a cup of tea made strong. If it is heavily adulterated with the compounds found in glucose, it will turn black, almost like ink. Another test is to pour alcohol and this poisonous compound together. Pure honey and alcohol will unite, but pure honey and this compound will separate like honey and water.

(NOTE.—The accuracy of the above test is not very apparent. If the glucose contained traces of iron the tannin of the tea would form a dark compound therewith. Alcohol in a solution of the mixture would precipitate dextrin.—II. W. W.)

### DETECTION OF CANE AND STARCH SUGAR IN HONEY. §

To detect starch sugar the author uses a 10 per cent solution of mercurous nitrate and pure commercial absolute alcohol as reagents. The mercurous nitrate solution is made from 1 g of the crystallized salt, and 9 cc of water. Two or three drops nitric acid are added. After standing several hours the clear liquid is poured off and is

---

* E. v. Raumer, Vers. d. bayer. Ver. d. angew, Chemic. 9; Pharm. Centralhalle, 31, 322 ; abs. Chem. Centralblatt, 1890, 2, 126.

† V. Planta. Dingl. polyt. Jonr, 238, 356; abs. Jour Chem. Soc., 1881, 40, 316.

‡ Rev. J. G. Teeter, Amer. Bee Journal, Aug. 26, 1885; ibid., Oct. 27, 1886.

§ II. Hager, Pharm. Centralhalle, 26, 327 ; Chem. Centralblatt, 1885, 764.·

ready for use. Before trial part of starch sugar should be dissolved in four parts of cold water, and starch sirup and honey in three. Place in a test tube 1 cm wide 4 cc. of the filtered solution and add 6 drops of the mercurous nitrate solution. Shake, and add 4 cc of the alcohol. Cork the tube and set aside. Honey solution gives a translucent, somewhat milky, solution, which remains in this condition for two days. The second day an extremely slight deposit may form. Starch sirup treated in the same way gives a cloudy solution, only slightly translucent. After the lapse of six to twelve hours a white, or whitish precipitate of from 3 cm. to 6 cm. in height forms. The supernatant fluid is usually clear. If a honey contain starch sugar the reaction can take place in two different ways, according to the content. With a large admixture (30 to 40 per cent) the precipitate forms within five to eight hours, and the supernatant liquid begins to clear. With a smaller amount the precipitate frequently refuses to form, but in the course of time it becomes opaque, being no longer translucent after twelve hours. Pure honey remains translucent for at least two days.

Another and easier test is that with absolute alcohol. Place in a test tube 1 cm. in diameter 1 or 2 cc. of a filtered 25 per cent solution of the honey, and allow half a cubic centimeter of alcohol to flow down the walls of the tube so as to form a clear overlying layer. The alcohol then remains clear and the line of contact shows a hardly noticeable opalescence, which soon disappears. When starch sugar is present the dividing line assumes a milky look, which lasts many hours. If only small amounts of the adulterant are present the turbidity is bluish white and shimmers.

To test for cane sugar place 1.5 or 2 cc of pure concentrated sulphuric acid in a test tube of 1 cm diameter, and add half a cubic centimeter of 25 per cent solution of honey in such a manner to make it form a layer above the acid. Allow to stand for an hour. Pure honey does not give a colored line of contact at first, and even after the lapse of an hour the color is yellow or clear brown. In the presence of cane sugar the line is successively brownish, brown, and, after half an hour, a nearly black layer is formed. Starch sirup behaves to this test like honey. After standing one to one and a half hours the pure honey may show a dark zone, but a gentle agitation which does not disturb the acid is sufficient to diffuse the coloring matter through the honey, which then appears brown yellow and transparent. With a honey containing cane sugar and similarly treated the supernatant liquid appears black, brown, and nontransparent. Blank experiments with known mixtures should be tried.

Another test is the microscopical. Take up half a drop of the honey with point of a needle, place it in a drop of glycerin on an object glass, and observe with a power of 100 to 200 diameters. The field of vision should include from 5 to 10 pollen grains.

DETECTION OF ARTIFICIAL HONEY.*

Dr. A von Planta originated a method depending upon the addition of alcohol to a solution of the honey to be tested. Under these circumstances an artificial honey gives a more or less deep cloudiness—provided the adulteration has been made with commercial starch sugar, which almost always contains more or less dextrin. Genuine honeys also occasionally give this reaction. A better method is that depending upon the use of tincture of iodine, which gives a deep brown red coloration with dextrin. Dissolve 10 grams of the honey in 50 cc. of distilled water, filter and add to half a test tube full 10 or 12 drops of a 2 per cent solution of iodine. Glucose honey gives a brownish red, but pure honey is colored only the wine yellow of the K I solution.

* G. Ambuhl, Schw. Wochensch. f. Pharm., 47-85, thence in Bienen Zeitung; Chem. Zeit., 1886, 70.

# BEESWAX AND ARTIFICIAL COMB AND COMB FOUNDATIONS.

## EXAMINATIONS OF PURE BEESWAX AND COMB FOUNDATIONS.

The samples of pure beeswax were made from the honeys accompanied with affidavits of their purity. They were analyzed as a check to test the purity of the wax in the comb foundations, the analyses of which occur in the next table.

The acid number as obtained by us with pure wax is slightly lower than that obtained by European analysts. The cause of this is not apparent. The analyses were conducted with the greatest care, and every precaution to prevent the admixture of any foreign substance was observed.

The samples of comb foundation labeled "Canadian" were obtained by request from Dr. Frank T. Shutt, chemist to the Central Experimental Farm of Ottawa.

The further description of the samples will be seen from my letter to Mr. Shutt and his answer.

As will be seen from the analytical data in the table, the three samples obtained from Mr. Shutt were heavily adulterated. On the other hand, all the comb foundations bought from dealers in the United States, as will be seen from the table following, appear to be pure beeswax.

U. S. DEPARTMENT OF AGRICULTURE,<br>
DIVISION OF CHEMISTRY,<br>
*Washington, D. C., July 28, 1891.*

DEAR PROF. SHUTT: I have received, with much interest, your report in the appendix to the report of the Minister of Agriculture, which you recently had the kindness to send me.

I am particularly interested in what you say in regard to the adulteration of comb foundation, and write to ask if you have any samples of this adulterated foundation left. If you have, will you kindly send to me a sufficient quantity of each of the adulterated samples to include in the analyses we are now making of comb foundations from different sources? We have purchased comb foundation from all the dealers to whom we can gain access, and have found no adulteration. I should be glad if we could include in our analyses a few adulterated samples, inasmuch as we are making a very thorough chemical examination of the waxes contained in comb foundations. I refer to your report on pages 150 and 151 of the publication mentioned above.

Hoping to receive in the future the publications which you issue on subjects connected with agriculture, I am,

Respectfully,

H. W. WILEY,<br>
*Chemist.*

Prof. FRANK T. SHUTT,<br>
   *Chemist, Experimental Farm, Ottawa, Canada.*

DOMINION OF CANADA, DEPARTMENT OF AGRICULTURE,
* CENTRAL EXPERIMENTAL FARM,
*Ottawa, July* 31, 1891.

DEAR DR. WILEY: In response to your request in favor of 18th instant I have very much pleasure in sending you by this mail three samples of adulterated foundation comb, which I trust will reach you safely. I trust that the quantity of each will be sufficient for your purposes. I would have sent more if I had had it. I think, however, there will be enough to take sp. gr. other extract after treatment with $H_2SO_4$ and fatty acids by saponification.

R. E. Smith, who sold the adulterated comb, claims to have purchased his stock in the United States.

Yours, faithfully,

FRANK T. SHUTT,
*Chemist, Dominion Experimental Farm.*

*Pure wax and comb foundations.*

| No. | Where bought. | Description. | Price per pound. |
|---|---|---|---|
| 8493 | Falconer Manufacturing Company, James- town, N. Y., per Gilman. | Light colored................................ | $1.05 |
| 8493 | .....do ................................. | Dark ..................................... | 1.05 |
| 8494 | J. Wallenstein, Kaukauna, Wis ........... | Surplus foundation made from light wax | .90 |
| 8495 | ......do ................................ | Surplus foundation made from dark wax. | .90 |
| 8496 | ......do ................................ | Runs 8 square feet per pound............ | .90 |
| 8497 | ......do ................................ | Runs 7 square feet per pound............ | .90 |
| 8498 | ......do ................................ | Runs 6 square feet per pound............ | .90 |
| 8499 | ......do ................................ | Runs 5 square feet per pound............ | .90 |
| 8500 | Wilbor G. Fish, Ithaca, N. Y.............. | Light colored wax, in half sheets....... | 1.50 |
| 8501 | ......do ................................ | Darker colored wax, in whole sheets.... | 1.50 |
| 8502 | E. Kretchmar, Red Oak, Iowa............. | Thin brood............................... | 1.08 |
| 8503 | ......do ................................ | Medium brood ........................... | 1.08 |
| 8504 | ......do ................................ | Thin surplus............................. | 1.08 |
| 8505 | ......do ................................ | Extra thin .............................. | 1.08 |
| 8506 | F. C. Erkel, Le Sueur, Minn ............... | Light colored, half sheets .............. | ........ |
| 8507 | ......do ................................ | Darker colored, whole sheets........... | ........ |
| 8508A | Chas. Dadant & Son, Hamilton, Ill ........ | ...................................... | ........ |
| 8508B | ......do ................................ | ...................................... | ........ |
| 8508C | ......do ................................ | ...................................... | ........ |
| 8508D | ......do ................................ | ...................................... | ........ |
| 8509A | J. Van Deusen & Sons, Spring Brook, N. Y. | ...................................... | ........ |
| 8509B | ......do ................................ | ...................................... | ........ |
| 8509C | ......do ................................ | ...................................... | ........ |

JAPAN WAXES.

| | | | |
|---|---|---|---|
| 8543 | Elmer & Amend, New York............... | Commercial Japan wax ................. | ........ |
| 8550 | McKesson & Robbins, New York ........ | .................................... | ........ |
| 8557 | W. H. Schieffelin & Co., New York....... | .................................... | ........ |
| 8603 | W. H. Bowdlear & Co., Boston, Mass.... | .................................... | ........ |

## CARNAUBA WAXES.

| No. | Where bought. | Description. | Price per pound. |
|---|---|---|---|
| 8540 | Elmer & Amend, New York............. | .................................................. | ........ |
| 8552 | McKesson & Robbins, New York ........ | .................................................. | ....... |
| 8554 | W. H. Schieffelln & Co., New York....... | .................................................. | ........ |
| 8609 | W. H. Bowdlean & Co., Boston, Mass .... | .................................................. | ........ |

## CERESINS.

| 8544 | Elmer & Amend, New York............. | Strong odor of petrolem ................ | ........ |
|---|---|---|---|
| 8551 | McKesson & Robbins, New York ........ | .................................................. | ........ |
| 8556 | W. H. Schieffelln & Co., New York....... | .................................................. | ........ |
| 8610 | W. H. Bowdlean & Co., Boston, Mass ... | Yellow-orange ceresin ................ | ........ |

## OZOKERITE.

| 8545 | Elmer & Amend, New York ........... | .................................................. | ....... |
|---|---|---|---|
| 8607 | W. H. Bowdlean & Co., Boston, Mass..... | .................................................. | ........ |

## PARAFFIN.

| 8541 | Elmer & Amend, New York............. | Commercial paraffin ...................... | ........ |
|---|---|---|---|
| 8547 | McKesson & Robbins, New York......... | .......do ..................................... | ........ |
| 8553 | W. H. Schieffelln & Co., New York....... | .......do ..................................... | ........ |

## AFFIDAVIT WAXES.

| 9009 | Honey bought from K. M. Thompson, Gaithersburg, Md. | .................................................. | ........ |
|---|---|---|---|
| 9010 | Honey bought from V. P. Hinkley, Gaithersburg, Md. | .................................................. | ........ |
| 9011 | Honey bought from A. O. Appleby, Germantown, Md. | .................................................. | ........ |
| 9012 | Honey bought from Edmund Gloyd, Gaithersburg, Md. | .................................................. | ........ |
| 9014 | ......do ............................ | .................................................. | ........ |
| 9015 | Honey bought from John W. Bauckman, Leesburg, Va. | .................................................. | ........ |

## SAMPLES FROM CANADA.

| 9019 | F. T. Shutt, chemist, Canadian Agricultural Department. | Adulterated comb foundation, bought of R. E. Smith. | ........ |
|---|---|---|---|
| 9020 | ......do ................................. | ......do .................................. | ........ |
| 9021 | ......do ................................. | ......do .................................. | ........ |

TABLES OF ANALYSES.

*Pure beeswax samples.*

| Number. | Cerotic acid. | Myricin. | Total. | Ratio. | Hübl's numbers. | | | | Iodine No. | Melting point. | Weight of 1 cc. at 100. | Weight times H₂O at 100. |
|---|---|---|---|---|---|---|---|---|---|---|---|---|
| | | | | | Acid No. | Ether No. | Total. | Ratio. | | | | |
| 9009 | 12.97 | 88.67 | 101.64 | 6.836 | 17.72 | 73.59 | 91.31 | 4.153 | 6.17 | 63.8 | .81223 | .84719 |
| 9010 | 13.82 | 90.74 | 104.56 | 6.565 | 18.88 | 75.31 | 94.19 | 3.999 | 6.23 | 63.7 | .81464 | .84973 |
| 9011 | 12.28 | 89.24 | 101.52 | 7.267 | 16.77 | 74.06 | 90.83 | 4.414 | 6.72 | 63.8 | .81290 | .84798 |
| 9012 | 13.71 | 90.05 | 103.76 | 6.568 | 18.73 | 74.83 | 93.56 | 3.999 | 8.61 | 63.6 | .81306 | .84815 |
| 9014 | 13.32 | 89.02 | 102.34 | 6.693 | 18.20 | 73.88 | 92.08 | 4.000 | 8.57 | 63.7 | .81491 | .85003 |
| 9015 | 13.12 | 89.69 | 102.81 | 6.836 | 17.92 | 74.43 | 92.35 | 4.159 | 6.59 | 63.8 | .81377 | .84884 |
| Average. | 13.20 | 89.57 | 102.77 | 6.786 | 18.03 | 74.33 | 92.36 | 4.122 | 7.15 | 63.7 | .81360 | .84697 |

*Comb foundation and other waxes.*

| No. | Cerotic acid. | Myricin. | Total. | Ratio. | Hübl's numbers. | | | | Iodine No. | Melting point. | Weight of 1 cc. at 100. | Weight times H₂O at 100°C. |
|---|---|---|---|---|---|---|---|---|---|---|---|---|
| | Per ct. | Per ct. | | | Acid No. | Ether No. | Total. | Ratio. | | | | |
| 8492 | 12.36 | 92.01 | 104.37 | 7.444 | 17.98 | 76.22 | 94.20 | 4.230 | 7.09 | 63.2 | 0.81435 | 0.84945 |
| 8493 | 12.70 | 88.93 | 101.63 | 7.000 | 17.35 | 73.63 | 90.98 | 4.244 | 8.24 | 63.2 | 0.81300 | 0.84790 |
| 8494 | 13.02 | 91.52 | 104.54 | 7.031 | 17.78 | 75.78 | 93.56 | 4.262 | 8.67 | 63.3 | ...... | ...... |
| 8495 | 13.11 | 92.12 | 105.23 | 7.027 | 17.91 | 76.31 | 94.22 | 4.261 | 8.15 | 62.8 | ...... | ...... |
| 8496 | 13.10 | 90.09 | 103.19 | 6.880 | 17.89 | 74.63 | 92.52 | 4.171 | 8.47 | 63.0 | 0.81560 | 0.85029 |
| 8497 | 13.03 | 94.61 | 107.64 | 7.261 | 17.80 | 78.37 | 96.17 | 4.403 | 8.37 | 63.2 | 0.81450 | 0.84950 |
| 8498 | 13.17 | 89.94 | 103.11 | 6.829 | 18.03 | 74.51 | 92.54 | 4.132 | 8.52 | 63.1 | 0.81435 | 0.84940 |
| 8499 | | | | | | | | | 8.54 | 63.1 | 0.81583 | 0.85080 |
| 8500 | 12.88 | 89.77 | 102.65 | 6.069 | 17.59 | 74.37 | 91.96 | 4.228 | 9.22 | 63.0 | 0.81467 | 0.84976 |
| 8501 | 12.96 | 88.59 | 101.57 | 6.825 | 17.73 | 73.39 | 91.12 | 4.139 | 9.43 | 62.8 | 0.81586 | 0.85053 |
| 8502 | 13.40 | 87.83 | 101.20 | 6.525 | 18.39 | 72.76 | 91.15 | 3.955 | 10.45 | 62.4 | 0.81495 | 0.84970 |
| 8503 | 13.33 | 89.34 | 102.67 | 6.702 | 18.21 | 74.01 | 92.22 | 4.064 | 10.16 | 62.7 | 0.81477 | 0.84982 |
| 8504 | 13.54 | 88.01 | 101.55 | 6.500 | 18.50 | 72.91 | 91.41 | 3.941 | 9.53 | 62.1 | 0.81449 | 0.85002 |
| 8505 | 13.55 | 89.38 | 102.93 | 6.506 | 18.51 | 74.04 | 92.55 | 4.000 | 9.50 | 63.1 | 0.81499 | 0.84998 |
| 8506 | 13.49 | 89.00 | 102.49 | 6.598 | 18.43 | 73.73 | 92.16 | 3.946 | 9.36 | 62.9 | 0.81427 | 0.84929 |
| 8507 | 12.93 | 88.65 | 101.58 | 6.856 | 17.66 | 73.44 | 91.10 | 4.159 | 9.36 | 63.3 | 0.81418 | 0.84935 |
| 8508 A | 13.15 | 88.15 | 101.30 | 6.703 | 17.96 | 73.02 | 90.98 | 4.066 | 9.54 | 62.9 | 0.81502 | 0.85070 |
| 8508 B | 13.78 | 87.17 | 100.95 | 6.223 | 18.82 | 72.21 | 91.03 | 3.837 | 10.36 | 62.7 | ...... | ...... |
| 8508 C | 13.68 | 88.58 | 102.26 | 6.256 | 18.69 | 73.58 | 92.27 | 3.937 | 10.47 | 62.8 | ...... | ...... |
| 8508 D | 13.63 | 88.92 | 102.55 | 6.524 | 18.62 | 73.66 | 92.28 | 3.956 | 10.27 | 62.8 | 0.81425 | 0.84933 |
| 8509 A | 13.85 | 86.31 | 100.16 | 6.232 | 18.92 | 71.50 | 90.42 | 3.779 | 10.64 | 62.7 | 0.81546 | 0.85064 |
| 8509 B | 13.19 | 87.66 | 100.85 | 6.646 | 18.02 | 73.62 | 90.64 | 4.029 | 9.04 | 62.6 | 0.81440 | 0.84950 |
| 8509 C | 13.59 | 86.77 | 100.36 | 6.377 | 18.55 | 71.88 | 90.43 | 3.821 | 10.66 | 62.7 | ...... | ...... |
| 9019 | 6.00 | 17.30 | 23.30 | 2.883 | 6.20 | 14.33 | 22.53 | 1.747 | 3.87 | 55.2 | 0.70232 | 0.79520 |
| 9020 | 10.01 | 43.31 | 53.32 | 4.331 | 19.06 | 35.89 | 49.55 | 2.627 | 7.34 | 57.3 | 0.77939 | 0.82344 |
| 9021 | 16.68 | 39.60 | 56.28 | 2.374 | 22.78 | 32.80 | 55.58 | 1.440 | 10.25 | 59.6 | 0.81322 | 0.84828 |
| 8543 | *8.88 | †94.28 | 103.16 | ...... | 20.20 | 196.50 | 216.70 | 9.727 | 14.87 | 40.5 | 0.88105 | 0.91889 |
| 8550 | *10.36 | †92.63 | 102.99 | ...... | 23.58 | 193.00 | 216.58 | 8.185 | 6.44 | 41.6 | 0.87452 | 0.91222 |
| 8557 | *10.28 | †92.76 | 103.04 | ...... | 23.94 | 193.30 | 217.24 | 8.070 | 10.25 | 41.3 | 0.87825 | 0.91612 |
| 8608 | *9.10 | †92.50 | 101.60 | ...... | 20.71 | 192.80 | 213.51 | 10.300 | 5.08 | 41.8 | 0.87435 | 0.91203 |
| 8546 | 1.45 | 86.79 | 88.24 | 50.85 | 1.98 | 73.10 | 75.08 | 36.920 | ...... | 82.8 | 0.83496 | 0.87001 |
| 8552 | | | | | | | | ...... | 10.64 | 82.9 | 0.83697 | 0.87311 |
| 8554 | | | | | | | | ...... | 10.30 | 82.8 | 0.83677 | 0.87287 |
| 8609 | .97 | 92.55 | 93.52 | 95.41 | 1.33 | 77.47 | 78.80 | 58.250 | 10.49 | 64.8 | 0.84118 | 0.87731 |
| 8544 | | | | | 1.00 | 0 | 1.00 | ...... | .00 | 64.8 | 0.74581 | 0.80036 |
| 8551 | | | | | 0 | 0 | 0 | ...... | 1.39 | 61.4 | 0.77232 | 0.80556 |
| 8556 | | | | | 0 | 0 | 0 | ...... | .56 | 62.9 | 0.77541 | 0.80871 |
| 8610 | | | | | 0 | 0 | 0 | ...... | .00 | 74.3 | 0.77010 | 0.80479 |
| 8545 | | | | | 0.18 | 0 | 0 | 0 | 3.12 | 68.9 | 0.79875 | 0.83310 |
| 8607 | | | | | 0.19 | 0 | 0 | 0 | ...... | 69.1 | 0.79530 | 0.82954 |
| 8541 | | | | | | | | | 0 | | | |
| 8547 | | | | | | | | | 0 | 54.3 | 0.75567 | 0.78817 |
| 8553 | | | | | | | | | 0.97 | 53.6 | 0.75487 | 0.78717 |

* Acid Palmitic.  † Palmitin.

## METHODS OF ANALYSIS ADOPTED FOR WAX.

*Acid and ether numbers.*—These were determined by the well-known method of Hehner (Analyst, 1883, 16, see abstracts, p. 844) using the acidimetric values as determined by titration with alcoholic potash. To set the potash and for back titration hydrochloric acid was used. This was standardized by weighing portions and precipitating the chlorine as silver chloride and weighing. This gave the per cent of hydrochloric acid by weight in the standard solution. The specific gravity of the solution was then taken at various temperatures by a specific gravity bottle, and from these two figures a table made out giving the content of acid of 1 cc at the prevailing temperatures. The method of titration in detail was:

Between 4 and 5 grams of wax were weighed and placed in a flask holding about 500 cc., covered with 100 cc of 95 per cent alcohol, a reflux condenser attached, and the alcohol boiled vigorously for two hours. While still hot it was titrated with alcoholic potash, using phenolphtalein as an indicator. A cubic centimeter of normal potash solution is equivalent to 410 milligrams of cerotic acid. Into the same flask were now run 50 cc of approximately half-normal alcoholic alkali, the condenser reinserted, and the alcohol heated to a brisk boil for five hours. The excess of alkali was then titrated by standard hydrochloric acid and the number of cubic centimeters required deducted from the number of cubic centimeters required to neutralize the potash in a blank which had received exactly the same treatment, except, of course, the addition of wax. The alkali which had disappeared was equivalent to the number of cubic centimeters of the standard hydrochloric acid thus obtained. One cubic centimeter of normal acid is equal to 676 milligrams of myricin.

*Melting points.*—Melting points were done by dipping the bulb of a thermometer into the melted wax for an instant, placing the thermometer (which now carried a thin film of wax on the bulb) through a perforation in the cork of a wide bottle, hanging the bottle in a beaker full of water kept heated to about 65°, and noting the temperature shown by the thermometer at the instant the wax runs down the bulb and forms a hanging drop. This was called the melting point. The experiment was tried of allowing the wax to remain on the bulb over night before making the determination, but the melting point did not differ from that shown by a fresh wax coating.

*Iodine number.*—This was determined according to the conventional method (Hübl's) for fats, except that owing to the low numbers found a greater weight (2 grams) was taken than is usual for fats (0.2 to 1.0 gram). More chloroform was also required. The method in detail is:

Two grams were weighed and placed in a glass-stoppered flask and dissolved in 40 cc of chloroform. Twenty-five cc of an iodine solution (containing 25 grams iodine and 30 grams of mercuric chloride dissolved in 95 per cent alcohol and made up to 1 liter) were then run in and the mixture shaken. In another similar flask 40 cc chloroform and 25 cc iodine solution (but no wax) were placed. The flasks were then placed in a dark closet, where they remained three hours. Fifteen cc of a 10 per cent solution of potassium iodide and 100 cc. of water were then placed in each flask and the free iodine titrated with standard solution of sodium thiosulphate. The iodine found in the first flask deducted from that found in the second, gave the amount absorbed by the 2 grams of wax. The "iodine number" expresses the per cent of iodine absorbed.

*Determination of specific gravity.*—The specific gravities were all taken at 100°. A specific gravity bottle was filled with distilled water, plunged neck deep in a bath of boiling water, and kept there for half an hour. The stopper, which was perforated, was then inserted, the bottle removed from the bath, allowed to cool to room temperature, and weighed. It was then emptied, washed with alcohol and ether, dried, and re-weighed. The difference between the weighings gave the weight of the water held at 100°. This, divided by 0.95865 (Rossetti's figure for the density of water at 100°) gave the capacity at 100° in cubic centimeters (true air). It was then filled with melted wax, again plunged into the bath, in which it was kept for half an hour, the stopper inserted, the wax wiped off, and cooled and weighed. The wiping off was facilitated by keeping the surface of the bottle hot by occasionally letting hot water from a tap run over it. The weight of the wax contained, divided by the weight of water contained at 100°, gave the figures put down in the column headed " times water at 100°." The weight of the wax was then divided by the number of cubic centimeters held by the specific gravity bottle at 100°, and the figures thus obtained placed under the head "weight of one cc at 100°."

### ABSTRACTS OF PAPERS RELATING TO WAX AND ITS ADULTERATIONS.

The literature relating to wax and its adulterations is so fragmentary and scattered as to make it desirable to collect brief abstracts thereof for convenience of reference. Such an attempt is beset with many difficulties, chief of which is the labor of condensing the material into a manageable space, retaining at the same time the essential features of the original articles.

It is proper to mention here that many of the tests and methods of analysis proposed in the following abstracts are valueless, and even misleading, but it is advisable that analysts be fully informed of the work already done, even if it be without value, in order that they may avoid its repetition. In many of the methods cited, moreover, no comparative tests have been made by this division, the inaccuracy of the methods being recognized from the work of others. All the more promising methods, however, have been tried, and the scheme of analysis finally adopted for our own work has been fashioned in accordance with the results of these tests. Fortunately the chemist has rarely presented for his examination a substance offering so many analytical difficulties as beeswax, and especially when he is called on to detect an adulterant which has been added to the extent of only 5 or 10 per cent. In such cases it is only after a thorough trial of all the approved methods of analysis that he is able to express an opinion which carries a reasonable degree of assurance. In the classification of the abstracts three categories have been made.

The first includes the different kinds of wax, their properties, methods of preparation, bleaching, etc.

The second embraces methods of the qualitative examination of waxes.

The third includes the methods of the quantitative analyses of waxes and their adulterants.

Many of the abstracts contain matter that belong to two or even all three of the above classes. These are placed according to the relative importance of their contents.

### KINDS AND PROPERTIES OF WAX.

#### EGYPTIAN WAX.*

This wax occurs in commerce as irregular cakes of a dirty light yellow color. The specific gravity is 0.955. A solution of 5 grams of wax in 5 cc. of chloroform, made by warming the two in a test tube, remained clear for an hour and then deposited granules, and the upper third became cloudy, though the lower remained clear for twelve hours. Although this reaction indicated the presence of vegetable wax, other tests gave no evidence of its presence. Tests for rosin gave negative results. Egyptian wax differs from Bohemian in that the chloroform solution does not remain clear, and that when it is boiled with dilute alcohol it gives a filtrate which becomes cloudy and that it is more easily bleached. The author found that some wax candles sent him for analysis contained Egyptian wax.

#### VEGETABLE WAX.†

This name, which formerly covered palm, carnauba, myrtle, and Japan wax, is now used to signify a kind of fat coming from India, which is no doubt the product of a kind of bassia. These fats, which are obtained in great quantities in India and parts of Africa, bear a number of different names. Galam butter, Bambuc butter, Bambara butter, or Shea butter is said to be obtained from the seeds of *Bassia parkerii* (according to some from *Bassia butyracea*); Bassia oil, or Illipe oil, from the seeds of the Indian mahwah or butter tree; *Bassia latifolia* and *longifolia* also give similar fats. The fat imported into Germany has an unpleasant rancid taste and a greenish color, soon disappearing under the influence of light. Under the microscope are seen in the green amorphous mass numerous crystalline granules. In places these crystals are so well developed that the fatty character disappears. The melting point of the amorphous mass is 33.6; that of the crystalline aggregates 55.6. Specific gravity is 0.9474. It is only slightly soluble in alcohol. Boiling absolute alcohol extracted 1.68 per cent; cold, 0.83 per cent. The chemical composition has been found very variable. O. Henry found it to consist principally of stearin; Pelouze and Bourdet mostly of olein. Buff found no palmitic acid. Thomson and Wood found a new acid, "bassiac," with a melting point of 70. According to Valenta, the fat from *Bassia longifolia* gave a mixture of fatty acids consisting of 63.49 per cent oleic and 36.51 per cent of a solid fatty acid of 62 melting point, probably mostly palmitic.

---

* K. Labler, Rundschau, 10, 289 ; abs. Chem. Centralblatt, 1884, 497.
† M. Buchner, Chem. Centralblatt, 1884, 257.

## MANUFACTURE OF ARTIFICIAL WAX.*

A French patent, granted to Pauvert, Moussay, and Chauvin, prescribes melting together one part rosin and one-half part paraffin. An alternative process is to melt rosin with one-third part soap or stearic acid and extract with potash. Copal or vegetable wax can also be used.

## CRYSTALLINE STRUCTURE OF BEESWAX.†

Besides an old observation of Dujardin's, that wax solidifying on an object glass under favorable circumstances shows under the microscope something of a crystalline structure, there seems to be no further notice of the subject in the literature of beeswax. The phenomenon may be demonstrated by melting a cake of white wax in a shallow porcelain dish three-fourths filled with water. When the wax is fully melted, the dish is allowed to cool as slowly as possible. Any bubbles in the wax are to be broken by approaching a piece of hot iron to them. Vibration must be avoided during this cooling. At the moment of solidification several opaque points form simultaneously and at almost equal distances apart. From these points crystallization begins. The surface of the solid cake will show well-defined crystals resembling in shape the cells of the honeycomb.

## CONSTITUTION OF BEESWAX. ‡

Schalfeef alleges that cerotic acid made from beeswax, according to Brodie's direction, when fractionally precipitated by lead acetate gives different acids, to one of which the formula $C_{34}H_{68}O_2$ is applied. The author, on repeating Schalfeef's work, obtained by fractional precipitation only one acid, the analysis of which gave results agreeing well with the formula of cerotic acid, $C_{24}H_{57}O_2$, but not with the formula $C_{34}H_{68}O_2$. The cerotic acid separated from a kilogram of yellow wax was a completely homogeneous substance.

## BLEACHING BEESWAX. §

Beeswax is most frequently bleached by simple exposure to the air. For this purpose it is cut into thin laminæ and exposed in an open place to the light and air. The coloring matter thus undergoes a complete combustion; the wax is completely decolorized in a period of time varying from ten to thirty days. Without the light the oxidation does not take place even in a current of ozonized air, but the presence of oxygenated or ozonized air causes the light to act more rapidly.

It is not, therefore, simply the ozone which effects the bleaching, as is generally supposed, but this agent only becomes effective in the presence of the solar rays. Even at a temperature of 60° ozone does not attack the coloring matter in darkness. Even in a vacuum or in an atmosphere of an inert gas, viz, $CO_2$, N, etc., the light will decolorize a wax, but more slowly than in the open air.

---

* Chem., Centralblatt 1876, 528.

† R. Röttger, Jahresber. d. phys. Ver. z Frankfurt a. M., 1876-'77, 23; abs. Chem. Centralblatt, 1878, 575.

‡E. Zatzeck, Monatsh. f. Chem., 3, 677; Chem. Centralblatt, 1882, 626.

§ Buisine, Bull. Soc. Chim., Oct. 20, 1890, 465.

Comparative analyses of pure unbleached and bleached wax afforded the following limiting data:

| | Melting point °C. | Free acid in m g KOH per g. of wax. | Total acids in m g K O H per g. wax. | Iodine absorbed. | Volume of H at 0° and 760 mm. furnished by 1 g. wax. |
|---|---|---|---|---|---|
| | | | | Per cent. | Cc. |
| Pure yellow wax .................... | 63 –64 | 19–21 | 91– 95 | 10–11 | 53. 5–55 |
| Pure yellow wax, bleached in open air................... | 63. 5–64 | 20–21 | 93–100 | 6– 7 | 54– 55 |

In air bleaching the yellow waxes lose only about 1 to 2 per cent of their weight. The melting point of the two kinds of wax rests sensibly the same. Only traces of acids soluble in water are formed during the bleaching process. The most notable differences are in the quantities of hydrocarbons, which fall from 13 to 14 in the yellow wax to 11 or 12 in the white variety, and the iodine number, which falls about four points in the white wax. The proportion of total acids in the white variety is slightly increased. In bleaching, some of the nonsaturated constituents of the wax fix oxygen and become saturated, thus diminishing their power of absorbing iodine. This is illustrated particularly in the hydrocarbons of the wax which, after bleaching, melt at 51.5 to 53 degrees, and fix 14.3 to 15 per cent of iodine, and before bleaching melt at 49.5 degrees and fix 22 per cent iodine.

In practice the pure wax is rarely bleached. The bleachers always add to the wax a certain quantity of suet, from 3 to 5 per cent. There are several reasons for this. The principle one is that pure wax when bleached is too brittle; moreover, in presence of a small quantity of suet, the bleaching goes on more rapidly, and without this suet it is difficult to obtain a product entirely white.

A series of yellow waxes to which a small quantity of suet had been added, fresh suet, and the same exposed to air and left for forty days, gave on analysis the following comparative and limiting data:

| | Melting point °C. | Free acids in mg KHO per g. | Total acids in mg KOH per g. | Iodine absorbed. | Volume of H at 0° and 760 mm furnished by g wax. | Hydro-carbons. |
|---|---|---|---|---|---|---|
| | | | | Per cent. | | Per cent. |
| Pure yellow wax ......... | 63–64 | 19–21 | 91–95 | 10–11 | 53. 5–55 | 13–14 |
| Wax bleached with 3 to 5 per cent suet .......... | 63. 5–64 | 21–23 | 105–115 | 6–7 | 52. 5–57 | 11–12 |
| Fresh suet................ | 47. 5 | 2. 75 | 202 | 36. 01 | 52. 5 | .......... |
| Same exposed for 40 days. | 48. 5 | 4. 86 | 213 | 27. 68 | 60. 4 | .......... |

These numbers illustrate the action of the suet in bleaching. It is due to the oleic acid it contains; easily oxidizable, thus aiding the combustion of the organic coloring matter. The essence of terebenthine added in small quantities acts in the same manner.

Other processes may be employed for the decoloring wax, e. g., bleaching with animal charcoal. The wax is kept in a fused state in contact with the black, and the white wax is obtained by filtration. Permanganate of potash or bichromate of potash may also be employed in acid solution with good results and even oxygenated water.

Reducing agents, such as sulphurous acid, sulphites, hydrosulphites, etc., do not act on the coloring matters of wax. Chlorine bleaches waxes, but the chlorine is absorbed as iodine and bromine are, and thus the constitution of the wax is profoundly modified. The composition of waxes bleached in various ways is illustrated in the following table :

| | Melting point °C. | Free acids in mg KOH per g. | Total acids in mg KOH per g. | Iodine, absorbed. | Volume of H at °0 and 76v mm furnished by g wax. | Hydro-carbons. |
|---|---|---|---|---|---|---|
| | | | | *Per cent.* | *CC.* | *Per cent.* |
| Pure yellow wax.......... | 63. 5 | 20. 17 | 93. 40 | 10. 87 | 53. 0 | 13. 54 |
| Wax bleached in air with 5 per cent terebenthine. | 63. 5 | 20. 20 | 100. 40 | 6. 78 | 54. 9 | 12. 39 |
| Wax bleached with oxygenated water .......... | 63. 5 | 19. 87 | 98. 42 | 6. 26 | 56. 1 | 12. 53 |
| Pure yellow wax.......... | 63. 0 | 20. 40 | 95. 06 | 11. 23 | 54. 5 | 14. 30 |
| Wax bleached with animal black............... | 63. 0 | 19. 71 | 93. 20 | 11. 36 | 53. 6 | 13. 30 |
| Wax by permanganate.... { | 63. 7 | 22. 63 | 103. 29 | 2. 61 | 53. 6 | 13. 30 |
| | 63. 5 | 21. 96 | 99. 24 | 5. 80 | 55. 5 | 13. 34 |
| Wax by bichromate....... { | 63. 2 | 21. 86 | 98. 90 | 7. 94 | 51. 0 | 13. 24 |
| | 64. 0 | 23. 43 | 107. 72 | 1. 08 | 53. 6 | 11. 77 |

The composition of waxes decolorized by chemical processes, as is seen from the table, is quite variable.

The numbers obtained show the modifications which are produced in waxes by the different processes followed in bleaching them. The data enable the analyst to decide within certain limits whether a white wax be pure, and by what process it has been bleached, and they will serve as a basis for a further investigation of adulterations.

BLEACHING OF WAX.*

The Jour. de phar. et de chim., 1891, May 15, contains a description of experiments on the bleaching of wax, by A. and P. Buisine. These gentlemen were the first to establish the fact that to obtain a rapid decoloration, both air and light are necessary, and that it is under the direct rays of the sun that the bleaching is best effected. They then state that the combustion of coloring matter is favored by ozone, but only in conjunction with the solar rays.

In 1885 I published a series of experiments whose results coincide with those of the authors just mentioned. Admitting that light plays a great part in the phenomenon, I wrote: "But it is not known if this part is preponderant; as for the exposure in the night, that is a vague expression. Besides, how does this exposure determine the bleaching, or at least contribute to it? In a word, what is the active agent?" Seeking to answer these questions, I first observed the influence of light alone, then the effect of light combined with exposure to the " exposure in the night," and, finally, the effect produced by this exposure without the action of light.

First experiment: Yellow wax was exposed in thin sheets to the action of light. or, to be more accurate, to the successive action of the sun and of diffused light. The action was nearly complete at the end of twelve days.

Second experiment: The same wax was exposed during the same time to the action of light on one side and the " exposure in the night " on the other. The bleaching was more nearly complete than before.

* M. H. Barnouvin, Jour. de phar. et de chim., 1891, July 1.

Third experiment: A third specimen of this wax was exposed to the "exposure in the night" and sheltered from the light during the day. The bleaching was less marked than in the first instance.

Still it remained to determine the cause which during the exposure to the "*exposure in the night*" produced the effect. Special research having revealed the constant existence of ozone in the same places where these experiments were most effectual, I tried to find if a connection existed between the occurrence of atmospheric ozone and the rapidity of the bleaching. I tested this by placing ozonoscopic paper by the side of the wax during the experiment. Comparison with an ozometric scale showed an evident relation between the progress of the bleaching and the quantity of ozone in the air. The ozone evidently played the leading part.

The results may be summed up as follows: Light bleaches the wax more rapidly than the "exposure in the night." On this subject I ought to add that the action of the direct solar rays alone possesses a great activity; in diffused light the bleaching is slow. The action which the "exposure in the night" produces is due principally to the ozone.

### SPECIFIC GRAVITY OF WAXES.*

| | | | |
|---|---|---|---|
| White wax | 0.973 | Rosin, French | 1.104–1.105 |
| Yellow wax | 0.963–0.964 | Cacao butter, filtered | 0.980–0.981 |
| Japan wax | 0.975 | Paraffin | 0.913–0.914 |
| Ceresin, white | 0.918 | Purified resin | 1.045 |
| Ceresin, half white | 0.920 | Beef tallow | 0.952–0.953 |
| Ceresin, yellow | 0.922 | Mutton tallow | 0.961 |
| Ozokerite (crude) | 0.952 | Stearin | 0.971–0.972 |
| Spermaceti | 0.960 | | |
| Rosin, American | 1.108 | | |

### BEHAVIOR OF WAX FROM THE RHUS FAMILY OF PLANTS.†

J. B. Batka‡ says that the most remarkable peculiarity of the above-named wax consists in the fact that when boiled with borax in water it dissolves fully, forming a gelatinous, quickly solidifying soap, from which acids precipitate a wax. This is not the case with beeswax, and therefore the reaction can be used to distinguish between them.

Japan wax is the most important of these waxes, being an exudation from the *Rhus succedanea*.

### VEGETABLE WAXES.§

Carnauba wax (Ceara or Brazil wax) is obtained from the leaves of *Copernicia cerifera* (Martius); comes from Brazil, is hard and brittle, and melts at 83.5° to 84°.

Pela wax (Chinese wax) is separated in China from the young branches of *Fraxinus chinensis* (Roxburg) by *Coccus pela* (Westwood), melts at 82.5° C., and has not been brought into commerce.

Koga wax is probably obtained from *Cinnamomum pedunculatum* in Japan. It is softer than Japan wax and has not yet come into commerce.

Ibota wax is produced from *Ligustrum ibota* by an insect. It is white, very solid, and is not met with in commerce.

Chinese vegetable tallow is obtained from the seeds of *Stillingia sebifera* (Martius). It is used in making candles, is an easily disintegrated substance, and melts at 37°.

Palm wax is collected from the trunks of *Ceroxylon andicola* (Humb.), indigenous to tropical America. It does not melt in its crude state till heated above 100°.

---

* Dieterich, Arch. Pharm. 3, 20, 454.

† Fres. Zeit. f. a. Chem., 1865, 491.

‡ Chem. Centralblatt, 1865, 12.

§A. Meyer, Arch. d. Pharm., Aug., 1879, 97, 129; Amer. Jour. Phar., Dec., 1879, 606; Proc. Am. Phar. Assoc, 1880, 293.

Myrtle wax is separated from the fruit of *Myrica cerifera* (wax myrtle), indigenous in the United States. It melts at 47.5° (Leroy) or at 49° (Chevreul). Japan wax is obtained from the dried fruit of *Rhu succedanea, R. vernicifera,** and *R. silvestris*, in Japan and China. Japan exported in 1877 wax worth about $238,600, Japan wax is nearly white or of a slightly yellowish green tint, has a sandy, short fracture, an unpleasant tallowy odor, is often coated with a fine white crystalline layer, and melts at 52° to 53°. When old it is soluble in boiling alcohol and ether, from both of which almost all again separates on cooling. It is used in polishing wood and in the preparation of wax matches and candles.

### COMPOSITION OF JAPAN WAX.[†]

The author regards the "wax" as a mixture of various glycerides and not as dipalmitin. The sample examined by him melted at 52°. When rapidly cooled after melting and again heated it melts at 42°. On standing some time it regains its original melting point. Melted with water it gives it an acid reaction. It readily dissolves in commercial absolute alcohol on heating, but mostly crystallizes out on cooling, leaving a softer and more fusible body in solution. The fatty acid obtained by saponification is mainly palmitic, but contains acids of higher melting point. One acid was found melting at a higher temperature than stearic. There was also found an oily acid in small quantity.

### NEW SOURCE OF WAX.[‡]

A wax has been isolated from *Sonchus oleraceus* and *Asclepias cornuti* possessing many of the qualities of beeswax, and these plants may be made a commercial source of the wax. One morgen of land planted with *Asclepias* should yield 50 centner of hay, 1.25 to 1.5 centner wax, and 0.80 centner of caoutchouc.

### CHINESE INSECT WAX. [§]

This wax is a compound of cerotyl alcohol with a wax acid. The wax-forming insects crawl on the under side of tender young twigs, probably of the *Fraxinus Chinensis*, and make an incision from which a liquid gushes forth, which soon coats the twig with wax.* In the course of three months the layer becomes about 0.25 inch thick. The twigs are then broken off and the wax stripped from them by hand. This wax is melted in boiling water to purify it. The stripped twigs are also thrown into hot water to get more wax. In this last operation the insects become detached from the wood and sink to the bottom of the containing vessel, whence they are gathered, pressed into a cake, and fed to hogs.

### QUALITATIVE EXAMINATION OF BEESWAX AND OTHER WAXES.

E. Donath ‖ proposes the following tests for adulterants in beeswax :

Boil a nut-sized piece of the suspected wax with concentrated solution of sodium carbonate for five minutes :

A. An emulsion is formed, remaining after cooling, indicating adulteration with rosin, tallow, stearic acid, or Japan wax. A new portion is now to be boiled with a strong solution of caustic potash for some minutes and then NaCl added : (*a*) The separated soap is in the form of a fine-grained magma : Japan wax. For complete certainty determine the specific gravity. If it is higher than 0.970, Japan wax is present. (*b*) The separated soap is flocculent : adulteration with rosin, or fatty substances.

---

* The wax from *R. vernicifera* is poisonous, and is the base of Japanese lacquer.

† E. Buri, Arch. f. Pharm, May, 1879, 403 ; Proc. Amer. Pharm. Assoc., 1879, 436.

‡ C. Kassner, Die Oel und Fettindustrie, 22–86 ; Chem. Zeit. 1886, 390.

§ C. Theilman, Amer. Bee Jour., Jan. 13, 1886, 24.

‖ Dingl. polyt. Jour., 205, 131 ; ab. Fres. Zeit. f. a. Chem., 1873, 325.

Rosin may be tested for by heating a fragment of the wax for fifteen minutes with concentrated nitric acid. Pour a little cold water on the wax swimming on the surface and decant the fluid. In the presence of rosin, a yellow, flocky body is thrown down on cooling or on dilution. Ammonia dissolves the flocks and becomes colored red brown. Stearic acid is tested for by Fehling's method, boiling the wax for forty-five minutes with twenty times its weight of alcohol, allowing the resultant solution to cool slowly, filtering and adding water to the filtrate. A precipitate or cloudiness indicates stearic acid. If a negative result is given, stearin should be sought for by Gottlieb's method, based on the solubility of oleate of lead in ether. Stearin if present is liable to influence the test given above for stearic acid. The distinction between the two can be made by means of an alcoholic solution of lead acetate, which causes no precipitate in the filtrate from pure wax or from that adulterated with stearin.

B. On cooling the wax floats on the top and the fluid remains clear and is but slightly yellow. If not adulterated with paraffin the wax is pure. If the specific gravity of the wax be less than 0.960 and no other adulterants have been found the presence of paraffin is assured.

To take specific gravity of waxes Donath keeps the wax melted for some time in order to extricate air bubbles and then pours into a potash mold. After fully cooling the wax is molded into the desired form, brushed over with a camel's hair brush wet with water and the specific gravity taken in a pycnometer.

### DETECTION OF ADULTERANTS. [*]

The author says that white wax contains 3 to 5 per cent of tallow, and that manufacturers add turpentine or resin in order to impart to wax the requisite tenacity. Hence these additions, unless present in large quantity, can not be regarded as adulterants. The specific gravity of wax when higher than 0.964, indicates the presence of stearin, resin, or Japan wax, and when lower than 0.956 paraffin, ozokerit, or tallow is present. Chloroform or fatty oils form a clear solution with dry wax and a slightly turbid one with moist wax. By treating pure beeswax with a saturated solution of borax at 80°, the aqueous solution is rendered turbid; when Japan wax or stearin is present, a milky solution is obtained, remaining opaque after cooling. By boiling wax in a solution of soda (1:6), pure wax gives a translucent solution. If milky, stearin is present; if pasty or stiff, Japan wax has been added. When the specific gravity is less than 0.956 and the wax behaves with borax and soda like pure wax, paraffin or ozokerit has been added; the same result is obtained when the specific gravity is correct and the borax or soda test indicates the presence of Japan wax. Ceresin (white or yellow) forms milky solutions in the borax or soda test, or behaves like beeswax, but has a lower specific gravity.

### METHOD OF DETECTING ADULTERATION OF BEESWAX. [†]

Adulteration of beeswax can be detected by the following methods:

To determine the specific gravity an egg-sized piece of wax is placed in a beaker with 33 per cent alcohol, shaken vigorously to remove adhering bubbles, and alcohol or water added until the wax just floats. The density of the mixture is then ascertained by a spindle.

To determine the mineral and coloring matters 10 grams are placed in a flask holding about 250 cc., together with 100 cc. of water, and the mixture boiled for several minutes. After cooling any mineral matter which may be present will be found in the bottom of the flask. On cooling if the water is yellow, turmeric may be present and can be tested for with ammonia. Starch can be tested for with iodine. For further testing Mr. Clarency prescribes the sodium carbonate test.

---

[*] Hager, Dingl. polyt. Jour., 233, 356 ; abs. Jour. Chem. Soc., 1881, 40, 316.

[†] A. Clarency, Journ. de pharm. et de chim. (6) 13, 27; Chem. Centralblatt, 1886, 174.

The specific gravity of yellow wax and also of the white varies between 0.956 and 0.964, and is on the average 0.960, although most samples are between 0.958 and 0.960. If the specific gravity exceeds these limits on either side it is suspicious, and should the variation be great adulteration can be considered as certain. If the specific gravity be above 0.964, stearic acid, Japan wax, rosin, water, heavy spar, sawdust, etc., may be present. If it lies below 0.956, paraffin, ceresin or fat may be present. Although the specific gravity affords some criterion for judging wax, yet samples lying within the limits are not necessarily pure, as the correct specific gravity can be easily obtained by double adulteration. For quantitative and qualitative work on wax the best method is that of Hübl.

### PETROLEUM BENZINE AS A QUALITATIVE REAGENT.†

This new method of testing depends on the behavior of beeswax toward petroleum benzine. If a cylinder of beeswax is placed in a test tube, and benzine poured over till it overtops it from 1 to 2 cm, the fluid gradually penetrates into the mass of wax, and very small flocks or pulverulent particles separate and collect at the bottom of the benzine. Finally, the whole mass disintegrates, and in an hour or two the contents of the test tube are arranged in two layers, the lower consisting of a homogeneous layer of wax particles, the upper of clear benzine. The conduct of adulterated wax with benzine is quite different. Wax containing foreign substances conducts itself with more or less resistance, according to the adulterant. Such a wax cylinder remains unchanged half a day, often from two to four days. With samples containing from 8 to 20 per cent of admixture, the wax cylinder swells somewhat more quickly, and the outside layer shows by degrees from 4 to 12 divisions lengthwise, which are separated from one another by narrow, transparent, or deeply shining lines. If the foreign substance is only a small per cent, flocks separate from the wax a few minutes after the addition of the benzine, and after a half or a whole day the wax sediment consists not of a homogeneous mass, but of flocks, interspersed with broken, lengthwise columns, or fragments of columns, showing transparent veins of benzine.

### DETECTION OF ADULTERATION IN BEESWAX. ‡

When pure beeswax is chewed it breaks up in the mouth; the adulterated acts like chewing gum.

### DETECTION of STEARIC ACID. §

Boil the suspected sample with distilled water, allow to cool, and test the aqueous layer with litmus. Stearic acid renders water slightly acid in reaction, which is not the case with pure wax. Regnard himself says that this method is not of great value as small amounts of sulphur dioxide remaining after bleaching could easily cause mistake. He also proposes a modification: Heat the sample with limewater in a flask having reflux condenser. With pure wax the limewater remains transparent; otherwise, a turbidity ensues and the precipitate of stearate of calcium falls. The fluid reddens litmus.

E. Geith's method ‖ is also based on the use of limewater, but according to him there is no precipitate, the fluid remaining perfectly clear, but the fluid loses its

* H. Röttger, Chem. Zeit., 1890, 37, 606.
† H. Hager. Central Org. f. Waarenkunde, 1891, 1, 239; abs. Chem. Zeit., 1891, 93, 307.
‡ A B C of Bee Culture, 290.
§ Regnard, Jour. de chim. med., 1844, 328.
‖ Dingl. polyt. Jour., 1847, 105, 445.

alkaline reaction. According to my own trials a turbidity always ensues in the beginning, but there is no precipitate. On longer heating the cloudiness disappears,
and the fluid again becomes clear. Whether the fluid becomes acid or remains alkaline naturally depends on the amount of stearic acid present and the strength of the
limewater.

Fehling* says: As pure wax contains cerotic acid, a body which conducts itself
toward alkali, limewater, alcohol, and other reagents recommended for the detection of stearic acid, very much as does the latter, it is not possible to detect admixtures of less than 10 per cent stearic acid by the known methods. Stearic acid is,
however, separated from its solution in cold alcohol on the addition of water, while
cerotic acid, though it dissolves in hot alcohol, separates almost completely on cooling
and the solution then contains so little that it is not much affected by the addition
of water. Fehling therefore boils the wax for four or five minutes with twenty
times its weight of alcohol, allows to stand for several hours in order to completely
cool, filters and adds water to the filtrate. If the wax be pure the liquid is only
slightly clouded, but in presence of stearic acid a flocky precipitate falls. One per
cent of stearic acid gives a strong, unmistakable turbidity. In detail the method is:
Boil 1 gram wax in a test tube with 10 cc. of 80 per cent alcohol for several minutes
and then allow to cool to about 18° or 20°. Filter into a cylinder, add water, and
shake. The stearic acid separates in flocks on the surface and the underlying fluid
becomes nearly clear.

### DETECTION OF TALLOW OR ANIMAL FAT IN BEESWAX.

Grease† can be detected by scraping a smooth surface on a cake of wax and at-
tempting to write on it with pen and ink, which can be readily done should the wax
be pure. Another plan is to scratch the wax with the finger nail. If pure the wax
will show a shining line along the scratch, but if tallow is present the line will be
dull. A fresh break will generally show the presence of tallow, if present, by the
smell.

Hager‡ shakes 1 to 1.5 grams of the chloroform solution of the wax with 12 to 15
grams of limewater. In the presence of stearic acid a mealy lime soap forms, assuming dendritic shapes, while the solution of pure wax in chloroform separates in
the form of a white emulsion. Even in this modification the method of Regnard can
not be recommended.

Benedikt§ proposes to boil the wax sample with carbonate of soda and allow to
cool. In the presence of stearic acid the solution solidifies from the formation of
stearate of soda. This method is good, but is not so certain in presence of small
quantities as that of Fehling.

### DETECTION OF PARAFFIN AND CERESIN.

Wagner‖ detects the presence of paraffin and estimates its quantity by the influence it exercises on the specific gravity of the wax. He says: Normal wax has a
constant specific gravity, and paraffins of very different origin show specific gravi-

---

* Dingl. polyt. Jour., 1858, 147, 227.
† Amer. Bee Jour., 21, 19, 298.
‡ Comment., Pharm. Germ., 1873, 436.
§ Analyse der Fette, 291.
‖ Dingl. polyt. Jour., 1867, 185, 72.

ties varying only within narrow limits. He gives a table of the specific gravity of various mixtures of wax of 0.969 specific gravity, and paraffin of 0.871.

| Wax. | Paraffin. | Specific gravity. |
|------|-----------|-------------------|
| 0    | 100       | 0. 871            |
| 25   | 75        | . 893             |
| 50   | 50        | . 920             |
| 75   | 25        | . 942             |
| 80   | 20        | . 948             |
| 100  | 0         | . 969             |

Pure wax (free from paraffin) should sink in alcohol of 0.961 specific gravity (33 per cent by volume, Tralles).

### DETECTION OF PARAFFIN IN WAX.[*]

For this purpose Landolt recommends heating a nut-sized piece of the wax, with excess of fuming sulphuric acid, in a porcelain dish. As soon as the wax melts a vigorous reaction sets in, enfeebled, however, by the presence of paraffin. Heat for two or three minutes after the evolution of gas begins to slacken, and then allow to cool. Paraffin is found as a transparent layer, easily removable. It is best to use enough acid to insure the mass remaining fluid at the end of the reaction, as otherwise the paraffin is contaminated with the decomposition products of the wax. In this case another treatment with acid will be found to make the paraffin colorless. By this method very small per cents of paraffin can be detected. Ordinary acid should not be used, as the decomposition with it is tedious.

According to Wagner,[†] Dullo,[‡] and Breitenlohner,[§] this method is seldom applicable, inasmuch as paraffin butter (vaseline), not solid paraffin, is used, and the former is destroyed by sulphuric acid. This method is unreliable, and not used at the present time.

### DETECTION OF PARAFFIN IN BEESWAX. ||

Payen recommends for this purpose the determination of the melting point. Wax mixed with paraffin melts at 48°, while the usual melting point of the wax of commerce lies between 61.5° and 62°. Paraffin has the property of lowering the melting point of beeswax. All kinds of paraffin, from whatever source, have melting points lower than 62°. [There is a paraffin found in Rangoon oil which has a melting point in the neighborhood of 61°, which is only 1° under that of wax, and according to Hofstatter paraffin from ozokerite has occasionally a melting point of 65.5°.] Boghead paraffin melts at 42°; that from turf tar at 49.5°, and that from shale (Autun) melts at 49°.

The fusibility of paraffin is changed by distillation, and the distilled paraffin always shows a lower melting point. If in distilling the distillation be broken off, when only about one-half or two-thirds has come over, the distillate invariably shows a lower melting point than the residue. Payen also recommends the method based on the fact that when an adulterated wax is saponified with alcoholic potash and the soap solution evaporated to dryness, the paraffin can be extracted with ether.

---

[*] Dingl. polyt. Journ., 1861, 160, 334, through Fres. Zeit. f. a. Chem., 1862, 116.

[†] Dingl. polyt. Jour., 1867, 185, 72.

[‡] Wagner's Jahresber., 1863, 670.

[§] Ibid., 1864, 662.

|| Journ. de pharm. et de chim., T. 2, sér. 4, 233, Fres. Zeit. f. a. Chem., 1865, 490.

### DETECTION OF PARAFFIN IN BEESWAX.*

Heat 50 cc. of amyl alcohol on the water bath to about 100° and add 5 grams of wax. When dissolved add 100 cc. of fuming sulphuric acid diluted with half its bulk of water, first heating the mixture to 100°. Heat till no more bubbles are given off, then cool. A cake is formed containing melissin, cerotate, and palmitate of amyl, and paraffin, if contained in the sample. Heat the cake on the water bath with a mixture of 50 cc. sulphuric acid and 25 cc. of Nordhausen acid. In about two hours the decomposition, which goes on quietly, is ended, but the treatment is to be continued until no more gas can be obtained on stirring up with a glass rod, when everything but the paraffin will have been completely carbonized. After cooling squeeze the cake and add it to 50 cc. of amyl alcohol heated to 100. Filter off the residue from the solution thus formed, using a hot filtration device, pour 50 cc. hot amyl alcohol on the filter, allow it to run through, and then add 50 cc. more. Heat the filtrate (150 cc.) to 100° and add 70 cc. of concentrated sulphuric acid to convert the amyl alcohol into amyl sulphuric acid, in which, according to Roard, paraffin is insoluble. If the carbonization of the wax has been complete, two purifications will insure the paraffin being in weighable condition. The author remarks that in using this method the paraffin is not attacked, which is always the case with Landolt's method, in which only fuming sulphuric acid is used.

### DETECTION OF PARAFFIN IN BEESWAX.†

Add to 2 grams of the wax 1.5 grams KHO and about 5 grams water and boil, shaking repeatedly till a complete mixture is obtained. Cool the mass almost to the crystallizing point of the acids and add 6 to 9 grams of petroleum ether, shaking till an emulsion is formed, from which the ether does not separate on standing. Add an excess of neutral lead acetate and stir with a glass rod ; separation of the ether from the other liquid ensues. Separate the two and reëxhaust the aqueous solution twice with fresh portions of ether. The ether extract is evaporated and the residue weighed. Pure yellow wax gives 14 to 16 per cent by this method, which is hardly a recommendation for it. There are also samples of wax which give 57 per cent. To obtain the paraffin pure, and free from the wax constituents, it is preferable to destroy these latter by fuming sulphuric acid.

[In the reference cited (Zeit. f. a. Chem.) the method described is wrongly attributed to Marggraf.]

### ADULTERANTS IN BEESWAX.‡

The paraffin-mixed wax described [in the preceding abstract] which gave 57 per cent to petroleum ether, it seems from Hager's article, was suspicious from its appearance and physical properties. It possessed a slippery, soapy feel, and on kneading showed little viscosity. Pure yellow wax has at 20° a specific gravity not lower than 0.965 nor higher than 0.975. The sample in question, however, did not sink in alcohol of higher specific gravity than 0.896 at 20°. Another trial gave the specific gravity as 0.896. Latterly, according to Hager,§ there has been coming into the trade wax adulterated with Japan wax and with paraffin, not differing greatly in looks from the pure wax. The specific gravity is near that of wax, 0.920 to 0.925. It is not made to imitate high-grade wax. A sample was analyzed by Hager. Three grams were boiled with a solution of 0.500 grams borax in 8 cc. of water.‖ This gave a complete, tolerably white emulsion, not changing in form on cooling. By this the pres-

* Lies-Bodart, Compt. rend, T. 62, 749 ; Jour. de chim. med., T. 2, sér. 5me, 297; Fres. Zeit. f. a. Chem., 1866, 252.

† H. Hager, Polyt. Centralblatt, 1869, 1406 ; Fres. Zeit. f. a. Chem., 1870, 133.

‡ Fres. Zeit. f. a. Chemie, 1870, 419.

§ Pharm. Centralhalle, 11, 209.

‖ Method for Japan wax first published by Hager in Pharm. Centralhalle, 3, 207.

ence of Japan wax, and, from the light specific gravity also of paraffin, was established, but the question of the presence of beeswax remained undecided.   To settle this the author used the difference in behavior of the different ingredients toward sulphuric acid and alcohol.   Japan wax, when added to twenty times its weight of concentrated sulphuric acid, the mixture warmed on the water bath and occasionally shaken, gives a clear dark, brown red solution, remaining fluid on cooling.   If this solution is again heated until it becomes brownish black and foams, and then added drop by drop to four or five times its volume of alcohol, a dark blackish red (often clear) mixture is obtained, depositing nothing on the surface, or at most a few easily disintegrated flocks.   The same test made on pure wax gave a dark brown, foaming, cloudy mixture, not liquid after cooling.   When again heated till foamed strongly, and then mixed with alcohol (thorough mixture may be obtained by pouring from one test tube to another repeatedly), there is formed on cooling a black, crumbly cake on the surface, which when dissolved in petroleum ether leaves a black powdery substance.   The decanted petroleum-ether solution on evaporation gives a black substance which climbs upward on the sides of the dish.   This black substance, heated to 300°, becomes solid again after cooling.   It is smeary and melts under the warmth of the finger.   It is of lower specific gravity than wax.

Paraffin treated with sulphuric acid gives a clear brown mixture, liquid while hot and solidifying on cooling.   When again heated and mixed with alcohol of 90 per cent it gives a solid grayish crystalline cake.   On evaporation it leaves clear gray margins (not black), and gives a residue of paraffin, completely volatile at 300° to 310°, with no bad smell.

The wax tested by the author gave, when treated in the same way, a black but more solid cake than had the yellow wax.   This, in dissolving in petroleum ether, left a black substance.   The decanted solution left, on evaporation, dark gray margins. The residue had a scarcely recognizable structure, and left, after heating in a mercury bath to 300°, a black, solid substance similar to that obtained from wax, of 0.930 specific gravity.   Further heating produced stifling vapors, but complete volatilization was not obtained until nearly 400°.

As by the foregoing tests the Japan wax remained dissolved in the sulphuric acid-alcohol mixture and the black cake indicated wax and paraffin, Hager concluded that the sample contained all three, probably in equal parts.   The color was very likely due to curcuma.

ADULTERATION WITH PARAFFIN.[*]

Beeswax is met with in the Philadelphia market adulterated with paraffin to the extent of 80 per cent.   It is a trifle translucent on the edges and rings somewhat on being struck.   It may also be recognized by a peculiar concavity on the tops of the cakes, beeswax cakes being always either flat or slightly convex, or else having vertical fissures running through the block.   Melting point, 146° F. (63°); specific gravity 0.929.   Beeswax cakes were also met with made of black earthy matter, neatly covered with yellow wax.

DETECTION OF CERESIN IN WAX. [†]

For the detection of ceresin (a mixture of "earth wax" and carnauba wax) M. Buchner recommends the determination of the specific gravity.   He found genuine wax to have a specific gravity of 0.959 for yellow and 0.955 for white wax, while the specific gravity of samples of ceresin examined by him was between 0.858 and 0.901.   Pure wax will sink in alcohol of 0.954 to 0.950, while ceresin will float.

---

* Proc. Amer. Pharm. Assoc., 1875, 498; Amer. Jour. Pharm., Nov., 1874.
† Dingl. polyt. Jour., 231, 272; Fres. Zeit. f. a. Chem., 1880, 240.

## PARAFFIN IN WAX.

A simple method is recommended by Hager* for detection of paraffin. Warm together in a test tube 2 grams of wax with 5 cc solution of sodium carbonate till the former melts, shake energetically and then while still shaking add gradually about 6 cc of benzol. An emulsion is produced. Place the test tube in a water bath heated to about 50° and allow to remain for an hour so that the mixture can stratify, then let it stand for some time at the ordinary temperature. With pure wax after cooling there is a fluid, scarcely cloudy layer of benzol. When this is the case it is not necessary to hunt farther for paraffin. In the presence of the latter the layer is not fluid and is also cloudy or white.

## DETECTION OF CERESIN AND PARAFFIN IN WAX.†

Boil 1 gram wax in a test tube with 1 part potash and 3 parts 90 per cent alcohol for several minutes. Place tube in a hot-water bath and allow to cool gradually. If the wax is pure the liquid remains clear, while in the presence of paraffin and ceresin an oily layer is formed.

## DETECTION OF CERESIN, OZOKERITE, AND PARAFFIN IN BEESWAX.‡

The determination of the specific gravity is an essential point. If the wax contains moisture it should be cut with a sharp knife into thin pieces, and these should be placed in a place the temperature of which does not exceed 30°. After one or two days the pieces are melted and the liquid wax dropped on clean lead foil. The solidified drops are thrown into diluted alcohol (40 cc alcohol, 90 per cent, and 60 cc water) and by addition of water or alcohol made to float in the liquid, any adhering gas bubbles being carefully removed. The specific gravity of beeswax varies between 0.956 and 0.964 (temperature not stated). A specific gravity below 0.954 indicates adulteration.

## EXAMINATION OF BEESWAX FOR PARAFFIN, ETC.§

Adulterations of beeswax with paraffin, ceresin, or ozokerite can be easily determined by subjecting the sample to the influence of heat. In a small porcelain capsule of about 5 cm diameter and 1 to 2 cm depth 2 grams of the wax, previously cut into shavings and dried by exposure to air, are placed and heated over a small flame; when vapors are evolved a beaker of same diameter as capsule and of one-half to two-thirds liter capacity is held over the capsule and completely filled with the vapor, when it is covered and set aside for condensation ; a second beaker is filled in the same manner and then the flame is removed. The condensation of the vapor requires about one hour, and when completed the deposit of one beaker is dissolved in 3 cc chloroform and poured into the second beaker, rinsing the first beaker with a small additional quantity of chloroform. With the chloroform solution of the sublimate the following tests are made: (1) One to 15 cc are evaporated in a test tube and, after adding 4 cc solution of sodium hydrate, heated to the boiling point ; after cooling the paraffin will float upon the colorless lye. (2) Several drops are allowed to evaporate spontaneously upon an object glass and the residue examined microscopically ; paraffin has the appearance of raised stars with curved or serpent-like rays. In this distillation the first portion of the vapor always consists of the paraffin, pure beeswax only producing volatile matter on heating to 300° to 320° C. ; the sublimate from beeswax is always colored, the chloroform solution being decidedly colored ;

---

* Pharm. Centralhalle, 18, 414.

† Peltz. Jour. de pharm. et de chim. (5) 5, 154; Arch. d. Pharm., June, 1882, 471 ; Proc Amer. Pharm. Assoc., 1882, 363.

‡ Hager, Chem. Centralblatt, 1889, 2, 815.

§ H. Hager, Pharm. Centralhalle, 1889, 565.

the soda lye is colored and also turbid; under the microscope the chloroform residue presents a wavy appearance without the stars. For a quantitative determination the results are only approximate; instead of 25 per cent there were obtained in three determinations 22.38, 23, and 23.70 per cent.

### DETECTION OF ROSIN IN BEESWAX.*

Determination of specific gravity of wax samples, in order to detect sophistication with rosin, can be rapidly made by using officinal " Liq. ammon. caustic " (German). In this pure wax floats, while that containing rosin sinks.

### DETECTION OF ROSIN IN BEESWAX. †

Five grams of the wax are introduced into a flask with four or five times as much crude nitric acid (1.32 to 1.33 specific gravity), the mixture heated to boiling and kept at that temperature for a minute. Then an equal bulk of cold water is added, and then ammonia till the fluid smells strongly of it. With pure wax the alkaline fluid is colored only yellow, but in presence of rosin, it is deep brown. A blank with pure wax should be run simultaneously. With mixures containing rosin, the action of the acid is much more vigorous than with pure wax. This method is exactly the same as that accredited to Donath.

### DETECTION OF ROSIN IN BEESWAX. ‡

In the literature are to be found:

(1) Method of Donath (given elsewhere).

(2) Schmidt's method (given elsewhere).

(3) Hager's method:§ Boil a sample of wax with fifteen times its volume of a mixture of 1 part water and 2 parts 90 per cent alcohol. Allow to fully cool, decant, or filter if cloudy, and mix with an equal volume of water. If rosin is present the liquid becomes cloudy or milky. With alcohol of the above strength the rosin can be entirely extracted, while the wax and stearic acid are unaffected.

(4) According to the results of the pharmacy commission ‖ wax containing rosin gives with soda solution a kind of emulsion which is tolerably permanent, remaining for several days. One gram wax should be heated with 10 cc water and 3 grams carbonate of soda to boiling for fifteen minutes.

(5) Sedna's method:¶ Three grams of wax are to be dissolved in ten to twelve times as much chloroform, 200 grams lime water added and the mixture shaken. Pure wax makes an emulsion, but in presence of rosin the fluid becomes yellowish brown and gray-brown flocks of rosin swim on the surface.

On a critical trial these methods gave the following results:

(1) Sedna's method is useless. Gray-brown flocks were not obtained even when working with wax containing 20 per cent of rosin.

(2) Hager's method is right in principle, but the sentence " with this strength of alcohol (1 part water to 2 parts 90 per cent alcohol = 60 per cent alcohol) rosin can be extracted, while wax and stearic acid are unaffected," is erroneous, inasmuch as ' stearic acid if present with rosin always goes into solution, at least partially. This, however, does not interfere with the test, as, under the conditions given, stearic acid separates on the surface while the rosin remains emulsified. Better results may be obtained by using 50 per cent alcohol instead of 60, as the former has no effect on stearic acid. Two per cent of rosin can be easily detected.

(3) The best method for the detection of rosin is that of Donath as modified by Schmidt. The assertion made that 1 per cent of rosin is easily detected in this way is correct.

* Chem. Centralblatt, 1876, 151.

† E. Schmidt, Ber. 10, 837 ; abs. Zeit. f. a. Chem., 1878, 509.

‡ H. Röttger, Chem. Zeit., 1891, 45.

§ Comment. Pharm. Germ., 1873, 436.

‖ Arch. Pharm., 1886, 224, 489.

¶ Sedna, Das Wachs und seine Verwendung, 14.

Rabineaud's † method is based on the varying solubilities of different waxes in ether. One part of wax is placed in 50 parts of ether and the whole shaken occasionally. When the pieces of wax have disappeared and a voluminous precipitate taken their place, this last is filtered into a weighed filter, washed with cold ether, the ether allowed to spontaneously evaporate and the filter and contents weighed. Beeswax should leave 50 per cent residue, vegetable wax (Japan wax) 5 per cent Dullo ‡ says, however: "It is not true that Japan wax (improperly 'plant wax') is always soluble in ether. There are several kinds of wax called ' vegetable wax' in trade, and while it is quite possible that there are kinds nearly completely soluble, still this can seldom be the case. Out of six varieties which I have examined not one has com-. pletely dissolved, but all have conducted themselves like beeswax with ether. Usually a trifle over 50 per cent has dissolved, but not very much more. A sample of wax containing over 50 per cent of Japan wax given me for investigation behaved with ether like pure wax."

Four samples of Japan wax were examined. One left a residue, causing slight opalescence of the solution but unweighable, the other three dissolved completely. As, however, other substances used in adulterating beeswax such as stearin (stearic acid) paraffin, rosin, and tallow (but not ceresin) are soluble in cold ether, this method is of little value as far as the detecting of vegetable wax (Japan wax) alone goes. If, however, the fact of the adulteration by this wax alone were established other-wise, this method could be used for an approximation of its extent, inasmuch as all pure beeswax samples behave nearly alike toward ether.

Dullo says (l. c.): "The best method for the detection of Japan wax is: Boil to-gether 10 grams of the suspected wax in 120 grams water and 1 gram soda (accord-ing to others 1 gram caustic potash) for one minute. If Japan wax is present, there is formed a soap, which on cooling becomes gradually solid or thick. Boiling for so short a time and with such a dilute alkali solution does not saponify beeswax, which separates at the surface of the liquid with its natural hardness and consistence. The soap produced by Japan wax is materially different from that produced from stearin and soda. The latter is slimy and gelatinous while the former is a magma of fine granules. The one can not be mistaken for the other by any one who has seen both. The Japan wax soap requires much alcohol, and must be heated before it will dissolve, and, on cooling, a portion of the wax separates, but the solution of the remainder does not solidify. For solution of sodic stearate, little alcohol and not much heat are required, but the solution ultimately solidifies even when quite di-lute."

According to investigations made, this method is useless, no matter whether soda or caustic potash be used. Pure beeswax heated this way gives a thick milky solu-tion, and no such thing as a solid wax cake separates.

Hager § says "the presence of Japan wax is established when a wax which is mostly soluble in chloroform to a clear solution is heavier than 0.980." Ch. MéncⅠⅠ says, "the detection of Japan wax in beeswax is only possible by means of the specific weight, and is not possible by means of determining either crystallization point or melting point. But reliance on specific gravity alone is unsafe."

In another article Hager¶ says, "the detection of Japan wax is easily accomplished by boiling .300 to .400 gram of wax in a solution of .500 gram borax in 6 to 8 cc water, shaking occasionally. The resultant cloudy solution on standing gradually

* H. Röttger, Chem. Zeit., 1890, 85, 1442, do. 87, 1473.
† Fres. Zeit. f. a. Chem., 1862, 115; Dingl. polyt. Jour., 1862, 163, 80.
‡ Dingl. polyt. Jour., 1864, 172–156.
§ Comm. Pharm. Germ., 1873, 436.
ⅠⅠ Dingl. polyt. Jour., 1874, 214–97.
¶ Chem. Zeit., 1890, 14–606.

separates into a clear liquid and a floating cake of wax, if Japan wax is not present. If it is present, it remains milky, and according to the extent of the adulteration becomes either thick or gelatinizes completely. I have tried this method. By treatment of pure beeswax with borax solution—I invariably used 7 cc of a solution of 5 grams borax in 100 cc. water and .350 gram wax—a solution is gotten which is at first milky, but separates after some hours into a fluid, opalescent at first, afterwards clear, a floating solid film and a layer of emulsion of equal size.

For the detection of foreign admixtures, especially Japan wax tallow, stearic acid, and rosin, the method is generally unreliable, for the separation into layers takes place not so easily as described. Only stearic acid and rosin can be detected in this manner. By a content of only 5 per cent stearic acid, no solid layer is obtained and a thick pasty emulsion is formed, nothing separating at first, though after several days a little clear liquid separates underneath. In the presence of only 5 per cent of rosin the thick emulsion does not separate in two layers and no solid cake is formed.

For the detection of small admixtures of Japan wax the above method, for the reasons given, is unreliable and misleading. In the presence of larger quantities of Japan wax (over 10 per cent) a solid layer separates on the surface, under which is a thick emulsion, separating after several days into a more or less clear liquid. Tallow behaves in a similar way, but the quantity of emulsion is smaller, and the method consequently less applicable.

For my own part I should think it would be better to abandon the use of the borax method, or at least be cautious in judging from its results.

The pharmacy commission of the Deutscher Apotheker Verein* recommends boiling 1 gram wax with 10 cc water and 3 grams sodium carbonate. On cooling, the wax should wholly separate, leaving only an opalescent solution below. Wax containing Japan wax, stearic acid, or rosin, gives an emulsion with the soda, not separating into a cake, and clear fluid, even after several days. Tallow, although not mentioned, behaves in a similar way. In its presence a cake forms, and underneath (with 5 to 10 per cent) a clear fluid, with emulsion in the upper layers. This emulsion is greatest in the presence of rosin; somewhat smaller with Japan wax and stearic acid, and slightest with tallow. From my results with personally-made mixtures, 2 per cent of Japan wax, stearic acid, or rosin, can be detected by the abnormal emulsion. Tallow does not become evident till the proportion reaches 5 per cent.

### MICROSCOPIC EXAMINATION OF WAX. †

By melting together 4 parts of vaseline with 1 part of ceresin, spermaceti, wax, ozokerite, etc., characteristic crystals are formed which may be of use in an analytical way. A drop of the mixture is to be placed on a microscope slide, a cover glass softly pressed down on it, and the whole allowed to stand for twelve hours, at a temperature which must not exceed 5° C. Examine in polarized light with a power of 20 diameters.

### METHODS OF ANALYSIS OF WAX. ‡

The methods of wax examination which have been proposed by different writers were examined by Mr. Morse in some detail. The method of the United States Pharmacopœia is: Boil 1 gram of wax with 40 grams of "solution of soda" (specific gravity 1.18) for half an hour. On cooling, the wax should entirely separate, leaving the fluid clear and HCl should produce no precipitate in a filtered portion (absence of fat, fatty acids, Japan wax, and resin). A mixture of 7 parts of a beeswax known

---

* Arch. Pharm., 1886, 24–490.

† E. Dieterich, Geschäftsber. der Papier und chem. Fabrik in Helfenberg, bei Dresden, 1883; abs. Fres. Zeit. f. a. Chem., 1884, 567.

‡ Thesis of C. M. Morse, Mass. College of Pharmacy, 1888.

to be pure and 3 parts of lard was made and treated as above. No precipitate was obtained with HCl. Mixtures of wax and Japan wax, wax and tallow, and wax and resin also yielded negative results, whence the author concludes the products of saponification are not soluble in alkali as strong as that prescribed. To prove this he boiled 5 grams of common yellow soap with 50 cc. of "solution of soda" (specific gravity 1.18) for half an hour, cooled, filtered and acidified as above. No precipitate was formed.

The Pharmacopœia test for paraffin (also ceresin) reads: "If 5 grams of wax be heated in a flask for fifteen minutes with 25 grams of sulphuric acid to 160° C. and the mixture diluted with water, no solid, wax-like body should separate (absence of paraffin)." In working this method it is found advantageous to use a tall 8-ounce beaker and to gradually heat the mixture on the steam bath, taking great care to stir it at first, as the reaction is liable to become unmanageable.

When the violence of the action is over raise the heat gradually to about 100° (instead of 160°) and keep it there for an hour and a half, stirring occasionally. Allow to cool gradually. When quite cold the paraffin will be found as a layer on top of the semisolid mass. Carefully remove and wash with water to remove as much as possible of the charred wax. Again heat with about 15 grams of sulphuric acid for about an hour. On cooling the paraffin may be again detached, washed, dried, and weighed. Trial with a known mixture containing 20 per cent paraffin gave 125 milligrams paraffin from 1 gram (= 200 milligrams paraffin).

A trial with a known mixture gave good results.

Morse found 20 samples of pure wax to be below 0.96 specific gravity. Prof. Bedford[*] gives another method resting on the use of sodium carbonate in dilute solution. Saponifiable bodies if present in the wax give emulsions. The author prefers the concentrated solution of Donath.

The London Pharmaceutical Journal[†] says: "Resin may be estimated by treatment with cold alcohol." A sample of wax of known purity yielded 6 per cent to cold alcohol, and 5 commercial samples an average of 5.6 per cent. Brodie[‡] and J. F. Babcock[§] say pure wax contains from 4 to 6 per cent of cerolein, which is soluble in cold alcohol. The foregoing test is therefore useless except with large quantities. Another test tried was :[ǁ] Melt 1 gram of wax with 3 drops concentrated sulphuric acid. A red color is produced in the presence of resin. On hardening, the wax assumes a violet shade. Trials with known mixtures of resin and wax gave the reaction, there however being no difference as to intensity of color between samples of wax with 5 and 15 per cent of resin. Pure wax did not give the reaction. Nine of the 87 samples of commercial wax gave the color. The author found that differences of 2 per cent could be distinguished by the depth of color produced. This was true up to 12 per cent resin, above which it required a difference of 4 per cent to make a perceptible change in the tint. The test indicates the presence of 0.25 per cent resin.

By heating 1 gram beeswax with 10 cc. of saturated solution of borax at 80° and cooling the aqueous solution becomes turbid. In presence of Japan wax or stearin a milky solution is produced remaining opaque after cooling. Pure wax gave a turbid solution ; a mixture of wax and Japan wax rendered the solution milky, and on cooling left a light flocculent mass, occupying nearly the whole bulk of the solution ; a mixture with stearin gave a white emulsion ; a mixture with paraffin behaved like pure wax and one with spermaceti gave a milky solution. On diluting each of these tests with 5 volumes of water at 80° and briskly shaking, that containing the stearin mixture was opaque as before, with a light curdy mass on the surface ; that contain-

* Proc. Amer. Pharm. Assoc., 1877, 144.
† September, 1870.
‡ Phil. Trans., 1878 ; Miller., Elements of Chemistry, III ; 263.
§ Proc. Amer. Pharm. Assoc., 1867, 374.
ǁ Amer. Jour. Pharm., 1881, 307.

ing the Japan wax was filled throughout with a thick flocculent substance, and those containing paraffin and spermaceti had the upper third occupied by a light flocculent mass.

Various authorities say that wax is adulterated with sulphur, yellow ocher, calcined bones, starch, tallow, paraffin, stearin, Japan wax, etc. No sampleswere found adulterated with sulphur, yellow ocher, calcined bones, or paraffin. Wheat starch to the amount of 11.4 per cent was found in one instance. It was estimated by treating the wax with a warm 2 per cent solution of sulphuric acid. The wax was then well washed, dried, and reweighed, and the loss calculated as starch. Japan wax was found in 7 samples, stearin in 4, resin in 9, and tallow in 3. The total number of samples examined was 87, of which 24 were adulterated.

The method used for mechanical admixtures was to dissolve the wax in turpentine. Any sediment remaining may be sulphur, yellow ocher, calcined bones or starch.

Wax is separated by boiling alcohol into three portions—myricin, which is insoluble; cerin, which crystallizes out on cooling, while the cerolein remains dissolved. J. F. Babcock* gives the proportions as myricin 30 per cent, cerin 65 per cent, and cerolein 5 per cent. According to Bloxam the proportion is, myricin about one-third, cerin nearly two-thirds, and cerolein about 4 per cent.

Ten grams of pure wax were boiled with alcohol. The larger portion settled to the bottom. The clear liquid was poured off, and the treatment repeated several times. On cooling, the alcohol white feathery crystals were deposited. These were filtered off and the filtrate evaporated to dryness.

The insoluble portion represented 65 per cent; that portion soluble in hot alcohol but not in cold, 29.50 per cent, and the portion soluble at all temperatures, 5.90 per cent. Total, 100.4.

Myricin fuses at 63°. It is insoluble in alcohol, soluble in warm chloroform, benzine, and ether. From the two latter solutions it mostly separates on cooling in light, feathery crystals, fusing at 67°. That portion soluble in cold ether is a bright lemon-yellow colored solid, fusing at 56°. Brodie confines the name myricin to the portion insoluble in cold ether.

Two grams of myricin fused with 1 gram caustic potassa become fluid, but harden on cooling. This melt, dissolved in water and decomposed with hydrochloric acid, gives a precipitate. This precipitate, when boiled with lime water, forms insoluble palmitate of calcium, and another wax-like body is liberated.

Brodie gives this body the name of melissylic alcohol, and the formula, $C_{60}$ $H_{61}$ O, HO. Hence, myricin is a compound ether—palmitate of melissyl—$C_{92}$ $H_{92}$ $O_4$ $=C_{60}$ $H_{61}$ O, $C_{32}$ $H_{31}$ $O_3$.

Others call this body melissin. It fuses at 104°, is of a light-yellow color, insoluble in alcohol and ether. According to Brodie, when melissylic alcohol is distilled with hydrate of potassa, it is decomposed, hydrogen is evolved and melissate of potassium is formed, the reaction being the same as that by which acetate of potassium is produced when ordinary alcohol is treated in a similar manner.

Cerin or cerotic acid as first separated from boiling alcohol fuses at 53°, but by repeated crystallization it may be raised to 70° C. The proportion varies in different samples, but the average is about 28.6 per cent.

Brodie finds it to be 22 per cent, and in one sample from Ceylon it was entirely wanting.

In order to produce the acid in a pure state, dissolve the cerin in boiling alcohol and add a boiling alcoholic solution of acetate of lead, by which a heavy, white precipitate of cerotate of lead is produced. This is filtered while still hot, and the precipitate boiled in strong alcohol and filtered. The precipitate was again boiled in ether and filtered. The filtrate from the alcoholic washing, on evaporating spontaneously, left a small amount of a waxlike body resembling myricin, but fusing at 61°. The lead salt was decomposed by strong acetic acid, and the body which

---

* Proc. Amer. Pharm. Assoc., 1867, 374.

separated was well washed with boiling water, dissolved in absolute alcohol, and filtered. On cooling, crystals of pure cerin separated. These had a fusing point of 67° C. (Brodie says 78° C.), and were soluble in six parts of boiling alcohol. Brodie's analysis with chromate of lead gives for the formula, $C_{54}H_{54}O_4=$carbon, 78.98 per cent; hydrogen, 13.12 per cent; oxygen, 7.90 per cent. Cerotic ether can be made by dissolving the acid in absolute alcohol and passing hydrochloric acid gas through the solution. It has the appearance of a soft wax, and fuses at 59° C. Cerolein, that portion which is soluble in cold alcohol, is a soft, greasy body, soluble in ether, chloroform, and benzine; fuses at 81.5° C., renders the alcoholic solution alkaline, and is not easily saponified. It has a strong balsamic odor, and seems to contain the odoriferous portion of the wax.

*Specific gravity.*—This is obtained by diluting alcohol until a drop of the wax, previously melted and cooled on glass, would float indifferently in it. By taking the specific gravity of the alcohol that of the wax was found. The average gravity of five samples of pure wax was 0.9547. Melting point was determined by several methods: First, by placing a drop previously melted and cooled on glass or any smooth surface on a volume of mercury and gradually heating by means of a steam or water bath; the instant the wax was seen to liquefy the temperature indicated by a thermometer previously placed in the mercury was noted. Second, by means of a thin glass tube, drawn out to a small opening, the finger was placed over the large end and the small end dipped just below the surface of the melted wax, removed, and the thin cap allowed to thoroughly cool. The tube was then partially filled with water, say from 1 to 3 cc, according to the diameter and size of the lower opening. This tube thus prepared was fastened to a thermometer by means of two rubber bands, so that the cap of wax and the thermometer bulb were on the same level. This was placed in a water bath and gradually raised to the temperature. Care was taken to have the water level of the tube above that of the bath (but not so much above that the pressure would break the cap of wax) until it was thoroughly fused. It was found that a tube one-quarter inch in diameter gave the best results when 2.5 cc. of water were placed in it and the water level kept 1.5 inches above that in the bath. When the water in the tube was seen to lower the thermometer was read. A third method was by means of a thin tube drawn out to a long point and filled with melted wax. When cold the point was broken off and the tube fastened to a thermometer, the same as in the previous case. The whole was so placed in cold water that the wax was about an inch below the surface. The water was now gradually heated until the pressure of the water forced the wax up in the tube. This was the time to read the thermometer. The last method was to dip a thermometer bulb in melted wax and remove, care being taken that the thermometer bulb should not be too cold, else too thick a coating would be formed. After this thin film of wax was thoroughly cooled, the thermometer was suspended in water and gradually heated until the wax became transparent and liquid and then the thermometer read.

The average fusing point of pure wax (5 samples) was found by these four methods to be 62.6° C.

| No. | First method. | Second method. | Third method. | Fourth method. |
|---|---|---|---|---|
| 1...... | 60 | 62.5 | 63 | 62 |
| 2...... | 62 | 63 | 63.5 | 63 |
| 3...... | 61 | 63 | 63.5 | 62.5 |
| 4...... | 63 | 63 | 63.5 | 62.5 |
| 5...... | 62.5 | 63 | 63 | 62.5 |

METHOD FOR QUALITATIVE EXAMINATION FOR VARIOUS WAXES. *

Heat the sample with ten times its volume of chloroform to boiling and, when completely dissolved, cool.

1. The chloroform solution remains clear after cooling.

A. Ether dissolves original wax completely.

(a) Alcohol solution of ferric chloride gives with the alcoholic solution of the wax a precipitate insoluble on heating. Wax from *Myrica quercifolia*.

(b) Ferric chloride colors the alcoholic solution black. Wax from an undetermined species of *Myrica*.

(o) Ferric chloride colors brownish, but gives no precipitate. Wax from *Myrica cerifera*; wax from Orizaba.

B. Ether dissolves only a part.

A sample is boiled with ten parts of caustic potash till saponification takes place and the soap is heated with 100 parts of water.

(a) The soap is completely soluble. Japan wax.

(b) The soap is partly soluble; beeswax. African beeswax.

2. The chloroform solution becomes cloudy on cooling.

A. Alcoholic solution of lead acetate gives with the alcoholic wax solution a cloudiness after a few minutes standing. Wax from stick lac.

B. Alcoholic solution of lead acetate gives no cloudiness.

(a) The ether solution of the wax becomes cloudy on the addition of an equal volume of alcohol. Brazil and Carnauba wax.

(b) The ether solution remains clear. Bahia wax.

RESULTS OBTAINED BY APPLYING QUALITATIVE TESTS TO PURE BEESWAX, OTHER WAXES, AND COMB FOUNDATION IN THE DEPARTMENT LABORATORY.

(1) Boil 1 gram of the wax with 10 cc. of water and 3 grams of $Na_2CO_3$. On cooling a pure wax should separate as a cake, leaving an opalescent solution below. Japan wax, stearic acid, and rosin give an emulsion and no cake.

Foundation comb, No. 8506, gave a cake of wax and soap and a translucent solution. No. 8507 gave a cake of wax and soap underlaid by a slightly milky solution. A Japan wax sample, No. 8543, gave a cake of soap and a milky solution. Stearic acid gave a layer of soap above an opalescent solution containing flocks of fine crystals. Rosin gave a cake of soap and a yellow underlying liquid.

(2) Pure beeswax gives, with a saturated solution of borax at 80°, a turbid aqueous solution. Japan wax and stearic acid, emulsions.

Foundation sample, No. 8506, gave a slightly turbid yellow solution. No. 8507, also a foundation, gave a slightly turbid but pale solution. A Japan wax gave an emulsion which, after standing forty-eight hours, only partially cleared up. Stearic acid gave a white emulsion, solid on cooling. Rosin gave a turbid yellow solution much like wax.

(3) Treat as above, but after saponification keep moderately warm for some hours to allow to stratify.

Foundation No. 8493 gave a soap and a slightly turbid solution. Foundation No. 8504 behaved similarly, but the solution was yellow. Foundation No. 8509A gave a cream-colored emulsion. No. 8509B gave a soap and a turbid solution. No. 8509C gave a soap and a clear yellow solution. Stearic acid gave a thick milky mass. Japan wax (No. 8543) gave a milky solution, nearly translucent, with a layer of soap on the surface. Another Japan wax (No. 8608) gave a milky or creamy mass of nearly uniform consistency. Tallow gave a cake and a slightly milky fluid, almost transparent. No. 8493, a foundation, gave a soap layer and a slightly turbid solution. No. 8505

* E. Hirschsohn, Phar. Jour. Trans., Mar. 28, 1880, 749; Proc. Amer. Pharm. Assoc., 1880, 291.

gave a soap layer and a yellow, turbid solution. No. 8508A gave a soap layer and a very turbid solution, only faintly translucent. No. 8509A gave a soap layer and a turbid mass which separated after twenty-four hours, showing a small portion of liquid at bottom, opaque or only slightly translucent. No. 8495 gave a cake and a turbid aqueous solution. No. 8499 behaved similarly, but the solution was more transparent. Nos. 8508B, 8508C, and 8508D gave a cake and an opaque yellow solution. Carnauba wax samples, Nos. 8546 and 8554, gave a cake and a perfectly clear solution.

(4) Boil a portion of wax with KOH solution and then add NaCl. Japan wax gives a soap separating in fine grains; rosin or fatty substances give a flocculent soap.

No. 8506 gave a soap that was slightly granular. Solution below was colored yellow and was translucent. A Japan wax (No. 8543) gave a granular soap and aqueous solution; on cooling set into a translucent jelly. Stearic acid gave a granular cake of soap and a clear aqueous solution. Rosin gave a sticky soap, smelling of rosin, and a clear brown solution.

(4) Heat portion of wax until fumes are given off. Collect the fumes in a flask and allow to condense. Dissolve in chloroform and evaporate the solution. Saponify the residue with caustic soda. Pure wax should give a colored solution. Paraffin gives a colorless solution, and on cooling separates on the surface as a cake. Another portion of the chloroform solution should be evaporated on a microscope slide and the residue examined. Wax gives a film; paraffin star-shaped crystals.

On heating, No. 8506 gave an odor of burning tallow. On saponifying the condensed fumes, a mass of flocks floating in a clear yellow solution was obtained. Some light-colored waxy matter floated on the surface. The microscopical test gave nothing definite. A paraffin sample (No. 8553) gave an odor of burning fat, and after saponification a brown waxy cake formed on the surface of the solution, not differing greatly from that formed with No. 8506. Microscopical test not satisfactory. A foundation, No. 8493, also gave an odor of burning fat. On saponifying the fumes and cooling, a few flocks appeared near the surface. Solution was colorless. Under the microscope the film showed lines running in every direction and dividing it into small portions. No. 8547, another paraffin, likewise gave the odor of burning fat. On saponification there was formed a brown cake on the surface. The solution was colorless. Under the microscope the film showed only a few irregular disks, but no star-shaped bodies.

(5) Boil sample fifteen minutes with nitric acid, dilute with water, and add excess of ammonia. In presence of rosin this procedure gives a liquid colored reddish brown or brownish red.

A sample of rosin tested gave a fine red color. No. 8506 gave a yellow solution. No. 8493 gave a faint red brown. Nos. 8497 and 8499 gave pale yellow solutions. Nos. 8508A and 8508B gave faintly red-brown solutions. No. 8508C also gave a reddish solution, but the color was fainter even than the preceding. No. 8509A gave a distinctly reddish brown solution, and 8509C one which was a little lighter in hue. To a light colored foundation 5 per cent of rosin were added and the mixture tested like the foregoing. The resulting solution was much darker in color than was given by any of the foundation samples tested. A carnauba wax (No. 8554) gave a brown solution and another (No. 8552) one a brownish yellow. The wax left floating on the surface after applying the method to the above two samples, on washing with hot water and cooling, in both cases gave lemon-yellow cakes having a faint odor of hydrocyanic acid. A ceresin sample (No. 6544) gave a yellow solution.

(6) Boil 10 grams of wax in 120 grams water containing 1 gram sodium carbonate, for one minute. Japan wax is saponified, but pure beeswax is not, by so weak an alkali in so short a time. It is sometimes directed to use one gram of caustic potash instead of the soda.

No. 8493 gave a pale yellow emulsion which did not separate on two hours standing. Nos. 8493, 8506, and 8509A behaved similarly. A Japan wax (No. 8608) gave a white emulsion. No. 8506, tested with the caustic potash solution, gave a pale yellow emulsion, and the Japan wax a thicker white one.

(7) *Paraffin.*—Warm 2 grams wax with soda solution, shake and add 6 cc. of benzol. Heat to 50° for an hour and then let cool. Pure wax gives a fluid layer of benzol, paraffin a cloudy or white benzol layer.

No. 8506 gave a layer of soap which mixed with the benzol layer, rendering it opaque; color, a dirty yellow. A paraffin (No. 8547) gave a clear layer of benzol, but on standing over night crystals appeared in it. A mixture of the above two samples, containing about 25 per cent of paraffin, gave a reaction similar to that of the foundation alone. The benzol solution was colored opaque, and of course no paraffin crystals could be seen.

(8) *Rosin.*—Melt 1 gram wax with three or four drops of concentrated sulphuric acid. Rosin gives a red color, changing to violet.

This color was given on heating a little rosin with the acid, but the mixture soon became so dark that the color could not be distinguished. The same trouble was encountered when working with a sample of wax. It was soon charred, and no distinctive color was observed.

## QUANTITATIVE EXAMINATION OF WAXES.

### METHOD FOR DETERMINING PARAFFIN IN WAX.[*]

The lately proposed method of Lies-Bodart,[†] based on the determination of the hydrocarbon ($C_{27}H_{54}$) contained in the wax, appears unreliable, because of the varying composition of beeswax and because of the uncertainty of the true composition of beeswax. The method of Payen,[‡] based on the determination of the melting points, is useful in confirming or disproving the genuineness of any particular sample of wax, but it gives no idea as to the amount of added paraffin, as the different paraffins possess very different melting points and the influence of the several kinds of mixtures with wax is not known. Of much greater importance, at least it so seems to me, is the determination of the specific gravity of such a mixture, as normal wax has a constant specific gravity and the specific gravity of paraffins of different origin vary only within narrow limits; and, finally, the specific gravities of paraffin and wax lie tolerably far apart. The following determinations were made with samples which were first melted for some time, to free them from adhering water, and after cooling were kneaded and pressed to free them from all water bubbles. The fluid in which the specific gravity was taken was a mixture of alcohol and water, as investigation had shown that such a mixture possessed practically no solvent effect on paraffin during the time of the experiment. Determinations of the specific gravities of different samples of beeswax, indisputably genuine in origin' and partly personally melted from the comb, gave the following numbers:

|  |  |  |  |
|---|---|---|---|
| Yellow wax No. 1 | .968 | White wax No. 1 | .968 |
| do. No. 2 | .965 | do. No. 2 | .966 |
|  |  | do. No. 3 | .969 |

For the following experiments, white wax (sample number 3) was used. Determinations of the specific gravities of the different samples of paraffin gave the following: Paraffin from Saxon brown coal, hard variety, 0.875, and soft variety, 0.871. Paraffin from Boghead coal, 0.873; paraffin from petroleum (so-called Belmoutin) from the London paraffin factory, 0.873; paraffin from Rangoon tar, (a) 0.869; (b) 0.870; paraffin from a German shale, (a) 0.877; (b) 0.853; (c) 0.876; paraffin from tar of red birch wood (made in the year 1832 and very likely by the discoverer of paraffin, Reichenbach himself), 0.874.

I was not able to note experiments made with paraffin made from turf of Derbyshire, devil's dung, Galician ozokerite or neftgil, nor could I find statements as to their

[*] R. Wagner, Fres. Zeit. f. a. Chem., 1866, 279.

[†] Compt. rend 62, 749; Fres. Zeit f. a. Chem., 1866, 252.

[‡] Fres. Zeit. f. a. Chem, 4, 490.

specific gravity in the literature at my command. According to Malaguti,* ozokerite consists of a mixture of two bodies similar to paraffin, one of which has a specific gravity of 0.957 and melts at 90°, while the other constituent, with a specific gravity of 0.945, melts in the neighborhood of 75°. Preliminary determination showed that the specific gravity of wax (0.965 to 0.969) and commercial paraffin (0.869 to 0.877) lie wide enough apart to enable quantitative determinations to be made on mixtures from the specific gravity. Pure, that is to say, paraffin-free beeswax should sink in alcohol of 0.961 specific gravity (33 per cent by volume Tralles or 15.8° Baumé, or 27.27 per cent by weight). If it floats in alcohol of this strength it is very likely adulterated with paraffin.

In the manufacture of candles, when using solid fat acids, paraffin up to 20 per cent is always added, and on the other hand, when manufacturing paraffin candles, stearic acid is always added. As, according to the text-books, the specific gravity of pure stearic acid is 0.956, it occurred to me that candles could be investigated by determination of specific gravity, but investigation has shown the contrary. The reason for this is that under the name stearic acid, in the technical sense, is not found the pure acid, but a mixture of various bodies, different in composition and physical properties according to the source of the original fat. This mass consists in part of neutral bodies. Stearic acid made from tallow by lime gave the following specific gravity :

No. 1 : 0.954      No. 2 : 0.962      No. 3 : 0.958

With other samples, made by means of sulphuric acid, subsequent determinations gave 0.892.

DETERMINATION OF THE SPECIFIC GRAVITY OF WAXES, ETC.†

Place in an accurately marked 50 cc. flask a weighed rod of the wax, about 1 to 1.5 cm long by 0.5 cm diameter, and allow water to flow into the flask from a burette till the water level reaches the mark. Fifty cc minus the burette reading represent the volume occupied by the wax. The rod should be made to lie flat on the bottom of the flask, so that the incoming water will force its ends against the sides and prevent the end from rising above the mark.

DETERMINATION OF PARAFFIN IN BEESWAX.‡

A wax mixed with paraffin is found in the trade under the name of "purified wax." The following method was tried on some of this product: 100 grams were heated with 30 grams concentrated sulphuric acid to 177° for between fifteen and twenty minutes, 100 cc. of water then added, and the whole allowed to cool. On the surface was now found a layer of paraffin, which weighed 80 grams. On repeating the experiment with a mixture of 20 parts of wax and 80 parts of paraffin, the same result was obtained. Paraffin alone treated in the same way remained unaltered. Carbonized particles adhering to the paraffin can be detached by remelting. Paraffin on cooling contracts so strongly that the surface becomes concave ; wax retains its horizontal surface.

Dieterich § gives a table of the specific gravity of various mixtures of wax and paraffin.

Sedua‖ tests wax for paraffin by shaving off thin layers of wax, covering them with twenty times their weight of ether, and allowing them to stand half a day. Paraffin dissolves, but very little wax goes into solution. The ether is decanted, evaporated, and the residue weighed. Five-sixths of the weight is calculated as paraffin.

* Annal. de chim et de phys., 4, 63, 390.

† A. Gawalowski, Oel u. Fettindustrie ; Chem. Centralblatt, 1890, 11, 502.

‡ A. W. Miller in Zeit. des österr. Apoth. Vereins, 1875, p. 49 ; abs. Fres. Zeit. f. a. Chem., 1875, 200.

§ Wagner's Jahresber, 1882, 1028.

‖ Das Wachs und seine technische Verwendung, 15.

## SPECIFIC GRAVITY OF PARAFFIN.*

According to E. Sauerlandt,† the specific gravity of paraffin varies between the limits of 0.869 and 0.943. Ozokerite paraffin of 56°C. crystallizing point has a specific gravity of 0.912; that of 61°C., one of 0.922; that of 67°C., one of 0.927; that of 72°C., one of 0.935; that of 76°C., one of 0.939; that of 82°C., one of 0.943. As the specific gravity of paraffin of different solidifying points is different, ozokerite and the ceresin prepared from it must also exhibit this characteristic.

### DETERMINATION OF CARNAUBA WAX. ‡

E. Valenta has investigated the melting point of mixtures of carnauba wax with stearic acid, mineral wax, and paraffin. He employed for this purpose samples having the following fusing points:

|  | °C. |
|---|---|
| Carnauba wax | 85.0 |
| Stearic acid, commercial | 58.5 |
| Mineral wax | 72.7 |
| Paraffin | 60.1 |

Mixtures were made having the following compositions and melting points:

| | Carnauba wax. | Melting point.[1] |
|---|---|---|
| Stearin: | | °C. |
| 95 | 5 | 69.75 |
| 90 | 10 | 73.75 |
| 85 | 15 | 74.55 |
| 80 | 20 | 75.20 |
| 75 | 25 | 75.80 |
| Mineral wax: | | |
| 95 | 5 | 79.10 |
| 90 | 10 | 80.56 |
| 85 | 15 | 81.60 |
| 80 | 20 | 82.53 |
| 75 | 25 | 82.95 |
| Paraffin: | | |
| 95 | 5 | 73.90 |
| 90 | 10 | 79.20 |
| 85 | 15 | 81.10 |
| 80 | 20 | 81.50 |
| 75 | 25 | 81.70 |

[1] Average of five determinations.

An addition of 5 per cent of carnauba wax raises the melting points of the other bodies mentioned quite appreciably, though increasing additions do not give a proportional increment. Mixtures made with it show greater luster and hardness than those without it. The sample of carnauba wax employed was yellowish gray, brittle, had a specific gravity of 0.9983 at 15° C., and left 0.43 per cent reddish ash, containing $Fe_2O_3$, $Al_2O_3$, CaO, $K_2O$, $SiO_2$, and slight quantities of $CO_2$. One gram required for saponification 94.5 to 95.0 milligrams of potash; stearic acid required 197.0; beeswax, 100.4; Japan wax, 122.0; paraffin and ceresin, none.

### ACETYL NUMBER IN WAXES. §

This method gives very good results in wax analyses. When a wax is saponified and the soap decomposed with hydrochloric acid, a mixture of fatty acids and higher

---

* Fres. Zeit. f. a. Chem., 1884, 256.

† Chem. Zeit. 7, 388.

‡ Fres. Zeit. f. a. Chem., 1884, 257; Zeit. f. landw. Gew. durch Pharm. Centralhalle, 24, 417.

§ Fres. Zeit. f. a. Chem., 1888, 528.

fat alcohols separates. If this mixture is acetylized the alcohols are converted into their acetic ethers, invariably giving a high acetyl number, differing for different waxes.

## BECKER'S METHOD.

Becker[*] recommends a method based on that of Koettstorfer for butter. About 2 grams of wax, which has been melted and filtered, are introduced into a flask (about 150 cc), covered with 25 cc of normal alcoholic potash. Close the flask with a rubber stopper bearing a 2-bulb safety tube containing enough mercury in its bend to make the saponification take place under a pressure equivalent to a column of 5 cm. This amount of pressure insures saponification after half an hour's heating on the water bath. When the wax melts it is best to swing the flask occasionally to insure the mixing of its contents. After saponification add 50 cc alcohol, some phenolphtalein and titrate with half normal HCl. If the contents of the flask begin to get solid before the end of the titration, momentary setting on the water bath will clear the solution. Investigation of 6 samples guaranteed pure gave figures representing the consumption of between 97 and 107 milligrams of potash for 1 gram of wax. Of the common adulterants paraffin and ceresin (except of course when containing carnauba wax) absorb no potash; 1 gram rosin equals 194.3 milligrams of potash; 1 gram Japan wax, 222.4; 1 gram carnauba wax, 93.1; 1 gram spermaceti, 108.1 milligrams; 1 gram tallow, 196.5.

### ANALYSIS OF BEESWAX—YELLOW.[†]

Hehner has attempted to apply to the examination of wax the well-known method of Koettstorfer for fats. A difficulty presents itself in its use, however, arising from the extraordinarily high molecular weights of both cerotic acid and myricin, respectively, 410 and 676. One cc, therefore, of normal alkali would equal 410 mg of cerotic acid and 676 mg of myricin, and titrations have to be made with the most extreme care, a difficulty enhanced by the dark solutions yielded by some foreign waxes. Another obstacle was found in the difficulty with which myricin saponifies. The most serious trouble of all, however, was the procuring of a wax which could be certified to as genuine. It would naturally be imagined that if honeycomb were purchased as it comes out of the hive the wax would be genuine, without doubt. But this is not so. Very many bee-keepers suspend in the hives sheets of wax stamped on both sides with hexagons, to induce the bees to utilize the hexagonal ridges as "foundations" for the cells, thus insuring the regularity of the comb. These foundations are obtained from certain dealers, some of whom warrant them to be composed of genuine wax. I have no doubt that genuine wax foundations are to be had, but the two samples which I obtained were mixtures, in spite of the warranty, as will be seen from results stated further on. Pure wax does not seem to be quite so plastic as certain mixtures. This may be one reason for their compound nature, but I suspect that since wax is dear and fats and paraffin are cheap, the chief inducement is not of an entirely unselfish character. As for 20 pounds of honey a hive only yields 1 pound of wax it is also intelligible why some bee-keepers are very liberal with the supply of foundation to the bees. Although generally a comb into which foundation has entered can be distinguished from the more irregular, pure comb, and although I have taken all possible care to exclude suspicious samples, I am not at all certain that the whole of the samples which I believed to be unmixed were absolutely pure and free from admixture. The method of analysis finally adopted was: First, make up alcoholic potash, using spirit rectified over potash of such a strength that 1 cc equals 0.3 to 0.4 cc normal acid. Weigh 3 to 5 grams of wax, transfer to a flask holding about 400 cc and heat on the water bath with 50 cc alcohol prepared as above. Add plenty of phenolphtalein solution and titrate with the alcoholic potash. Next run in

---

[*] Corr. Bl. Ver. analyt. Chem., 2, 57; through Fres. Zeit. f. a. Chem., 1880, 240.
[†] Otto Hehner, Analyst, 1883, 16.

an excess of the alkali, 50 cc being a convenient quantity. The whole is then briskly boiled under a reflux condenser for an hour, shaking occasionally. The solution should be clear, or nearly so. Titrate back the excess of alkali with standard acid, keeping the liquid boiling. From the data thus obtained, the free acid, calculated as cerotic acid, and the saponifiable substance—calculated as myricin—are obtained. The following results were obtained:

| No. | Cerotic acid. | Myricin. | Sum. | Description of sample. |
|---|---|---|---|---|
| | Per cent. | Per cent. | | |
| 1 | 14.35 | 88.55 | 102.90 | Hertfordshire wax. |
| 2 | 14.86 | 85.95 | 100.81 | Do. |
| 3 | 14.79 | 87.76 | 102.55 | |
| 4 | 13.22 | 86.02 | 99.24 | Surrey wax; not quite pure. |
| 5 | 13.56 | 88.16 | 101.72 | Lincolnshire wax. |
| 6 | 14.64 | 87.10 | 101.74 | Buckingham. |
| 7 | 15.71 | 89.02 | 104.73 | Do. |
| 8 | 15.02 | 88.83 | 103.85 | Hertfordshire. |
| 9 | 14.96 | 89.87 | 104.83 | New Forest. |
| 10 | 15.49 | 92.08 | 107.57 | Lincoln ; made from comb containing foundation. |

The following samples were obtained from dealers:

| No. | Cerotic acid. | Myricin. | Sum. | Description of sample. |
|---|---|---|---|---|
| | Per cent. | Per cent. | | |
| 11 | 14.64 | 87.49 | 102.13 | |
| 12 | 15.11 | 89.05 | 104.16 | |
| 13 | 13.12 | 88.66 | 101.78 | |
| 14 | 15.91 | 87.21 | 103.12 | |
| 15 | 12.15 | 89.58 | 101.73 | |
| 16 | 13.76 | 87.70 | 101.46 | |
| 17 | 13.49 | 87.76 | 101.25 | |
| 18 | 14.28 | 86.73 | 101.01 | |

The eighteen samples, the results of which are given above, are all English. The following are foreign waxes, obtained direct from the importers:

| No. | Cerotic acid. | Myricin. | Sum. | Description of sample. |
|---|---|---|---|---|
| | Per cent. | Per cent. | | |
| 19 | 15.16 | 88.09 | 103.25 | United States; brown wax. |
| 21 | 13.56 | 88.11 | 101.67 | Madagascar. |
| 22 | 13.04 | 88.28 | 101.32 | Mauritius; brown wax. |
| 23 | 12.17 | 95.68 | 107.85 | Mauritius; dark brown. |
| 24 | 13.72 | 96.02 | 109.73 | Do. |
| 25 | 13.74 | 95.04 | 108.78 | Mauritius. |
| 26 | 13.44 | 92.67 | 106.11 | Mauritius; light brown. |
| 27 | 13.49 | 85.12 | 98.61 | Jamaica; bright yellow. |
| 28 | 14.30 | 85.78 | 100.08 | Do. |
| 29 | 13.44 | 89.00 | 102.44 | Mogadore. |
| 30 | 13.93 | 102.44 | 116.37 | Do. |
| 31 | 13.02 | 117.86 | 130.88 | Mogadore; very soft, acrid, and hot. |
| 32 | 16.55 | 83.73 | 100.28 | Gambia; dark brown. |
| 33 | 13.92 | 89.24 | 103.16 | Melbourne; gray wax. |
| 34 | 13.18 | 87.47 | 100.65 | Melbourne; pale yellow. |
| 35 | 13.06 | 92.79 | 105.78 | Sydney; gray wax. |
| 36 | 13.16 | 88.62 | 101.78 | Sydney; pale yellow. |

The foregoing results may be conveniently examined in two divisions: samples 1 to 18 comprising samples from various English sources, and 19 to 35, exotic productions.

Excluding sample No. 4, fused from the comb, on account of the sample having been palpably impure with suspended matters which could not be separated, the size of sample being too small; and sample 10 as having been made from comb containing foundation, it is at once seen that the figures fluctuated only between narrow limits. Only one of the samples contained less than 13 per cent of free acid calculated as cerotic, 4 between 13 and 14, 7 between 14 and 15, and 4 between 15 and 16, the average amount being 14.40 per cent. The saponifiable matter, calculated as myricin, was in one case less than 86, in one between 86 and 87, in 6 between 87 and 88, in 4 between 88 and 89, and in 4 between 89 and 89.6, the average being 88.09 per cent. In all cases is the sum of myricin plus cerotic acid somewhat higher than 100, it reaching on the average 102.49. While these figures prove conclusively that English beeswax consists almost completely of cerotic acid and myricin, they also corroborate the existence of a substance of low molecular weight in wax in small quantity. It is probably cerolein. It was thought possible that during the prolonged boiling of the alcoholic potash solution, some of the alkali might be neutralized by the silica of the glass, the quantity destroyed of course counting in the analysis as myricin, and thus bringing the total above 100. But this is not the case, for in a blank experiment not the slightest diminution of strength could be observed after 50 cc of alcoholic potash had been kept briskly boiling for one hour. It must be considered as established by these results that the composition of wax is remarkable for its constancy. In English wax the ratio of cerotic acid to myricin is 1: 6.117. In the foreign samples the fluctuations are much more extensive, but due allowance should be made for the fact that they were derived from a great variety of different insects, yet the discrepancies are more likely due to the men who collected and put the samples into marketable form, than to the insects that produced them. For this belief testifies the fact that while some of the samples of Mogador and Mauritius wax corresponded closely to the English samples, others showed a great increase in the saponifiable matters calculated as myricine. The soft, smeary Mogadores were obviously mixed with some fat; some of the Mauritius specimens appeared burnt in process of melting out of the comb. And lastly, it is not a little significant that the price of the normal samples is considerably above that of the specimens which gave excessive totals.

### SUBSTANCES USED FOR ADULTERATING.

These may be grouped in three classes: (1) acid substances; (2) neutral but saponifiable substances; and (3) matters indifferent to potash.

The first class embraces the solid fatty acids, mainly palmitic and stearic, and the acids which constitute resin, particularly sylvic acid. The second class is made of neutral solid glycerides—viz, stearin and palmitin—of Japan wax, spermaceti, and carnauba wax. The only representative of the third division for all practical purposes is paraffin. Solid alcohols of high molecular weight, such as cetylic or myricylic, also belong to this class, but being unmarketable they need not be taken into account.

Both compounds constituting the wax possess a higher equivalent weight than any other substances belonging to the fatty series occurring in nature, excepting a fatty acid recently discovered by Mr. Kingzett in cacao butter.

A substance of the first class, say stearic acid, would inordinately increase the apparent per cent of cerotic acid (1 per cent of stearic acid possesses the neutralizing power of 1.443 per cent of cerotic) and depress the myricin. One part of palmitic acid corresponds to 1.601 of cerotic and 1 part of resin to 1.246. The two fatty acids, stearic and palmitic, never being found alone, but always mixed and in variable ratio, an average between the two in approximating to the per cent of added fatty acids, viz, 1.518, should be taken.

By addition of a body belonging to the second class, saponifiable substances, the apparent amount of myricin is increased and that of cerotic acid decreased. Averaging the molecular weights of tri-palmitin and tri-stearin, one part of added fat will correspond to 2.391 parts of myricin. Japan wax is stated to consist entirely of palmitin. A pure sample gave free acid corresponding to 6.21 per cent palmitic acid and a saponification number corresponding to 94.12 per cent palmitin, total 100.33. Another somewhat yellow sample gave figures representing 11.93 and 91.38, and a total of 103.31 per cent. An addition of Japan wax to fat would therefore amount to addition of both free fatty acid and fat, and in consequence to an apparent increase in both myricin and cerotic acid. Spermaceti is too high priced to be used in adulterating wax, but, on the other hand, wax is often added in making sperm candles. Several samples tried were found to be free from free acid. They gave saponification numbers corresponding on the average to 109.68 per cent of cetyl palmitate. Carnauba wax has been little studied. One specimen was examined which showed an acidity equal to 6.09 per cent of cerotic acid and a saponification number corresponding to 92.58 per cent myricin, total 98.67. With alcoholic potash, therefore, carnauba wax closely corresponds to beeswax. Its physical properties are, however, so different and remarkable that it could hardly be largely used as an adulterant, except possibly in hardening and giving consistence to wax containing fats. The foregoing substances saponify with different degrees of rapidity. Fat, including Japan wax, breaks up very readily; next comes spermaceti; carnauba wax much more slowly, its melting point being higher than the boiling point of alcohol. Ordinary wax is the most tenacious of all.

Of the third class, represented by paraffin, little need be said. An addition of paraffin decreases both the myricin and cerotic acid, their proportions not being altered. A mixture of wax and paraffin, containing nothing else, offers no difficulty in estimating, as the paraffin may be taken to represent the number left after deducting the sum of myricin and cerotic acid from 100. Its presence can hardly be overlooked in saponification, paraffin being but little soluble in alcohol. It adheres to the sides of the flask in a characteristic way. The specific gravity would also be lower than that of pure wax. But it is quite easy to imagine a mixture of fatty acids, fat and paraffin quite devoid of wax, yet giving analytical results identical with those of wax. A mixture of 9.48 per cent fatty acids, 36.84 per cent of fat, and 53.68 per cent of paraffin would show on analysis 14.40 per cent of cerotic acid and 88.09 of myricin.

Paraffin may be estimated directly by heating a weighed quantity of the wax with from five to ten times its volume of sulphuric acid to about 130°. Volumes of sulphur dioxide are given off, the fluid frothing and rising considerably. After about ten minutes heating the mass becomes almost solid, it is allowed to cool, the acid washed out with water, and the residue exhausted with ether. The paraffin thus obtained is re-treated with a little sulphuric acid to destroy particles of wax escaping the first treatment, again washed, and extracted.

Having obtained the per cent of paraffin in any mixture, the other ingredients may be obtained by the use of the following formulæ: Let A be the per cent in the paraffin-free mixture of free acid calculated as cerotic, and B the per cent of saponifiable matter calculated as myricin; let X be the unknown per cent of cerotic acid, Y that of fatty acid, Z that of myricin, and W that of fat, in a mixture containing fatty acid, fat, and wax, either separately or all together. Now,

$$\text{1.} \quad X + 1.518\,Y = A, \text{ whence } Y = \frac{A - X}{1.518}$$

$$\left.\begin{array}{l}\text{2.} \quad Z + 2.391\,W = B \\ \text{3.} \quad Z = 6.117\,X\end{array}\right\}\text{whence } W = \frac{B - 6.117\,X}{2.391}$$

$$\text{4.} \quad X + Y + Z + W = 100$$

By substituting the values of X, Z, Y, and W in equation 4, are obtained the equations:

$$X + \frac{A - X}{1.518} + 6.117 \, X + \frac{B - 6.117 \, X}{2.391} = 100$$

$$X = \frac{362,954 - 2.391 \, A - 1.518 \, B}{14.151}$$

$$X = 25.694 - (0.1689 \, A + 0.1703 \, B)$$

In this way is obtained the per cent of cerotic acid. This multiplied by 6.117 gives the myricin, the sum of both being the per cent of wax in the mixture. Deducting the real cerotic acid from A, and dividing the residue by 1.518, gives the per cent of fatty acids. The real myricine deducted from B, and the result divided by 2.391, gives the true per cent of fat. Thus are found the per cent of the paraffin-free mixture. An artificial mixture of 80 per cent wax and 20 per cent lard, gave, wax, 80.42 per cent (cerotic acid, 11.30 per cent, myricine, 69.12), and fat, 19.58 (fatty acid, 0.46, and fat, 19.07).

One of the samples of comb foundation alluded to gave 8.35 per cent of cerotic acid and 35.67 of myricin. It contained much paraffin. Assuming the absence of fat, the composition of the samples calculates: Cerotic acid, 5.83 per cent; myricin, 35.67 (together equaling 41.50 per cent); fatty acid, 1.66 per cent, and paraffin, 56.84. Another foundation gave cerotic acid, 11.99; myricin, 73.36 (together, 85.35 per cent wax); fatty acid, 4.31 per cent; paraffin, 10.34 per cent. The paraffin of commerce generally contains a small proportion of fatty acid, added to diminish its transparency, whence probably the slight proportion found above. A paraffin candle contained 12.4 per cent of fatty acids.

A light yellow sample of wax, warranted genuine by the vendor, gave 10.47 per cent of cerotic acid, and 69.30 per cent myricin. From this it follows that the sample consists of wax 79.77 per cent and paraffin 20.23. Another sample obtained by purchase gave wax 70.60 per cent, fatty acid 5.42 per cent, and fat 24.38. It was free from paraffin.

In conclusion, Hehner warns analysts against adopting his figures in working on bleached wax. In a discussion of the paper before the Society of Public Analysts, the president, Mr. Wigner, stated that many of the combs received from America were entirely artificial. Dr. Muter said that paraffin was practically the only adulterant used in wax.

About a half a year later than Hehner, but apparently independently, Hübl[*] published a wax method based on a similar principle. He heated 3 or 4 grams of the substance with about 20 cc. neutral, 95 per cent alcohol, titrated hot with seminormal potash and phenolphtalein to estimate free acid, added 20 cc. more of potash and saponified by gentle boiling for about forty-five minutes on the water bath without the use of mercury pressure. Excess of alkali was titrated with seminormal hydrochloric acid. Hübl called the number of milligrams of potash required to saturate the free acid of 1 gram of wax the "acid number," that required to decompose the wax ethers the "ether number." According to his experiments, which were not numerous, the potash required to neutralize the free acids of 1 gram of wax is equivalent to 19 to 21 milligrams; that for the ethers, 73 to 76. The relation of the acid to the ether numbers varied between 1.36 and 1.38. For the complete saponification Hübl took between 92 and 97 milligrams of potash.

---

* Dingl. polyt. Jour., 249–338.

Trials with wax substitutes gave—

|  | Acid No. | Ether No. | Saponifi- cation No. |
|---|---|---|---|
| Japan wax[1]............................ | 20 | 200 | 220 |
| Carnauba............................. | 4 | 75 | 79 |
| Tallow[2]............................... | 4 | 176 | 180 |
| Stearic acid........................... | 195 | 0 | 195 |
| Fir resin.............................. | 110 | 1.6 | 112 |
| Ceresin.............................. | 0 | 0 | 0 |
| Yellow beeswax ........... ......... | 20 | 75 | 95 |

[1] Acid number varied from 15 to 24.
[2] Acid number varied from 2 to 7.

E. Dieterich's investigations* confirm Hübl's statement of the applicability of the method. In filtered wax he found the specific gravity never below 0.962 and never over 0.966. Unfiltered wax (130 samples) gave figures between 0.963 and 0.967.

EXAMINATION OF WAX. †

For the examination of beeswax the method of Hübl, which is an evolution of Keettstorfer's method for examination of butter, is recognized as the most convenient and the best.

From numerous experiments the acid number for pure yellow beeswax is found to lie between 19 and 21, and the ether number between 73 and 76, and the saponification equivalent between 92 and 97, and the ratio of the acid number and the ether number is found to be 1 to 3.7. Lately, Buchner ‡ has published a paper in which the numbers given above do not seem to agree with those obtained for white, chemically bleached wax. Buchner examined yellow and, as he says, undoubtedly pure white wax bleached either in the sunlight or by chemical means. As the result of his researches, he concludes that the chemically bleached wax shows a higher acid number, viz, 23.01, and a higher saponification equivalent, 98.36. There, however, may be some doubt about the wax examined by Buchner being perfectly pure. In the Helfenberger laboratory some researches were undertaken to determine this point. Two kinds of yellow wax were taken, and they were decolorized, the one with bone black and the other with permanganate of potash.

Results of this examination are as follows :

|  | Specific gravity. | Acid No. | Ether No. | Saponifica- tion equiv- alent. | Ratio. |
|---|---|---|---|---|---|
| Yellow wax No. 1.............................. | .966 | 19.6 | 74.0 | 93.6 | 3.77 |
| No. 1 decolorized with bone black.............. | .963 | 20.1 | 74.0 | 94.1 | 3.68 |
| No. 1 decolorized with permanganate of potas- sium ..................................... | .963 | 18.1 | 72.8 | 90.9 | 4.00 |
| Yellow wax, No. 2 ............................ | .964 | 20.1 | 74.8 | 94.9 | 3.72 |
| No. 2 decolorized with bone black.............. | .963 | 19.6 | 74.0 | 93.6 | 3.77 |
| No. 2 decolorized with permanganate of potas- sium ..................................... | .964 | 19.1 | 74.0 | 93.1 | 3.87 |

According to these numbers the specific gravity of the bleached wax is not higher, as Allen affirms it is, but in three cases at least it was lower. It likewise appears that the acid, ether, and saponification numbers are not raised in the bleached wax, but

*Geschaftsber. der Papier und chem. Fabrik in Helfenberg, 1884, 13.
† Dr. H. Röttger, Chem. Zeit., 1889, 1375.
‡ Chem. Zeit., 1888, p. 1276.

the same are found within the limits for pure yellow wax. Recently, Helfenberger, in the examination of numerous samples of wax tested also chemically bleached wax, which bleaching took place by means of sulphurous acid. In this sample of wax the specific gravity was 0.966, the acid number 20.2, the ether number 76.7, the saponification number 96.9, and the ratio 3.79. Two samples designated as "pure wax" were purchased in open market and on analysis they yielded the following numbers, showing that they were highly adulterated.

|  | I. | II. |
|---|---|---|
| Acid number ........................... | 29.7 | 31.46 |
| Ether number ......................... | 87.5 | 67.66 |
| Saponification number................. | 117.2 | 99.10 |
| Ratio ................................. | 2.9 | 2.14 |

ANALYSIS OF WHITE BEESWAX.*

I stated two years ago that bleached beeswax would show occasionally higher acid and saponification numbers than have been accepted for white wax, alike whether bleaching had been done chemically or in the natural way. I made the statement in order to warn chemists against hastily concluding that because a wax gave these figures somewhat high that it was necessarily adulterated, inasmuch as I had obtained similar figures in analyzing undoubtedly pure wax. I did not intend to convey the idea that a bleached wax must necessarily show higher numbers, but that this was occasionally the case. My views were not corroborated by some investigations published in the Helfenberger Annalen (1888), and Dr. Röttger obtained numbers from chemically bleached wax not agreeing with mine, whence Dr. Röttger doubted my having worked with pure wax. I have not since had occasion to pursue this investigation farther, but I have recently read a very interesting article,† by A. & P. Buisine, confirming my statements, as they also found higher numbers in bleached wax.

To repeat, analytical chemists should not condemn a white wax showing up to 20 or 30 acid number and as high as 100 saponification number on that account. All samples of bleached wax do not necessarily show these high numbers, but this is of frequent occurrence.

WHITE WAX.‡

In a paper read before the Versammlung bayerischer Vertreter der angewandten Chemie, R. Kayser stated that from the results of numerous investigations he had come to the conclusion that the bleaching of wax by the various processes made no material difference in its composition. The acid number varies only between 19.1 and 20.4, the ether number between 74 and 76.5, the ratio between 3.61 and 3.81. He confirmed the results arrived at by Röttger.§ The detection of the commoner adulterations of white wax with Japan wax, paraffin, ceresin, tallow, stearic acid, etc., is easily and certainly arrived at by this method. Medicus states that wax coming from southern countries was very frequently adulterated with vegetable wax. Röttger remarks that lately very little pure wax was to be had. Borgmann ascribes this to the fact that among bee-keepers the use of artificial comb was becoming general.

---

* G. Buchner, Chem. Zeit., 1888, 12, 1276 ; ibid., 1890, 101, 1707.
† Chem. Zeit., 1890, 14, 319.
‡ R. Kayser, Chem. Zeit., 1890, 42, 686.
§ Chem. Zeit., 1889, 13, 1375.

COMPOSITION OF BEESWAX.*

Beeswax is formed chiefly of two immediate principles, which can be separated, owing to the difference of their solubility in alcohol into cerin and myricin. Brodie, in his classic work on the constitution of beeswax, has shown that cerin, the parts of beeswax soluble in hot alcohol, is formed essentially of a high fatty acid, viz, cerotic, and that the insoluble part, myricin is the palmitic ether of melissic alcohol.

Nafzger and Schwalb have shown that the wax contains small quantities of acids related to cerotic, such as melissic acid, as well as some nonsaturated acids of the oleic series, and of alcohols related to cerylic alcohol, such as melissic alcohol, etc., and also some saturated hydrocarbons, such as heptacosane ($C_{27} H_{50}$) and hentriacontane ($C_{31} H_{64}$).

Hübl, Becker, and Hehner have pointed out methods of estimating the free acids and combined acids in wax. They have thus established two particular numbers for wax, which, according to them, characterize it.

MM. Buisine have sought many methods for determining the other classes of bodies in wax, notably the nonsaturated acids of the oleic series, the fatty alcohols, and the hydrocarbons. They did not seek to find methods of determining each one of these bodies separately, which would have been a very difficult thing, and of very little practical value; but only for reactions, which would permit each class of bodies to be estimated as a whole and by simple processes, based upon reactions easy to produce, and which could be applied to the practical examination of the wax of commerce. The methods are as follows:

*Determination of free acids.*—Hübl was the first who indicated a practical process for the estimation of free acids in wax, and of fatty bodies in general. It consists in treating the bodies in solution in alcohol by a standard solution of soda, with phenolphtalein as indicator. It is found that 1 gram of wax requires from 19 to 21 milligrams of potash to saturate the free acids which it contains. This number corresponds to a content of from 13.22 to 15.71 per cent. of cerotic acid. The authors applied this process to numerous samples of pure French beeswax, and found a variation of from 13.5 to 15.5 per cent in cerotic acid.

*Estimation of all the acids and of the combined acids of wax.*—Becker has shown that the potash required for the complete neutralization of the acids contained in 1 gram of yellow wax is from 97 to 107 milligrams.

Hübl, operating in the same manner as Becker upon wax prepared in the laboratory and perfectly washed, has found somewhat smaller numbers, viz, 92 to 97 milligrams of potash for 1 gram of wax. It is believed that this difference is due to the fact that Becker worked upon wax imperfectly washed and retaining traces of honey. If from the above number be subtracted the number representing the free acids (19 to 21 milligrams of potash) the number found for the combined acids varies from 73 to 76 milligrams of potash for 1 gram of wax.

Hübl takes the proportion of the two numbers thus found and shows that the proportion should be 1 : 3.6 and 1 : 3.8.

Hehner translates the results of the titration of the free acids into cerotic acid and the quantity of combined acids into palmitate of myricyle. Wax of English origin examined by Hehner, contained from 13.12 to 15.91 per cent of cerotic acid and from 85.95 to 92.08 per cent of palmitate of myricyle. The authors have made this determination upon a certain number of samples of yellow French wax, and the results obtained are given in the following table:

---

* MM. A. & P. Buisine, Bull. de la Soc. Chim. de Paris, T. 5, 1890, 867.

*Free and combined acids of yellow wax.*

| Free acids. | | Total acids in milli-grams for 1 gram of wax. | Combined acids. | | | Ratio of free and combined acids. |
|---|---|---|---|---|---|---|
| Milligrams KHO for 1 gram of wax. | Per cent of cerotic acid in the wax. | | Milligrams KHO for 1 gram of wax. | Per cent myricin in wax. | Per cent palmitic acid in wax. | |
| 10 | 13.50 | 91 | 72 | 86.76 | 32.85 | 3.5 |
| 21 | 15.50 | 97 | 76 | 91.58 | 34.67 | 3.8 |

These results agreed with those of Hübl and Hehner, but the means obtained by the French chemist are somewhat lower than those obtained by the other authors. They found some few samples indicating a total acid content corresponding to 91 to 92 milligrams of potash for 1 gram of wax, although the lowest limit given by them is 92. On the other side they did not find a quantity of fatty acids corresponding to a number above 94.7 milligrams of potash for 1 gram of wax. The greater part of the samples examined by them contained a quantity of fatty acids corresponding to 92 to 95 potash for 1 gram of wax. The ratio of the two numbers representing the free and combined acids was also found somewhat lower than that indicated by Hübl. The wax which is the least rich in fatty acids is always found to be that which is the most colored, and in proportion as the color of the wax grows faint it is noticed that the content of fatty acids increases.

*Estimation of nonsaturated acids of the oleic series.*—The method of Hübl for the absorption of iodine was applied for this determination. It must not be supposed, however, that the acids of the oleic series present are the only compounds in wax which are capable of absorbing iodine. The authors have shown that the hydrocarbons of wax contain a certain number of bodies nonsaturated which are capable of fixing iodine. However this may be, it must be allowed that by a treatment with iodine a new number is obtained for beeswax, which is of considerable value for analytical purposes. From 1 to 2 gram of wax are taken for each determination, and the method is the same as that ordinarily used. The French yellow waxes are capable of absorbing from 8.2 to 11 per cent of iodine; that is to say, they contain from 9 to 12 per cent of nonsaturated acids calculated as oleic acid. The difference in the amount of iodine absorbed by the different samples examined did not exceed 3 per cent.

*Determination of the alcohols.*—The alcohols belong to the same series and possess consequently the same chemical properties. The authors determined them *en bloc* by submitting them to a reaction which is common to them and which is easily measured. This is the important reaction of fatty alcohols described by Dumas and Stas, viz, the reaction which they give when heated to a moderate temperature with hydrate of potash. Under these conditions these alcohols are transformed into the corresponding acids and at the same time they disengage hydrogen. The other principles of wax, viz, the fatty acids, oleic acids, hydrocarbons, etc., are not changed in the above operation, and by measuring the volume of hydrogen set free the proportion of alcohol contained in the wax can be approximately determined. The operation is carried on as follows:

From 2 to 10 grams of the wax are melted in a porcelain capsule and mixed with an equal weight of caustic potash finely pulverized. The mass is afterward treated with three or four times its weight of potash, pulverized. The mixture is introduced into a small flask or into a test tube, which is heated on a mercury bath to 250° for two hours. The reaction begins at about 180°, and after two hours of heating at 250° the evolution of hydrogen is completed. The gas is received in an apparatus invented by M. Dupre. The evolution tube, fixed by a stopper in the neck of the flask, conducts the gas to the upper part of the receiving flask, and another tube joined to this conducts the gas to the inferior tubulure in the same way. These two tubes are each furnished with a stopcock. The apparatus being thus disposed, and containing air at atmospheric pressure, the two stopcocks are closed and the receiving flask is filled with water. The stopcock is then opened which connects the flask with the interior tubulure of the receiving flask and heating takes place. The gas is collected in the superior part of this flask. When the evolution of hydrogen stops the heating of the flask ceases, and it is left to cool by opening the cock by which the flask communicates with the upper part of the vessel and by closing the other. When the temperature has reached that at which the operation was commenced, the stopcock is closed and the gas evolved is driven out into a graduated tube, its volume and temperature noted, and likewise the barometric pressure. One has thus exactly the volume of gas disengaged in the reaction and it is not necessary to take count of the air remaining in the apparatus, its volume being the same as before the operation. The volume of hydrogen, calculated to zero at a pressure of 760 millimeters, is then calculated for 1 gram of wax. Afterward the result is calculated into terms of melissic alcohol by means of the equation, $C_nH_{2n+2}O + KOH = 4H + KC_nH_{2n} - _1O_2$. The proportion of the melissic alcohol first found is then calculated to the amount of palmitic acid previously determined. The following table indicates between what limits the results vary:

| Volume of hydrogen at 0° and 760 mm., furnished by 1 gram of wax. | Per cent melissic alcohol in the wax. | Ratio of the melissic alcohol to the palmitic acid. |
|---|---|---|
| 53.5 to 57.5 | 52.5 to 56.5 | 1.58 to 1.65 |

In the palmitate of myricyle, the proportion of melissic alcohol to palmitic acid is 1.71.

*Determination of hydrocarbons.*—This determination is made very easily and very rapidly upon the product of the action of the potash and of the potash lime upon the wax; that is to say, upon the residue from the preceding operation. In this operation, indeed, all of the acids of the wax and the alcohols themselves are transformed into acids and are fixed in the state of alkaline salts. The hydrocarbons of the wax alone remain free. To remove them, it is sufficient to treat the resulting mass from the above reaction by an appropriate solvent—ordinary ether or rectified petroleum ether of a low boiling point. There is found in wax an almost constant quantity of hydrocarbons. The different samples examined contained from 12.72 to 13.78 per cent. These numbers are in all cases very much above those indicated by Schwalb; according to him, wax contains only about 5 to 6 per cent of hydrocarbons; nevertheless the hydrocarbons thus isolated are pure. They present themselves under the form of a waxy mass, scarcely colored, fusible at 49°.5; they are soluble in ether and petroleum spirit, benzine, chloroform, etc. These solutions are neutral and allow the product to be deposited in the form of a crystalline mass. Treated by potash lime, they evolve only a trace of hydrogen, which indicates the complete absence of alcoholic products. The hydrocarbons of wax are not wholly formed from saturated hydrocarbons as Schwalb has said. Those examined by the authors were capable of absorbing bromine and iodine; 100 parts of the hydrocarbon in a solution of chloroform were capable of absorbing 22.05 parts of iodine.

*General conclusions.*

Pure beeswax, melting point, 63° to 64°; entirely soluble in hot chloroform.

*Acids of the wax.*

Free acids correspond to from 19 to 21 milligrams potash for 1 gram of wax, or to 13.5 to 15.5 per cent cerotic acid.
Total acids correspond to from 91 to 97 milligrams potash for 1 gram of wax.

Combined acids correspond to 71 to 72 milligrams potash for 1 gram of wax, equivalent to 32.85 to 34.67 per cent palmitic acid in the wax. Ratio between the free and combined acids, 3.5 to 3.8. Percentage of iodine absorbed by wax, 8.3 to 11; corresponding to oleic acid, 9 to 12 per cent.

### Alcohols of wax.

Hydrogen evolved for 1 gram of wax, under the influence of potash, 53.5 to 57.5 cc; corresponding to per cent of melissic alcohol, 52.5 to 56.5; ratio of melissic alcohol to palmitic acid, 1.58 to 1.65.

### Hydrocarbons of wax.

Per cent, 12.5 to 14. Melting point, 49°.5. Percentage iodine absorbed by the hydrocarbons, 22.05.

MM. A. and P. Buisine* state further that besides these two processes (Hehner and Hübl.) they are in the habit of using three others. They take the iodine number and determine the alcohols and hydrocarbons. The results it is true vary within certain limits, but, on the whole, these methods permit the detection of fraud, both qualitatively and quantitatively, provided the numbers corresponding to the various adulterants are once determined.

With this end in view they have studied the substances oftenest employed in adulteration, using a method already described, for yellow† and white‡ wax. Having found a series of numbers peculiar to these bodies and representing quantitatively their composition, we determined their variance from those given by pure wax and the degree in which they modify the results when added to it. The following table shows the results:

| | Melting point. | Mg. of KHO for 1 gram of substance. | | | Iodine fixed by 1 gram of the wax. | Volume of H at 0° and 760 mm. given by 1 gram wax. | Hydrocarbons from 1 gram of the wax. |
|---|---|---|---|---|---|---|---|
| | | Acids soluble in water. | Free acids. | Total acids. | | | |
| | | | | | | Cc. | |
| Japan wax......... | 47 to 54 | 2 | 18 to 28 | 216 to 222 | 6 to 7.55 | 69 to 71 | 0 |
| China wax......... | 53.5 | 2 | 22 | 218 | 6.85 | 72.3 | 0 |
| Vegetable wax .... | 47 to 54 | 2 | 17 to 19 | 218 to 220 | 6.6 to 8.2 | 73 to 74 | 0 |
| Carnauba wax..... | 83 to 84 | 0 | 4 to 6 | 79 to 82 | 7 to 9 | 73 to 76 | 1.6 |
| Mineral wax....... | 60 to 80 | 0 | 0 | 0 | 0 to 0.6 | 0 | 100 |
| Paraffin............ | 38 to 74 | 0 | 0 | 0 | 1.7 to 3.1 | 0 | 100 |
| Suint wax ......... | 62 to 66 | 0 | 95 to 115 | 102 to 119 | 13 to 18.5 | 0 | 14 to 18 |
| Waxy acids of suint | 50 to 62 | 0 | 155 to 185 | 159 to 189 | 2.6 to 2.8 | 0 | 0 |
| Tallow............. | 42 to 50.5 | 0 | 2.75 to 5 | 196 to 213 | 27 to 40 | 52 to 60 | 0 |
| Stearic acid........ | 53.5 | 0 | 204 | 209 | 4 | 0 | 0 |
| Resin............. | 53.5 | 0 | 168 | 178 | 135.6 | 35 | 0 |
| Yellow beeswax ... | 62 to 64 | 0 to 1 | 19 to 21 | 91 to 97 | 8 to 11 | 53 to 57.5 | 12.5 to 14.5 |
| White beeswax.... | 63 to 64 | 0 to 2 | 20 to 23 | 93 to 11 | 2 to 7 | 53 to 57 | 11 to 13.5 |

Comparing these numbers to those given by pure wax, it is apparent that the introduction of any foreign body modifies more or less the results, and since different waxes give varying figures the nature of the impurity can be detected.

(1) The melting point of beeswax is lowered by the addition of Japan or China wax, by certain kinds of paraffin, by stearic acid and tallow. On the contrary, it

---

* Bull. Soc. Chim., 1891, 3d ser., t. 5, p. 654.
† Bull. Soc. Chim., 3d sér., t. 3, p. 867.
‡ Bull. Soc. Chim., 3d sér., t. 4, p. 465.

is raised by carnauba wax and certain mineral waxes. Again, the addition of some mineral waxes, of suint wax, and of various mixtures does not change the melting point.

(2) The addition of mineral waxes, paraffin, tallow, and carnauba wax diminish the free acids, which, on the other hand, increase with the addition of suint wax, suint acids, resin, and stearic acid. With China and Japan wax they do not pass the prescribed limits.

(3) The entire quantity of acids is diminished by mineral wax, paraffin, and somewhat by carnauba wax. They increase slightly with suint wax, and in a greater degree with the waxy acids of suint, with resin, tallow, stearic acid, and vegetable waxes.

VON HÜBL'S METHOD FOR EXAMINING WAX*.

v. Hübl's method possesses many advantages, but is attended with the disadvantage that many kinds of wax saponify with difficulty. Half an hour's boiling under the inverted condenser seldom suffices, and it is generally necessary to heat the sample in an open flask on the water bath until the alcohol is nearly completely expelled. Waxes containing ceresin almost invariably give saponification numbers much too low. The method gives good results only after long practice. Indeed the commercial chemists using it have often adjudged waxes as adulterated which more carefully examined have been found genuine. For this reason we propose the following alterations in it: First, determine the acid number in the usual way with aqueous seminormal potash. It seems, however, desirable to take 7 to 10 grams, requiring 5 to 7 cc seminormal potash; for with only 3 or 4 grams, the quantity prescribed by v. Hübl, errors in titration have too great an influence.

Instead of determining the "saponification number," we estimate the "total acid number," or, in other words, the amount of potash (calculated as tenths per cents) required by 1 gram of a mixture of fat acids and alcohols obtained by first saponifying a wax with potash and then decomposing the soap with hydrochloric acid. We call this mixture "opened wax" ("anfgeschlossenes Wachs"). The detailed procedure is: Dissolve about 20 grams potash in a hemispherical porcelain dish of 350 to 500 cc. capacity, in 15 cc. of water, heat over a Bunsen burner to incipient boiling, add 20 grams of the wax sample, which should have been fused over a water bath, and stir. Continue heating over a low flame, stirring constantly, for ten minutes. Dilute with 200 cc. water, heat and acidify with 40 cc. hydrochloric acid, previously diluted slightly. Boil till the floating layer is completely clear; cool and purify the cake by thrice boiling with water, adding a little hydrochloric acid the first time. Finally lift the cake, wipe with filter paper, dry in the air bath and filter. The filtered wax while still fused is to be poured into a cover glass and after cooling broken in fragments. Six to 8 grams of this "opened wax" are heated with neutral alcohol and titrated, using phenolphtalein as an indicator. The saponification, even with samples containing much ceresin, is complete. The "total acid number" is somewhat lower than v. Hübl's "saponification number." Calling the acid number $s$, the total acid number $S$ and the ether number $a$, $a + s$ represents the saponification number of Hübl, and:

$$a = \frac{56100\ (S-s)}{56100 - 18S}. \quad . \quad (1).$$

$$S = \frac{56100\ (a+s)}{56100 + 18\ a}. \quad . \quad (2).$$

---

* R. Benedikt u. K. Mangold, Chem. Zeit., 1891, 28, 474.

For the average acid number ($s=20$) for example the saponification number ($a+s$) and the total acid number ($S$) have the following values:

| $a$ | $a+s$ | $S$ | $S$ | $a$ | $a+s$ |
|---|---|---|---|---|---|
| 69 | 80 | 87.07 | 87 | 68.91 | 88.91 |
| 70 | 90 | 88.02 | 88 | 69.96 | 89.96 |
| 71 | 91 | 88.97 | 89 | 71.02 | 91.02 |
| 72 | 92 | 89.92 | 90 | 72.08 | 92.08 |
| 73 | 93 | 90.87 | 91 | 73.14 | 93.14 |
| 74 | 94 | 91.82 | 92 | 74.19 | 94.19 |
| 75 | 95 | 92.77 | 93 | 75.25 | 95.25 |
| 76 | 96 | 93.72 | 94 | 76.30 | 96.30 |
| 77 | 97 | 94.67 | 95 | 77.36 | 97.36 |
| 78 | 98 | 95.61 | 96 | 78.41 | 98.41 |

If the proportions are not taken from the ether and acid numbers (v. Hübl), but from the acid and total acid numbers, a value is obtained for v. Hübl's normal wax, and the saponification number 95, of $S - s : s = 72.77 : 20 = 3.64$.

Still these proportions are not as constant for pure wax as v. Hübl assumes. According to our own results a wax of 18 acid number and 90 saponification number can not be pronounced adulterated. A large number of samples of yellow wax of different origins gave values between 88 and 93 for the total acid number.

*Determination of ceresin and paraffin in wax.*—Calculating the wax content of a ceresin mixture from the total acid number $S$ according to the formula

$$W = \frac{100S}{92.8} \quad \ldots \quad (3)$$

in which 92.8 represents the average total acid number (corresponding to the saponification number 95) a small error is encountered from the fact that the wax has taken up 2.33 parts of water in saponifying. Therefore it is more exact to calculate,

$$W = \frac{100wS}{92.75 - S(1 - w)} = \frac{92.72}{92.75 - 0.02285} \quad \ldots \quad (4)$$

whence

$$W = 100 : 102.33 = .9772.$$

However, as the error at most amounts to only .7 per cent, it may be neglected, especially when the saponification number of the wax contained in the mixture is unknown.

The results of four mixtures made from ceresin and wax are given below in tabular form:

| No. | Wax. | Ceresin. | Total acid number. | Wax according to formula. (3) | (4) |
|---|---|---|---|---|---|
| 1 | 100 | 0 | 92.3 | 100 | 100 |
| 2 | 80 | 20 | 74.3 | 80.1 | 79.7 |
| 3 | 60 | 40 | 55.3 | 59.7 | 59.1 |
| 4 | 40 | 60 | 37.1 | 40.0 | 39.4 |
| 5 | 20 | 80 | 18.1 | 19.4 | 19.1 |
| 6 | 0 | 100 | 0 | 0 | 0 |

As the saponification numbers vary between 90 and 97, neither the original v Hübl method nor this modification can certainly distinguish the addition of less than 6 per cent of ceresin. This can, however, be done by the method of Buisine, which has been thoroughly tried by Mangold.

Additions of resin or stearic acid can be distinguished by the increased acid number. If $R$ be the known average acid number of the adulterant, $s$ the acid number of the sample, the amount of addition can be obtained from the known formula,

$$K = \frac{100\,(s - 20)}{R - 20} \quad \cdots \quad (5)$$

using for commercial stearic acid $R = 200$, the per cent of added stearic acid is

$$K = \frac{10\,(s - 20)}{18} \quad \cdots \quad (6)$$

*Determination of fats.*—If $s$ equals total acid number as obtained by titration, $Sw$ the number 92.8 (taken as the average total acid number of pure wax), $Sf$, the total acid number of the fats, and further, if $A$ parts of wax give 1 gram of "opened wax" and $B$ parts of fat 1 gram of insoluble fatty acids, then approximately,

$$W = \frac{100\,(S - Sw)}{Sf - Sw} \quad \cdots \quad (7)$$

or more exactly

$$W = \frac{100\,(Sf - S)\,a}{(Sf - S)\,a + (S - Sw)\,b} \quad \cdots \quad (8)$$

For example, with tallow, $Sf = 205$, $b = 1.05$, and with wax $Sw$ averaged 92.8 and $A = .9772$, in consequence of which in a mixture of tallow and wax the latter can be gotten from the equation,

$$W = \frac{100\,(S - 92.8)}{112.2} \quad \cdots \quad (9)$$

or more exactly

$$W = \frac{97.72\,(205 - 8)}{103.20 + .073\,S} \quad \cdots \quad (10)$$

The difference between the formulæ 9 and 10 amounts at the maximum to about 2 per cent.

### ANALYSIS OF BEESWAX.[*]

An adulteration of beeswax with less than 6 per cent of paraffin can be detected neither by Hübl's method nor by the modification of it proposed by Benedikt and myself,[†] for the reason that acid and ether numbers and their ratio vary within wide limits even with yellow wax. The detection of small amounts of paraffin is only practicable by direct determination of the amount of hydrocarbons present in the wax. A. and P. Buisine described some time since[‡] a method for this purpose which has appeared to me so important for the technical investigation of wax that I have subjected it to a careful trial. C. Holl,[§] and his pupils Sturcke[||] and Schwalb,[¶] deter-

[*] Karl Mangold, Chem. Zeit., 1891, 46, 799.

[†] Chem. Zeit., 1891, 15, 474.

[‡] Bull. Soc. Chim., 1890, 3 Ser. 3, 567 ; Chem. Zeit. Repert, 1890, 14, 226.

[§] Lieb. Ann. Chem., 1884, 223 ; Chem. Zeit., 1884, 8, 859.

[||] Lieb. Ann. Chem., 1884, 223, 295; Chem. Zeit., 1884, 8, 860.

[¶] Lieb. Ann. Chem., 1886, 235, 106.

mined the fatty alcohols and hydrocarbons in beeswax in an essentially similar way long before MM. Buisine, whose principal service consists in having simplified the apparatus and accurately studied the conditions of success. The principle of the method lies in the fact that fatty alcohols are converted into fatty acids on fusion with caustic potash, hydrogen being evolved. Saponified wax is heated with potash lime and the liberated hydrogen measured. The melt is pulverized, the hydrocarbons extracted by solvents and weighed.

I have estimated the hydrogen by this method on several samples and have gotten numbers somewhat lower than those of Buisine. As, however, the estimation of the hydrocarbons was of more interest to me, I did not follow the matter farther. I have however observed that the gas evolved does not reach a constant volume until after three hours' heating, instead of the two prescribed by Buisine. On the completion of the operation the flask is taken from the apparatus, allowed to cool, broken, the sintered mass powdered and, with the fragments of the flask, placed in a Soxhlet extractor, extracted for several hours with petroleum ether, the excess of ether distilled from the extract, and the latter dried at 110° and weighed. Unadulterated beeswax always contains hydrocarbons. Schwalb[*] claimed the amount of these to be about 6 per cent. Buisine found between 12.5 and 14, and the numbers which I have obtained, excepting for two samples (Nos. 15 and 21 in the following table), fall between these.

The numbers obtained are found in the following table:

| No. | Kind of wax. | Hydro- carbons. | Acid No. s. | Total acid No. S. | S—s. | Ratio v.[1] |
|---|---|---|---|---|---|---|
| 1 | Ausaeo | 13.51 | 19.79 | 92.30 | 75.51 | 3.66 |
| 2 | Domestic wax | 13.75 | 20.44 | 91.09 | 70.65 | 3.46 |
| 3 | ....do | 14.72 | 20.42 | 88.26 | 67.84 | 3.32 |
| 4 | Dalmatian | 14.51 | 18.81 | 90.80 | 71.99 | 3.83 |
| 5 | Hungarian | 14.60 | 23.04 | 89.50 | 66.55 | 2.89 |
| 6 | Bosnian (Banjaluka) | 14.27 | 19.31 | ............ | ............ | |
| 7 | Slavonian | 13.76 | 20.95 | 91.18 | 70.23 | 3.35 |
| 8 | Krain | 13.64 | 20.08 | 89.70 | 69.62 | 3.46 |
| 9 | Bosnian (Dolna-Tuzla) | 13.32 | 20.02 | 89.39 | 70.37 | 3.45 |
| 10 | Lower Styria | 14.34 | 18.26 | 90.76 | 72.50 | 3.97 |
| 11 | Lower Austria | 13.72 | 20.58 | 88.41 | 67.83 | 3.29 |
| 12 | Mozambeck | 13.37 | 19.42 | 91.20 | 71.78 | 3.70 |
| 13 | Chile | 13.35 | 19.99 | 90.00 | 70.01 | 3.50 |
| 14 | Monte Cristo | 13.50 | 20.24 | 87.69 | 67.45 | 3.33 |
| 15 | Morocco | 11.02 | 21.66 | 98.68 | 77.02 | 3.56 |
| 16 | Bombay | 14.04 | ............ | ............ | ............ | |
| 17 | Madagascar | 11.77 | 20.03 | 92.88 | 72.85 | 3.64 |
| 18 | Saffi | 12.20 | 19.92 | 93.40 | 73.48 | 3.72 |
| 19 | Oran | 11.55 | 19.91 | 99.90 | 79.99 | 4.02 |
| 20 | Massowa | 12.80 | 21.11 | 90.60 | 69.49 | 3.29 |
| 21 | Mogador | 11.40 | 20.85 | 96.40 | 75.55 | 3.62 |

$$^1 V = \frac{S-s}{s}$$

On inspection of the above it will be seen that, with exception of Nos. 15 and 21 the hydrocarbons vary only between 12.5 and 14 per cent. Taking these results as a standard, it follows that this method permits determination of added hydrocarbons when in amount greater than 2 per cent. Using the average figure, 13.50, the amount of ceresin added to a beeswax can be obtained according to the formula

$$C = \frac{100\ (K-k)}{100 - K}$$

---

[*] Lieb. Ann. Chem., 1886, 235, 149.

iu which $K$ represents the amount of hydrocarbons found, $k$ the amount natural to wax (13.50) and $C$ the ceresin or paraffin. Using the average figure 13.50 the equation becomes

$$C = \frac{100\ K - 1350}{86.5}$$

A specimen of wax from Siebenbürgen gave an acid number of 16.66, and a total acid number of 72.68, being evidently adulterated with paraffin. Direct estimation of the hydrocarbons gave 28.12 per cent, which, calculated according to the second formula, is equivalent to an addition of 17 per cent of ceresin.

Some samples of white wax were also tried. Two were purely white and showed normal numbers, being probably bleached in the natural ways. According to Röttger,[*] Valenta,[†] and Dieterich,[‡] white wax should not differ from yellow if the bleaching is not done chemically. The two samples gave the following numbers:

| | | Hydrocarbons. | Acid No. s. | Total acid No. S. | S—s. | Ratio v.[1] |
|---|---|---|---|---|---|---|
| 1 | Smyrna | 10.93 | 20.87 | 89.20 | 68.33 | 3.28 |
| 2 | Egyptian | 11.35 | 20.04 | 89.08 | 69.04 | 3.49 |

[1] Bull. Soc. Chim., 1890, 3 aer., 465; Chem. Zeit. Repert, 1890, 14, 320.

A. & P. Buisine[§] also found somewhat lower per cents of hydrocarbons in white waxes than in the yellow.

Two more white samples, probably chemically bleached and not perfectly pure, gave:

| | | Hydrocarbons. | Acid No. s. | Total acid No. S. | S—s. | Ratio v.[1] |
|---|---|---|---|---|---|---|
| 1 | Siebenbürgen | 13.61 | 24.68 | .......... | .......... | .......... |
| 2 | Hungarian | 15.48 | 23.05 | 102.54 | 74.49 | 3.45 |

$$[1]\ V = \frac{S-s.}{\kappa.}$$

ANALYSIS OF A MIXTURE OF WAX, PARAFFIN, STEARIN, AND STEARIC ACID. §

(1) *Determination of stearic acid.*—Introduce into a flask 3 or 4 grams of the wax and 60 cc of 96 per cent alcohol and boil. Allow to cool and titrate with a seminormal solution of alkali, using phenolphtalein as indicator. Wax is very slightly soluble in cold alcohol and it is unnecessary to take into account its acidity. 7.8 cc of seminormal alkali equal 1 gram of commercial stearic acid.

(2) *Determination of paraffin.*—Add to the neutralized solution in the flask 3 or 4 cc of a 50 per cent solution of caustic soda. Attach a reflux condenser and heat the solution for an hour to saponify the fats and waxes. Distil off the bulk of the alcohol and transfer the residue to a capsule containing a mixture of dried silica and short asbestos. Dry at 100. Pulverize and exhaust with warm chloroform (or petroleum ether), which dissolves the whole of the paraffin and the myricyl alcohol of the wax.

For the separation of myricyl alcohol and paraffin, Horn has suggested acetylization and the solution of the resultant ether in glacial acetic acid, in which paraffin

[*] Chem. Zeit., 1889, 13, 1375.

[†] Centr. Org. für Waarenk u Technol., 1891, 112.

[‡] Helfenberger Ann., 1889, 21.

[§] F. Jean, Bull. Soc. Chim., 1891, p. 3.

is insoluble. According to him, wax after saponification yields 50 per cent of matter soluble in glacial acid (myricyl alcohol). In following his directions we have not been able to separate the paraffin nor to obtain a constant quantity for the part of the wax soluble in chloroform.

Our method is to distil off most of the chloroform, transfer the residue to a tared capsule, evaporate, dry at 100, and weigh. A weighed portion of this dried residue is to be transferred to a small flask (with a reflux condenser attached), together with 4 or 5 cc of anhydrous acetic acid to etherify the myricyl alcohol, which becomes soluble in it on warming, and the whole heated for an hour. After the completion of the reaction the product is transferred to a glass tube marked for 10 cc, and graduated to tenths. Rinse the flask with a little boiling acid, and add to the preceding. The total volume should be about 9 cc. Close the tube with a cork, place in a water bath kept at 90°, and shake till complete emulsification is effected. Let it remain quiet in the bath till it becomes clear again, and then read of the volume of paraffin floating on the surface of the acid. Reëmulsify, allow to become clear, and read, and so on till the readings give concordant results. One gram of paraffin equals 1.35 to 1.40 cc. On deducting the weight of the paraffin from the total weight of the chloroform extract, the residue represents the portion of the wax dissolved in the chloroform (myricyl alcohol).

(3) *Determination of the stearin.*—The portion of the saponified product insoluble in chloroform is composed of the soaps formed from the stearin and stearic acids, and from the cerotic acid. To determine the first, dissolve this residue in boiling water, filter to separate the silica and asbestos, and decompose the filtrate by a slight excess of dilute nitric acid to set free the fatty acids. Again filter, and in the filtrate titrate the glycerine, after neutralization and precipitation by acetate of lead, by means of potassic bichromate. Five grams of glycerine are equivalent to 95 grams of stearin. In cases where the percentage of stearin is but slight, it would be preferable to saponify 10 to 25 grams, and determine glycerine in the product by the bichromate method.

By the above method can be determined :

(1) Stearic acid by alkalimetry.

(2) Paraffin by volume of matter insoluble in glacial acetic acid.

(3) Part of the wax by deducting the paraffin from the weight of the residue soluble in chloroform.

(4) Stearine by titrating the glycerin.

(5) The residual portion of the wax (cerotic acid) by difference.

# PATENTS RELATING TO THE MANUFACTURE OF ARTIFICIAL COMB FOUNDATION.

Fifteen patents have been issued for the manufacture of artificial comb and comb foundation. Arranged chronologically follows a brief description of them:

### No. 32258, ISSUED MAY 7, 1861.

This being the first one on record it is given almost in full.

SAMUEL WAGNER.—ARTIFICIAL HONEYCOMB.

*Specification forming part of Letters Patent, No. 1254. Whole No. 32258, dated May 7, 1861.*

*To all whom it may concern:*

Be it known that I, Samuel Wagner, of York, in the county of York, and State of Pennsylvania, have invented a new and useful article of manufacture; and I do hereby declare that the following, taken in connection with the drawings which accompany and form part of this specification, is a description of my invention so full and exact as to enable those skilled in the art to practice it.

My new manufacture consists in a substitute for the central division or foundation of the comb built by bees, either with or without the whole, or any portion of the walls forming the hexagonal cells projecting from the division, which substitute is artificially and suitably formed upon both sides or faces, and of any suitable material which is susceptible of receiving the desired and necessary configuration.

A mold is prepared, similarly to those used in the production of printers' type, in which solids are cast which will accurately fill the interior of a newly-formed cell of a natural comb of the kind of which it is desired to form the central division. Numbers of type or solids being produced they are "locked together" into a "form" like printers' type, and facsimiles of the assemblage are produced by either of the well-known processes of stereotyping or electrotyping.

Two of these stereotypes or electrotypes are made to act, by means of a press or otherwise, upon the opposite sides or faces of an interposed sheet of suitable material, which action gives the sheet the configuration desired. It is best to obtain in this division or foundation sheet a uniform degree of tenuity, which can only be done by closely imitating the natural waxen comb, which is effected by so placing the dies that the apices formed at the juncture of the three rhomboidal facets of each hexagon shall be exactly opposite the juncture of the sides of three facets of adjacent hexagons forming the reverse side. The angles of the rhomboidal facets should be as nearly as possible 109° and 71°, and the dies should not be permitted to approach each other so nearly as to reduce the thickness of the interposed material much less than the one-hundredth part of an inch. Should it be deemed desirable to form the hexagonal walls of the cells, or any portion of them, the type or solids should be formed with a band or projection around them of about the one two-hundredth part of an inch in thickness, and some taper may be given to the type from the band toward the rhomboidal facets. If the walls of the cells are to be extended to any considerable distance from the central web or division provision should be made for the admission of air into

861

the spaces left vacant by the withdrawal of the dies from the material being formed, which can be accomplished by making a cavity in each hexagonal projection of the die, and with a removable valve in one of the facets of each hexagon, or at the apex formed by the juncture of the facets. Amongst the many materials which may be used may be mentioned compounds of which wax forms a part—rubber and gutta-percha, and compounds of which they or either of them are components, papier-maché, etc. Thin sheets of metal, reduced to the tenuity of foils, may be used, though I prefer good nonconductors of heat improved by being rendered waterproof if not so.

Very many materials and compounds not mentioned may be used, but it is unnecessary herein to attempt to specify them, as my invention is not confined to, and is independent of any particular material. It may be mentioned that with some materials heat as well as pressure may be used in shaping the artificial comb foundation. Many variations may be made in my invention which, though not improvements upon it, embody its essence. For example the relative arrangement of the impressing dies may be varied so as to produce a different arrangement of cells on the obverse and reverse sides of the comb foundation from that shown in the drawings, in which case the thickness of the division plate would have to be increased provided the pyramidal depressions made by the three rhomboidal facets terminating each hexagon were retained. Such depressions might be dispensed with and the foundation sheet might be impressed so as to leave slightly projecting ridges of the material from which the sides of the cells can be extended on each side of the sheet. But I do not recommend any departure from the closest imitation possible of the natural central sheet of the comb as formed by bees. To render the artificial comb foundation acceptable to the bees it is not requisite that any portion of the sides of the cells should be formed thereon as the salient angles on either side formed at the edges of the described depressions are a sufficient guide to the bees, and from them they will commence the waxen sides of their hexagonal cells. By the employment of my invention in beehives perfect regularity of combs and their kind is insured, and the production of drones prevented to any extent desired. I propose to take honey from store combs built upon my artificial foundations by removing the full combs from the hives and by slicing off the natural waxen superstructure ; the artificial central portion of the comb being then replaced in the hive will be again built upon by the bees, saving to them always the elaboration of wax and the time required for the construction of this part of the comb which consumes more time in its natural construction than other parts of the comb of equal weight, because fewer laborers can be engaged upon it at one time than on other portions.

I claim as a new article of manufacture, an artificial substitute for the central division of comb built by bees, which presents to them, on both sides thereof, guides for the construction or continuation of the sides of the comb cells whether the same is constructed with or without the whole or any portion of the sides of the cells.

SAM. WAGNER.

Witnesses :
    D. S. WAGNER,
    JOHN A. URLSEN.

No. 115066, ISSUED MAY 23, 1871.

Homer A. King, of New York, claims a machine for making a comb, having about one-third of the cell ready for completion by the bees. To prevent the dies from sticking to the wax, they are kept moistened with vinegar.

No. 134411, ISSUED DECEMBER 31, 1872.

Joseph Williams, of Bean Station, Tenn., claims a device for making artificial comb, in which the cells, instead of standing perpendicular to the foundation, are inclined toward the center of the comb, as is the case with the natural product. His apparatus was designed to produce a comb in every respect resembling the natural comb built by bees.

When the dies described in the drawings have been properly adjusted the " honeycomb is produced by pouring through an opening in the top of the die casings and frame melted beeswax. This fills the dies, and when the latter are separated a perfect comb appears.

" This comb may then be placed in the hive and will be used by the bees, thus saving the insects the labor of building combs, and causing them to spend the time otherwise appropriated to the above work in the gathering and storing of honey."

No. 198648, ISSUED DECEMBER 25, 1877.

A. E. McConnell, of New Orleans, claims an invention for supplying thin strips of wax, at certain distances apart in the hive, whereby bees are enabled to economically and rapidly construct their combs. This device is hardly to be considered as an artificial comb or foundation, but is so classed by the Patent Office.

No. 200549, ISSUED FEBRUARY 19, 1878.

This is the invention of Alfred B. Lawther, of Chicago. The object of the invention is to " provide combs of suitable form and material, ready-made, for honey bees to store their honey in, thus saving them the labor of preparing the wax and constructing combs in the usual manner, thereby greatly increasing their power to gather honey."

The comb is made complete of a web of paper, cloth, or suitable material, which after molding is saturated with melted wax. The excess of coating is thrown off by a centrifugal machine. The " advantage arising from my invention is that combs constructed accordingly can be filled and emptied repeatedly without breaking, the honey being extracted by means of a centrifugal machine, or as commonly done with other honeycombs when it is desired to use them a second time."

No. 207057, ISSUED AUGUST 13, 1878.

Martin Metcalf, of Battle Creek, Mich. The foundation is made of cloth saturated with starch, so that when stamped it will retain the impression of the dies. The whole is then coated with wax.

" The ordinary wax foundation now used frequently softens with heat and will sag by reason thereof, and its own weight added to that of the gathering bees causing an elongation of the indentations and consequent enlargement of the completed bee cells. Such enlarged cells are totally unfit for the cradles of working bees, and the queen will but seldom deposit her eggs in them, and when she does drones only hatch therefrom." This defect, it is claimed, this invention will avoid.

No. 208595, ISSUED OCTOBER 1, 1878.

In favor of John E. Hetherington, of Cherry Valley, N. Y. This invention consists in the " combination with a comb foundation of wires which pass through the foundation and prevent it from sagging and stretching and also strengthen it, making it less liable to breakage while being handled."

No. 215336, ISSUED MAY 13, 1879.

By John Y. Detwiler, of Toledo, Ohio. This patent claims an improvement in artificial bases for honeycombs. The object of the invention is to overcome the difficulties which pertain to foundations made wholly of beeswax. The base of metallic foil is coated on both sides with beeswax, and this forms the base of the comb. It is claimed that only a minimum quantity of wax is required by this kind of foundation and that it is not subject to the serious objections that arise in using an interposed textile fabric or paper. When these substances are used the bees spend most of their time endeavoring to pull out the threads or particles of paper, or in cutting the threads, as they can easily do. The indentations of a hexagonal shape for the cells are made with the usual machinery.

## No. 234226, ISSUED NOVEMBER 9, 1880.

By Andrew F. Bonham, of Seven Mile Ford, Va. This invention employs two semimolds, made preferably of plaster of Paris, and provided upon their faces with triangular pyramidal projections fitting together nicely, so as to produce the impressions required. The molds are first soaked in water till they are thoroughly moist and their faces are then dipped in melted wax, which will adhere without sticking, owing to the faces having been soaked. Next, the molds are closed together and some pressure exerted, so as to form of the wax adhering to the mold a single sheet or cake. After permitting these to cool for a short time the apparatus is dipped into cold water and cautiously opened, when the foundation sheet may be readily removed and the operation repeated. It is claimed that the foundation sheet produced in this manner is stronger, more easily handled, and freer of defects than those made by other processes.

## No. 246049, ISSUED AUGUST 23, 1881.

By Frances A. Dunham, of De Pere, Wis. The material for the foundation, beeswax, is fed to the rolls of a machine, which is described, and of such a nature that, after passing through, the result is a sheet of beeswax impressed with a series of cells having cylindrical walls and three-sided or triangular bottoms, those on one side breaking joints with the bottoms of the cells on the other, and the tops of the walls of the cells lying in one and the same horizontal plane, at right angles to the sides of the cells. By making the cells complete it is claimed that the time of the bees is saved and they at once begin to secrete honey without taking up the time for forming comb, as is usually the case. It is claimed that the base of the foundation requires very little filling, as the queen will immediately deposit eggs, and that the work of feeding the larvæ and lengthening up the walls of the cells goes on together, without interfering with the gathering of the main honey crop. It is also claimed that the comb can be finished without generating so great a heat in the hives that the bees are forced into swarming.

## No. 258251, ISSUED MAY 23, 1882.

By Wm. C. Pelham, of Maysville, Ky. This is a machine for manufacturing honeycomb foundations. The dies are arranged as rolls upon a cylinder. The dies are made of type metal, although any hard metal may be used. The dies are not set perpendicular, but slightly inclined, so that they may be more readily withdrawn from the wax after the impressions are made. The dies are so arranged as to leave a portion of the cell wall complete, at least one-tenth of an inch in height, and more if possible. The cells made are of the regular hexagonal shape.

## No. 283442, ISSUED AUGUST 21, 1883.

By E. Beverly Weed, of Detroit, Mich. The inventor claims that by a peculiar construction and arrangement of die rolls he is able to make a comb foundation with cells of any desired depth and in any state of perfection. His improvement in the machine consists in constructing dies with uncut cell formers and in covering them with a substance adhesive to water, which prevents the wax from sticking to the dies. The substance used is dental rubber and the die rolls are so arranged as to have both of them immersed in water. He claims that he can make comb foundation with high walls and still have it discharge freely from the dies.

No. 397046, ISSUED JANUARY 29, 1889.

By Lewis Augs. Aspinwall, of Three Rivers, Mich.  The inventor claims that efforts have been made to produce artificial honeycombs, but difficulties have arisen preventing such combs being fully available.  If the artificial comb is of wax it is liable to become too soft in hot weather for handling, and can not be used a second time.  If made of tin, celluloid, hard rubber, or similar material, it is expensive and not acceptable to the bees, which require a surface of wax upon which to deposit their honey, and where efforts have been made to coat such combs with wax the comb was liable to scale and become injured.  When paper has been formed into a comb, the same has not the strength necessary for handling, and where such artificial combs have been placed in centrifugal separators for removing the honey, they have collapsed and become unfit for further use.  The inventor finds that a strong comb, adapted to repeated use, can be made of a slab of end-grain wood, with holes bored into the same parallel to the grain of the wood.  These can be coated with wax by dipping into the melted material and the excess thrown off with a centrifugal machine.  The inventor prefers basswood, but does not limit himself to this particular kind.  The slab is about the usual thickness of a honeycomb, and the holes are bored into the same of about the same size and in about the position of those in the natural honeycomb.  In all instances the holes are parallel to the grain or fiber of the wood so that the partitions between the cells may be as thin as possible and the walls smooth.  After the holes are bored the prepared slab is introduced into the molted wax and the wax penetrates and fills the pores of the wood, and the whole of it will be coated with a thin film of wax.  A combination of beeswax with rosin or other gums, which is less expensive, may be employed instead of natural wax—this compound being acceptable to the bees and accomplishing the same result.

## METALLIC COMB.

A honeycomb made wholly from metals and afterwards coated with wax, is described in Quinby's Bee Keeping by L. C. Root, edition of 1884, page 193.  The author of the book also says, speaking of artificial comb, "That cells of full depth with such comb have not yet been offered for commercial purposes."  He expresses his belief that such artificial comb will yet be made, and says that as long ago as 1870 Mr. Quinby made extensive experiments in this direction.

Comb was made out of tin plate by crimping it and placed in the center of a piece of worker comb, when "the queen occupied it, filling it with eggs, just as she did the natural cells adjoining, and in due time the young bees matured equally well. * * * Sheet iron was also used. * * * The bees would lengthen the artificial cells with wax."

The American Bee Journal of July 25, 1888, however, says that artificial comb was made at that time with cells one-half inch in depth, which is the full depth and a little more, of the natural cell.  It is therefore seen that Mr. Quinby's anticipations have been realized at an earlier date, even, than he anticipated.

### LIST OF MANUFACTURERS OF COMB AND COMB FOUNDATION.

J. V. Caldwell, Cambridge, Ill.

Charles Dadant & Son, Hamilton, Hancock County, Ill.; 1889, production 59,551 pounds; 1890, product 85,000 pounds.

F. C. Erkel, Le Sueur, Minn.

W. T. Falconer Manufacturing Company, Jamestown, N. Y.

Wilbur G. Fish, Ithaca, N. Y.; 40 and 50 cents per pound.

M. H. Hunt, Bell Branch, Mich.

E. Kretchmar, Red Oak, Iowa.
T. G. Newman & Son, 246 East Madison street, Chicago, Ill.
Novelty Company, Rock Falls, Ill.
Smith & Smith, Kenton, Ohio.
E. B. Weed, Grand River avenue, Detroit, Mich.
Jacob Wollerskeim, Kaukauva, Wis.

## BIBLIOGRAPHY OF BEESWAX—ARRANGED BY YEARS.

**1848.**
Composition of beeswax. Brodie, Phil. Trans., 1848, 1, 159.
**1858.**
Detection of stearic acid in beeswax. Fehling, Dingl. polyt. Jour., 1858, 147, 227.
**1860.**
Detection of adulterants in beeswax. Rabineaud, Jour. de pharm. d'Anvers, 1860, 531; Wittstein's Vierteljahreschrift, 1861, 409; Fres. Zeit. f. a. Chem., 1862, 115; Dingl. polyt. Jour., 1862, 163, 80.
Adulterations of beeswax. H. Hager, Pharm. Centralhalle, 1862, 3, 207.
Detection of paraffin in beeswax. Landolt, Dingl. polyt. Jour., 1862, 160, 224; Fres. Zeit. f. a. Chem., 1862, 116.
**1863.**
Detection of adulterants of beeswax. Dullo, Wagner's Jahresber., 1863, 670; Fres. Zeit. f. a. Chem., 1864, 510.
**1864.**
Detection of vegetable wax in beeswax. Dingl. polyt. Jour., 1864, 172, 156.
Detection of paraffin in beeswax. Payen, Jour. de pharm. et de chim., t. 2, 4, 233; Fres. Zeit. f. a. Chem., 1865, 490.
**1866.**
Determination of paraffin in beeswax. Lies-Bodart, Comptes rend., 1866, 62, 749; Fres. Zeit. f. a. Chem., 1866, 252; Jour de chim. med., t. 2, ser. 5, 297.
Determination of paraffin in beeswax. R. Wagner, Fres. Zeit. f. a. Chem., 1866, 279.
**1867.**
Detection of paraffin in wax. R. Wagner, Dingl. polyt. Jour., 1867, 185, 72.
Bleaching beeswax. J. F. Babcock, Proc. Amer. Pharm. Assoc., 1867, 98 and 372.
**1869.**
Adulteration of beeswax. H. Hager, Pharm. Centralhalle, 1869, 10, 49; Polyt. Centralblatt, 1869, 1406; Chem. News, 1869, 19, 310; Fres. Zeit. f. a. Chem., 1870, 133 and 419.
**1870.**
Adulteration of beeswax. E. Davies, Pharm. Jour. Trans., Sept., 1870; Amer. Jour. Pharm., Nov., 1870; Proc. Amer. Pharm. Assoc., 1871, 312.
Adulteration of beeswax with Japan wax. H. Hager, Pharm. Centralhalle, 1870, 11, 209; Jour. de pharm. et de chim., May, 1870; Proc. Amer. Pharm. Assoc., 1871, 311.
Detection of resin in beeswax. Pharm. Jour. Trans., Sept., 1870.
**1871.**
Optical analysis of beeswax. H. Pocklington, Pharm. Jour. Trans., 1871, 2, 81.
**1872.**
Detection of ceresin in beeswax. Pharm. Centralhalle, 1872, 371; Amer. Jour. Pharm., 1873, 11; Proc. Amer. Pharm. Assoc., 1873, 487.
Formation of beeswax. W. v. Schneider, Ann. Chem. Pharm., 162, 235; Jour. Chem. Soc., 1872, 25, 639; Bienen Zeitung, 1872, 281.

1873.

Detection of adulterants in beeswax. H. Hager, Comment. Pharm. Germ., 1873, 435.

Specific gravity of waxes used as adulterants. E. Dieterich, Arch. Pharm., 1873, 20, 454.

Tests for adulterants of beeswax. E. Donath, Dingl. polyt. Jour., —, 205, 131; Jour. Chem. Soc., 1873, 26, 194; Fres. Zeit. f. a. Chem., 1873, 325; Apoth. Zeit., 1873, No. 1; Proc. Amer. Pharm. Assoc., 1873, 267.

1874.

Adulteration of beeswax. Amer. Jour. Pharm., 1874, 510; Proc. Amer. Pharm. Assoc., 1875, 232.

Detection of Japan wax in beeswax. Ch. Mene, Comptes rend., 1874, 78, 1544; Dingl. polyt. Jour., 1874, 214, 87; Jour. Chem. Soc., 1874, 27, 1026.

Wax adulterated with paraffin. Rep. de Pharm., Nov., 1874; Amer. Jour. Pharm., 1875, 66; Proc. Amer. Pharm. Assoc., 1875, 498.

1875.

Adulteration of beeswax with paraffin. A. W. Miller, Zeit. d. österr. Apoth. Ver., 1875, 49; Fres. Zeit. f. a. Chem., 1875, 200.

1876.

Crystalline structure in beeswax. R. Röttger, Jahresber. d. phys. Ver. z. Frankfurt a. M., 1876, 77, 23; Chem. Centralblatt, 1878, 575; Jour. Chem. Soc., 1879, 36, 171.

Composition of beeswax. Schalfejeff, Ber. d. chem. Gesell., 1876, 9, 278, and 1688.

Detection of resin in beeswax. Chem. Centralblatt, 1876, 151; Jour. Chem. Soc., 1877, 365.

Manufacture of artificial wax. Chem. Centralblatt, 1876, 528.

1877.

Adulteration of beeswax. Bedford, Proc. Amer. Pharm. Assoc., 1877, 444 and 513; Pharm. Jour. Trans., 1877, 316.

Action of iodine on beeswax. T. A. Edison, Amer. Chemist, 1877; Chem. News, 1877, 36, 138.

Detection of paraffin in beeswax. H. Hager, Pharm. Centralhalle, 1877, 18, 414.

Detection of rosin in beeswax. E. Schmidt, Ber. d. chem. Gesell., 1877, 10, 837; Jour. Chem. Soc. 1877, 642; do. 1879, 283; Fres. Zeit. f. a. Chem., 1878, 509; Arch. f. Pharm. 1878, 212; Proc. Amer. Pharm. Assoc., 1879, 434.

1878.

Estimation of paraffin in beeswax. W. T. Thompson, Chem. News, 38, 167; Jour. Chem. Soc., 1878, 1010.

1879.

Analysis of wax. F. Becker, Corr. Blatt. Ver. analyt. Chem., 2, 57; Chem. Zeit., 1879, No. 12; Amer. Jour. Pharm., 1879, 555; Proc. Amer. Pharm. Assoc., 1880, 292; Fres. Zeit. f. a. Chem., 1880, 241.

Detection of paraffin in wax. M. Buchner, Schweiz. Wochenschrift f. Pharm., May 2, 1879, 149; Zeit d. österr. Apoth. Ver., 1879, 154; Amer. Jour. Pharm., 1879, 302; Dingl. polyt. Jour., 1879, 231, 272; Chem. Centralblatt, 1879, 267; Jour. Chem. Soc., 1879, 36, 675; Fres. Zeit. f. a. Chem., 1880, 240.

Electrical properties of beeswax. W. E. Ayrton, Phil. Mag. [5], 6, 132; Jour. Chem. Soc., 1879, 36, 427.

Is beeswax a rancid fat? Pharm. Zeit., 1879, 220; Amer. Jour. Pharm., 1879, 302.

1880.

Examination of wax. H. Hager, Pharm. Centralhalle, 1880, 119; Amer. Jour. Pharm., 1880, 447; Dingl. polyt. Jour., 1880, 238, 356; Jour. Chem. Soc., 1881, 40, 316.

1881.

Determination of hydrocarbons in beeswax. A. H. Allen and W. T. Thomson, Chem. News, 1881, 43, 267.

Detection of resin in beeswax. Jean, Chem. Zeit., 1881, 303; Amer. Jour. Pharm., 1881, 307.

1882.

Constitution of beeswax. E. Zatzeck, Monatsh. f. Chem. —, 3, 677; Chem. Central-
blatt, 1882, 626; Fres. Zeit. f. a. Chem., 1883, 618.
Detection of paraffin in beeswax. E. Dieterich, Wagner's Jahresber., 1882, 1028.
Detection of ceresin in beeswax. Peltz, Jour. de pharm. et de chim [5], 5,154; Arch.
d. Pharm., 1882, 471; Proc. Amer. Pharm. Assoc., 1882, 363.
Manufacture of wax by the bees. Hutchinson, Pharm. Jour. Trans., 1882, 24.

1883.

Adulteration of beeswax. Amer. Bee Jour., May 23, 1883.
Analysis of beeswax. O. Hehner, Analyst, 1883, 16; Jour. Chem. Soc., 1884, 779;
Dingl. polyt. Jour., 1884, 251, 168; Fres., Zeit. f. a. Chem., 1886, 441.
Analysis of beeswax. F. Hübl, Dingl. polyt. Jour., 1883, 249, 338; Amer. Jour.
Pharm., 1884, 479; Proc. Amer. Pharm. Assoc., 1885, 200; Jour. Chem. Soc.,
1884, 46, 506.
Detection of tallow in beeswax. Amer. Bee Jour., 1883, 298.
Determination of carnauba wax in beeswax. E. Valenta, Pharm. Centralhalle, 1883,
24, 417; Fres. Zeit. f. a. Chem., 1884, 257.
Microscopic examination of wax. E. Dieterich, Geschäftsber. d. Papier u. Chem.
Fabrik in Helfenberg, bei Dresden, 1883; Fres. Zeit. f. a. Chem., 1884, 567.
Tests for purity of beeswax. P. F. Resch, Bienenvater,—; Amer. Bee Jour., 1883,
211.

1884.

Acid constituents of beeswax. F. Nafzger, Lieb. Ann., 1884, 224, 225; Chem. Central-
blatt, 1884, 886; Jour. Chem. Soc., 1884, 46, 297.
Analysis of beeswax. Stürcke, Lieb. Ann., 1884, 283, 295; Chem. Zeit., 1884, 8, 860.
Composition of beeswax. C. Hell, Lieb. Ann., 1884, 223, 269; Chem. Zeit., 1884, 8, 859.
Non-acid constituents of beeswax. F. Schwalb, Inaug. Diss., Stuttgart, 1884; Chem.
Centralblatt, 1885, 16, 354; Jour. Chem. Soc., 1885, 48, 962.
Tests for purity in beeswax. Chas. Dadant, Amer. Bee Jour., 1884, 84.

1885.

Bleaching of wax. M. H. Barnouvin, Rep. de pharm., 1885, 6; Pharm. Jour. Trans.,
1885, 616; Proc. Amer. Pharm. Assoc., 1885, 201.
Detection of animal fat in beeswax. Amer. Bee Jour., 1885, 19 and 298.
Purification of beeswax. Pharm. Jour. Trans., 1885, 448.

1886.

Analysis of wax. Pharm. Commission d. deut. Apoth. Ver., Arch. f. Pharm., 1886, 24,
490.
Analyse der Fette u. Wachsarten. Benedikt, published in Berlin, 1886.
Composition of beeswax. F. Schwalb, Lieb. Ann., 1886, 235, 106; Jour. Chem. Soc.,
1887, 124; Proc. Amer. Pharm. Assoc., 1887, 182.
Das Wachs u. seine technische Verwendung. Louis Sedna, Vienna, A. Hartleben,
1886.
Detection of adulterations in beeswax. A. Clarency, Jour. de Pharm. et de Chim.,
[6], 13, 27; Chem. Centralblatt, 1886, 17, 174.
Determination of purity of beeswax. C. L. Lochman, Proc. Penna. Pharm. Assoc.,
1886, 204.
Feeding of wax to bees. N. W. McLain, Rep. of Entomologist, U. S. Dept. of Agriculture; Amer. Bee Jour., 1886, 296.

1887.

Determination of specific gravity of waxes. E. Dieterich, Pharm. Zeit., 1887, 32, 37;
Arch. d. Pharm., 1887, 132; Proc. Amer. Pharm. Assoc., 1887, 183; Pharm. Rec-
ord, Feb. 15, 1887; Pharm. Jour. Trans., Mar. 19, 1887, 770.
Dimethylamidoazobenzol for coloring beeswax. Fres. Zeit. f. a. Chem., 1887, 106.

1888.

Acetyl number in waxes. Fres. Zeit. f. a. Chem., 1888, 528.
Adulteration of beeswax. Amer. Bee Jour., Aug. 1, 1888, 499.

Analysis of beeswax.  Buchner, Chem. Zeit., 1888, 1276.
Analysis of beeswax.  F. Hübl, Chem. Zeit., 1888, 1277; Pharm. Zeit. f. Russl., 1888,
   579; Proc. Amer. Pharm. Assoc., 1888, 653; Amer. Jour. Pharm., 1888, 561.
Analysis of beeswax.  C. M. Morse, Thesis for Mass. College of Pharmacy, 1888.
                                    1889.
Analysis of beeswax.  E. Dieterich, Helfenberger Annalen, 1889, 21.
Detection of paraffin in beeswax.  H. Hager, Pharm. Centralhalle, 1889, 565; Amer.
   Jour. Pharm., 1889, 564; Chem. Centralblatt, 1889, 2, 815; Fres. Zeit. f. a.
   Chem., 1889, 480; Proc. Amer. Pharm. Assoc., 1890, 505; Jour. Chem. Soc., 1891,
   122.
Analysis of beeswax.  Röttger, Chem. Zeit., 1889, 1375.
Apparatus for the investigation of fats, waxes, etc.  Schädler, Chem. Centralblatt,
   1889, 2, 861.
                                    1890.
Analysis of beeswax.  Buchner, Chem. Zeit., 1890, 1707.
Analysis of beeswax.  A. and P. Buisine, Bull. Soc. chim., Par., 1890, 3 ser., t. 3, 567;
   Chem. Zeit. Repert., 1890, 226.
Analysis of beeswax.  A. and P. Buisine, Bull. Soc. chim., Par., 1890, 3 ser., t. 3, 867;
   do. t. 4, 465; Chem. Zeit. Repert., 1890, 320.
Analysis of beeswax.  R. Kayser, Chem. Zeit., 1890, 686.
Analysis of beeswax.  Röttger, Chem. Zeit., 1890, 606; do., 1442; do., 1473.
Bleaching of wax.  U. S. patent, 421,904, Feb. 25, 1890.
Detection of rosin in beeswax.  Chem. Zeit., 1890, 1474.
Determination of specific gravity of waxes.  A. Gawalowski, Oel u. Fett. Industrie;
   Chem. Centralblatt, 1890, 2, 502.
Test for specific gravity of beeswax.  Amer. Bee Jour., 1890, 629.
                                    1891.
Analysis of beeswax.  Benedikt u. Mangold, Chem. Zeit., 1891, 474.
Analysis of beeswax.  A. and P. Buisine, Bull. Soc. chim. Par., 1891, 3 ser., t. 5, 654;
   Chem. Centralblatt, 1891, 2, 10; Jour. Soc. Chem. Ind., 1891, 10, 729.
Analysis of beeswax.  Valenta, Centr. Org., f. Waarenkunde, 1891, 112.
Analysis of beeswax.  F. Jean, Bull. Soc. chim. Par., 1891, 3 ser., t. 5, No. 1.
Analysis of beeswax.  K. Mangold, Chem. Zeit., 1891, 799.
Bleaching of wax.  A. and P. Buisine, Jour. de pharm. et de chim., May 15, 1891, 526.
Bleaching of wax.  M. H. Barnouvin, Jour. de pharm. et de chim., July 1, 1891, 6.
Determination of paraffin in waxes, F. M. Horn, Zeit. f. angew. Chem. 63; Chem.
   News, 1891, 63, 165.
Detection of paraffin in beeswax.  Phar. Jour. Trans., 1891, 851.
Detection of rosin in beeswax.  Röttger, Chem. Zeit., 1891, 45.
Petroleum benzine as a reagent for waxes.  H. Hager, Central Org. f. Waarenkunde,
   1891, 1, 239; Chem. Zeit., 1891, 307.

----

# BIBLIOGRAPHY OF WAXES USED IN ADULTERATING BEESWAX— ARRANGED BY YEARS.

                                    1863.
Melting points of various waxes.  B. S. Proctor, Chem. and Drug., 1863; Amer.
   Jour. Pharm., 35, 527.
                                    1865.
Sumach wax.  J. Batka, Fres. Zeit. f. a. Chem., 1865, 491; Chem. Centralblatt,
   1865, 12.
                                    1868.
Adulteration of Japan wax with water.  Arch. f. Pharm., Jan. and Feb., 1868, 144;
   Proc. Amer. Pharm. Assoc., 1868, 179.

Black wax from Madras. Chem. News, May 22, 1868; Proc. Amer. Pharm. Assoc., 1868, 205.

### 1869.

Carnauba wax. N. S. Maskelyne, Chem. News, March, 1869, 145.

### 1870.

Carnauba wax. Jour. f. prakt. Chem., 1869; Arch. d. Pharm., April, 1870; Proc. Amer. Pharm. Assoc., 1871, 308.

### 1874.

Collection of Japan wax. Pharm. Jour. Trans., 1874, 425; Proc. Amer. Pharm. Assoc., 1875, 218.

### 1876.

Collection of Japan wax. Gehe's Handelsber., Arch. Pharm., 1876, 374; Pharm. Jour. Trans., 1876, 1003; Proc. Amer. Pharm. Assoc., 1876, 193.
Reactions of Carnauba wax. Rep. de pharm., 1876, 710; New Remedies, 1877, 109; Proc. Amer. Pharm. Assoc., 1877, 283.

### 1877.

Collection of Japan wax. Amer. Jour. Pharm., Sept., 1877, 452; Proc. Amer. Pharm. Assoc., 1878, 295.

### 1878.

Wax contained in the leaves of *Ilex paraguayensis*. P. N. Arata, Gazzeta chimica italiana, 7, 366; Jour. Chem. Soc., 1878, 2, 324.

### 1879.

Japan wax. E. Buri, Arch. d. Pharm., May, 1879 (3), 14, 403; Proc. Amer. Pharm. Assoc., 1879, 436; Amer. Jour. Pharm., 1879, 361; Jour. Chem. Soc., 1879, 36, 1037.
Vegetable wax. A. Meyer, Arch. d. Pharm., 1879, 97, 129; Amer. Jour. Pharm., Dec., 1879, 606; Proc. Amer. Pharm. Assoc., 1880, 293.

### 1880.

Collection of Chinese insect wax. Gardener's Chron., Oct. 2, 1880; Pharm. Jour. Trans., Oct. 16, 1880; Proc. Amer. Pharm. Assoc., 1881, 305.
Qualitative reactions of various waxes. E. Hirschsohn, Zeit. d. österr. Apoth. Vereins, 18, 306; Pharm. Jour. Trans., 1880, 749; Proc. Amer. Pharm. Assoc., 1880, 291; Amer. Jour. Pharm., 1880, 303.

### 1882.

Specific gravity of waxes. E. Dieterich, Arch. d. Pharm., June, 1882, 455; Proc. Amer. Pharm. Assoc., 1882, 363.
Myrtle wax. Pharm. Jour. Trans., 1883, 61.

### 1884.

Constituents of carnauba wax. H. Störcke, Lieb. Ann., 1884, 223, 225.
Egyptian wax. K. Labler, Rundschau, 10, 289; Chem. Centralblatt, 1884, 497.
Specific gravity of paraffin. E. Sauerlandt, Chem. Zeit., 1884, 7, 388.
Specific gravity of paraffin. Fres., Zeit. f. a. Chem., 1884, 256.
Vegetable wax. M. Buchner, Chem. Centralblatt, 1884, 257.

### 1885.

Chinese insect wax. Muth-Rasmussen, Amer. Bee Jour., 1885, 50, 787.
Ocotilla wax, from *Fonquieria splendens*. H. C. De S. Abbott, Amer. Jour. Pharm., 1885, 81; Proc. Amer. Pharm. Assoc., 1885, 179.
White insect wax. Pharm. Jour. Trans., Mar. 14, 1885, 755; Proc. Amer. Pharm. Assoc., 1885, 201.

### 1886.

Asclepias wax. C. Kassner, Die Oel u. Fett-Industrie, 22–86; Chem. Zeit., 1886, 390.
Chinese insect wax. C. Theilmann, Amer. Bee Jour., 1886, 24.
Glycerine, determination in waxes by permanganate. Wanklyn and Fox, Chem. News, 1886, 53, 15.

1888.
Composition of Japan wax. Eberhard, Rundschau, 1888, 844; Proc. Amer. Pharm. Assoc., 1889, 654.

1890.
African insect wax. Chem. and Drug., May 17, 1890, 667; Proc. Amer. Pharm. Assoc., 1890, 506.
Japan wax. O. Kleinstück, Chem. Zeit., 1890, 1303; Jour. Chem. Soc., 1890, 9, 1072.

---

## BIBLIOGRAPHY OF HONEY—ARRANGED BY YEARS.

1867.
Adulteration of honey. Proc. Amer. Pharm. Assoc., 1867, 61, 341.

1868.
Adulteration of honey. Pharm. Jour. Trans., Sept., 1868; Proc. Amer. Pharm. Assoc., 1869, 186.

1870.
Honey trade of the United States. B. F. Stacey, Proc. Amer. Pharm. Assoc., 1870, 141.
Tinted honey. Pharm. Jour. Trans., Dec., 1870; Proc. Amer. Pharm. Assoc., 1871, 313.

1871.
Tinted honey. Pharm. Jour. Trans., Jan. 7, 1871; Amer. Jour. Pharm., 1871, 88.

1872.
Adulteration of honey. F. Molitor, Bienen Zeitung, 1872, 73.
Artificial honey. C. T. V. Siebold, Bienen Zeitung, 1872, 280.
Artificial honey and honey substitutes. Dzierzon, Bienen Zeitung, Jan., 1872, 1.
Fermentation of honeys. J. Boussingault, Ann. de chim. et de phys. [4], 26, 362; Jour. Chem. Soc., 1872, 25, 906.
Mehring's artificial honey. W. S. Schuller, Bienen Zeitung, 1872, 76.

1873.
Use of locust flowers for flavoring artificial honey. Proc. Amer. Pharm. Assoc., 1873, 480.

1874.
Constituents of honey. E. Erlenmeyer and A. v. Planta, N. Report. Pharm., —, 23, 610; Chem. Centralblatt, 1874, 5, 790.

1875.
Adulteration of honey. Schweitz. Wochenschrift, Jan. 15, 1875; Amer. Jour. Pharm., 1875, 346; Proc. Amer. Pharm. Assoc., 1875, 232.
Boxwood-flower honey (artificial). J. M. France, Pharmacist, 1875, 322; Proc. Amer. Pharm. Assoc., 1876, 405.
Colloids and crystalloids in honey. E. Dieterich, Chem. Centralhalle, 1877, 318; Amer. Jour. Pharm., 1877, 448; Proc. Amer. Pharm. Assoc., 1878, 528.
Honey dew. H. Hoffman, Landw. Versuchs. Stat. ——, 20, 61; ab. Jour. Chem. Soc., 1877, 2, 210.
Poisonous honey in Armenia. Pharm. Jour. Trans., 1877, 184; Proc. Amer. Pharm. Assoc., 1878, 529.
Prosecution for adulterating honey. [England.] Analyst, 1877, 2, 167.

1878.
Adulterated honey. Amer. Bee Jour., 1878, 29.
Composition of honey. J. C. Brown, Analyst, 1878, 3, 267; Jour. Chem. Soc., 1878, 2, 969.

**1879.**

American honey. Amer. Jour. Pharm., 1879, 102.

California honey. Amer. Jour. Pharm., 1879, 320.

Ethiopian honey. E. Villiers, Comptes rend., 1879, 88, 292; Ber. d. chem. Gesell., 1879, 12, 671; Jour. Chem. Soc,, 1879, 36, 450.

Fennel honey. Pharm. Zeit., 1879, 719; Amer. Jour. Pharm., 1880, 132; Proc. Amer. Pharm. Assoc., 1880, 60.

**1880.**

Adulteration of honey. v. Planta, Dingl. polyt. Jour., 1880, 238, 356; abs. Jour. Chem. Soc., 1881, 40, 316.

Use of glucose for adulterating honey. Amer. Bee Jour., 1880, 10.

**1881.**

Artificial honey. Prof. A. J. Cook, Amer. Bee Jour., 1881, 315.

Artificial honey. Amer. Bee Jour., 1881, 244.

Test for adulteration in honeys. Amer. Bee Jour., 1881, 13.

Use of glucose for mixing honeys. Amer. Bee Jour., 1881, 393.

**1882.**

Adulteration of honey. v. Planta, Zucker Ind., 1882, 388; Bied. Centralblatt, 1882, 575; Jour. Chem. Soc., 1882, 42, 1327; Chem. Centralblatt, 1883, 16.

**1883.**

Adulteration of honey. Amer. Bee Jour., 1883, 526.

Artificial comb honeys. Century, Oct., 1883; Amer. Bee Jour., 1884, 211.

Canadian honey. Canad. Pharm. Jour., Sept., 1883; Pharm. Jour. Trans., Nov. 10, 1883, 365; Proc. Amer. Pharm. Assoc., 1884, 203.

Detection of glucose. Amer. Bee Jour., 1883, 377.

Aconite flower honey. Pharm. Jour. Trans., Sept. 29, 1883, 242.

Orange-blossom honey. Amer. Bee Jour., 1883, 377; ibid., 1883, 421.

Poisonous honey. Pharm. Jour. Trans., Dec. 29, 1883, 504.

**1884.**

Adulteration of honey. Amer. Bee Jour., 1884, 51.

Adulteration of honey. Amer. Bee Jour., 1884, 229.

Analysis of honey. O. Hehner, Analyst, 1884, 9, 64; Jour. Chem. Soc., 48, 444.

Analytical methods for honey. J. Sieben, Fres. Zeit. f. a. Chem., 1884, 24, 137.

Analytical methods for honey. W. Lenz, Fres. Zeit. f. a. Chem., 1884, 24, 135.

Formic acid in honey. Pharm. Jour. Trans., Nov. 1, 1884, 343.

Gallisin. E. Schmidt, Ber. d. chem. Gesell., 1884, 17, 1000 and 2456.

Lecture on the adulteration of honey. O. Hehner, Analyst, 1884, 9, 181.

Poison of the hymenoptera. Carlet, Comptes rend., 1884, 1550.

Spurious California honey. Stearns and Smith, Amer. Bee Jour., 1884, 339.

Test for purity of honey. Prof. W. C. Preston, Amer. Bee Jour., 1884, 36.

**1885.**

Adulteration of honey. H. Hager, Pharm. Centralhalle, 1885, 26, 327; Chem. Central-blatt, 1885, 764; Jour. Chem. Soc., 1886, 50, 282.

Adulterations of honey. Doc. sur les falsifications des matieres alimentaires, 1885, 590.

Adulteration of honey. H. W. Wiley, Amer. Apiculturist, 1885, 3, No. 12.

Analysis of honey. W. Bishop, J. Pharm., —— [5], 10, 459; Jour. Chem. Soc., 1885, 48, 444.

Artificial honey. Amer. Bee Jour., 1885, 423; ibid., 627.

Analytical methods for honey. M. Barthe, Pharm. Centralhalle, 1885, 26, 87.

Ash of honey. O. Hehner, Analyst, 1885, 10, 217.

Composition and adulteration of honey. J. Sieben, Bied. Centralblatt, 1885, 134; Jour. Chem. Soc., 1885, 48, 693; Analyst, 1885, 10, 34.

Detection of glucose in honeys. Rev. J. G. Teeter, Amer. Bee Jour., 1885, Aug. 26; ibid., 1886, Oct. 27.

Dextro-rotary honeys. Amthor. Repert. anal. Chem., 1885, 163.
Estimation of water in honeys. H. W. Wiley and F. V. Broadbent, Chem. News, 1885, 52, 280; Jour. Chem. Soc., 1886, 50, 282.
Fermentation of honey. E. Dieterich, Geschäftsber. d. Papier u. Chem. Fabrik in Helfenberg, bei Dresden, 1885–'86; Helfenberger Annalen, 1886–'87; Fres. Zeit. f. a. Chem., 1888, 231.
Poisonous honey from gelsemium. Pharm. Jour. Trans., Aug. 29, 1885, 188; ibid., 448; Laucet, Aug. 22, 370; Pharm. Zeit., Nov. 25, 1885.
Proper time to harvest honey. K. Zwilling, Bied. Centralblatt, 1885, 67; Jour. Chem. Soc., 1885, 48, 590.

### 1886.
Adulterated honeys. Amer. Bee Jour., 1886, 216.
Artificial honeys. Amer. Bee Jour., 1886, 307.
Characteristics of honeys from different sources. C. S. Commings., Amer. Jour. Pharm., 1886, 539; Proc. Amer. Pharm. Assoc., 1887, 182.
Detection of artificial honey. G. Ambuhl, Schweitz. Wochenschrift f. Pharm., ——, 47, 85; Chem. Zeit., 1886, 70.
Fermentation of honey. R. Kayser, Ber. über d Vers. bayr. Vertretr. d. angew Chem., 1886, 91; Fres. Zeit. f. a. Chem., 1888, 231.
Nectar of flowers. A. v. Planta, Zeit. f. physiol. Chem., 1886, 10, 227; Chem. Centralblatt, 1886, 17, 367.
Poisonous. Chem. Zeit., 1886, 27.

### 1887.
Adulterated honeys. Report on adulteration of food, Ottawa, Canada, 1887, 58.
Eucalyptus honey. Thomas Caraman, Progres medicale, April 16, 1887; Pharm. Jour. Trans., 1887, 1016; Proc. Amer. Pharm. Assoc., 1887, 182.
Examination of honey. R. Kayser, Fres. Zeit. f. a. Chem., 1887, 27, 2; Chem. News, 1888, Aug. 24, 97; Proc. Amer. Pharm. Assoc., 1889, 499.
Poisonous constituents of Trebizonde honeys. Pharm. Jour. Trans., 1887, 397; ibid, 540; Proc. Amer. Pharm. Assoc., 1888, 411.

### 1888.
Adulterations of honey. Amer. Bee Jour., 1888, 682, ibid., 810.
Analytical methods for honeys. Fres. Zeit. f. a. Chem., 1888, 28, 231.
Artificial English honey. Amer. Bee Jour., 1888, 691.
History of adulteration of honey. Chas. Dadant, Amer. Bee Jour., 1888, 537.
Composition of honey. Bensemann, Jour. de chim. et de pharm., 1888, 20.
Honey-canning factory (A. Christie, Smithland, Iowa). Amer. Bee Jour., 1888, 100.
Food juice of bees. A. v. Planta, Chem. Centralblatt, 1888, 673.
Examination of honey. R. Kayser, Fres. Zeit. f. a. Chem., 1888, 231.
Production of honey in California. Amer. Jour. Pharm., 1888, 126; Proc. Amer. Pharm. Assoc., 1888, 410.
Artificial honey. Amer. Bee Jour., 1888, 709.
Protection wanted against adulteration. Amer. Bee Jour., 1888, 265.
Strained honey, purity, adulteration, etc. Amer. Bee Jour., 1888, 587.
Use of oleomargarine for adulterating honey. Amer. Bee Jour., 1888, 739.

### 1889.
Analysis of honey. v. Raumer, Zeit. f. angew. Chem., 1889, 607.
Eucalyptus honey. Arch. d. Pharm., 1889, 873; Proc. Amer. Pharm. Assoc., 1890, 505.
Eucalyptus honey. Maquenne, Ann. de chim. et de phys., 1889, t. 17, 6 ser., 495.
Food of bees. A. v. Planta, Chem. Centralblatt, 1889, 299.
Right-rotary honeys. v. Lippman, Zeit. f. angew. Chem., 1889, No. 20; Analyst, 1889, 14, 20.
Right-rotary honeys. Amthor and Stern, Zeit. f. angew. Chem., 1889, 575; Analyst, 1889, 14, 238; Amer. Jour. Pharm., 1890, 13; Proc. Amer. Pharm. Assoc., 1890, 505.

1890.

Action of phenols on honey. A. Ihle. Chem. Zeit., 1890, 14, 3; Chem. Centralblatt, 1890, 1, 390.

Adulterated honey. Amer. Bee Jour., 1890, 211.

Adulterated extracted honey. Amer. Bee Jour., 1890, 244.

Bogus honey. C. C. Miller, Amer. Bee Jour., 1890, 505.

Examination of honey. Chem. Zeit., 1890, 42, 686.

Honey. Vierteljahreschrift f. Chem. d. Nahr. u. Genussmittel, 1890, 2, 188.

Orange blossom honey not likely to be pure. Amer. Bee Jour., 1890, 580.

1891.

Presence of dextrin in pure honey. W. Mader, Arch. Hyg., 1890, 399; Vierteljahre-schrift über Nahrungs. u. Genussmittel, 1890, 311.

Date honey (date sirup). Karl Gaab, Chem. Zeit., 1891, 118.

Dextro-rotary honeys. O. Haenle, Analyst, 1891, 79.

Examination of honeys. Mansfeld, Vers. d. Nahrungs Chem. u. Mikroskopiker in Wien, Oct. 13, 1891; Chem. Zeit., 1891, 1053 and 1544.

Eucalyptus honey. Pharm. Era, Feb. 15, 1891, 107.

# INDEX.

## A.

I

## M.

## N.

## O.

## P.

○

www.ingramcontent.com/pod-product-compliance
Lightning Source LLC
Chambersburg PA
CBHW020850270326
41928CB00006B/637